BIOGRAPHICAL DATA
from
BALTIMORE NEWSPAPERS
1817 - 1819

BIOGRAPHICAL DATA
from
BALTIMORE NEWSPAPERS
1817 - 1819

Robert W. Barnes

CLEARFIELD

Copyright © 2011 by
Robert W. Barnes
All Rights Reserved

Reprinted for Clearfield Company by
Genealogical Publishing Company
Baltimore, Maryland
2011

Made in the Untied States of America

Biographical Data from Baltimore Newspapers, 1817-1819

Contents

Introduction..vii

Unusual Obituaries..vii

Marriage Statistics...viii

Bibliography and Abbreviations Used...viii

Acknowledgements...ix

Biographical Data from Baltimore Newspapers, 1817-1819..............1

People with One Name..129

Notes on Ministers...135

Notes on Cemeteries..149

Index...153

Biographical Data from Baltimore Newspapers, 1817-1819

Introduction

When I published *Marriages and Deaths from Baltimore Newspapers, 1796-1816*, I found I still had notes on similar items for the period 1817 through 1819. For many years I did nothing with those index cards until I decided I would incorporate them into another book.

I did not limit my findings to people who were married or died in Baltimore City or Baltimore County, but included items concerning people from the surrounding states of Delaware, Pennsylvania, and Virginia, and the District of Columbia, and items concerning people from Baltimore and Baltimore County who may have moved farther away.

This book would be more than just vital statistics. It would contain data on estates, runaway servants, apprentices, wives, and soldiers. Information on executors or administrators selling property, notices seeking the whereabouts of lost relatives, places of burial (where known), and in the case of foreign-born decedents, information pertaining to their naturalization, would all be included.

A separate section was included for people with just one name. These were not just slaves, but occasionally indentured servants. Runaway slaves who had two names were included in the main section of the text.

Originally I used microfilm copies of newspapers found at the Maryland State Archives and the Maryland Historical Society, but latterly I culled data from the scanned images of newspapers found on such websites as Early American Newspapers ®.

Unusual Obituaries

Many obituaries simply gave the date of death and age of the deceased. Others gave more information, such as this one:
Hale, Mrs. Jane, d. lately at a very advanced age; for fifty years of her life had kept a Toy, Fruit and Cake Table at the market near Gay St. She was born in Eng., and raised a family of children and grandchildren. She refused to remove to the Alms house, and lived in a wooden tenement which she held on a ground rent [a long obit follows] (*BPAT* 22 Nov 1819). Jane Hale, aged 92 years, was buried 6 Nov 1819 from St. Paul's Parish (from St. Paul's Parish (ReamySP). For the will of Jane Haile, filed in 1820, see BAWB 11:126.

Biographical Data from Baltimore Newspapers, 1817-1819

Marriages

As I compiled the marriages it became apparent that an inordinate number of marriages were performed on Thursdays, and a similar unusually large number occurred in the evenings. In all, 1293 marriages were found; 646 (49.9%) were performed in the evening, and 486 (37.5%) were performed on Thursdays. Deducting the number of marriages for which the day of the week could not be ascertained, I found that 1139 rites of matrimony were performed on known days. Of these, 664 (58.3%) were performed in the evening, and 486 (42.7%) were held on Thursdays. One possible explanation for these statistics might be that most people were working class, and the evening was the best time when their friends could gather to witness the nuptials. Setting aside the fantastic idea that ministers liked to play golf on Fridays (just as doctors are popularly believed to play golf on Wednesdays), perhaps the reason Thursdays were so popular was that many people could take Fridays off even if they did not go on extended wedding trips.

Bibliography and Abbreviations Used

AAWB: Anne Arundel Co. Register of Wills (Will Books).
BA: *Baltimore American.*
BACDA: *Baltimore American and Commercial Daily Advertiser.*
Barnes, Robert W. *Marriages and Deaths from the Maryland Gazette, 1727-1839.* Baltimore: Genealogical Publishing Co. © 1973.
BMC: Baltimore *Maryland Chronicle.*
BPAT: *Baltimore Patriot and Mercantile Advertiser.*
BAWB: Baltimore Co. Register of Wills (Will Books).
Erdman, Lorrie A. E. *Abstracts of Marriages and Deaths in the (Baltimore) American and Commercial Daily Advertiser, 1831-1836.* Westminster: Willow Bend Books, 2003.
FGBA: *Federal Gazette and Baltimore Advertiser.*
Grogaard, Hans, and Mary Warfield. *Burials in Pro-Cathedral and Cathedral Cemeteries, Baltimore, Maryland, 1791-1874.* Westminster: Willow Bend Books, 2004. In 1815 those with relatives buried in the Pro-Cathedral Cemetery were able to transfer their remains to the new graveyard on North Fremont Avenue.
Hayward, Mary Ellen, and R. Kent Lancaster. *A Guide to the Markers and Burials, 1775-1943* [of Baltimore's Westminster Cemetery Westminster Presbyterian Church]. Baltimore: Westminster Preservation Trust, 1984.
Kanely: Edna Agatha Kanely. *Directory of Ministers and the Maryland Churches They Served.* 2 vols. Westminster: Family Line Publications, 1991.
Md. Gaz. Annapolis *Maryland Gazette.*
MOLL: Interment Records of Mt. Olivet Cemetery, Frederick Road, Baltimore; available at www.lovelylane.net.
Oszakiewski: Robert Andrew Oszakiewski. *Maryland Naturalization Abstracts: Volume 1: Baltimore County and Baltimore City, 1784-1851.* Westminster: Family Line Publications, 1995.
Oszakiewski: Robert Andrew Oszakiewsi. *Maryland Naturalization Abstracts: Volume 2: The County Court of Maryland, 1779-1851; The U.S. Circuit Court for Maryland, 1790-1851. Covering All of Maryland Except for Baltimore and County.* Westminster: Family Line Publications, 1996.
PedenM: Henry C. Peden, Jr. *Methodist Records of Baltimore City, Maryland, Volume 1, 1799-1829.* Westminster: Family Line Publications, ©1994.
ReamySP: Bill and Martha Reany. *Records of St. Paul's Parish.* Volume Two. Westminster: Family Line Publications, ©1989 by Bill and Martha Reamy.
Who Was Who in America, 1607-1896. Chicago: A. N. Marquis Co., 1963.

Biographical Data from Baltimore Newspapers, 1817-1819

Acknowledgements

It has been said that it 'takes a whole village to raise a child' and no one person is responsible for bringing forth a book. As author I am responsible for doing the research, keying in the data, and preparing the manuscript for publication, but I have been assisted by a number of people. I thank Allender Sybert for technical assistance, and also for encouragement. He, Robert K. Headley, and Dolly Ziegler have provided the 'listening ears' whenever I wanted to discuss the project.

I am also grateful to Edward C. Papenfuse, State Archivist, and Michael McCormick, Director of Reference and Research at the Maryland State Archives, and to Patricia Anderson and Francis O'Neill at the Maryland Historical Society. They have all created research facilities for many people engaged in research.

Finally I must thank Michael Tepper, Eileen Perkins, and Joe Garonzik of the Genealogical Publishing Company for their technical assistance and encouragement.

Biographical Data from Baltimore Newspapers, 1817-1819

"A"

Abbott, John, dec.: his admx., Ann Abbott, conv. two contiguous lots of ground at the northwest intersection of North St. and Wagon Alley to Patrick Kelly; a commission will meet on Tues., 16th inst., to establish the lines of the lots (*BPAT* 9 March 1819).
Abell, Samuel, was m. at Hagerstown, to Miss Nancy Flora (*BMC* 28 May 1819; *BPAT* 29 May 1819).
Abercrombie, Rev. James, D.D., Senior Assistant Minister of Christ's Church, St. Peter's and St. James', was m. at Philadelphia by the Rev. Dr. Pilmore, to Miss Mary Mason of the Island of Barbados (*BPAT* 9 June 1817).
Ackey, John, of Charleston, S. C., seeks information on his father, an aged man, who left the country with a design of going to Tennessee, and has not been heard of since (*BPAT* 6 Aug 1817).
Acworth, Capt. William, of Washington, d. at Hayti on 19 May 1817 (*BPAT* 15 Feb 1819).
Adam, Elizabeth, d. 1st inst., of a lingering illness, aged 37 years and 6 mos., wife of Jacob Adam (*BPAT* 4 Dec 1819).
Adam, Jacob, was m. at Hagerstown, on Tues., 15th inst., by Rev. J. R. Reily, Miss Sarah Bernheiser (*BPAT* 26 June 1819).
Adams, Miss Susannah, dau. of the late Thomas Reeder, of St. Mary's Co., and wife of William Adams of Baltimore, d. last Friday after a long and painful illness (*BA* 21 Jan 1817; *BPAT* 22 Jan 1817).
Addington, Rt. Hon. John Hilby, d. Thursday night of a mortification in his stomach (*BPAT* 3 Aug 1818).
Adkison, John, was m. Thurs. eve. by Rev. Waugh, to Miss Sarah M'Comas, both of Baltimore (*BPAT* 12 June 1819).
Aikens, William, was m. on Sat. by Rev. Glendy, to Mss Susan Martin, all of Baltimore (*BA* 15 April 1817; *BPAT* 17 April 1817).
Aisquith, Edward, has died. A commission will be held to establish the lines of the three adjoining lots of land on Pitt St., between Front and High Sts. (*BPAT* 29 Aug 1817).
Aisquith, Rev. Grandison, of York, was m. Tues. eve. last by Rev. Mr. Henshaw, to Miss Charlotte Wall of Baltimore (*BPAT* 10 Sep 1819).
Aisquith, Robert C., merchant, was m. last Thurs. by Rev. Mr. Henshaw, to Miss Eleanor Elizabeth Warfield, all of Baltimore (*BA* 29 Sep 1817; *BPAT* 29 Sep 1817 gives the bride's name as Winfield).
Aitken, Robert, of Baltimore Co., is an insolvent debtor (*BPAT* 14 Oct 1819).
Alberger, Mr. Samuel, Jr., and Mrs. Eleanor Rebecca Cook, all of Baltimore, were m. last Thurs. eve. by Rev. Mr. Hagerty (*BPAT* 6 Nov 1819).
Albers, Samuel, was m. last Thurs. by Rev. Bartow, to Miss Mary Travis, both of Baltimore (*FGBA* 27 Jan 1818; *BPAT* 27 Jan 1818).
Alexander, James, and **John Alexander** of Harford Co. are to have an Act of the Assembly to confirm their certain lands herein mentioned (*BPAT* 10 Feb 1817).
Alexander, William, of Harford Co. is to have an act of the Assembly for his benefit (*BPAT* 10 Feb 1817).

1

Biographical Data from Baltimore Newspapers, 1817-1819

Allbright, Hetty, dau. of John Allbright, d. Wed., 28th ult., in her 25th year (*BPM* 1 Dec 1818).

Allen, Adam T., was m. last Thurs. eve., by Rev. Wells, to Miss Susannah Purdy, all of Baltimore (*BA* 10 Nov 1817; *BPAT* 10 Nov 1817).

Allen, James, was m. last Sat. eve. by Rev. Bartow, to Miss Elizabeth Curtis, all of Baltimore (*BA* 5 Jan 1819; *BPAT* 5 Jan 1819).

Allen, John, son of Capt. James Allen, formerly of Baltimore, d. 10th inst., at the house of his step-father, James Land, near Carlisle, PA, in his 26th year (*BA* 26 Feb 1817; *BPAT* 26 Feb 1817).

Allen, Mrs. Mary Susan, consort of Capt. Ethan A. Allen of the U.S. Artillery, d. [date not given] near Norfolk (*BPAT* 4 Nov 1818).

Allen, Michael, aged about 23 years, deserted from the U. S. Ship *Alert* lying at the navy hard in this city [Washington] on the 10th inst. /s/ Edmund P. Kennedy, Commander (*BPAT* 26 Dec 1817).

Allen, William W., was m. 19th ult. [Wed.] by Rev. Slemmons, to Miss Mary Whittington, all of Somerset Co. (*BPAT* 2 June 1819).

Allenson, [-?-], a child of Mr. Allenson, was buried in St. Ingles' Ground in Sep 1817 (See *MGSB* 30 (3) 293).

Allender, Mr. William, was m. Thurs., 25th inst., by the Rev. Mr. Richardson, to Miss Tabitha Allen, all of Baltimore Co. (*BPAT* 27 Sep 1819).

Alley, Micajah, of Baltimore Co., is an insolvent debtor (*BPAT* 23 Dec 1819).

Allison, Mr. William, merchant, of Richmond Va,, was m. Thurs., 30 Sep, by Rev. Mr. Hoskinson, to Miss Ann Waters of Montgomery Co., Md. (*BPAT* 7 Oct 1819).

Allmond, Jacob, was m. last Sun. eve. by Rev. Mr. Parks, to Miss Clemence McComas (*BA* 3 Sep 1817; *BPAT* 3 Sep 1817).

Alvis, Peter M., was m. Thurs. eve. by Rev. Mr. Force, Miss Sarah Neighbours, all of Baltimore (*FGBA* Feb 1819; *BPAT* 5 Feb 1819).

Amos, James, was m. last Thurs. eve. last by Rev. Roberts to Sarah Towson, both of Baltimore (*BPAT* 25 May 1818).

Amoss, Joshua, was m. last Thurs. eve. by Rev. Dr. Roberts, to Miss Ann Catherine Omesetller, both of Baltimore (*BPAT* 12 June 1819).

Anderson, Catherine, of Holliday St, killed herself by poison. The inquest was yesterday (*BA* 27 April 1818).

Anderson, Elizabeth Parker, youngest child of William J. and Mrs. Sybella Anderson, died last eve., aged two years and one mo. (*BPAT* 9 Oct 1818).

Anderson, Ellen, a bound girl, about 15 years old, light color for a Negro, ran away, but as she is completely worthless, "I shall not . . . thank any person for bringing her home (*BPAT* 4 April 1817).

Anderson, George, was m. Thurs. by Rev. Hargrove, to Martha Harley, all of Baltimore (*BA* 15 Aug 1818; *BPAT* 14 Aug 1818).

Anderson, George, has died. E. F. Chambers, trustee, advertises a sale of Anderson's real estate, located in Chestertown (*BPAT* 23 Nov 1817). His real estate consists of four tenements now in the possession of James E. Barroll, Esq., William Harris, Thomas Walker, and James Dawson (*BPAT* 15 Nov 1817).

Anderson, John, merchant of Norfolk, Va., d. 21st inst., in Baltimore, aged 32 years (*BPAT* 26 Nov 1819). For the will of John Anderson, filed in 1820, see BAWB 11:130.

Anderson, Major John, of the U.S. Engineer Corps, was m. in Washington, Miss Julia Taylor of the latter place (*BPAT* 18 May 1818).

Anderson, Michael, was m. last Thurs. by Rev. Bartow, to Mrs. Christiana Folger (*BA* 8 Dec 1818; *BPAT* 8 Dec 1818).

Anderson, Robert, or **Bob,** about 17 years old, ran away from Chas. Crook and Co., No. 21, Cheapside, His brother **Matthew,** about 20 years of age, ran away in Aug 1816; one or both may be in the state of Delaware, near Milford where they were raised (*BPAT* 28 Oct 1817).

Biographical Data from Baltimore Newspapers, 1817-1819

Anderson, Robert, d. at his farm on Bush Creek, after a short illness, aged 56 years (*BPAT* 27 Oct 1819).

Anderson, William, merchant, of the Island of Dominica, was m. Wed. eve. by the Right Rev. Bishop Kemp, Miss Maria Louise Sanders, of Philadelphia (*BA* 21 Nov 1817).

Andeslouis, Adrian, was m. last Sat by Rev. Mr. Luck, to Miss Harriet Stedel [Steel?], both of Baltimore (*FGBA* 4 Sep 1817).

Angelucci, N. J. M., His Most Christian Majesty's Consul for Baltimore, was m. on Sat., 25th ult., at the country seat of Hyde de Nevulle, near New Brunswick, N. J., to Mlle. L. Villaret (*BPAT* 7 Nov 1817).

Anloes, George, apprentice to the Morocco business, ran away from Lewis Kalbfus, living one mile from Baltimore on the Reisters' Town Road (*BPAT* 20 June 1817). [His name might really be Inloes].

Annan, Robert, D.D., d. at Lancaster, Pa., as a result of a fall from his gig, in his 79th year (*BPAT* 31 Dec 1819).

Anthony, Lieut. Charles, of the U. S. Army, and aide de camp to Brig.-Gen. Moses Porter, d. last Mon. at Philadelphia (*BPAT* 1 July 1818).

Appleton, William G.; his creditors are to apply to Nath'l Williams, his trustee, to receive a dividend of $8,500.00 on his estate (*BPAT* 21 May 1818).

Appold, Frederick, was m. Thurs. eve. by Rev. Valiant, to Miss Ann Maria Joyce (*BA* 9 March 1818; *BPAT* 7 March 1818).

Arcambal, Felix, m. last Tues. eve. by Rev. Moranville, to Miss Louisa Figuieres, all of Baltimore (*BA* 12 Dec 1818; *BPAT* 11 Dec 1818).

Argilanders, John, about 5' 2", apprentice, ran away from John Griggs (*BPAT* 15 Dec 1818).

Armistead, Col. George, who defended Fort McHenry, d. 25th inst., at Baltimore (long obit) (*FGBA* 27 April 1818; *BA* 27 April 1818). Col. George Armistead, aged 39 years, was buried 25 April 1818 from St. Paul's Parish (ReamySP). An ordinance was proposed to exempt certain plate, presented him by the Citizens of Baltimore from taxation (*BPAT* 8 June 1818).

Armistead, Robert, a midshipman in the U.S. Navy, d. at Norfolk (*BPAT* 4 May 1819).

Armitage, Benjamin, a native of Baltimore, d. in New Orleans on 4 Sep, in his 18th year (*BA* 15 Oct 1817; *BPAT* 15 O ct 1817).

Armor, Mr. David, formerly of Baltimore, was m. at Westminster last Tues. by Rev. Jonathan Forrest, to Miss Maria Moore of the latter place (*BPAT* 7 Sep 1819).

Armstrong, Mr. Daniel, and Miss Ann Welden, all of Baltimore were m. last Thurs. eve. by Rev. Bartow (*BPAT* 9 Nov 1819).

Armstrong, Henry, was m. Sat, eve. by Rev. Fenwick, to Emilie Vallette, both of Baltimore (*BA* 31 Aug 1818; *BPAT* 31 August 1818).

Armstrong, Silas, d. at Washington, on 8th inst., after an illness of about 20days. He was aged 23 years, and chief of the Delaware tribe of Indians, one of the deputation of several tribes which had arrived at that city on public business a month ago (*BPAT* 11 Dec 1817; *BA* 11 Dec 1817).

Arnest, Mrs. Ann, d. 23 May in her 29th year, in Westmoreland Co., VA, consort of Dr. John Arnest, late of Baltimore (*BA* 4 June 1818).

Arnold, Francis, aged 19, indented apprentice, ran away from James F. Winchell, baker, at No. 59 South St. (*BPAT* 1 Jan 1818).

Arnold, Francis, was m. 15th inst. [Tues.], by Rev. George Dashiell, to Miss Margaret Long (*FGBA* 25 June 1819; *BPAT* 24 June 1819).

Arthur, Mrs. Damaris, native of the Island of Barbados, but a resident of Baltimore for the last 12 years, d. 23rd inst., aged 61 (*FGBA* 29 Sep 1818; *BPAT* 30 Sep 1818). Mrs. Arthur was buried 24 Sep 1818 from St. Paul's Parish (ReamySP). For her will, filed in n1818, see BAWB 10:507.

Ashe, Bernard D., was m. Thurs. eve. by Rev. Bartow, to Miss Ann Johnson (*BA* 14 Dec 1818; *BPAT* 14 Dec 1818).

Biographical Data from Baltimore Newspapers, 1817-1819

Ashley, David, about 40 years old, a stevedore, his wife Jane, 35 years old, and their dau. Jane, about 8 years old; all three ran away from Robert Bilus, No. 44, S. Charles St. (*BPAT* 11 July 1817).

Askew, Alexander, was m. last Thurs. eve. by Rev. Bartow to Miss Pamela Lynch (*BA* 14 Dec 1818; *BPAT* 14 Dec 1818).

Askew, Robert, m. last Thurs. by Rev. D. E. Reese to Miss Mary Ann Armstrong (*FGBA* 3 Oct 1818; *BPAT* 3 Oct 1818).

Asquith, Eli, was m. last Tues. by Rev. Bartow to Miss Mary Swain, all of Baltimore (*BA* 13 May 1819; *BPAT* 13 May 1819).

Atkinson, Anselow, aged about 16 years, and stout, an apprentice to the ship joiner's business, ran away from William Denny, Wolf St., Fell's Point; a reward of $20.00 was offered (*BPAT* 25 Aug 1818).

Atkinson, Isaac C., of Elk Ridge, was m. Tues. eve. by Rev. Dr. Inglis, to Amelia C. Stables, of Baltimore (*BA* 6 May 1819; *BPAT* 5 May 1819).

Atkinson, Thomas, of Easton, was m. at Friends Meeting House on Lombard St., on [Wed.], 15th inst., to Hannah Hussey, youngest dau. of George Hussey, Sr., late of Baltimore (*BPAT* 30 Dec 1819).

Attlesperger, John, about 27 years old, a counterfeiter, escaped from the custody of Miles Bunn, Constable, Shippensburg, Carlisle, Pa., on Fri., 31st ult., on the Walnut Bottom Road leadings from Carlisle to Shippensburg; had been a resident of Baltimore (*BPAT* 17 Aug 1818).

Augustine, Henry, d. 31 Jan 1818 in his 71st year. His res. was at Lombard St. (*FGBA* 14 Feb 1818; *BPAT* 14 Feb 1818).

Augustine, Samuel, of Baltimore, d. yesterday in his 27th year. His funeral will be from the residence of Mrs. Myers, 7 Union St., Old Town (*BA* 13 June 1818; *BPAT* 13 June 1818).

Aull, John W., was m. last Thurs. by Rev. Rev. D. E. Reese to Miss Elizabeth Benner, both of Baltimore (*BA* 16 July 1818; *BPAT* 16 July 1818).

Ayres, Capt. James, merchant, of Steubenville, Ohio, d. there last 21 Dec., in his 23rd year, son of Thomas Ayres, of Harford Co. (*BA* 3 Jan 1817).

"B"

Babe[?], Luke, and Miss Elizabeth Babe [sic], all of Philadelphia, were m. there on Thurs. eve,. last by Rev. Dr. Abercrombie (*BPAT* 19 Nov 1819).

Bacon, James, d. At Wood Lawn, Harford Co., last 15 March, in his 45th year (*BA* 16 April 1817; *BPAT* 17 April 1817).

Bacon, Dr. James [or John], formerly a respectable practitioner of this place, died at the Baltimore Hospital a few days since (*BPAT* 17 Feb 1818; *FGBA* 16 Feb 1818).

Baconais, Mr. Louis, for 24 years an inhabitant of Baltimore, and a teacher, died yesterday at 3:00 at his country seat. He resided on South Charles St. (*BA* 25 Aug 1817). He was 48 years old, died of an apoplectic fit, and was a native of St. Domingo, He was buried in the Cathedral Cemetery (Grogaard).

Badab, Henry, of Baltimore, was m. last Mon. by Rev. Badab to Joanna Parentiere, of Philadelphia (*BPAT* 1 Oct 1818).

Baden, Lieut. N., of the U.S. Ordnance Corps, was m. Mon. eve. by Bishop Kemp to Miss [E?]. Frances E. Collins, dau. of James W. Collins, of Baltimore (*BA* 26 July 1817; *BPAT* 26 July 1817).

Baer, William & Co., advertise 200 tons of stoves, consisting of Cooking, Nine Plate, Franklin, and Box Stoves at Pratt St., between Charles and Hanover (*BPAT* 9 Nov 1819).

Baggett, Ignatius, aged 54, was m. in Washington to Miss Julia [Baggett?], aged 15, both of Baltimore (*BPAT* 24 April 1819).

Bailey, Elisha T., was m. last Thurs. by Rev. Dr. Jennings to Miss Jane Ann Donaldson, both of Baltimore (*BA* 2 May 1818).

Biographical Data from Baltimore Newspapers, 1817-1819

Bain, George W., was m. Thurs. eve. by Rev. Valiant to Miss Jane Cox, all of Baltimore (*FGBA* 9 June 1818; *BPAT* 6 June 1818).

Bailey, Robert, a debtor, last Thurs., broke and made his escape from the Washington jail in the District of Columbia. He is about 50 years of age and is the same Major Bailey who kept boarding houses at Berkeley Springs, and last, the Bell Tavern in Washington. He is a notorious gambler and a black leg. /s/ Tench Ringgold, Marshal, Dist. of Columbia (*BPAT* 10 Aug 1818).

Baker, Charles, owes taxes for the years 1813, 1814, 1815, on 1 a., part *Grindon* in the 4th Dist. (*BPAT* 7 Jan 1819).

Baker, George C., was m. last Sun. by Dr. Roberts to Miss Eliza Williams, all of Baltimore (*BA* 16 Sep 1818; *BPAT* 16 Sep 1818 gives the groom's name as George W. Baker).

Baker, James, of Baltimore Co., is an insolvent debtor (*BPAT* 29 Sep 1819).

Balderston, Elizabeth, wife of Jonathan Balderston, d. 10th inst., in her 32nd year (*BA* 13 Nov 1818; *BPAT* 13 Nov 1818).

Balderston, Isaiah, d. yesterday, in the 65th year of his age (*BPAT* 6 Sep 1817; *BA* 6 Sep 1817). For his will, filed in 1817, see BAWB 10:357.

Balderston, Jonathan, dec.; his furniture at his late dwelling, 64 Lombard St., will be sold, Tues., 2nd inst. (*BPAT* 1 Nov 1819).

Baldwin, Mr. Abraham, was m. Sun. eve. last, by Rev. Mr. Healey to Miss Mary Proctor, both of this city (*BPAT* 29 Aug 1817).

Baldwin, Mr. Charles, was m. Sunday morning by Rev. Mr. Healey to Miss Elizabeth White, both of Baltimore Co. (*BPAT* 1 Sep 1817).

Baldwin, Mrs. Hannah, consort of William Baldwin, d. Sun., 21st inst., in Harford Co., aged 70 (*FGBA* 27 March 1819).

Baldwin, Capt. Pierson, was m. last Tues. by Rev. Mr. Glendy to Miss Sophia Gardner, all of this place (*BPAT* 21 May 1818).

Ball, Elisha, of Baltimore, was m. Thurs., 22nd inst. by Rev. Dr. Jennings to Miss Mary Divers of Baltimore Co. (*BA* 22 May 1817).

Ballard, William, merchant, d. yesterday, aged 34. A native of Boston, he had lived in Baltimore, for 12 years (*BA* 25 Dec 1818; *BPAT* 26 Dec 1818). His personal estate and furniture at his property at his residence in Hanover St., three doors south of Conway St., will be sold on Friday, 8th inst. Property to be sold included Brussels and Kidderminster carpets, elegant cut glass, and India and Staffordshire dining services, and one Washington Timepiece (*BPAT* 5 Jan 1819).

Balling, William, was m. last Tues. by Rev. D. E. Reese to Miss Hannah Richmond, all of Baltimore (*BA* 27 Nov 1818; *BPAT* 27 Nov 1818).

Baltzell, Charles, was m. last eve. [Mon.] by Rev. Hinshaw to Miss Maria Virginia Ringgold (*BA* 26 Nov 1818; *BPAT* 25 Nov 1818).

Bangs, Mr. Thomas, and Miss Ann Few, all of Baltimore, were m. last Tues. eve. by Rev. Mr. Force (*BPAT* 4 Dec 1819).

Banks, John, owes taxes for the year 1815, on 1 a. Name unknown in the 7th Dist. (*BPAT* 7 Jan 1819).

Bankson, John C., was m. last eve. [Tues.] by Rev. Mr. Henshaw, to Miss Sarah Ann, eldest dau. of George Maris, all of Baltimore (*BPAT* 31 March 1819).

Banning, Henry, aged 84, d. 20 Aug., near Easton, MD. When the Revolutionary War began, he was one of the first colonels to form a regiment. He served in the Legislature, and was a Justice of the Peace, and a County Commissioner (*BPAT* 8 Sep 1818).

Bannon, Hugh, born in Ireland, aged 23 years old, a laborer, deserted from the detachment under my command at Fort Covington o the 3rd of March. /s/ James H. Cook, Capt. (*BPAT* 13 April 1818).

Bantz, Mrs. Catherine, d. 21st inst., in her 31st year, widow of the late Jacob Bantz (*BA* 23 Aug 1817; *BPAT* 23 Aug 1817).

Biographical Data from Baltimore Newspapers, 1817-1819

Barber, James, was m. 27 May [Tues.] by Rev. Glendy to Mrs. Mary Davis, both of Baltimore (*BA* 30 May 1817; *BPAT* 30 May 1817).

Barber, Col. Thomas, of St. Mary's Co., was m. Thurs., 11th inst., by Rev. Henshaw to Miss Margaret Wellmore of Baltimore (*FGBA* 16 Feb 1819; *BPAT* 12 Feb 1819).

Barnard, Sarah, advertises herself as a poor broken woman, the widow of John Barnard, with two small children, states the properties advertised for sale by Thomas Hamlin were the property of John Barnard and lately of Priscilla Barnard, dec. (*BPAT* 21 June 1818).

Barnard, William, formerly lived in Canada. If he or any person who may know where he now happens to reside will inform the Postmaster of Baltimore, something of interest will be communicated to Barnard (*BPAT* 23 Nov 1818).

Barney, Charles, child of William B. Barney, d. yesterday when he fell into a well (*FGBA* 28 July 1819). Chase [*sic*] Barney, aged 10 years, was buried 28 July 1819 from St. Paul's Parish (ReamySP).

Barney, Commodore Joshua, a native of Baltimore, d. at Pittsburgh about 1 Dec. He was born on 6 July 1759, and served in the Revolutionary War and in the late war. He was wounded at Bladensburg (*BA* 8 Dec 1818). Members of his family are buried in Westminster Presbyterian Churchyard, Baltimore (HaywardW). For his will, filed in 1819, see BAWB 10:543.

Barnman, Mr. Henry, was m. last eve. [Tues.], by Rev. Mr. Kurtz, to Miss Elizabeth Huveler, all of Baltimore (*BPAT* 22 Dec 1819).

Barrett, Mr. George H., was m. Thurs. eve. at Marietta, PA, to Miss Mary Hopkins, dau. of James Hopkins of Lancaster, Pa, (*BA* 4 Sep 1818; *BPAT* 4 Sep 1818).

Barrett, Lieut. John M., lately the captain of the elegant corps of Regular Blues of Baltimore, now of the 4th Regt., U. S. Infantry; d. 16th Oct., of the yellow fever on his passage from Orleans to Mobile; aged 34 years; he had been appointed to an honorable station on the Southern frontier, where he was bound with his family. He leaves a wife and children. Long obit (*BPAT* 16 Nov 1819).

Barron, Mrs. Elizabeth, relict of Commodore Samuel Barron of the U.S. Navy, d. 26 Oct at Hampton, Va. (*BA* 9 Nov 1818; *BPAT* 4 Nov 1818).

Barron, Mr. Wm. H. merchant, of Washington City, was m. Sun., 11th inst., at Analostan Island, to Miss Leeanah Mason, of Prince William Co., Va. (*BPAT* 15 May 1817).

Barry, Miss Ann, sister of Rev. Dr. Barry, d. Sat., 23rd Aug. after a long illness (*BPAT* 4 Sep 1818). Ann Barry, aged 50 years, was buried 7 Oct 1819 from St. Paul's Parish (ReamySP).

Barry, Rev. E.D., D. D., of Baltimore Co., was m. at St. Paul's Church in Huntington, Conn., on 4th inst., [Mon.] to Miss Cornelia Shelton, dau. of Dr. Shelton of Huntington (*FGBA* 12 Jan 1819; *BPAT* 12 Jan 1819).

Barry, Mrs. H., wife of Rev. E. D. Barry, recently of New York, d. yesterday, leaving a husband and children (*FGBA* 24 April 1817). Hepzibah Barry, aged 43 years, was buried 23 April 1817 from St. Paul's Parish (ReamySP).

Barry, Capt. John Jones, was m. last Thurs. by Rev. Dr. Kurtz to Sophia Ratien, eld. dau. of Richard Ratien, all of Baltimore (*FGBA* 7 Feb 1818; *BPAT* 7 Feb 1818).

Barry, Thomas J., Baltimore merchant, was m. Tues. eve. by Rev. Mr. Endress, to Miss Maria Lemaz, dau. of Jacob Lemaz of Lancaster, PA (*BA* 2 Oct 1817; *BPAT* 2 Oct 1817 gives the bride's name as Leman).

Bartleson, William, d. yesterday at the Hospital (*FGBA* 12 Feb 1817; *BPAT* 13 Feb 1817).

Bartlett, Mr. Jonathan, was m. to Miss Mary Ann Jordan, dau. of Capt. William Jordan (*BPAT* 21 April 1817).

Bartlett, Mr. William, was m. last Sun. eve. by the Rev. Dr. Roberts to Miss Aley Robinson (*BPAT* 28 June 1817).

Barton, John, owes taxes for the year 1817 on 10½ a. part *Stout* in the 1st Dist. (*BPAT* 3 Aug 1819).

Biographical Data from Baltimore Newspapers, 1817-1819

Basford, David, of Boston, was m. last Thurs. by Rev. Dr. Roberts to Miss Catherine Fowler, all of Baltimore (*FGBA* 26 Sep 1818; *BA* 26 Sep 1818; *BPAY* 25 Sep 1818).

Batchelder, Mr. Smith, was m. Tues., 23rd inst., by Rev. Mr. Kurtz to Miss Mary Swaney, all of Baltimore (*BA* 29 Dec 1817; *BPAT* 29 Dec 1817).

Bateman, William L., was m. last Tues. eve. by Rev. Dr. Jennings to Miss Catherine R. Dallas, all of Baltimore (*BPAT* 30 Nov 1818).

Bauer, David, was m. last Thurs. eve. by Rev. Dr. Roberts to Miss Nancy James, all of Baltimore (*BPAT* 21 May 1818).

Bauhgn, Mrs. Dorothea, aged 108 years, lacking nine days, d. 3rd inst., within one mile of the White Chimnies, Caroline Co., Va. She was never known to have taken medicine of any kind. She had ten children, nine of whom she raised to be men and women; the other died at the age of eight (*BPAT* 21 Oct 1819).

Baxley, Mr. Elisha T., Jr., was m. to Miss Jane Ann Donaldson, all of Baltimore on last Thurs. eve. by Rev. Dr. Jennings (*BPAT* 1 May 1818).

Baxley, Miss Sally Phillips, dau. of John Baxley, d. last Sat. morning, in her 18th year (*FGBA* 3 June 1818).

Bayard, James, a free-born black boy, son of Mingo Bayard, was born in Appoquitiminck Hundred, New Castle Co., Del., in June 1804. He was bound by his father to Wm. F. Corbit, who sold him to a certain Benjamin Johnson, where he lived, until missing. His father asks for information about his whereabouts (*BPAT* 14 Feb 1818).

Bayley, Elisha T., Jr., was m. last Thurs. eve. by Rev. Dr. Jennings to Miss Jane Anne Donaldson, all of Baltimore (*BPAT* 1 May 1818).

Bayley, Sarah Ann, eld. dau. of Henry E. Bayley of Baltimore Co., d. 29th ult., in her 14th year (*BA* 2 Dec 1817; *BPAT* 2 Dec 1817).

Bayly, Elisha, heirs of, owes taxes for the year 1815, on land in the 1st Dist. (*BPAT* 7 Jan 1819).

Bayly, Girdin C., was m. last Thurs. by Rev. Dr. Roberts, to Miss Cassandra Ann Leek, both of Baltimore (*BA* 21 Oct 1818; *BPAT* 19 Oct 1818).

Baynard, John, merchant, was m. last eve. [Thurs.], by Rev. E.J. Reis, to Miss Eliza, dau. of George Heide, Esq., of Baltimore (*FGBA* 6 June 1817; *BPAT* 6 June 1817).

Baynard, John, aged 34, of the House of Baynard and Dickenson, d. last Sat., aged 34 (*BPAT* 13 Oct 1819).

Bayne, John F., of Accomac Co., VA, was m. last 24 Sep [Tues.] to Miss Ann C. Bailey of the same place (*BA* 17 Oct 1817; *BPAT* 27 Oct 1817).

Bays[?], Mr. William, d. at Fredericktown, after a short illness, in the 50th year of his age (*BPAT* 30 Aug 1819).

Beacham, Miss Eliza, d. last Mon. eve. aged 20 years and 5 mos. (*FGBA* 30 April 1817; *BPAT* 30 April 1817).

Beacham, William, aged 19 years old, apprentice to the boot and shoemaking business, ran away from Wm. Davis, who asks that the boy be returned to the Baltimore Co. gaol. a reward of ten dollars is offered (*BPAT* 25 Feb 1818).

Beacham, William, was m. last Sun. by Rev. Dr. Roberts to Mrs. Mary Kithcart, both of Baltimore (*BA* 9 May 1818; *BPAT* 8 May 1818).

Beall, Elizabeth Caroline, only dau,. of Mrs. Margaret Beall, d. on Fri., 28th Sep last, near Port Tobacco, Charles Co., after a tedious and painful illness, in the 19th year of her age (*BPAT* 23 Nov 1819).

Beall, Mr. Zadock W., late of Prince George's Co., was m. Thurs., 11th inst., by Rev. Neale H. Shaw to Miss Susan R. Morton, dau. of Mr. Samuel Morton of St. Mary's Co. (*BPAT* 19 Dec 1817).

Beam, Conrad, of New York, was m. Sun eve. by Rev. Mr. Bartow, to Miss Maria Hurst, of Baltimore (*BA* 17 June 1817; *BPAT* 17 June 1817).

Beam, Major George, dec.; his son, Mr. William Beam, has purchased from the executor of his father's estate, the tavern establishment and the farm connected

Biographical Data from Baltimore Newspapers, 1817-1819

therewith; the sale is postponed, and William Beam will continue his father's business (*BPAT* 24 Nov 1818). For the will of George Beam, filed in 1815, see BAWB 10:18.

Beam, Mrs. Sarah, d. this morning after a lingering illness, in the 52nd year of her age (*BPAT* 28 Nov 1817). For her will, filed in 1817, see BAWB 10:392,

Beam, Miss Susannah H., dau. of the late Major George Beam, d. 16 Aug, aged 5 years (*BA* 18 Aug 1818; *BPAT* 11 Aug 1818).

Beans, Major Wm. B., d. at Upper Marlboro, Prince George's Co., in his 42nd year (*BPAT* 8 Jan 1818).

Beatty, Mr. Lewis A., and Miss Sarah B. Marshall, of Frederick Co., were m. at Frederick Town (*BPAT* 8 Nov 1819).

Beatty, Mr. Samuel, d. 27th Oct., in Dorchester Co., in his 30th year; late of Baltimore Co., where he was born. He leaves a widow and three children (*BPAT* 6 Dec 1819)

Beausey, Charles, aged about 18 years of age, slender made, light hair, fair complexion, five feet five inches tall, apprentice to the Cedar Coopering Business, has run away from Samuel Robertson, 20 N. Howard St. (*BPAT* 27 July 1819).

Beck, Samuel, son of Paul Beck, Esq., of Philadelphia, d. at New York on 7th inst., after a lingering illness (*BPAT* 10 Dec 1817).

Beck, Samuel, died at Kent Co., on the 16th inst., in his 83rd year. He took part in the Revolutionary War (*BA* 19 March 1818; *BPAT* 18 March 1818).

Beck, Sarah, sister of Darius Gamble, of Kent Co., dec,, is suing Samuel Beck, and William G. Lowman, who reside outside the State of Md., William Strong, Simon Wickes, Greenbury Gamble, and Robert S. Gamble, concerning the estate of said Darius Gamble (*BPAT* 4 Aug 1817).

Beck, William C., of Philadelphia, was m. last Friday to Miss Sarah Matilda McCoy of Baltimore (*BMC* 31 May 1819; *BPAT* 29 May 1819).

Becker, Rev. Dr. Christian L., d. 12 July 1818 in his 63rd year; he resided on Second St. (*FGBA* 3 July 1818; *BPAT* 13 July 1818).

Beckett, John, was m. Sun, eve. by Rev. Davis to Mrs. Sarah Scaplander (*BA* 4 Aug 1818; *BPAT* 4 Aug 1818).

Beckham, Armistead, master armourer of the U.S. Manufactory of Arms at Harper's Ferry, was m. to Miss Jane Frame of Charleston, VA, on Thurs., 22nd inst. by Rev. Benj. Allen (*BPAT* 29 Jan 1818; *BPAT* 29 Jan 1818).

Beedle, Mr. Thomas, of Cecil Co., but for many years a resident of this city, d. last Friday. In the course of his illness he was visited by Rev. Mr. Wyatt who performed the funeral obsequies in Christ Church on Sunday evening. He left a wife and daughter (*BPAT* 25 March 1817).

Beemis, Nathan S., of Chester Co., PA, was m. to Susannah Ashmore of Harford Co. on Thurs. 13th Aug. by Rev. Dr. Inglis (*BA* 26 Aug 1818; *BPAT* 26 Aug 1818).

Bell, Elisha, of Baltimore, was m. Thurs. eve., 22nd inst., by Rev. Dr. Jennings, to Miss Mary Divers of Baltimore Co. (*BPAT* 27 May 1817).

Bell, Hugh, was m. to Miss Ann Chambers, both of Baltimore on Thurs. eve. by Rev. Dr. Jennings (*FGBA* 15 May 1818; *BPAT* 15 May 1818).

Bell, Mr. John, was m. [at Hagerstown?}, [date not given], to Miss Catherine Caphart (*BPAT* 8 Oct 1819).

Bell, Peter, was m. to Miss Ann Bird, both of Somerset Co. last Wed. by Rev. Glendy (*BPAT* 8 April 1819; *BMC* 10 April 1819).

Bell, Thomas, of VA, was m. Thurs. eve. by Rev. Roberts, to Miss Matilda Barney of Baltimore (*BA* 24 May 1817; *BPAT* 24 May 1817).

Bell, William D., editor of the *Torch Light,* and Miss Susanna Harry, both of Hagerstown, were married there, on Tues., 10th inst.. (*BPAT* 14 Dec 1818)

Bemont, Silas, late of Pittsfield, MA, d. last Sun. He was drowned with four others by the upsetting of a boat in passing from Fort McHenry to the city (*BPAT* 23 May 1817).

Biographical Data from Baltimore Newspapers, 1817-1819

Bender, Henry, d. this morning, aged 9. His funeral will be from the dwelling of Peter Fowble, at the corner of Paca St. and Whiskey Alley (*FGBA* 2 Oct 1817; *BOPAT* 3 Oct 1817).

Benjamin, Miss Emily, a native of Stratford, Conn., d. last Sat. at the residence of Josiah Meigs at Washington (*BPAT* 19 March 1818).

Bennet, John M., was m. 25 Sep [Thurs.] 1817 by Rev. Kemp to Mrs. Margaret Thomson, both of Baltimore (*BA* 29 Sep 1817; *BPAT* 27 Sep 1817).

Bennett, Anthony B., of Somerset Co., was m. to Maria Louisa, dau. of Dr. James Derickson, of Laurel, Del., at the latter place on Wed., 16th June (*BPM* 21 June 1819).

Bennett, Mr. Edmund T., clerk of the court of Concordia Parish, La., d. at there at the residence of the Hon Judge Dunlap of La., of the yellow fever, after an illness of three days. Bennett was formerly a resident of Snowhill, Somerset Co. (*BPAT* 16 Oct 1819, 18 Oct 1819).

Benning, William, of Trinidad, was m. to Miss Ann White of Boston, last eve. [Tues.] by Rev. Inglis (*BA* 6 Jan 1819).

Bentley, Israel, was m. to Miss Mary Herback, both of Union Town, Frederick Co., on Tues. last by Rev. Lauston (*BA* 20 Nov 1818; *BPAT* 19 Nov 1818).

Benson, Levin, was m. Thurs., 16th inst., at Little Falls Meeting House in Harford Co. to Miss Rachel Lancaster (*BPAT* 22 Sep 1819).

Benton, Richard, was m. to Mrs. Susan Eddy, both of Baltimore, last eve. [Thurs.] by Rev. Dr. Roberts (*BA* 30 April 1819; *BPAT* 30 April 1819).

Berge, Joseph, a native of France, d. 27th inst., aged 45 years. He was long known to many in Baltimore and Annapolis as a teacher of languages. Born and educated under the smiles of affluence, he came to our shores after seeing his father butchered in St. Domingo (*BPAT* 30 Dec 1819).

Berkley, Robert, owes taxes for the year 1816 on land transferred from Carter's estate in the 1st Dist. (*BPAT* 3 Aug 1819).

Bernard, Capt. Louis, d. 27th inst., in his 76th year, long an inhabitant of this county (*BPAT* 5 Feb 1819).

Berridge. Mr. William, d. at the Trappe (*BPAT* 2 Nov 1819).

Berry, Benjamin, Jr., was m. by Rev. McCormick, to Miss Eleanor Brooke Eversfield Forbes, of Washington (*BA* 22 May 1817; *BPAT* 21 May 1817).

Berry, John, took from Thos. Wentz' livery stable in Lancaster, Pa., on Monday, 10th a horse and gig (*BPAT* 5 Nov 1817).

Bersch, Henry, was m. Thurs. by Rev. Baker to Miss Mary Hoffman, all of Baltimore (*FGBA* 26 July 1817; *BPAT* 28 July 1817).

Bestpitch, Joseph, of Dorchester Co., dec. William Craft, admin., will settle the estate (*BPAT* 27 June 1818).

Betts, Catherine, wife of Enoch Betts, d. Sun., 30th inst., in her 39th year (*FGBA* 31 Aug 1818; *BPAT* 31 Aug 1818).

Betts, Enoch, was m. to Miss Elizabeth Ball, all of Baltimore, last Thurs. eve. by Rev. Mr. Bartow (*FGBA* 27 March 1819; *BPAT* 27 March 1819).

Betune, Joseph, a yellow boy, about 17 or 18 years of age, ran away from Job West on or about the 25th of last month (*BPAT* 8 July 1818).

Betz, George W., d. Wed., 30th ult., in his 42nd year, a respectable officer of Baltimore, leaving a wife and two children (*BA* 4 Aug 1817; *BPAT* 4 Aug 1817).

Biays, James, Jr., of Baltimore, was m. at Philadelphia on 23rd ult., [Tues.] by Rev. Dr. Neill, to Miss Margaretta McMullen, dau. of John McMullen of Philadelphia (*BPM* 1 Jan 1818; *BPAT* 1 Jan 1818).

Bicknell, Thomas W. T., was m. last Wed. eve. by Rev. Mr. Read to Miss Ann Baker, both of Baltimore (*BA* 5 Sep 1817; *BPAT* 5 Sep 1817).

Biddison, Jeremiah, was married Tues., 9th inst. by Rev, Healey, to Miss Ann Vears of Baltimore Co. (*FGBA* 20 March 1819; *BPAT* 19 March 1819).

Biographical Data from Baltimore Newspapers, 1817-1819

Bidgood, Wm. Rodman, of Philadelphia, d. at St. Bartholomew's on the 12th of Feb., after five days' illness, in his 22nd year, leaving a brother and sister and other relatives (*BPAT* 17 March 1817).

Biggs, Benjamin, d. 5th inst. in Frederick Co. in his 59th year (*BMC* 22 May 1819).

Billington, William, d. last Mon., 26th Jan., aged 65, formerly of England; he resided on the York Road (*FGBA* 3 Feb 1818; *BPAT* 2 Feb 1818). For his will, filed in 1818, see BAWB 10:412.

Binns, Mr. John A. was m. in Leesburg, VA, to Miss Mary Ross, youngest dau. of Capt. John Rose (*BPAT* 25 Nov 1818).

Bird. Charles, of Tenn., was m. to Julia Ann Merkle, of Baltimore, on Thurs. eve. by the Rev. Mr. Hershberger (*BA* 17 Oct 1818; *BPAT* 16 Oct 1818)).

Bird, Capt. Jacob, of New York, was m. to Miss Ann Maguire of Baltimore by Rev, Glendy last Sunday (*BPAT* 22 Sep 1818).

Blackburn, Mrs., wife of Professor Blackburn of Asbury College, died when her room caught fire last wed. Her two daughters were also injured (*FGBA* 27 April 1818).

Black, Vachel, was m. Thurs. eve. by Rev. Dr. Jennings, to Miss Catherine Berry, all of Baltimore (*BA* 11 Oct 1817).

Blackiston, Michael, dec., in his lifetime was indebted to Thomas Stinson. He died possessed of a house and lot, of about six acres, in Queen Anne's Co. and about sixty acres of land in the same county. His heirs at law, including John Blackiston who died without issue, are James. Michael, Ebenezer, Jabez, Harriot, Mary, and Doretha M. Blackiston, and John Berbage are being sued by Stinson. The bill of complaint sates that Michael, Ebenezer, Elizabeth, and Mary Blackiston, and John Berbage, all reside without the state of Md. (*BPAT* 22 Sep 1818; see also *BPAT* 8 Oct 1818).

Blair, William, d. yesterday, after a short illness, in his 36th year (*BA* 8 Oct 1817; *BPAT* 8 Oct 1817).

Blake, Dr. James H., d. at Washington City, Thurs. morning after a painful indisposition that lasted 14 mos., in the 52nd year of his age. He was a native of Calvert Co., Md., had dwelt in Va. for some years, and for the last ten years had lived in this city [Wash.]. He leaves a wife and children.. He was a Magistrate in Va., and in the District of Columbia, and had been a Representative in the Legislature of Va. ; for several years he was Mayor of Washington, D,C,, and part of the time was Collector of The Internal Revenue. At the time of his death he was Register of Wills for Washington Co. (*BPAT* 31 July 1819).

Blatchford, Miss Harriot P., d. in the village of Lansingburgh in her 24th year, second dau. of the Rev. Samuel Blatchford, D.D. Her death is supposed to have been caused by the rupture of an artery in the brain (*BPAT* 31 March 1819).

Blatchley, Thomas, owes taxes for the years 1814 and 1815, on 4 a. *Matthews Farm* in the 4th Dist. (*BPAT* 7 Jan 1819).

Blick, William H., of Va., and Mary Ann Feinour, eld, dau. of Charles Feinour of Anne Arundel Co. were m. Tues., 7th inst., by Rev, Henshaw (*BA* 10 Dec 1818; *BPAT* 9 Dec 1818).

Bliss, Capt. Calvin, was m. Thurs. eve., 24 April, by Rev. Nathaniel Greenleaf to Miss Catherine Ling, all of Baltimore (*BPAT* 2 May 1817).

Bloomfield, Charles, and his two sons, Michael and Antony, coopers by trade, emigrated from the city of Limerick, Ireland, and set up business in either Baltimore or Philadelphia. Anyone knowing of the same is asked to contact with his [Charles'] son, John Bloomfield of Norfolk, Va. (*BPAT* 11 March 1818).

Blow, John, aged 35, a native of England, d. leaving a wife and two children (*BPAT* 2 Feb 1819).

Blow, Joshua, is an insolvent debtor of Baltimore (*BPAT* 5 Jan 1819).

Blue, Harry, a Negro man, about 33 years of age, and about 5 feet 9 inches tall, ran away from John Mathews, near Annapolis, Md. (*BPAT* 4 Aug 1817).

Biographical Data from Baltimore Newspapers, 1817-1819

Blunt, John S., was m. last eve. [Thurs.] by Rev. D. E. Reese to Miss Sarah Morris, both of Baltimore (*BA* 28 Nov 1817; *BPAT* 28 Nov 1817).

Boblitz, Michael, owes taxes for the years 1813, 1814, 1815, on 117 a. *Edwards 'Choice* in the3rd Dist. (*BPAT* 7 Jan 1819).

Boddily, John, and Miss Mary Ann Turner, all of Baltimore, were m. last Mon. eve. by Rev,. Davis (*BPAT* 27 Jan 1818).

Bodenverber, John, aged 38, a baker, a servant, a Dutch Redemptioner, ran away from Henry Freburger, 59 Lexington St. (*BPAT* 19 Jan 1819).

Bogen, Dr. John A., d. Wed., 27th ult., at Carlisle (*BPAT* 8 Nov 1819).

Boggs, Alexander L., merchant, was m. last Tues. eve. by Rev. Dr. Inglis to Miss Susan Green, both of this city (*BPAT* 14 Feb 1817; *BA* 15 Feb 1817).

Bohn, Mr. Chas., and Mrs. Caroline Tepkin, all of Baltimore, were m. 7th inst. [Sun.], at Beach Hill, Baltimore Co., by Rev. Dr. Kurtz (*BPAT* 9 Nov 18190.

Bohn, Mrs. Elizabeth, wife of Charles Bohn, formerly a respectable merchant of this city, died 30th ult., in her 60th year (*BA* 8 Dec 1818; *BPAT* 4 Dec 1818).

Boisseau, Joseph, of Alexandria, and Miss Ann Jenkins of MD, were m. last Thurs., at Alexandria by Rev. Mr. Farclough (*FGBA* 24 Feb 1819; *BPAT* 25 Feb 1819).

Bollman, Thomas, d. this morning, aged 44. He resided at the corner of Water St. and Public Alley (*FGBA* 17 April 1819; *BPAT* 17 April 1818). His property, at the corner of Water St. and Public Alley, has been taken over by John M. Rudenstein and [-?-] Breuning for their grocery and baking business (*BPAT* 10 June 1819). For his will, filed in 1819, See BAWB 11:364.

Bolton, Capt. Henry, of Fells Point, d. 28th inst. He resided at Market St., Fells Point (*BA* 29 Sep 1818; *BPAT* 29 Sep 1818). His death was recorded in the records of the East Baltimore Station of the Methodist Church (PedenM) For his will, filed in 1818, see BAWB 10:510.

Bond, Jacob H., owes taxes for the years 1813, 1814, 1815, on 2¾ a. *Spring Garden* in the 7th Dist. (*BPAT* 7 Jan 1819).

Bond, Rev. John Wesley, d. last night at the house of his brother, after a painful illness of 15 days, in his 35th year. He had been an itinerant minister of the Gospel in the Methodist Episcopal Church for ten years. He had been the faithful attendant of the late Bishop Asbury for the two years. The funeral will be tomorrow morning from the residence of Dr. Bond in Charles St., and the funeral discourse will be delivered at Light St. Church (*BPAT* 23 Jan 1819). For his will, filed in 1819, see BAWB 11:11.

Bond, Josiah, and Miss Mary Blaney were m. last Sun, eve. by Rev. Mr. Valiant (*BPAT* 17 April 1818).

Bond, Lambert, was m. last eve. [Thurs.] by Rev. Mr. Healey, to Miss Susannah Lauderman, both of Baltimore (*BPAT* 9 Jan 1818).

Bond, Oliver, son of James Bond, d. Sat., 28th inst., after a short severe illness, aged 18 years and 19 mos., a student of Physic under Dr. Clendenin. Washington and N. C. papers please copy (*FGBA* 2 Sep 1819; *BPAT* 1 Sep 1819).

Bond, Thomas, of Baltimore and Mary Jane Franklin, dau. of John Franklin of N. Y., were m. in the latter city on 11th inst. [Mon.], by Rev. Dr. Milledollar (*FGBA* 15 Jan 1819; *BPAT* 16 Jan 1819).

Bonfanti, Joseph, lately arrived from Europe, has opened a shop at 34½ Baltimore St., second door below Frederick St., where he sells a large variety of Fancy Articles (*BPAT* 9 Aug 1817).

Bonfield, James, purchased part of *Cole's Harbor* or *Todd's Range* on 15 June 1759. A commission will meet to establish the liens of the tract (*BPAT* 24 Aug 1818).

Bonsall, John M., and Miss Mary Everett, all of Baltimore, were m. Wed., 2nd June, by Rev. Dr. Roberts (*BPAT* 7 June 1819).

Boone, Mr. Robert, of Frederick Co., was m. at Washington on 15th inst. [Tues.], by the Right Rev. Leonard Neale, Archbishop of Baltimore, to Miss Catherine Francis Queen, of the District of Columbia (*BPAT* 18 April 1817).

Biographical Data from Baltimore Newspapers, 1817-1819

Booth, Joseph, was m. Thurs. eve. last by Rev. D. E. Reese to Miss Mary Carmichael, both of this city (*BPAT* 7 June 1817).

Bose, Mr. William, co-editor of the *American*, and Miss Mary Goulding, all of Baltimore, were m. last Tues. eve. by Rev. Mr. Fenwick (*BPAT* 27 Nov 1819).

Bosley, Ann, owes taxes for the years 1813, 1814, 1815, on 109 a. Name Unknown in the 7th Dist. (*BPAT* 7 Jan 1819).

Boss, Hezekiah, Sr., a respectable citizen of Baltimore, for many years a branch pilot of the *Chesapeake*, and an affectionate husband and tender parent, d. at Norfolk (*BPAT* 12 April 1817).

Bouldin, Charles D., and Miss Mary Gover Wilson, were m. last eve. [Thurs.] by Rev. Fenwick (*FGBA* 23 April 1819; *BPAT* 24 April 1819).

Bounds, John, of Somerset Co., died; Daniel Davis, exec., advertised he would settle the estate (*BPAT* 3 Feb 1817).

Bourke, Mrs. Bridget, wife of John Bourke, d. yesterday, after a lingering illness. Her funeral will be from her late residence, Star Alley, Fells Point (*BA* 29 March 1817; *BPAT* 29 March 1817).

Bourke, Mr. William Y., of Queen Anne's Co., was m. at Easton, to Mrs. Rebecca Dunn (*BPAT* 21 April 1817).

Bourry, Mr. Lewis, d. last night of a lingering illness. His funeral will be from his late residence in Market Space (*BPAT* 17 Aug 1819, 18 Aug 1819). For the will of Louis Boury, filed in 1819, see BAWB 11:40..

Bowen, Josias, of Baltimore Co., died, leaving a valuable mill property located near the Baltimore and York Turnpike, containing 9 or 10 acres in the neighborhood of Bellona Powder Mills. The property is to be sold by a decree of the Chancellor of Md. /s/ Saml. J Donaldson, trustee (*BPAT* 20 July 1818).

Bowers, Daniel, owes taxes for the year 1816 on 1 lot in Hookstown in the 1st Dist. His heirs owed taxes on the same land in 1817 (*BPAT* 4 Aug 1819).

Bowie, Gov. Robert, d. at Nottingham, Md., on Friday, in his 68th year; an old Revolutionary officer, and formerly Gov. of Md.. He leaves a widow, three daus. and a son (*FGBA* 12 Jan 1818; *BPAT* 12 Jan 1818: long obit is given).

Bowly, Daniel, owned a lot of ground, situate on the n. e. side of Granby St., between Polly and Wilkes Sts., which was sold by Thomas Buchanan, his trustee, to Whitley Barnes; the City Commissioners will meet to determine the boundaries of the lot (*BPAT* 17 March 1817).

Bowman, Capt. Samuel, a Patriot of the Revolution, d. at Wilkesbarre, PA., on the 25th inst. at an advanced age, when he was killed by a bull (*BPAT* 2 July 1818).

Boyd, John, and Miss Margaretta Isler, of Baltimore, were m. last Tues. eve. by Rev. Dr. Roberts (*FGBA* 1 Aug 1818; *BPAT* 3 Aug 1818).

Boyd, Mr. Patrick, and Miss Jane May, all of Baltimore, were m. Mon. eve. by Rev. Dr. Glendy (*BPAT* 16 Dec 1819).

Boyle, Patrick, aged 38, born in Ireland, a plasterer, lately resided in Chambersburg, deserted from the Carlisle Barracks on 17th inst. /s/ James Pratt, Captain of Superintendent Recruiting Services, 5th Regiment (*BPAT* 2 Sep 1817).

Boyle, Thomas, a recruit of the 5th Infantry, 38 years of age, by profession a plaisterer, late place of residence: Chambersburg; he was born in Ireland. /s/ James Pratt, Captain, Superintending [sic] recruiting Service, 5th Infantry at the Carlisle Barracks (*BPAT* 4 Sep 1817).

Bradburn, Samuel, and Miss Sarah Wheeler, both of Baltimore Co., were m. Thurs., 4th inst. by Rev. Mr. Tydings (*FGBA* 10 Feb 1819; *BPAT* 10 Feb 1819).

Braderhouse, Mr. William, was m. to Miss Louisa Lannay, all of Baltimore on Thurs. eve. by Rev. Bishop Kemp (*BPAT* 11 March 1818; *BA* 11 March 1818).

Bradford, John, and Ann Eliza, dau. of Gen. Stricker, all of Baltimore, were m. last eve. [Tues.] by Rev. Inglis (*FGBA* 9 Dec 1818; *BA* 10 Dec 1818; *BPAT* 10 Dec 1818).

Bradford, William, of Frederick Town, and Miss Jane Ringgold of Baltimore, were m. last eve. [Mon.] at St. Peter's Church by Rev. Henshaw (*BPAT* 5 May 1818).

Biographical Data from Baltimore Newspapers, 1817-1819

Bradley, Capt. Peregrine, late commander of the Indiaman *Bingham* of Philadelphia, d. at Havana of the yellow fever *(BPAT* 2 Nov 1819).

Brady, Mr. Felix, was m. at Washington, to Miss Susan Dougherty, all of that place *(BPAT* 12 June 1817).

Brady, Francis, of Baltimore, native of Ireland, was m. to Miss Martha Lafilly of Charleston, S. C., at that place on 21 May [Thurs.] *(BA* 20 Aug 1818; *BPAT* 18 Aug 1818 gives the bride's name as Lavilly).

Bragdon, John, aged about 11 years, apprentice to the silk making business, ran away from John Healey. a reward of 25 cents is offered *(BPAT* 21 Aug 1818).

Brand, Mr. David, was m. last eve. [Sun.], by Rev. Dr. Kurtz, to Miss Ann Wells, all of Baltimore, *(BPAT* 27 Sep 1819).

Brandt, Mrs. Mahalia, wife of David W. Brandt, d. 12th inst., in her 22nd year *(BPAT* 13 Oct 1818).

Brannan, Mr. Pritchard, was m. Thurs. eve. by Rev. Glendy to Miss Margaret Mann *(BPAT* 21 June 1817; *BA* 21 June 1817 gives the groom's name as Branslan).

Brant, J., merchant of Baltimore, and Miss Hannah Arianna Blake of Queen Anne's Co., were m. last eve. [Mon.] by Rev. Duncan *(BPAT* 5 May 1818).

Brashears, Richard B., of the U. S. Navy, and formerly of Washington, d. at Charleston a few days ago,*(BPAT* 15 Sep 1817).

Brass, Joseph, aged 19, and Miss Ann Hagon, aged 58, all of Baltimore, were m. last Thurs. by Rev. E. I. Reis *(FGBA* 12 Aug 1818).

Brent, Mrs. Eliza, d. yesterday afternoon, in the 21st year of her age, of consumption, dau. of John Carrere, Esq., of Baltimore *(BPAT* 12 Feb 1817; *FGBA* 12 Feb 1817). She was buried in the Cathedral Cemetery (Grogaard).

Brent, Robert, Esq., late Paymaster General of the Army, and Judge of the Orphans Court of for the county of Washington Co. d. at Washington City, after a long and protracted illness *(BPAT* 10 Sep 1819).

Brereton, Thomas, of Montgomery Co. d. after a short illness (St. Anthony's Fire), in the 34th year of his age *(BPAT* 18 Dec 1817).

Brevitt, Benjamin S., merchant, was m. last Thurs.,25th inst., by Rev. Mr. Dodson, to Miss Eliza Rebecca Hynson, of Kent Co., Eastern Shore *(BPAT* 2 Dec 1819).

Brewer, Mr. Lewis, was m. on Thurs. eve. by Rev. Helfenstein to Miss Catherine Neppard, both of Baltimore *(BPAT* 26 July 1819).

Brewer, Nicholas, Jr., of Annapolis, was m. Thurs. eve. by Rev. Duncan to Miss Julia Stewart, of Anne Arundel Co. *(BA* 3 Nov 1817; *BPAT* 1 Nov 1817).

Brewster, Mr. Edward, portrait painter of Philadelphia, was m. at Louisville, Ky. [date not given], to Miss Lydia Stevens *(BPAT* 15 Jan 1819).

Brian, William, and Miss Catherine Clackner, all of Baltimore, were m. Sun. eve. by Rev. Bartow *(BA* 5 Jan 1819; *BPAT* 5 Jan 1819 gives the groom's name as William Briar).

Bridges, Mr. Elias, was m. at Port-Gibson, Mississippi, [date not given], to Miss Tennessee Tannehill, dau. of Mr. George Tannehill of this county *(BPAT* 15 Dec 1818).

Bridges, Harriet, advertises that she and her sister Sarah Bridges, keep a millinery shop. Harriet was to have married John Tyler, recently dec. Certain persons have circulated [anonymously] certain reports injurious to her character. She asks that if any person knows of any misconduct or bad behavior by her, [he or she] will openly declare it *(BPAT* 2 Oct 1818).

Bridges, James, of Georgetown, was m. in Washington, to Miss Mary McKim of Baltimore *(BPAT* 25 April 1817).

Bridport, Mr. George, d. at Havana on the 2nd inst., a native of England, an eminent artist, and late of Philadelphia. He had long suffered from a pulmonary complaint *(BPAT* 26 March 1819).

Briguin, James, native of France, and Miss Annette Ricaud of Baltimore, were m. last Friday by Rev. D. E. Reese *(BPAT* 2 June 1819).

Biographical Data from Baltimore Newspapers, 1817-1819

Briscoe, George, Esq., d. at his residence at Nottingham, Prince George's Co., on Thurs., 1st, inst., aged 67 years, collector for the port of Nottingham, which station he has filled ever since the Revolutionary War (*BPAT* 9 April 1817).

Briscoe, Moses, died recently in Kent Co., possessed of considerable real state, and leaving the following people as his hers at law: Samuel Briscoe, George Briscoe (who lives outside the state of Maryland), Maria Briscoe, and Ann, wife of Thomas Bevans. John Maxwell and Margaret Briscoe were appointed administrators. They are being sued in chancery by James M. Anderson, Jr., John Whaland, Edward Scott, Joseph Harper, and Ann Hynson (*BPAT* 19 June 1819).

Briscoe, Samuel, Esq., d. last Sat. of the prevailing disease, merchant of Baltimore, leaving a wife and children (*BPAT* 2 Oct 1819).

Britten, Edward, and Miss Ariel Hutchins, both of Baltimore Co., were m. last Thurs. by Rev. Mr. Johnson (*FGBA* 9 May 1818; *BA* 9 May 1818; *BPAT* 8 May 1818).

Bromwell, Henry B., and Miss Henrietta Holmes, all of Baltimore were m. last Tues. by Rev. Jenkins (*BA* 20 Aug 1818; *BPAT* 20 Aug 1818).

Brook, Elizabeth, wife of Samuel Brook, chief clerk in the office of the Treasury of the United States, d. in Washington (*BPAT* 11 Aug 1819).

Brook, Rev. Thomas, M.A., d. 29 June. He resided on South Eutaw near Lombard St. (*BA* 30 June 1818; *BPAT* 30 June 1818).

Brooke, Lieut. Edmund, of the U.S. Marine Corps, was m. in Prince George's Co., to Miss Ellen Young, only dau. of the late Benjamin Young, Esq., dec. (*BPAT* 10 Feb 1817).

Brooke, Richard, Esq., d. at his residence in Frederick, last Sat. night in his 44th year, a distinguished member of the bar in the Sate of Md. (*BPAT* 14 May 1819).

Brooke, Robert, d. last Sat., in his 44th year, at his residence in Frederick; he was a member of the Maryland Bar (*BA* 15 May 1819; *BMC* 15 May 1819).

Brooks, Major Alexander B., of the U. S. Regiment of Light Artillery, was m. to Miss Sarah Turner (*BPAT* 7 June 1817).

Brooks, R., aged 4 years, was buried in Glendy's Ground about Sep 1817 M*GSB* 30 (3) 293).

Brooks, William, was m. last Tues. eve., by Rev. Mr. Neale to Miss Sophia, second dau. of Mr. Samuel Matthews, all of this city (*BPAT* 13 Feb 1817; *FGBA* 13 Feb 1817).

Broom, Lieut. C. R., was m. Mon. eve., to Miss Mary E. Hewitt, all of Baltimore (*BA* 12 March 1817; *BPAT* 12 March 1817),

Broom, T. R., of New York, was m. last eve. [Fri.] to Miss Rozetta E. Dashiell, second dau. of Rev. George Dashiell, of Baltimore (*FGBA* 11 Jan 1817).

Brotherton, Miss Mary, d. Sun., 22nd, inst., in her 17th year (*FGBA* 26 Feb 1818).

Brotherton, Miss Sarah, d. Sun., in her 17th year (*BA* 26 Feb 1818; *BPAT* 26 Feb 1818). Sarah Brotherton, aged 17 years, was buried 23 Feb 1818 from St. Paul's Parish (ReamySP).

Broughan, John, was m. yesterday eve. [Thurs.], by Rev. Dr. Chilton to Rachel Hainks [*sic*], of Baltimore Co. (*BPAT* 18 Jan 1817; *FGBA* 17 Jan 1817).

Broughton, Mr. Henry, of Cecil Co., d. Sun., 31st ult. (*BPAT* 12 Nov 1819).

Brown, Amos, of Baltimore Co., is an insolvent debtor (*BPAT* 23 Dec 1819).

Brown, Mr. Benjamin, was m. last Wed. eve. by Rev. Mr. Fenwick, to Miss Sarah K. Mullan of Baltimore (*BPAT* 9 Oct 1819).

Brown, Mrs. Caroline S., wife of Dr. Morgan Brown, d. Thurs., 27th inst., at Chestertown, on the Eastern Shore of Md. She had resided for many years in Baltimore. She left a husband and adopted children [Long obit] (*BPAT* 3 Sep 1818).

Brown, Mrs. Catherine, wife of Charles Brown of Baltimore and dau. of the late Valentine Hoffman, d, last Fri. at Philadelphia (*FGBA* 4 March 1818; *BPAT* 3 March 1818).

Biographical Data from Baltimore Newspapers, 1817-1819

Brown, Rev. Clarke, Rector of William and Mary Parish, Charles Co., d. 12 Jan (*FGBA* 27 Jan 1817; *BPAT* 28 Jan 1817).

Brown, Mr. Elias, and Miss Susanna Brown, all of Baltimore Co., were m. Tues., 7th inst., by Rev. Mr. Jackson (*BPAT* 14 Sep 1819).

Brown, George, of Baltimore, and Isabella, only dau. of the late John McLanahan, were m. 17th inst. [Wed.], at Prospect Hall, near Green Castle, PA, by the Rev. Lind (*BA* 23 Dec 1818; *BPAT* 23 Dec 1818).

Brown, Jedediah, was born in Springfield, Vt., in Nov 1793; he left his father's house in April 1809, came to Boston, and made a voyage to Africa, returned in April 1810 and ailed in the employ of Mr. Francis Lincoln to some of the West Indian Islands and returned the July following. He wrote his father, saying that he was sailing to the East Indies in the ship *Hunter*. He did not sail on that ship and ha snot been heard of since. Any information concerning him should be sent to Major Benjamin Russell, Boston (*BPAT* 23 April 1817).

Brown, John, dec.; his executors, on 23 Oct 1805, leased a lot, on the west side of High St., to Thomas Skipper, and was sold on 7 April 1819 by order of the Orphans Court to Benjamin Chandler and Robert Holloway. A commission will meet to determine the bounds of a lot (*BPAT* 4 May 1819).

Brown, John D., owes taxes for the years 1813, 1814, 1815, on 15 a. *Ashmead's Delight* in the 6th Dist. (*BPAT* 7 Jan 1819).

Brown, John M., formerly of Baltimore, d. 1st Dec. last at Buenos Aires, in his 29th year (*FGBA* 25 March 1818; *BPAT* 25 March 1818).

Brown, Mrs. Margaret, relict of Dr. G. R. Brown of Port Tobacco, d. in Washington, NC, on the 4th inst. She was living with her only dau., the wife of Thomas H. Blount (*BPAT* 26 Dec 1818).

Brown, Mary, a Negro girl, aged about 12 years, ran away and if found, should be brought to No. 90, Bond St., Fell's Point (*BPAT* 8 July 1817).

Brown, Mary, Negro, aged 16 years, ran away from John E. Wall; if found she is to be left at the Exchange Hotel, Water St. (*BPAT* 11 Dec 1819).

Brown, Miss Mary, d. at Taneytown, aged 16 years, 6 mos. and 10 days; on the day of her death she walked six miles from home to church; she was a friend of Miss Elizabeth Reifsnider (*BPAT* 27 Oct 1819).

Brown, Mr. Morgan, was m. last eve. [Sat,] by Rev. Hargrove, to Miss Margaret M'Clain, all of Baltimore (*BA* 5 May 1817; *BPAT* 5 May 1817).

Brown, Major Moses, of Baltimore Co., d. 3rd inst., leaving a family of young children (*FGBA* 8 Sep 1817). For his will, filed in 1817, see BAWB 10:350.

Brown, Nicodemus, of Ohio, was m. Sun. eve., 12th inst., by Rev. Mr. Hemphill, to Eliza Baile [Baily?] of this city (*BPAT* 16 Jan 1817; *FGBA* 17 Jan 1817).

Brown, Peter, was m. last evening [Wed.] by Rev. Dr. Roberts to Miss Sarah Gardiner, all of Baltimore (*BPAT* 9 July 1819).

Brown, Capt. Samuel, and Miss Mary McKinnen, all of Baltimore, were m. last Thurs. eve. by the Rev. Dr. Glendy (*BPAT* 27 Nov 1819).

Brown, Stewart, and Miss Sarah Muncaster, all of Baltimore, were m. last eve. [Wed.], by Bishop Kemp (*FGBA* 18 Sep 1818; *BPAT* 19 Sep 1818).

Brown, William, was m. on Deer Creek, 5th inst. [Thurs.], by Rev. Stevenson, to Miss Pamela Bennett (*BA* 7 June 1817; *BPAT* 7 June 1817).

Brown, Mr. William, was m. to Miss Henrietta Markland, both of Talbot Co. (*BPAT* 29 Dec 1817).

Brown, William, for Isaac McKinley's heirs, owes taxes for the year 1815, on 2¾ a. *Ellicott's Mills* in the 1st Dist.(*BPAT* 7 Jan 1819).

Brown, William, was m. last Sun. eve. by Rev. D. E. Reese to Elizabeth Brown (*FGBA* 3 April 1819; *BPAT* 3 April 1819).

Browne, Mrs. Caroline S., wife of Dr. Morgan Browne, d. 27th inst., at Chestertown, Md. (*BPAT* 3 Sep 1818).

Biographical Data from Baltimore Newspapers, 1817-1819

Browning, P. G., dec.; Mary Browning, extx., advertises the sale of a two story brick house and lot in Lombard St., opposite the friends Meeting House (*BPAT* 20 March 1817). For the will of Peregrine G. Browning, filed in 1816, see BAWB 10:166.

Brunelot, Capt. Francis, for several years a resident of Baltimore, d. last Sat. at the house of Dr. Chatard (*BA* 27 Jan 1817; *BPAT* 27 Jan 1817). Francois Bernardin Brunelot, native of the Republic of France, was naturalized on 24 Nov 1796 (Baltimore Co. Court Naturalization Docket 1:2). As Francois Brunlot, he was buried in the Cathedral Cemetery (Grogaard).

Brundige, Mrs. Jane M., wife of William, of Baltimore, d. 3 Dec at Dumfries, Va., aged 23 (*BA* 21 Dec 1818; *BPAT* 21 Dec 1818).

Brunner, Elias, was m. last eve. [Thurs.] by Rev. Mr. Valiant, to Miss Gaynor Dungan, all of Baltimore (*BPAT* 3 July 1818).

Bryan, Santy, a black slave, ran away on 13th ult. from Jacob Michael in Harford Co. (*BPAT* 4 Sep 1818).

Bryant, Thomas, M.D., d. at New Orleans on the 15th ult., in the 42nd year of his age; formerly of Philadelphia (*BPAT* 18 Nov 1819).

Bryson, Nathan G., is an insolvent debtor of Baltimore (*BPAT* 15 Nov 1819). Nathan Greg. Bryson, native of Co. Antrim, Ireland, was naturalized on 16 April 1799 (General Court of the Eastern Shore Naturalization Record 1796-1805, fol. 5).

Buchanan, Mr. George, native of Ireland, and recently from Baltimore, d. at New Orleans, of a lingering illness, in his 21st year (*BPAT* 12 March 1817).

Buchanan, Jane, second dau. of James Buchanan, d. Sun. of consumption, after a severe illness of eight months, in her 27th year (*BPAT* 15 Sep 1817). Jane Buchanan, aged 27 years, was buried 14 Sep 1817 from St. Paul's Parish (ReamySP).

Buchanan, William, Jr., son of William of Baltimore, d. Wed. in his 17th year (*BA* 3 Oct 1817; *BPAT* 3 Oct 1817).

Buckingham, Samuel, of Baltimore, was m. last Thurs., by Rev. E. J. Reis to Ann Mitchell of Harford Co. (*FGBA* 5 Dec 1818).

Buckley, Mr. Henry, was m. last eve. [Thurs.] by Rev. Mr. Valiant, to Miss Susan Wheeler (*BPAT* 27 Nov 1818).

Buckmaster, Benjamin, of Calvert Co., was m. last Tues., 9th inst., by Rev. Valliant, to Miss Mary Jones of Baltimore (*BPAT* 12 March 1819; *FGBA* 31 March 1819).

Buell, William S., of Baltimore Co., is an insolvent debtor (*BPAT* 6 Oct 1819).

Buffum, Mrs. Jane, consort of John Buffum, formerly a merchant of Baltimore, d. 7 Nov at Cincinnati, Ohio (*FGBA* 23 Nov 1818; *BPAT* 24 Nov 1818).

Bunker, Mrs. Rachel, widow of Capt. Samuel Bunker of Baltimore, d. last Wed. eve. (*FGBA* 23 March 1819; *BPAT* 22 March 1819).

Burcket, Mr. Thomas, was m. 30 Jan. [Thurs.], by Rev. Mr. Willis to Miss Jane Carney, all of Loudon Co., Va. (*BPAT* 14 Feb 1817).

Burgess, Mr. Bazil, was m. to Ann, dau. of Caleb Merryman of Baltimore Co. on the eve. of 20th inst. [Tues.] by the Rev. James Smith, at the residence of Caleb Merryman (*BPAT* 22 Jan 1818).

Burgess, Mr. George, was m. Thurs., 6th inst., by Rev. Mr. Diver, to Miss Elizabeth Earlougher, all of AA Co. (*BPAT* 14 March 1817).

Burk, Mr. John, merchant of New York, was m. Thurs. eve. by Rev. Dr. Inglis, to Miss Margaret Nicholson, of Richmond, VA (*BPAT* 1 Dec 1818).

Burk, Mr. Richard, was m. last Tues. eve. by Rev. Mr. Valliant, to Miss Mary Dungan, all of Baltimore (*BPAT* 3 Dec 1818).

Burke, James, a black man, formerly the property of Wm. Doran, Prince William Co., Va., about 34 years of age, ran away from Thomas Seales; he was on his way to Sparta, Ga.; had been a runaway for several years, and was taken up in Philadelphia and sold by order f the court last Oct (*BPAT* 23 Jan 1818).

Burke, John, merchant of New York, was m. Thurs. eve. by Rev. Dr. Inglis to Miss Margaret Nicholson of Richmond, Va. (*BA* 1 Dec 1818).

Biographical Data from Baltimore Newspapers, 1817-1819

Burke, Mr. Joshua, of Baltimore, was m. last eve. [Sun.] by Rev. Mr. Valliant to Miss Elizabeth Bowman of Delaware (*BPAT* 21 Dec 1818; *BA* 23 Dec 1818).

Burke, Patrick, lived in Baltimore until 1805. If living he should apply to this office, where he will hear something to his advantage (*BPAT* 25 Sep 1819).

Burling, Thomas, printer, a resident of Richmond for 13 years, d. leaving a wife and child "From the Richmond *Compiler*" (*BPAT* 9 Jan 1818).

Burn, Mr. Henry, was m. at Hagerstown [date not given] to Miss Magdalena Kuhn (*BMC* 17 May 1819).

Burnes, Mr. James, d. Monday, 6th inst., after a short but painful illness, in the 30th year of his age, He leaves a disconsolate sister and a numerous train of relatives to mourn his loss (*BPAT* 9 Jan 1817).

Burneston, Mrs. Mary, wife of William J Burneston, of Baltimore Co., d. Sun., 16th inst. (*BA* 20 Nov 1817; *BPAT* 20 Nov 1817).

Burnett, Mr. Asa, was m. last eve. [Fri.] by Rev. D. E. Reese, to Miss Sarah Atkinson, both of Harford Co. (*BPAT* 2 May 1817).

Burns, Francis, of Baltimore, was m. at Philadelphia [date not given] to Miss Elizabeth Weylands of the latter place (*FGBA* 20 Jan 1819; *BPAT* 19 Jan 1819 gives the bride's name as Elizabeth Heylands).

Burns, Robert, of Rochdale, Eng., was m. at Philadelphia [date not given], to Miss Mary Campbell Wurts, dau. of Maurice Campbell Wurts (*BPAT* 22 Dec 1819).

Burns, William, brick maker, d. at Philadelphia on 12th inst. in his 51st year (*FGBA* 15 May 1819).

Burroughs, Mr. George, merchant, late of Baltimore, was m. at Cape Henry, Hayti, by Rev. Mr. Morton, to Miss Caroline M. Harper (*BPAT* 2 April 1818).

Busey, Samuel F., was m. last Sun. night by Rev. Mr. Fechtig, to Miss Rebecca Richardson, both of Baltimore (*BPAT* 1 April 1818; *BA* 1 April 1818).

Bush, Mr. James, was m. to Mrs. Catherine Coliden [or Culliden] last Tues. eve. by Rev. Mr. Reise (*BPAT* 13 Feb 1818; *FGBA* 13 Feb 1818).

Busk, Mr. John, was m. last Thurs. eve. by the Rev. Mr. Rev. Bartow, to Mrs. Hester Dobbin, all of Baltimore (*BPAT* 26 Dec 1818; *BA* 25 Dec 1818).

Butler, John, was m. last eve. [Fri.] by Rev. Rossell, to Miss Margaret Cronmiller, all of Baltimore (*FGBA* 6 June 1817; *BPAT* 6 June 1817).

Butler, Capt. John R., of Philadelphia., age 23, was m. there [date not given] to Miss Pauline Leuba, age 16, dau. of Mr. Piere [*sic*] Henry Leuba of the Canton of Vaux, Switzerland (*BPAT* 15 Jan 1819).

Butler, William, of the firm of Pease and Butler of Baltimore, was m. in New York to Miss Alice M. Morris of the latter city (*BMC* 12 April 1819; *BPAT* 10 April 1819).

Buttman, David, an indented apprentice, ran away from George Wheelwright (*BPAT* 5 Sep 1817).

Byer, Henry, about 17 years of age, an apprentice to the stone cutting business, ran away from Cook & Taylor (*BPAT* 6 April 1818).

Byrd, Francis Otway, Esq. of the U. S. Army, was m. at Philadelphia, to Miss Elizabeth R. Pleasants of that city (*BPAT* 12 June 1817).

Byrne, Catherine, dau. of Lawrence Byrne of Baltimore d. yesterday; the funeral will be from her father's residence on Federal Hill (*BA* 6 May 1818; *BPAT* 6 May 1818). Her death was the result of burns. She was buried in the Cathedral Cemetery (Grogaard).

Byrnes, Lawrence, will not pay the debts of his wife Teressa, who has left his bed and board without cause (*BPAT* 19 Nov 1817).

"C"

Cabell, Col. Samuel Jordan, d. 4th inst., in Nelson Co., Va., a hero of the Revolution, in his 62nd year (*FGBA* 30 Sep 1818; *BPAT* 1 Oct 1818).

Biographical Data from Baltimore Newspapers, 1817-1819

Cadle, Ambrose, about 19 years old, 5 feet, 8 or 9 inches tall, round shouldered, apprentice to the Carpenter's Business, ran away last 21 Dec. from Thomas Davis of Baltimore (*BPAT* 12 Feb 1819).

Caffert, Mr. Thomas, was m. last Thurs. eve. by Rev. D. E. Reese, to Miss Catherine Roe, all of Baltimore (*BPAT* 29 Sep 1819).

Cain, A., was m. Sun., 5th inst., by Rev Mr. Davis, to Mrs. Ann Magness, all of Baltimore (*FGBA* 13 July 1818).

Cain, John, aged about 18, apprentice to the boot and shoemaking business, ran away from Edw. Hagthrop, Bond St., F. P. [Fell's Point], Baltimore. A reward of twelve and a half cents is offered (*BPAT* 11 June 1818).

Caldwell, James H., Esq. manager of the Theatres of Va, and New Orleans, was m. Thurs. eve. last, by Rev. Mr. M'Guire, to Mrs. Maria Carter Wormsley, widow of the late Warner Wormsley. Esq., of Rose Hill, Va. (*BPAT* 1 Dec 1819).

Caldwell, John, of Harford Co., is to have an act to confirm his title to certain lands therein (*BPAT* 10 Feb 1817)

Caldwell, Mr. Jonathan, Printer, of Philadelphia, was m. last Sat. by Rev. Mr. Rutter to Miss Rebecca Storts of Delaware (*BPAT* 5 Dec 1817).

Caldwell, Mr. Joseph, Jr., editor of the *Virginia Reformer,* was m. on Sun., 14th ult., by the Rev, Reuben Finnell, to Miss Ann, dau. of the late Capt. John Mitchell of Shenandoah, near Front Royal (*BPAT* 7 Dec 1819).

Calhoun, James, a Brigade Major in the Baltimore Troops, and son of the late James Calhoun, d. last eve. in his 49th year. In the late war he was a Brigade Major of the Baltimore troops (*FGBA* 31 Aug 1819; *BPAT* 31 Aug 1819, 1 sep 1819). He is buried in a pyramidal vault, inscribed Buchanan and Calhoun that covers lots 18 and 14 in Westminster Presbyterian Churchyard, Baltimore (HaywardW).

Calhoun, John, was m. last Wed. by Rev. D. E. Reese, to Miss Sarah Cowley, both of Baltimore Co. (*BA* 19 June 1818; *BPAT* 11 June 1818).

Calhoun, Miss Lydia, 3rd dau. of the late William Calhoun of Baltimore, d. 7 April at Charleston, S. C., in her 19th year (*FGBA* 16 April 1818; *BPAT* 15 April 1818).

Callender, Thomas, a merchant of Philadelphia, but late of Baltimore, d. last Sat., aged 42. He leaves a wife and six children (*FGBA* 23 June 1818; *BPAT* 24 June 1818). His household furniture will be sold at auction at his late residence opposite the Methodist Meeting House, Green St., Old Town, on Sat., 8 Aug, by Nicholas Strike, auctioneer. /s/ Martin F. Maher, admin. (*BPAT* 30 July 1818).

Cameron, Hugh, owes taxes for the year 1815, on one lot on York Road (*BPAT* 1 Jan 1819).

Camper, Moses, a Negro man, 30 years of age, but says he is 38, five-feet-five or six inches high; had been purchased from Mr. Charles Pritchard of New Market by Jesse Schaeffer of Easton, and sold to Austin Woolfolk, Sr., from whom he has run away (*BPAT* 20 Dec 1819).

Campbell, Daniel W., of St. Mary's Co., was m. yesterday [Thurs.] by Rev. Henshaw, in St. Peter's Church, to Miss Sarah Ann V. B. Jolley, of Baltimore (*FGBA* 22 Jan 1819; *BPAT* 22 Jan 1819).

Campbell, Mrs. Elizabeth, relict of the late Archibald Campbell of Baltimore, d. yesterday, aged 63 (*FGBA* 16 Feb 1818; *BPAT* 17 Feb 1818). Elizabeth Campbell, aged 63 years, was buried 15 Feb 1818 from St. Paul's Parish (ReamySP). For her will, filed 1818, see BAWB 10:431.

Campbell, George, merchant, and Miss Julia Bedford, all of Baltimore, were m. 28th inst [Thurs.] by Rev. Bishop Kemp (*BPAT* 30 Oct 1819).

Campbell, Levin H., d. at his residence in Cambridge on Tues. morning, 3rd inst., of a sudden bilious disease, leaving a wife and infant family (*BPAT* 27 Aug 1819; a long obit in *BPAT* 28 Aug 1819).

Campbell, William, d. Sun. last at Monkton Mills, Baltimore Co., aged about 6 5 years. He was a native of Pa., and was a brother-in-law to William Gwynn. In early life he took an active part in the Revolutionary War (*BPAT* 4 Oct 1819).

Biographical Data from Baltimore Newspapers, 1817-1819

Cannon, William, native of London, and a resident of Baltimore, d. yesterday in his 37th year, leaving a wife and two children (*BA* 27 May 1817; *BPAT* 27 May 1817).

Cantler, David, advertises he will not pay the debts of his wife Louisa, who has left his bed and board, without any cause on his part (*BPAT* 25 Nov 1817).

Cantler, Capt David, of Cecil Co., was m. last eve. [Tues.] by Rev. Mr. Parks, to Miss Louisa Townsley of Harford Co. (*BA* 10 Sep 1817).

Canoles, Mr. Charles, was m. last Wed. eve. by Rev, Mr. Healey to Miss Elizabeth Bywater, all of Baltimore Co. (*BA* 9 Oct 1817; *BPAT* 8 Oct 1817).

Canoles, William, was m. last Thurs. eve. by Rev. D. E. Reese, to Miss Nancy Fuller, all of Baltimore (*BA* 22 Feb. 1817).

Care [?], William R. Esq., of Port Royal, Va., was m. Thurs. eve. last by Rev. Mr. Duncan, to Miss Eliza Maxwell of Baltimore (*BPAT* 3 July 1819).

Carnighan, Catharine, consort of James Carnighan, d. after a painful and protracted illness. (*BPAT* 1 Feb 1819).

Carns, Capt. John, was m. Thurs. eve. by Rev. Bartow, to Miss Eliza Snow, all of Baltimore (*BA* 19 July 1817; *BPAT* 19 July 1817).

Carpenter, Emanuel, was m. last Thurs. by Rev. Mr. Jennings, to Mrs. Eliza Sansgton (*BPAT* 11 April 1818).

Carpenter, Richard, apprentice to the tailoring business, ran away 15th inst. from Richard Higdon, 20 Hanover St. (*BPAT* 16 June 1819).

Carr, George, was m. last Tues., by Rev. John Glendy, to Miss Sarah Wark (*BA* 21 June 1817).

Carr, Mr. James, Esq., and his daughter, aged 9, drowned on the 24th Aug last, below Louisville, Ky. The family was intending to settle in the West, when the daughter fell overboard and her father jumped in to save her. Both drowned. Mr. Carr was a representative in congress from the District of Maine, and very recently a merchant from Baltimore (*BPAT* 14 Sep 1818).

Carr, Mr. John, was m. last Thurs. eve. by Rev. M. Valiant, to Miss Eliza Wilson, all of Baltimore (*BPAT* 7 Aug 1819).

Carr, Mr. Joseph, was m. Sun. eve. by Rev. Dr. Roberts, to Miss Mary Husk, all of Baltimore (*BPAT* 5 Oct 1818).

Carr, Mr. Joseph, d. last Wed. night, in his 80th year. He was a native of Eng., but had resided in this city for the last 25 years. He was an affectionate husband and father (*BPAT* 2 Nov 1819). Joseph Carr of Great Britain was naturalized on 21 Aug 1797 (Baltimore Co. Court Naturalization Docket 1:7).

Carrell, Mrs. Mary, wife of John Carrell, d. Tues. eve. in her 51st year. "Philadelphia, 20 March" (*FGBA* 21 March 1817).

Carrington, Paul, d. Tues., 22nd June, at his seat in Charlotte Co., Va., in the 86th year of his age, perhaps the oldest, and one of the few surviving patriots who took an active part on the Councils of his country (*BPAT* 11 July 1818).

Carroll, Charles, son of Daniel Carroll of Duddington, d. at his residence in Baltimore Co. (*BPAT* 14 Dec 1819).

Carroll, Mrs. Margaret, d. at Mt. Clare, on 14 March, in her 76th year (*BACDA* 22 March 1817). Margaret Carroll, aged 76, was buried 14 March 1817 from St. Paul's Parish (ReamySP). For the will of Marguerite Carroll, filed 1817, see BAWB 10:294.

Cars, Capt. Thomas, late master of the New York Packet Schooner *Mark Time,* d. last Fri. at his residence in Petersburg. He had scarcely attained his 45th year and was blessed with a wife and three children, when he fell a victim to a bilious fever (*BPAT* 21 July 1818)

Carson, Mr. George, of Alexandria, was m. last Tues. eve. by the Rev. Mr. Duncan, to Miss Ella Knox, of Baltimore (*BPAT* 15 May 1817).

Biographical Data from Baltimore Newspapers, 1817-1819

Carson, John, was m. last Thurs. eve. by Rev. D. E. Reese, to Miss Corrilla Hobbs, all of Baltimore (*BA* 6 Aug 1817).

Carter, Robert, dec.; his heirs owe taxes for the years 1813, 1814, 1815, on two lots of the Company's lands in the 1st Dist. (*BPAT* 7 Jan 1819). For the will of a Robert Carter, filed in 1804, see BAWB 7:264.

Carter, Sophia, owes taxes for the year 1816 on property in the 1st Dist. transferred from Carter's estate (*BPAT* 3 Aug 1819).

Carter, Thomas Burton, moved from Harrisonburg, Rockingham Co., Va., to Ohio about five years ago, and was last heard from in Cadiz, Oh. He is about 25 years ago, and a tailor by trade. There is a vague rumor that he is dead. A letter containing information about him, directed to Henry Tutweiler, P.M., will confer a peculiar kindness on his aged, infirm and widowed mother (*BPAT* 22 July 1818).

Carvalho, Rev. Emanuel Nunes, the respectable and much esteemed pastor of the Hebrew congregation of Philadelphia, d. last Thurs., in the 4th year of his age (*BPAT* 22 March 1817).

Carver, Mrs. Elizabeth, d. at Havre de Grace, on the 6th inst., in her 51st year, after a long and painful illness (*BPAT* 12 Oct 1819).

Casey, Dr. John A., a native of Md., d. at Savannah, Ga., for many years a resident of Ga. (*BPAT* 20 Sep 1819, 4 Oct 1819).

Cassat, Miss Elizabeth, d. 6th inst., aged 15 years (*BPAT* 10 Aug 1818).

Cassell, Joseph, was m. last eve. [Mon.] by Rev. Dr. Samuel K. Jennings, to Miss Rebecca Jane Ing, all of Baltimore (*FGBA* 15 July 1817; *BPAT* 26 July 1817).

Casson, Mr. Henry, was m. [date not given] to Miss Baynard of Caroline Co.(*BPAT* 21 April 1817).

Cathcart, James Leander, of Washington City, advertises that when he settled in Cadiz as Consul of the United States, he left his eldest son, George Latimer Cathcart at his grandfather's house in the City of Washington, for the benefit of his education. He was to be sent to the military school at West Point when a vacancy should occur. He remained until 19 Oct 1816 when he disappeared. He went to Alexandra [Alexandria], where he remained for some days, and has not been heard of since. He may have gotten to Baltimore or some other seaport and been enticed away by some unprincipled persons. George Latimer Cathcart was born at Leghorn on 28 Jan 1803 when I was Consul of the United States for Tripoli, and has lived with his family at Madeira during the eight years I was Consul there. He was educated by Mr. Mackey and speaks the Portuguese language tolerably well.(*BPAT* 16 sep 1817).

Cavanagh, Mr. Bernard, was m. last Thurs. eve. by Rev. Mr. Fairclough to Miss Ann M'Kanna, both of Baltimore (*BPAT* 18 April 1818).

Cavenaugh, Bernard, a native of Ireland, and for several years a resident of Baltimore, d. in Amelia Island (long obit) (*BA* 18 Oct 1817).

Cavanaugh, Peter, aged 30, formerly of this city, d. lately at St. Mary's, Ga., of a fever supposedly contracted at Savannah. He was an officer of the corps of volunteers under the command of Major Barney at the time of the British attack [on Baltimore], and was esteemed as a good citizen. He had accepted a commission under M'Gregor, and was on his way to join him when he was cut down in the vigor of life (*BPAT* 14 Oct 1817). He may be the Peter Cavenagh of Ireland who filed his declaration of intent on 1 May 1812 (Baltimore Co. Court Minutes, folio 186). Peter Cavanaugh, a native of Ireland, filed his Declaration of Intention to become a citizen of the United States on 1 May 1812 (Baltimore Co. Court Minutes, 1810-1814: 186).

Chalmers, John, Esq., late Sheriff of Baltimore Co., d. 19th June, in his 67th year of age (*BACDA* 2 July 1817; *BPAT* 30 June 1817).

Chamberlin, Philip, and Miss Eliza Foster, all of this city, were m. Sun. eve. last by Rev. Mr. Beare (*BPAT* 8 May 1819).

Biographical Data from Baltimore Newspapers, 1817-1819

Chambers, Dyne, was m. to Miss Ann Ramsay, all of Baltimore last Thurs. by Rev. Dr. Jennings (*BA* 13 June 1818; *BPAT* 13 June 1818).

Chambers, Thomas, a Negro man, about 19 years of age, five-feet-two or three inches in height. He ran away from Jno. Page; he ran off with some clothes he got off his mother, who lives in Baltimore or on the Point; she is a free woman named Jenny Bradley (*BPAT* 4 Jan 1817).

Chandler, Capt. Samuel V., was m. last Wed. by Rev. Mr. Waugh to Miss Harriet Trimble (*BPAT* 29 May 1819).

Chappell, John G., was m. last Thurs. eve. by Rev. Wells, to Miss Rebecca Pitt, dau. of Capt. William Pitt (*FGBA* 18 July 1817; *BPAT* 19 July 1817).

Chase, William, a bright mulatto fellow, aged 18 or 19, ran away from A. & S. Woodcock, in Alexandria, D. C.; he was raised by Mr. Carr, a music seller on Baltimore St. (*BPAT* 16 Oct 1819).

Chavis, George, was m. last Wed. eve. by Rev. D. E. Reese to Miss Mary Ann Byrnes, all of Baltimore (*BA* 11 May 1819).

Chelly, William, was m. Thurs. eve. by Rev. Moranville to Maria, dau. of Daniel Cheston, all of Baltimore (*BA* 19 Sep 1818; *BPAT* 18 Sep 1818).

Chenoweth, Mr. John, was m. yesterday morning [Thurs.], by Rev. Mr. Childs, to Miss Ann, dau. of William Perine, Esq., all of Baltimore Co. (*BPAT* 3 Sep 1819).

Chesley, Mr. Z. C., was m. [date not given] in Washington to Miss Jane E. B. Thornton (*BPAT* 3 Nov 1817).

Chew, Mr. Richard. was m. Thurs. eve. last, by Rev. Mr. Healey to Miss Delilah Lightner, all of Baltimore (*BPAT* 5 March 1818).

Chibester (or Chidester), Dr. Thomas, of the U. S. Navy, d. near Chaptico, Md., on the 6th inst. He was a native of Pennsylvania, and entered the late war in the service of his country (*BPAT* 29 Aug 1818).

Child, Mr. William, was m. on Thurs. eve., 10th inst., by Rev. Mr. Richards, to Mss Sarah Jane Wilson, all of Baltimore (*BPAT* 12 June 1819).

Childs, Mr. Benjamin, of Baltimore, was m. at Annapolis on Tues. eve. by Rev. Job Guest to Miss Elizabeth, dau. of John Monroe of Annapolis (*BPAT* 8 May 1818)

Childs, Mr. Samuel, merchant of Georgetown, was m. last Thurs. eve. by Rev. Nelson Reid to Rebecca, dau. of Jacob Myers, merchant of Baltimore (*BPAT* 8 May 1818).

Chinn, John Y., owes taxes for the year 1816 on property in the 1st Dist. transferred from Carter's estate (*BPAT* 3 Aug 1819).

Chotard [Chatard?], Maj. Henry, of the U. S. Army, was m. Thurs., 27th May at Natchez, Mi., by E. Turner, Esq., to Miss Frances Minor, dau. of the late Major Stephen Minor (*BPAT* 6 July 1819).

Chrisfield, Mr. Peregrine, was m. on Sun., 1st inst., by Rev. Mr. Kurtz, to Miss Sarah M'Intire, both of Baltimore (*BPAT* 14 March 1818; *BA* 4 March 1818).

Clackner, Adam, d. 26 Nov, in his 46th year. He resided at George and Exeter Sts. (*BPAT* 27 Nov 1818).

Clagett, Mrs. Ann Louisa, wife of Darius Clagett, of Georgetown, d. there on Sat. eve. last, after a short but painful illness (*BPAT* 26 Nov 1819).

Claggett, William D., of Prince George's Co., and Miss Sarah Young, only dau. of Nicholas Young, were m. [date not given] at Nonesuch (*BPAT* 26 April 1819).

Claghorn, John, d. at Frederick, on Tues., 3rd inst., at the house of Col. John Houston, in his 35th year. He was a native of England *FGBA* 21 Feb 1818).

Clark, Elizabeth, owes taxes for the years 1813, 1814, 1815, on 23½ a. *Marshall's Desire* in the 6th Dist. (*BPAT* 7 Jan 1819).

Clark, James Cooke, was m. by Rev. D. E. Reese last Thurs. eve. to Miss Ann Jane Aull, both of Baltimore (*BPAT* 13 Dec 1817; but see James Cook Clarke below).

Clark, John, was m. last Tues., by Rev. Mr. Bartow, to Miss Agnes Clark, both late of Liverpool, Great Britain (*BA* 2 Oct 1817).

Biographical Data from Baltimore Newspapers, 1817-1819

Clark, John, born in Alexandria, aged about 25 years old, a papermaker, deserted from the detachment of James H. Cook, Capt., at Fort Covington on 3 March (*BPAT* 13 Sep 1818).

Clark, John, aged about 22 years of age, born in England, a seaman, deserted from the detachment of James H. Cook, Capt., at Fort Covington on 3 March; may have gone to Norfolk, kin expectation of working his way to England; he was accompanied by his wife and a child (*BPAT* 13 Sep 1818).

Clark, Joseph, druggist, was m. last Tues eve., by Rev. D. E. Reese, to Miss Elizabeth Clayton Brow—[?], all of Baltimore (*BA* 8 Aug 1817).

Clark, Joshua, of Talbot Co., and Mrs. Ann Clift of Baltimore, were m. last Tues. eve. by Rev. Markland (*BPAT* 20 Nov 1819).

Clark, Nelson, was m. last Tues. by Rev. Richards to Miss Lucretia Thomas, both of Baltimore (*BA* 6 Aug 1818; *BPAT* 6 Aug 1818).

Clark, Patrick Hale, aged about 18 years old, apprentice to the butchering business, ran away from Adam Seltzer on the Hooks Town Rod, near the Seminary; a reward of one cent is offered (*BPAT* 29 May 1817).

Clarke, Daniel, owes taxes for the years 1813, 1814, 1815, on 1½ a. *Brotherly Love* in the 7th Dist. (*BPAT* 7 Jan 1819).

Clarke, Elizabeth, owes taxes for the years 1813, 1814, 1815, on 23 a. part *Deliver* in the 7th Dist. (*BPAT* 7 Jan 1819).

Clarke, James Cook, was m. last Thurs. by Rev. D. E. Reese, to Miss Ann Jane Ault, both of Baltimore (*BA* 13 Dec 1817; but see James Cooke Clark above).

Clarke, Mr. L., lived in Baltimore last Fall, perhaps with a Mr. Clarke, an Englishman; he was a teacher in a female academy, and more recently kept a grocery store. If he will call on the Post Master, he may hear of something to his advantage (*BPAT* 26 Aug 1818).

Clarke, Capt. Matthew, of Baltimore, d. Sat. 18th inst., in his 58th year (*FGBA* 20 July 1818; *BPAT* 20 July 1818). For the will of Matthew Clarke, filed in 1818, see BAWB 10:416.

Clarke, Nicholas, about 22 years old, deserted from the U. S. Ship *Alert* lying at the Navy Yard in this city on Fri., 19th inst. (*BPAT* 26 Dec 1817).

Classen, Mrs., dec.: A constable's sale of her property, taken for house rent due Job Davidson, Esq., will be held 9th inst., at Mrs,. Dean's, opposite the Fell's Point market (*BPAT* 1 Nov 1819).

Claxton, Lt. Comm. Alexander, of the U.S. Navy, formerly of Washington, and Miss Rodolphe Lavall of Baltimore were m. at the latter place a few days ago (*BPAT* 3 July 1819).

Clayton, Joseph, owes taxes for the years 1813, 1814, 1815, on 18 a. *Clarkson's Hope* in the 2nd Dist. (*BPAT* 7 Jan 1819).

Clayton, Richard, apprentice to the Carpenter Business, ran away from George Bushey on 8th inst. (*BPAT* 10 Sep 1819).

Clayton, Samuel, and Miss Hannah O'Hare, all of Baltimore, were m. yesterday [Thurs.] by Rev. Mr. Hargrove (*FGBA* 25 June 1819; *BPAT* 25 June 1819).

Cleghorn, John, d. at Frederick Town, Md., 2nd inst., at the house of Col. John Houston, He was a native of Eng., and arrived here a few weeks since (*BPAT* 21 Feb 1818).

Clemm, William, was m. last Sun. eve. by Rev. Mr. Wyatt, to Maria Poe (*FGBA* 18 July 1817; *BPAT* 19 July 1817).

Clendinen, Alexander, M.D., was m. last Thurs. eve. by Rev. Mr. Glendy, to Miss Mary Belt (*BPAT* 24 Oct 1818; *BA* 24 Oct 1818).

Clendinen, Mrs. Elizabeth, wife of William H. C. Clendinen, of Baltimore, d. Sat., in her 29th year (Long obit is given) (*BA* 19 June 1818; *BPAT* 20 June 1818).

Clerklee, James, d. 4th inst., at his seat in Charles Co. (*Maryland Gazette or Baltimore General Advertiser* 19 March 1819; *BPAT* 20 March 1819).

Clerklee, Margaret Russell, native of London, consort of James Clerklee, of Bromont, Charles Co., d. 23 Nov (*BA* 27 Nov 1818; *BPAT* 27 Nov 1818).

22

Biographical Data from Baltimore Newspapers, 1817-1819

Clifton, Mr. Arthur, was m. last eve [Fri.] by the Right Rev. Archbishop Marechal, to Miss Alphonza Ringgold of Baltimore (*BPAT* 2 Jan 1818; *BPM* 2 Jan 1818).

Clinch, Col. D. L., of the U. S. Army, was m. at St. Mary's, [Geo.?], on Wed., 8th last, by Rev. Mr. Bell, to Miss Eliza B., youngest dau. of J. H. McIntosh (*BPAT* 27 Dec 1819).

Cline, William, aged 17 years, was m. Wed. eve. at Falmouth, VA, by Rev. William James, to Miss Clary Pusey, aged 45, all of Falmouth (*FGBA* 27 Jan 1817).

Coal, Skipwith H., M.D., was m. last eve. [Thurs.] by Rev. Wyatt to Mrs. Eliza Dugan, all of Baltimore (*FGBA* 30 Jan 1818).

Coale, Mrs. Ann, relict of Dr. Samuel Stringer Coale, d. Sat., aged 71. A native of Philadelphia, she was the last surviving member of the family of the Hon. Thomas Hopkinson (*FGBA* 28 April 1817; *BPAT* 29 April 1817). Mrs. Ann Coale, aged 71, was buried 26 April 1817 from St. Paul's Parish (ReamySP). For her will, filed in 1817, see BAWB 10:322.

Coale, Daniel, was m. last eve. [Thurs.] by Rev. Mr. Hargrove, to Miss Catherine Heagen, all of this city (*BPAT* 14 Feb 1817; *BA* 14 Feb 1817).

Coale, John, d. 11 Jan, aged 34, leaving a widow and mother. The funeral will be from his late residence in Baltimore Co., about eight miles from Baltimore (*FGBA* 11 Jan 1817; *BPAT* 11 Jan 1817). For his will, filed in 1817, see BAWB 10:416.

Coale, William, d. 5 Jan, aged 61 years, leaving a widow and five children (*FGBA* 11 Jan 1817; *BPAT* 11 Jan 1817). For his will, filed in 1817, see BAWB 10:276.

Coates, John, was m. to Miss Martha Ann Stocksdale, all of Baltimore Co., last Wed. by Rev. C. Frye (*BPAT* 15 Jan 1819; *FGBA* 15 Jan 1819).

Coats, Frederick, of Baltimore Co., is an insolvent debtor (*BPAT* 14 Oct 1819).

Coblentz, Dr. Jacob, was m. in Frederick Co. [date not given] to Miss Melinda Staley (*BPAT* 29 Nov 1819).

Cochran, John G., dec.; his handsome fee simple property will be sold at auction on Sat., 12th June (*BPAT* 5 June 1819).

Cochran, William, merchant of Baltimore. d. at Philadelphia on Mon., 16th inst., aged 55. He resided in Market St, (*FGBA* 20 Feb 1818; *BPAT* 21 Feb 1818). He is buried in Westminster Presbyterian Churchyard, Baltimore (HaywardW). For his will, filed in 1818, see BAWB 10:438.

Cochrane, Mr. James, was m. last eve. [Sun.] by Rev. Mr. Hagerty, to Miss Eliza de Buller, all of this city (*BPAT* 3 Feb 1817).

Cockey, John C., was m. in Baltimore last Friday morning by Rev. Dr. Becker to Miss Mary Hooper, all of Frederick Co. (*BPAT* 6 June 1818; *FGBA* 9 June 1818).

Cockey, Thomas, Jr., d. 30 Dec 1816, after an illness of four days, in the 27th year of his age (*FGBA* 11 Jan 1817; *BPAT* 11 Jan 1817).

Cocks, Richard John, only son of Capt. John Cocks, d. 5th inst., aged 8 years, 7 mos. (*BA* 14 May 1817; *BPAT* 14 May 1817).

Cockshot, Mr. Arthur R., was m. Tues. eve. by Rt. Rev. Bishop Kemp, to Miss Margaret Hook, all of Baltimore (*BPAT* 9 Dec 1819).

Coffee, Mr. Charles, and Miss Catherine Reily, of Washington Co., were m. Thurs. morning, 17th inst. by Rev. J. H. Reily, in Hagerstown (*BPAT* 26 June 1819).

Coffey, Mr. Joseph, died at his residence in Brandywine Twp., Pa., aged 85 years (*BPAT* 2 April 1819).

Cohen, Mr. Benjamin I., was m. last eve. [Wed.] by Rev. L. B. Seixas of Richmond, to Kitty, dau. of Solomon Etting, Esq., all of Baltimore (*BPAT* 16 Dec 1819).

Coit, Capt. P. L., was m. last Sat. eve. in Georgetown, D. C., by Rev. Mr. Healey, to Mrs. Mary Broom, all of this city (*BPAT* 26 Dec 1818; *BA* 28 Dec 1818).

Coker, Polly, a negro girl, aged 14 years, apprentice, ran away from Jeremiah Garey Light St. A reward of six cents is offered (*BPAT* 3 Sep 1818).

Biographical Data from Baltimore Newspapers, 1817-1819

Colbert, Mr. Levin, was m. last eve. [Thurs.] by Rev. Mr. Hemphill, to Miss Rebecca Kelley, all of this city (*BPAT* 17 Jan 1817; *BA* 18 Jan 1817).

Colburn, Milton Francis, and Miss Mary Theresa Murdock, both of Baltimore, were m. at White Marsh, Prince George's Co. [date not given] by Bishop Coleman (*BPAT* 30 April 1819).

Cole, James, aged about 28, born in the state of New York, a laborer, deserted from the detachment of James H. Cook, Capt., at Fort Covington on 3 March (*BPAT* 13 Sep 1818).

Cole, Capt. Thomas, dec.; an auction of his household effects will be held at his dwelling on Fells Point; John Carrerre and Dr. Samuel B. Martin, execs. (*BPAT* 8 Jan 1817).

Cole, Mr. Vachel, was m. Thurs., 11th inst., by Rev. Mr. Butler, to Miss Jemima Ensor, all of Baltimore Co. (*BPAT* 27 Dec 1817; the issue of 26 Dec 1817 had erroneously given Jemima's name as Enton).

Coleman, Miss Ann C., dau. of Robert Coleman, Esq., of Lancaster, d. last Thurs. morning, in her 23rd year of age, while visiting friends in Philadelphia (*BPAT* 15 Dec 1819).

Coleman, Mr. John, was m. last Mon. by Rev. Mr. Healey to Miss Catherine Keeho, both of Baltimore Co. (*BPAT* 26 May 1818; *FGBA* 27 May 1818).

Coleman, Thomas, was m. last Sun, by the Rev. D. E. Reese, to Miss Charlotte Whiffen, all of Baltimore (*BA* 29 April 1817; *BPAT* 29 April 1817).

Colestock, Henry, of Harrisburg, PA, was m. last Tues. eve. by Rev. Glendy, to Miss Rebecca Gill of Baltimore (*BA* 18 Dec 1817; *BPAT* 17 Dec 1817).

Colman, Mr. Edward, was m. last Thurs. eve. by Rev. Mr. Smith to Miss Julia Ann Chatterton, both of Baltimore (*BPAT* 18 July 1818; *FGBA* 20 July 1818).

Colquohon, Charles W., of Va., and Ann, dau. of R. C. Long, were m. Tues. by Rt. Rev. Bishop Kemp (*BA* 24 Sep 1818).

Colvin, John, d. yesterday, aged about 51. He resided at Potter and Low Sts., Old Town *BA* 26 May 1818). For his will, filed in 1818, see BAWB 471.

Colwell, Mr. Elijah, was m. last eve. [Mon.] by Rev. Healey to Miss Elizabeth Jones, both of Baltimore Co. (*BPAT* 26 May 1818; *FGBA* 27 May 1818).

Comegys, Ann Worrell, is to have an act for her benefit (*BPAT* 10 Feb 1817).

Comegys, Bartus, was m. last Tues. eve. by Rev. Mr. Henshaw to Miss Evelina Mary Dorsey, both of Baltimore (*BPAT* 15 Oct 1818).

Comegys, John G., of the House of Wm. Cochran and Comegys, merchants, of Baltimore, d. Fri., 5th inst. (*FGBA* 10 Feb 1819; *BPAT* 11 Feb 1819). For his will, filed in 1819, see BAWB 10:572.

Comerly, Daniel, Negro man who calls himself Daniel Smothers, about 25 years of age, ran away from Nehemiah Birckhead, living near Friendship, Anne Arundel Co.; left Baltimore on 27 March with a black man named Richard sparks, and may be in the neighborhood of Havre de Grace (*BPAT* 7 April 1818).

Compton, Elias, late of Philadelphia, and Miss Eliza Jeffrey, from Baltimore, were m. [date not given] at Louisville, Ky. By Rev. Mr. Banks (*FGBA* 3 April 1819; *BPAT* 2 April 1819).

Compton, John, tailor, late of Baltimore, d. 22nd Oct in his 39th year, on his passage to S[outh] A[merica] (*BPAT* 11 Nov 1818).

Conaway, Solomon, late of Baltimore Co., dec.; his personal property, including livestock, crops, slaves, and household furniture, will be sold at a Public Sale, by order of the Baltimore Co. Orphans Court on 24th inst. /s/ John Conaway, Charles Conaway, and Philip Gore, execs. (*BPAT* 16 Nov 1818). For his will, filed in 1818, see BAWB 10:531.

Biographical Data from Baltimore Newspapers, 1817-1819

Cone, Mr. Joseph, was m. last eve. [Mon.] by the Rev. Mr. Cone, to Miss Mary Ann Cave, both of this city (*BPAT* 11 March 1817; *BA* 12 March 1817).

Conkling, Capt. William H., and Elizabeth, dau. of Capt. James Gibson, of Fells Point, were m. last eve. [Thurs.] by Rev. Glendy (*FGBA* 2 July 1819; *BA* 3 July 1819; *BPAT* 3 July 1819).

Conley, John, of Harford Co. is to have an act for his relief (*BPAT* 20 Feb 1817).

Conn, William D., was m. last Thurs. eve. by Rev. Jennings, to Miss Mary Ann Bond, all of Baltimore (*BA* 15 Dec 1817; *BPAT* 15 Dec 1817).

Connell and Gregory, lately arrived fro Philadelphia, where they were employed at the principal Paper Hanging Manufactories, have begun the manufacturing of Paper hangings and have opened a store at the corner of Gay and Market Sts., next door to the Looking Glass store of Sanderson and Ward (*BPAT* 27 Oct 1818).

Connell, Edward, a blacksmith in the U. S. Ordinance department, born in Cork, Kingdom of Ireland, deserted from the U. S. Arsenal near Baltimore /s/ N. Baden, 1st Lieut, of Ord. (*BPAT* 7 Aug 1819).

Connell, Mr. John, was m. [date not given] to Miss Rebecca Parrott, both of Washington, D.C. (*BPAT* 29 Dec 1817).

Connelly, Mr. William, was m. last Sat. eve. by Rev. Healey to Miss Eliza Bullen, all of Baltimore (*BPAT* 26 May 1818; *FGBA* 27 May 1818).

Connor, Mrs. Mary, late of this city, and relict of James Connor, of Cork, Ireland, d. at the latter place on 2nd Aug last, in her 68th year (*BPAT* 27 Oct 1817).

Conrey, Capt., a citizen of the U. S., lost his vessel near the Philippine Islands. He arrived in Manila, got command of a vessel trading in Acapulco, and died on his return to the Marianne Islands. If his heirs or representatives should recognize him, they may hear something to their advantage by applying to the Custom House in Baltimore (*BPAT* 30 April 1818).

Contee, Mrs. Ann Russell, wife of Philip A. L. Contee, d. at Port Tobacco on 24 May, in her 24th year (*FGBA* 9 June 1819).

Contee, Mr. Philip A. L., of Westmoreland Co., Va., was m. on 2nd inst. [Thurs.], by Rev. Mann. to Ann Russel, eld. dau. of James Clerklee of Charles Co. *BPAT* 11 July 1818; *FGBA* 10 July 1818).

Conradt, Mr. G. M., was m. at Frederick Town, [date not given] to Miss Margaret Fessler (*BPAT* 8 Nov 1819).

Cooch, Mr. Zebulon H., was m. on Tues. eve. last by Rev. Mr. Richards to Miss Ann Maria Heide, all of Baltimore (*BPAT* 24 Dec 1818; *BA* 24 Dec 1818).

Cook, Anthony L., was m. last Sun. eve. by Rev. D. E. Reese, to Miss Mary Ratcliff, all of Baltimore (*BA* 25 Oct 1817; *BPAT* 25 Oct 1817).

Cook, Henry, and Mary Warner, all of Baltimore, were m. 27th ult. [Sat.] by Dr. Glendy (*FGBA* 6 April 1819; *BPAT* 3 April 1819).

Cook, Mrs. Margaret, consort of William Cook of Baltimore, d. leaving a husband and ten children; she was in her 48th year (*BA* 19 May 1818; *BPAT* 19 May 1818).

Cook, Philip, an apprentice to James P. Soper, bound to Soper for five years, had to stay 12 mos. from 13th Dec last (*BPAT* 14 Jan 1819).

Cook, Richard L., of Baltimore, d. at Raleigh, N. C., on 26th April (*FGBA* 6 May 1818; *BPAT* 7 May 1818).

Cook, Robert, of Kent Co., Del., is to have an act to authorize a certain portion of lands therein mentioned (*BPAT* 10 Feb 1817).

Cook, Samuel, an insolvent debtor, will have his property sold by Samuel Cole, auctioneer, on Sat., 19th inst., under the direction of David Delacour, trustee for said Cook (*BPAT* 5 June 1819).

Cook, Thomas, of Baltimore Co., and Miss Ann Rose of Baltimore were m. last Thurs. by Rev. Dr. Roberts (*BA* 29Aug 1818; *BPAT* 28 Aug 1818 gives his name as Cooke).

Cook, Thomas, of Dorchester Co., and Miss Mary Rankin, of Baltimore, were m. last eve. [Thurs.] by Rev. Birch (*BPAT* 24 Dec 1819).

Biographical Data from Baltimore Newspapers, 1817-1819

Cook, Mr. William, of Georgetown, was m. [date not given] to Miss Mary Beall (*BPAT* 15 May 1817).

Cooke, William, d. this morning, aged 71 (*BPAT* 24 July 1817; *FGBA* 25 July 1817). William Cook [*sic*], aged 71, was buried 24 July 1817 from St. Paul's Parish (ReamySP). For his will, filed in 1817, see BAWB 10:338.

Coolidge, William, Jr., was m. yesterday morning [Mon.] by Rev. Bishop Kemp, to Mrs. Eliza . Mullikin, all of this city (*BPAT* 11 March 1817).

Cooper, Mr. Isaiah, of Cecil Co., was m. Thurs., 18th inst., in York Co., Pa., to Miss Tylinda Delia Boyd, dau. of John Boyd, Esq., of the latter place (*BPAT* 22 June 1818; *BA* 22 June 1818).

Cooper, Mr. William, d. at Alexandria, merchant, aged about 30, a native of England; for the past few years a resident of this town (*BPAT* 30 Aug 1819).

Corkrell, Mr. William., d. in Talbot Co. (*BPAT* 29 Nov 1819).

Correy, Capt. a citizen of the U. S, lost his vessel near the Philippine Islands; he afterwards arrived in Manila, and got the command of a vessel trading in Acapulco. If his heirs or representatives should recognize him by this information they may hear something to their advantage by applying to at the Custom House, Baltimore (*BPAT* 30 April 1818).

Corrie, J., [dec.? insolvent debtor?]; George Dashiell, a trustee of his estate and John Diffenderfer and Isaac Causten advertise the sale of *Bachelor's Study*, 73 a. in Baltimore Co., *Stewart's Sylvania,* 24 a., and two-fifths of one tract in Bedford Co., Pa., cont. 1200 a. If not dispose of by next 1 March, they will be offered at public auction on that day by Messrs. Hazlehurst & Dorsey, auctioneers (*BPAT* 13 March 1817).

Corry, Mr. Ebenezer, of this city, was m. in Portland [date not given] to Miss Abigail Baker of the former place (*BPAT* 12 Aug 1818; *BA* 13 Aug 1818).

Corse, Barney, d. at Chestertown, last Mon. in his 71st year (*FGBA* 1 Sep 1817).

Cosden, George B., and Miss Eliza. eld. dau. of George Byrnes, were m. 27th inst. [Tues.], at Elkton, Md., by Rev. John Sharpley (*BPAT* 3 May 1819).

Coskery, Miss Elizabeth, dau. of Bernard Coskery, d. yesterday, aged 17 (*FGBA* 27 Feb 1819; *BPAT* 1 Feb 1819).

Cotner, Dion, of Caroline Co., is to have an act to alter and change the name to Dion Downes (*BPAT* 10 Feb 1817).

Cottingham, Daniel, of Worcester Co., dec.; a trustee's sale of all his lands will be held on 28 Aug next. /s/ Thomas Hopper, Trustee (*BPAT* 3 Aug 1819).

Coudon, Mrs. Rachel, d. 7 Aug, near Newark, Del., in her 62nd year, relict of the late Joseph Couden, of Cecil Co. (*FGBA* 20 Aug 1817; *BPAT* 20 Aug 1817).

Coulter, Mr. James, d. at Havana of the yellow fever (*BPAT* 2 Nov 1819).

Courtlan, James, was m. last Thurs. eve. by Rev. Mr. Valiant, to Patience Cole, all of Baltimore (*BA* 27 May 1817; *BPAT* 26 May 1817).

Courtney, Mary, dec.; Elizabeth Duesbury, admx., will settle the estate (*BPAT* 3 Feb 1819). (For the will of Mary Courtney, filed in 1818, see BAWB 10:598).

Courtney, Patrick, and Miss Mary Kain, both of Baltimore, were m. Sun., 10th inst., by Rev. Fenwick (*FGBA* 13 Jan 1819; *BPAT* 13 Jan 1819).

Cow, Michael, was m. Tues., 23rd inst., by Rev. Mr. Parks, to Miss Susannah Fairbank, eldest dau. of John Fairbank of Elk Ridge (*BA* 27 Dec 1817; *BPAT* 27 Dec 1817).

Cox, Jesse R., was m. last Friday by Rev. Kurtz, to Miss Catherine [Zeig], all of Baltimore (*BA* 2 Nov 1818; *BPAT* 2 Nov 1818).

Cox, John, d. 2nd inst., in his 36th year, leaving a widow, five children, and aged parents (*BPAT* 6 Aug 1818).

Cox, MacDonald, only son of James Cox of Baltimore, d. Tues. in his 21st year (*BA* 30 April 1818; *BPAT* 30 April 1818). Macdonald Cox, aged 20 years, was buried 28 April 1818 from St. Paul's Parish (ReamySP).

Cox, Capt. Samuel, formerly a merchant of Washington, D. C., d. at New Orleans in the 26th year of his age (*BPAT* 21 Dec 1819).

Biographical Data from Baltimore Newspapers, 1817-1819

Cox, William, merchant of Washington, was m. Tues. eve. by Rev. Mr. Wyatt, to Miss Mary Ann Dawson of Baltimore (*BA* 18 Dec 1817; *BPAT* 18 Dec 1817).

Coxe, Edward D., Esq., d. Sun., 3rd Oct last, at his father's country seat in Lower Dublin; one of the representatives for Philadelphia in the General Assembly of Pa., and a counselor at law (*BPAT* 7 Oct 1819).

Cramer, Mr. Cornelius, and Miss Amelia Fulton were m. [date not given] at Frederick Town (*BMC* 31 May 1819).

Crandal, Mr. Allison, was m. on 23rd inst. [Fri.] to Miss Maria Ann White of Cecil Co. (*BPAT* 31 Oct 1818; *BA* 31 Oct 1818).

Crane, Jesse, native of Baltimore, d. at sea on 19 July 1818, on board the Brig *Orleans*, bound from New Orleans to Gibraltar (*FGBA* [24?] Feb 1819; *BPAT* 24 Feb 1819).

Craper. John, owes taxes for the years 1813, and 1814 on 112 a., part *Stiltz's Deer Park*, in the 6th Dist. (*BPAT* 7 Jan 1819).

Crapster, John, Jr., and Miss Frances Shorb were m. [date not given] at Taneytown (*BMC* 17 May 1819).

Crassey, William, was m. last Wed. eve. by Rev. D. E. Reese, to Miss Keziah Roberts, all of Baltimore (*BA* 20 Sep 1817).

Crassmer, William, and Miss Caroline Maurer, dau. of John Peter Mauer of Baltimore, were m. last eve. [Tues.] by Rev. Kurtz (*FGBA* 26 May 1819; *BPAT* 27 May 1819).

Crawford, James, was m. last Sun. by Rev. Wyatt, to Miss Isabella Weir, all of Baltimore (*BA* 9 May 1817; *BPAT* 8 May 1817).

Crawford, John F., a person of Genteel appearance and small stature, of the District of Washington, came to the Stable of William Marks, at the Shakespeare Tavern, and took a pair of horses and a gig out for [a trial run, and never returned them (*BPAT* 3 April 1817).

Crawford, Col. Joseph, aged 83, a native of Ireland, and a Revolutionary patriot, d. at Chambersburg, Pa., 1st inst. (*BPAT* 15 Jan 1819).

Crawford, Mr. William H., of Baltimore was m. in Philadelphia last Mon. eve. by Rev. Mr. Parker to Miss Sarah V. Merritt (*BPAT* 12 March 1818; *BA* 12 March 1818).

Creager, Mr. John, was m. at Hagerstown, [date not given], to Miss Nancy McCall (*BPAT* 6 Aug 1819).

Creagh, John, and Miss Sarah Stewart, were m. last Sun. (*FGBA* 10 April 1819; *BPAT* 10 April 1819).

Crevenston, George, and Miss Martha Greenfield, both of Harford Co., were m. last Tues. by Rev. Finney (*BA* 27 April 1818).

Crever, Mr. Jacob, Jr., was m. last Wed. morning by Rev. Albert Helfenstein, to Miss Margaret Decker, dau. of Jacob Decker of Baltimore Co. (*BPAT* 21 Oct 1819).

Crew, Richard, and Miss Delilah Lightner, all of Baltimore, were m. Thurs., 26th ult., by Rev. Mr. Healey (*BA* 6 March 1818).

Cromwell, [-?-], and [-?-] Whelan, trustees for [-?-] M'Cubbin, owe takes 1813, 1814, 1815, on 488 a. in the 1st Dist., under a special demurrer (*BPAT* 7 Jan 1819).

Cromwell, Capt. Joseph H., and Miss Margaret Parrish, both of this city, were m. last eve. [Sun.] by Rev. Dr. Roberts (*BPAT* 27 April 1818; *BPM* 27 April 1818; the *FGBA* of 28 April 1818 gives his name as John H. Cromwell, but corrects it in the issue of 29 April 1819).

Crompton, Thomas, d. at Pleasant Valley, Washington Co. [date not given] (*BMC* 28 May 1819).

Crosby, James, and Miss Mary Hunter, all of Baltimore, were m. Tues. eve. by Rev. Glendy (*FGBA* 31 July 1819; *BPAT* 31 July 1819).

Cross, Lieut. Joseph, of the Navy, was m. in Washington City on Tues. eve. last, by Rev. Mr. Hyatt, to Miss Cecilia Duval, dau. of the late Charles Duval of Prince George's Co., MD (*BPAT* 21 Feb 1817).

Cross, Truman, and Miss Margaret, dau. of Charles Bohn, Esq., all of Baltimore, were m. last Tues. eve. by Rev. Dr. Kurtz (*BPAT* 28 March 1818).

Biographical Data from Baltimore Newspapers 1817-1819

Cross, William, owes taxes for the years 1814, 1815, on 68 a. *Hard Fare* in the 6th Dist. (*BPAT* 7 Jan 1819).
Crouch, Mrs. Elizabeth, d. 15th inst., in her 44th year (*FGBA* 16 July 1817; *BPAT* 17 July 1817).
Crouch, Samuel, aged about 18, apprentice to James Stewart of 96 Hanover St., has left his master's service without leave (*BPAT* 22 March 1817). Crouch has returned, and Stewart states he has always found Crouch to be worthy of his confidence and of the best disposition (*BPAT* 25 March 1817).
Croxall, James, late of Baltimore, was m. at Louisville, KY on Wed., 28th ult., by Rev. D. C. Banks, to Maria Aglae Duborg, dau. of William Duborg, merchant (*BACDA* 21 May 1819; *BPAT* 21 May 1819).
Croxall, Richard, son of John, d. Sat., 18 Jan 1817, in his 22nd year. The funeral will be from his father's dwelling in N. Charles St. (*FGBA* 20 Jan 1817; *BPAT* 20 Jan 1817).
Cuinand, Mr. F. E., was m. last Tues., by Rev. Mr. Barnhard, to Miss Mary C. Dewn (*BPAT* 10 Jan 1817).
Cully, Mr. Samuel, and Miss Ann Wilson, all of Baltimore, were m. Mon. eve. by Rev. D. E. Reese (*BPAT* 17 July 1819).
Cummins, Jno., and Miss Charlotte Sellers, all of Baltimore, were m. Thurs., 21st inst., by Rev. Gibson (*FGBA* 26 Jan 1819; *BPAT* 27 Jan 1819).
Cunningham, Mr. James, was m. last Sun. eve. by Rev. E. J. Reis, to Miss Sophia Gorsuch, all of Baltimore (*BA* 3 Sep 1817; *BPAT* 2 Sep 1817, 3 Sep 1817).
Cunningham, Mr. John, of Harford Co., d. on Wed., in his 23rd year (*BA* 8 Jan 1819; *BPAT* 8 Jan 1819).
Cunningham, John, late of Baltimore, d. at Bethlehem, PA, on 3rd inst. (*FGBA* 7 July 1819). For the will of John Cunningham, filed in 1818, see BAWB 10:435.
Curey[?], Mr. Henry, was m. last Sun. eve. by Rev. Mr. Rev. Bartow, to Miss H. Grisas, both of Kent Co. (*BPAT* 20 Dec 1819).
Curtain, James, and Miss Eliza Josephine Pilch, were m. last Tues. by Rev. Mr. Moranville (*BPM* 9 April 1818; *BPAT* 8 April 1818).
Cushing, Dr. Thomas H., one of the Assistant Surgeons of the U. S. Ship *Franklin,* d. at Philadelphia, 1st inst. He was interred on Monday afternoon with military honors (*BPAT* 5 June 1817).
Cuthbert, Mrs. Mary T., relict of the late William Cuthbert, d. [date not given] [prob. in Va.] (*BPAT* 4 Nov 1818).
Cutler, Mr. Robert C., formerly of Washington City, was m. [date not given] in Nelson Co., Va., to Miss Rebecca E. Powell (*BPAT* 2 April 1818; *BPM* 2 April 1818).
Cutler, Samuel, aged about 18, apprentice to the cordwaining business, ran away from James Ackland, 31 Water St.; a reward of six cents is offered (*BPAT* 11 June 1818).

"D"

Daffin, Sarah, of the Alms House, was buried 2 Sep (*FGBA* 3 Sep 1819).
Dailey, John and Miss Mary Roache, both of Baltimore, were m. last Sun. eve. by Rev. Mr. Craney [Carney?] (*FGBA* 21 April 1818).
Daily, Mr. John, was m. last Sun. eve. by Rev. Mr. Carney to Miss Margaret Crothers, both of Baltimore (*BPAT* 21 April 1818).
Dall, John R., and Meliora O., second dau. of Thomas Buchanan of Washington Co., were m. at Woodburn Seat, near Hagerstown, on Tues., 23rd Feb., by Rev. Mr. Clay (*FGBA* 4 March 1819; *BPAT* 5 March 1819).
Dallas, The Hon. Alexander, d. in Philadelphia on the 16th inst., in his 54th year [Long obituary (*FGBA* 20 Jan 1817; *BPAT* 22 Jan 1817).
Dalrymple, John, d.; the funeral will be from his late residence at the corner of King George and Albemarle Sts. (*FGBA* 7 May 1817). John Delrymple [*sic*], aged 60

years, was buried 7 May 1817 from St. Paul's Parish (ReamySP). For the will of John Dalrymple, filed in 1817, see BAWB 10:365.

Dalrymple, Mr. William P., d. this morning, in the 25th year of his age, of an inflammation of the brain (*BPAT* 4 Sep 1819). Mr. Dalrymple, aged 29 years, was buried 4 Sep 1819 from St. Paul's Parish (ReamySP).

Dalrymple, William P. of Baltimore Co., is an insolvent debtor (*BPAT* 18 Sep 1819).

Daly, Mrs. Mary, wife of Mr. James Daly of this city, d. last Sat., after a short but severe illness (*BPAT* 17 Aug 1819).

Dance, Mr. Thomas, of the Island of Jamaica, was m. last eve. [Tues.] by the Rev. Dr. Inglis to Miss Augusta Temple Sterrett, eld. dau. of Thomas Sterrett, Esq. of Baltimore (*BPAT* 6 May 1818;).

Dancker, John J., was m. last Tues., by Rev. D. E. Reese, to Miss Ann Jarvis, all of Baltimore (*BA* 6 Sep 1817).

Danneman, C. H., of the House of Brune and Danneman, and Miss Elvira W. Yeiser, of Baltimore, were m. last Thurs. by Rev. Wyant (*FGBA* 27 March 1819; *BPAT* 27 March 1819). Conrad Henry Danneman of Germany was naturalized on 25 May 1813 (U.S. Circuit Court Minutes 1790-1828).

Dante. John Baptiste, of Baltimore, a native of France, d. yesterday, 8th inst., in his 65th year (*BPAT* 9 June 1819).

D'Arcy, John M., was m. last eve. [Thurs.] at the seat of Henry Didier, Esq., near Baltimore, by Rt. Rev. Bishop Kemp, to Miss Amelia, youngest dau. of H. Didier, Esq. (*BPAT* 30 Jan 1818).

Darden, John, and Miss Mary Moale, were m. last Thurs. eve. by Rev. Rev. Bartow (*BMC* 29 May 1819; *BPAT* 28 May 1819).

Dare, E., dec.; recently occupied a tailor's shop on Pratt St., near the water J. D. Richardson, at 84 Bowly's Wharf, advertises that the premises are to let (*BPAT* 20 March 1819).

Darling, John, a native of Scotland, d. yesterday; funeral will be from [his residence, near?] the corner of Petticoat Alley (*BA* 14 Dec 1818; *BPAT* 14 Dec 1818).

Darrell [Darnel?], Capt. Sampson, dec.; James Gunteaume, administrator, will settle the estate (*BPAT* 23 Oct 1819). For the will of Sampson Darnel, filed in 1819, see BAWB 11:33.

Dashiell, George Washington, and Mary, only dau. of the late James Corrie, were m. last Tues. at St. John's Episcopal Church by the Rev. Dashiell (*FGBA* 31 March 1819; *BPAT* 31 March 1819).

Davey, Henry, and Mrs. Elizabeth Wheedon, all of Baltimore, were m. last Sun. by Rev. Davis (*BA* 18 March 1818; *BPAT* 17 March 1818).

Davidge, Francis H., and Anna Maria, eld. dau. of Judge Dorsey, were m. last eve. [Tues.] at Manor Vale, by Rev. Mr. Henshaw (*FGBA* 5 May 1819; *BPAT* 6 May 1819).

Davidge, Dr. John B., and Mrs. Rebecca Polk, both of Baltimore, were m. last Thurs. by Bishop Kemp (*FGBA* 28 Aug 1819; *BPAT* 30 Aug 1819 says last Tues.).

Davidge, Mrs. W. H., consort of Dr. Davidge of Baltimore, and youngest dau. of the late John Hathorn Stewart, Esq., of Physgill House, Wigtonshire, Scotland, d. 12th inst. in Harford Co. (*BPAT* 18 July 1818; *BA* 18 July 1818; *BPAT* 18 July 1818).

Davidson, Mr. Thomas, Esq., formerly of Bernholm, Denmark, and Miss Rachel Gough of Baltimore were m. 4th inst. [Sat.], by Dr. Elbert (*BPAT* 7 Dec 1819).

Davis, [-?-], child of R. Davis, aged two months, was buried 2 Sep 1819 (*FGBA* 3 Sep 1819).

Davis, Caleb, of Baltimore Co., and Miss Louisa W. Brown, eld. dau. of the late John R. Brown, also of Baltimore Co., were m. at *Good Fellowship,* Anne Arundel Co., last Tues. by the Rev. Linthicomb (*FGBA* 12 March 1819; *BPAT* 12 March 1819).

Davis, Mr. Charles, and Mrs. Catherine Worts, all of Baltimore, were m. 7th inst. [Sun.] by Rev. Dr. Glendy (*BPAT* 13 Nov 1819).

Biographical Data from Baltimore Newspapers 1817-1819

Davis, David, was m. last Thurs. eve. by Rev. Bartow, to Miss Mary Shane, both of Baltimore (*BA* 26 April`1817; *BPAT* 26 April 1817).

Davis, David, was m. last Thurs., by Rev. Mr. Healey, to Mrs. Rhoda Dougherty, both of Baltimore (*BPAT* 30 July 1817).

Davis, David, aged about 17, apprentice to the house carpenter's business, ran away from John Bahler, Howard St., opp. the Com. and Farmer's Bank (*BPAT* 29 Sep 1818).

Davis, Lieut. E. R., of the U.S. navy, died yesterday; the funeral will be from Mrs. Cannon's in South St. (*BA* 31 March 1818; *BPAT* 30 March 1818).

Davis, Elizabeth, offers a reward for the apprehension of Samuel van Winckle and Jeremiah Lyons who on 15th inst, led a band of ruffians who forcibly entered her house, set about her with clubs and destroyed her property (*BPAT* 20 May 1817).

Davis, Mr. George, d. (at Easton, Md.?) (*BPAT* 2 Nov 1819).

Davis, James, of York St., aged 45, d. last Sun. (*FGBA* 6 April 1819; *BPAT* 6 April 1819). James Davis, aged 45, was buried 5 April 1819 from St. Paul's Parish (ReamySP). For the will of James Davis, filed in 1819, see BAWB 10:594.

Davis, John N., will not pay the debts of his wife Sarah Ann Davis, who has eloped from his bed and board (*BPAT* 6 Dec 1819).

Davis, William, aged 26 years, a laborer, well known in New York, deserted from Fort Covington on 21st inst. /s/ James H. Cook, Capt., 4th Inf. (*BPAT* 24 Jan 1818).

Davis, William M., merchant of London, was m. last Tues. by Rev. Henshaw, to Miss Sarah Rutter of Baltimore (*BA* 14 Aug 1817; *BPAT* 14 Aug 1817).

Davison, Mr. Samuel, and Miss Caroline Dinges, all of Baltimore, were m. Sun. Eve., 31 Oct by Rev. Dr. Roberts (*BPAT* 16 Nov 1819).

Dawes, Edward, d. 30 Sept. after a short illness (*BPAT* 3 Oct 1818). For the will of Edward Dawes, filed in 1818, see BAWB 10:537.

Dawes, Harrison, of Baltimore Co., is an insolvent debtor (*BPAT* 6 Oct 1819).

Dawson, William, states that his wife Mary Dawson, formerly Mary Rogers, whom he married in July 1814, left his bed and board on 30 January 1819 and was again married by the Rev. Mr. David, to a man named John Handle. Dawson will not pay the debts of her and will apply for a bill of divorce (*BPAT* 17 Feb 1819).

Day, Sarah, who formerly lived in Albany and is the mother of Everett Day, or George Day, silversmith, who lived in Philadelphia three years ago, are asked to address a letter to Capt. James H. Hook at Baltimore, to learn some information that concerns them. The editors of the *Franklin Gazette* at Philadelphia and the Albany *Argus* are requested to publish the above lines (*BPAT* 30 June 1818).

Dealing [?}, Mr, Abner, d. at Easton, Md. (*BPAT* 5 July 1819).

Deane, James, of St. Mary's Co. will have an act passed for his benefit (*BPAT* 10 Feb 1817).

DeButts, Mr. John, of Prince George's Co. was m. on last Mon. to Miss Sophia Forrest, dau. of Josiah Forrest, Esq., of Washington (*BPAT* 13 Aug 1818).

Dechert, Mr. Peter S., of Chambersburg, Pa., and Miss Mary Harry, dau. of Mr. David Harry, were m. at Hagerstown [date not given] (*BPAT* 27 Dec 1819).

Dejarnatt, Mr. Daniel, was m. [date not given] at Washington, to Miss Huldah Coleman, both of Caroline Co., VA (*BPAT* 29 Dec 1817).

Dejean, Peter, Esq., of Prince George's Co., was m. [date not given] to Miss Henrietta McPhereson of the same county (*BPAT* 1 May 1817).

DeKrafft, Edward and Eleanor, dau. of Wm. de Wees, were m. [date not given] (*BPAT* 14 June 1819).

Delacour, James, d. Sat., 11th inst., after a long and painful illness, aged 74 year (*BPAT* 17 July 1818; *BA* 18 July 1818).

Delaplaine, Mr. John, and Miss Sophia Carlton, both of Frederick Co., were m. at Fredericktown [date not given] (*BPAT* 27 Oct 1819).

Delius, Arnold, plaintiff, sued Johann Denker, of St. Thomas, defendant, for debt in the High Court of Justice of the Free Hanseatic City of Bremen. Denker did not appear and the 'Burgmasters' and Council of Bremen found for the plaintiff on 4 Nov 1816 (*BPAT* 22 March 1817).

Dell, Peter, owes taxes for the years 1813, 1814, 1815, on one-half a. *Bond's Meadows* in the 6th Dist. (*BPAT* 7 Jan 1819).

Delowshew, Alex., of Baltimore Co., is an insolvent debtor (*BPAT* 27 Oct 1819).

Demaray, Mr. Joseph, Jr., of Baltimore, was m. Thurs. eve., 15th inst., at Kinder Hook, by the Rev. Jacob Sickles, to Miss Maria Crane of the latter place (*BPAT* 25 Feb 1817).

Den Bork, Abraham, a native of Holland, d. Sunday, 24th inst., in his 49th year; for many years he was a respectable inhabitant of Baltimore (*BPAT* 28 Oct 1819). Abraham Den Boer [*sic*], of Holland, a resident of Baltimore, renounced his allegiance to the Emperor of France on 20 May 1812 (U. S. Circuit Court Minutes 1790-1828).

Dennys (or Denys), Benjamin, d. Wed., in his 50th year he resided at Lexington and North Sts. (*BA* 2 Jan 1818' *BPAT* 2 Jan 1818). His funeral will be from St. Peter's church next Mon. (*FGBA* 24 July 1818). For the will of Benjamin Denys, filed in 1818, see BAWB 10:402.

Dent, Major J. T., was m. in Charleston, at St. Philip's Church last Wed. eve., by the Rev Mr. Gadsden, to Catherine Ann Cooper, dau. of Major Samuel Cooper of New York (*BPAT* 7 March 1817).

Dent, William H., of Baltimore, d. Sun., 1st inst., in his 31st year. He was a native of Charles Co., where he had practiced medicine for over eight years. He had come to Baltimore to attend a series of lectures at the Medical College of Maryland (*BPAT* 3 Feb 1818; *BA* 4 Feb 1818).

Derstedt, Capt. John, aged about 40, a native of Sweden, d. last Thurs. in Baltimore (*FGBA* 26 Dec 1817).

Despeaux, John, was m. last eve. [Wed.] by Rev. Hargrove, to Miss Anne Isabell Ardery, all of Baltimore (*BA* 30 Jan 1817).

Develin, Mr. Patrick, was m. last Sun. eve. by Rev Mr. Moranville to Miss Mary Ann Moore, both of Fells Point (*BPAT* 4 Aug 1818; *BA* 5 Aug 1818). Patrick Develin of Ireland was naturalized on 7 Nov 1808 (Baltimore Co. Court Naturalization Docket 1796-1851, f. 37).

De Viar, Don Joseph Ignacio, Charge d'Affairs and Consul General from His Catholic Majesty to the United States, d. at Philadelphia, 24th inst., after a lingering sickness (*BPAT* 28 Dec 1818).

DeVille, Miss, from Paris, and who has been established in Philadelphia for three years, has just arrived in Baltimore, where she intends to make dresses and millinery in a style that she hopes will win the approbation of the ladies of Baltimore. She will take a few young Ladies to learn the trade. She is at No. 2, Harrison St., next door to the *American* office (*BPAT* 14 Dec 1819).

Dew, Mrs. Henrietta Maria, consort of James C. Dew, and a dau. of Gen. T. E. Stansbury, d. of a rapid pulmonary complaint, Sun., 21st inst., aged 34 years (*BPAT* 25 Feb 1819).

Dew, James C., and Miss Ann Williams, all of Baltimore, were m. Tues. morning by Rev. Dr. Jennings (*FGBA* 14 July 1819; *BPAT* 14 July 1819).

Dias, Mr. Lopes, of Baltimore, was m. last Sat. in Philadelphia, to Miss Ann, dau. of the late Mr. James Hamm of the latter city (*BPAT* 6 May 1818; *BA* 8 May 1818). Joseph Lopez Dias, possibly from Portugal, was naturalized in Montgomery Co. (Montgomery Co. Court Minutes, Nov 1794, no p. given).

Dickhut, George, d. last Sat. in his 40th year (*FGBA* 7 Jan 1817).

Dickinson, Mrs. Rebecca Ann, d. last Wed. eve. after a short illness; aged 23, wife of Mr. William Dickinson. She left a husband and three small children (*BPAT* 12 Dec 1817).

Biographical Data from Baltimore Newspapers 1817-1819

Dickman, T., editor of the *Hampden Federalist*, was m. on 13 March [Thurs.] by Rev. Samuel Osgood, to Miss Brewer, dau. of Chancy Brewer. From the *Hampden Federalist* (*BPAT* 27 March 1817).

Diffenderfer, Mrs. Catherine, consort of Mr. John Diffenderfer of Baltimore, d. last evening in her 30th year, after a tedious indisposition (*BPAT* 1 July 1818; *FGBA* 1 July 1818).

Diffenderfer, Daniel, who resided in Great York St., opposite the New Jerusalem Church, d. yesterday in his 73rd year (*FGBA* 17 April 1819; *BPAT* 17 April 1818). (For the will of Daniel Diffenderfer, filed in 1819, see BAWB 10:598)

Diffenderfer, Michael, dec., Dorothy Diffenderfer, John Diffenderfer, and Charles Diffenderfer, administrators, announce the sale of two houses: one was a two story brick dwelling house located at 50 N. Frederick St., and the other a frame house at the corner of Albemarle and Prince Sts. (*BPAT* 6 Feb 1817).

Diffenderfer, Dr. Michael, was m. Thurs., 22nd inst. by Rev. Mr. Duncan to Miss Salome, eld. dau. of George Decker, of Baltimore (*BPAT* 26 Oct 1818; *BA* 27 Oct 1818).

Diggs, Mrs. Esther, d. Fri. eve., at Frederick Town, in her 96th year. She retained the use of her senses and of her eyes until the last moment. She attended church every Sunday (*BPAT* 6 Feb 1818; *BA* 6 Feb 1818).

Dimmitt, Mrs. Catherine, d. Thurs., 16th inst., after a short but painful illness, in her 50th tear (*BPAT* 21 July 1818; *FGBA* 20 July 1818). Catherine Dimmitt, aged 50 years, was buried 17 July 1818 from St. Paul's Parish (ReamySP).

Dirickson, Gen. Samuel, d. at Middletown, Ky., on 7thinst.,aged 53 years, a venerable Revolutionary Whig; he had moved to KY only a few years ago from Del. (*BPAT* 28 June 1817).

Disbrow, Mr. William, a native of Conn., d. at Still Pond, Kent Co., Sun., 24 Oct last, in his 23rd year, a teacher of the youth of Still Pond (*BPAT* 15 Nov 1819).

Disney, Mr. Wesley, and Miss Margaret Ann Sank were m. last eve. [Mon.] by Rev. Mr. Bare (*BPAT* 21 Dec 1819).

Dismukes, Mr. John, a native of Va., died at Milledgeville, Ga., on 4th inst., in his 93rd year; he fought in Braddock's War and was a soldier of the Revolution (*BPAT* 24 March 1818).

Dison, William, and Miss Ann Darnald, were m. at Frederick Town [date not given] (*BMC* 31 May 1819).

Dixson, Mr. Thomas, d. in Somerset Co., Md., on the 14th inst. (*BPAT* 30 Sep 1819).

Dobbin, John, and Miss Susan M. Dupuy, all of Baltimore, were m. 17th inst, [Sun.]. by Rev. Force (*FGBA* 20 Jan 1819; *BPAT* 21 Jan 1819).

Donaldson, Mrs. Rebecca. wife of Richard, d. last Sat., in his 32nd year (*BA* 9 Oct 1817; *BPAT* 9 Oct 1817).

Donaldson, Stephen P., was m. last Thurs. eve. by Rev. Dr. Elliott, to Miss Priscilla Sharpless, both of Baltimore (*BA* 11 Oct 1817; *BPAT* 10 Oct 1817).

Donnellin, Thomas, has just arrived from Ireland, and is seeking a situation in a respectable private family, who engages to act as a storekeeper, and keep accounts correct. He can produce satisfactory credentials from the County and City of Limerick. Any gentleman wishing to employ a correct young man of my description should apply to Mr. E. Sandeler [?], watchmaker, corner of Calvert and Market Sts. (*BPAT* 25 Aug 1819).

Donohoe, James, aged about 16 years, and stout, apprentice to the ship joiner's business, ran away from William Denny, Wolf St., Fell's Point; a reward of $20.00 was offered (*BPAT* 25 Aug 1818).

Donovan, William, aged about 20, and **James Donovan**, aged about 18, sons of William Donovan of Trinity Place, Dublin, in the kingdom of Ireland, goldsmith, quit their father's residence and went beyond the seas, , the former to the United States of North America, and the latter to the East Indies. These boys and their sisters Mary Anne and Margaret Donovan have lately been bequeathed a considerable personal

Biographical Data from Baltimore Newspapers 1817-1819

property, amounting to £1400 to £1500 each, by their late uncle, Kingsmill Dean, Esq. The two boys, who were .born in the City of Philadelphia [*sic*], should contact Mr. William Hope, No. 50, Dawson St., Dublin (*BPAT* 29 July 1818).

Doonin, Peter, who sometime since has lived in Baltimore, Lancaster, and Norfolk, is informed that his wife and children have just arrived from Ireland and need his immediate assistance; they are now in Baltimore at the house of Mr. Hamilton McDowell (*BPAT* 14 Oct 1818).

Dorry, Dr. Henry, of Baltimore City, dec.; F. Hurxthal, administrator, will settle the estate (*BPAT* 13 Oct 1819). [Cf. with Dr. Henry Dorsey, below].

Dorsey, Edward, owes taxes for the years 1813, 1814, 1815, on 125 a. *Bachelor's Refuge* in the 6th Dist. (*BPAT* 7 Jan 1819).

Dorsey, Elisha, owes taxes for the years 1813, 1814, 1815, on 61 a. *Hart's Goodwill* in the 5th Dist. (*BPAT* 7 Jan 1819).

Dorsey, Mrs. Elizabeth, wife of Hammond Dorsey, Esq., all of Baltimore Co., d. 11 Aug (*FGBA* 13 Aug 1819).

Dorsey, Dr. Henry W., d. Last Tues., of the prevailing disease, at his residence on Fell's Point, in the 45th year of his age (*BPAT* 16 Sep 1819). [Cf. with Dr. Henry Dory, above].

Dorsey, Mr. Hill, dec.; his property and farm *Dorsey's Manor* will be sold at auction this afternoon (*BPAT* 29 April 1817).

Dorsey, John H., of Baltimore, was m. last eve. [Tues.] by Rev. Joshua Wells, to Miss Harriot P. Byus, dau. of Capt. William Byus of Dorchester Co. (*BPAT* 24 June 1818; *BA* 25 June 1818).

Dorsey, Dr. John Syng, Professor of Anatomy at the University of Pennsylvania, died 12 Nov. A long obituary was published (*BPAT* 14 Nov 1818; *BA* 16 Nov 1818).

Dorsey, Mrs. Margaret, wife of John E. Dorsey, d. yesterday in her 59th year. The funeral will be from Lansdowne (*BA* 7 Aug 1817; *BPAT* 7 Aug 1818). Margaret Dorsey, aged 58 years, was buried 6 Aug 1817 from St. Paul's Parish (ReamySP).

Dorsey, Mrs. Mary, wife of Dr. Archibald Dorsey, d. 25th ult., leaving a husband and four children (*BPAT* 26 Oct 1818).

Dorsey, Mr. Nicholas, of Baltimore Co. was m. 9th inst. [Tues.] by Rev. Joshua Wells to Miss Eliza C. Long of Baltimore (*BPAT* 24 June 1818; *BA* 25 June 1818).

Dorsey, Nicholas, of Anne Arundel Co., and Miss Sarah Hyatt of Prince George's Co., were m. [[date not given] by Rev. Walch (*BPAT* 24 June 1819).

Dorsey, Samuel, formerly of Baltimore, d. in New Orleans on 23rd ult., in his 23rd year (*FGBA* 26 Jan 1818). For the will of Samuel Dorsey, filed in 1818, see BAWB 10:414.

Dorsey, Mr. William and Miss Mary Grant, all of Baltimore were m. last Tues. eve. by Rev. D. E. Reese (*BPAT* 17 Sep 1819).

Dorsey, Mr. William E., was m. Thurs. eve. at Mount Independence by Rev. James Magraw to Miss Catherine M., dau. of Mr. Nathaniel Lightner, all of Cecil Co. (*BPAT* 2 Feb 1818; *FGBA* 31 Jan 1818).

Dougherty, John, of Baltimore, and Miss Elizabeth Greenwood of Chestertown, were m. at the latter place last Friday by Rev. James Smith (*BPAT* 7 Jan 1818).

Douglas, Mr. Isaac, of Huntingdon, Pa., was m. Thurs. eve. by Rev. Mr. Markland, to Miss Ann Milliard of Baltimore (*BPAT* 14 Aug 1818; *BA* 14 Aug 1818).

Dove, William G., living on Gunpowder Neck, Harford Co., advertises for the return of a bay mare, strayed or stolen from him (*BPAT* 11 Oct 1817).

Dowell, Mr. John, of Calvert Co. was m. Sun. eve. last by Rev. Mr. Davis to Miss Elizabeth Pardy of Baltimore (*BPAT* 29 Dec 1818).

Dowlin, Thomas, aged 13 or 14 years, an apprentice boy to the shoemaking trade, ran away from James Summer; a reward of six cents was offered (*BPAT* 20 Aug 1818).

Downey, Mr. William A., printer, d. near Rockville, in Montgomery Co., aged 24 years and nine mos. (*BPAT* 23 Aug 1819).

Biographical Data from Baltimore Newspapers 1817-1819

Downing, John, of Seneca Co., N. Y., and Miss Sarah Tatham of Baltimore Co., were m. Mon. eve. by Rev. Beverly Waugh (*FGBA* 17 Feb 1819; *BPAT* 17 Feb 1819).

Downs, Ann, states that she did not leave the bed and board of her husband Joshua Downs, as he claimed, "until his brutal and inhuman treatment of me ...forced me to seek refuge under the protection of an aged widowed parent" (*BPAT* 27 May 1818).

Downs, James, owes taxes for the years 1813, 1814, 1815, on 30 a. *Organ's Forest* (*BPAT* 7 Jan 1819).

Downs, Robert, and Miss Margaret, dau. of Alexander McClanahan of Baltimore, were m. last eve. [Tues.] by Rev. Valiant (*FGBA* 14 July 1819; *BPAT* 15 July 1819).

Dowson, Henry, died. Robert H. Dowson forewarns any Persons not t buy a house and lot in Pitt St., or an unimproved lot adjacent. Each lot fronts 25 feet on Pitt St., and runs back 100 feet (*BPAT* 25 Feb 1818).

Drinkhouse, George, of Reading, Pa., and Miss Louisa Hands of Baltimore were m. last eve. [Tues.] by Rev. Dr. Roberts (*BPAT* 7 July 1819).

Druit, James, was m. [date not given] in Washington, to Miss Susan Maul (*BPAT* 24 March 1817).

Drury, Mr. William, was m. last Thurs. eve. by Rev. Mr. Davis, to Miss Elizabeth Evans, all of Baltimore (*BPAT* 2 May 1818; *FGBA* 4 May 1818).

Dubois, Nicholas, d. last Mon., aged 35 years (*FGBA* 16 Jan 1819; *BPAT* 15 Jan 1819).

Duchemin, Francis, d. last Fri., aged about 70, formerly a merchant of St. Domingo, and for 25 years a resident of Baltimore. He leaves a wife and three children (*BA* 5 May 1818; *BPAT* 5 May 1818). For the will of Francis A. C. Duchemin, filed in 1818, see BAWB 10:466.

Duffin, James, aged between 35 and 40 years, a black man, ran away from Eleanor Gotts, living in Montgomery Co. (*BPAT* 12 June 1817).

Duffin, James, owes taxes for the year 1814 on 68 a. in the 5th dist. on unknown land (*BPAT* 7 Jan 1819).

Duhamel, Rev. Charles, Pastor of the R. C. Church at Emmitsburg, d. 6th inst at St. Mary's Seminary near Emmitsburg (*BA* 2 March 1818).

Duhamel, James, and Miss Martha O'Bryan, both of Queen Anne's Co., were m. [date not given] (*BPAT* 25 Jan 1819).

Duke, Mr. Basil, was m. on Tues. eve. by Dr. Roberts to Miss Juliet Wilson, all of Baltimore (*BPAT* 13 Nov 1817).

Dukehart, Henry, merchant, and Miss Mary Ann Murphy, were m. on the 20th [Thurs.], by Rev. Bare (*FGBA* 22 May 1819; *BPAT* 21 May 1819).

Dukehart, Capt. Thomas, and Miss Mary Matthews, were m. last eve. [Thurs.] by the Rev. Mr. Helfenstein (*BPAT* 20 Aug 1819).

Dulany, Col. Daniel, d. Mon., 2nd inst. a hero of the Revolutionary War (*FGBA* 10 Nov 1818; BA 10 Nov 1818; *BPAT* 10 Nov 1818).

DuMaine, Charles M. Toubert, d. yesterday in his 60th year, a native of La Rochelle, France. He went to St. Domingo until 1803. He taught at St. Mary's Seminary (*BPAT* 24 Feb 1819). Charles Mary Goubert [sic] Dumaine, aged 69 years, an ancient inhabitant of St, Domingo, was buried in St. Mary's College Burial Ground (Grogaard).

Dumas. Peter, was m. last eve. [Wed.] by Rev. Fenwick, to Miss Rose Beauzamy, both of Baltimore (*FGBA* 10 April 1817; *BPAT* 10 April 1817 gives the bride's name as Reuzamy).

Duncan, Capt. David W., d. in this city last Friday, of the prevailing disease, aged 28 years (*BPAT* 21 Sep 1819).

Dungan, Capt. Abel S., was m. last Thurs. eve. by Rev. Mr. Rev. Bartow to Miss Jane Traverse (*BPAT* 27 June 1818; *BA* 29 June 1818; *FGBA* 29 June 1818).

Dunn, Arthur, owes taxes for the years 1813, 1814, 1815, on 89 a. *Wells Manor* (*BPAT* 7 Jan 1819).

Biographical Data from Baltimore Newspapers 1817-1819

Dunning, Mr. Samuel, was m. last Thurs. eve. by Rev. Mr. Parks, to Miss Mary Card, all of Baltimore (*BPAT* 6 June 1818; *FBBA* 6 June 1818; *BA* 6 June 1818 gives the bride's name as Cord).

Duntze, George, a native of Germany, d. yesterday in his 32nd year (*FGBA* 2 Nov 1818; *BA* 3 Nov 1818; *BPAT* 2 Nov 1818).

Dupont de Nemours, Samuel Peter, d. 6th inst. at Eleuthrerian Mills on the Brandywine, near Wilmington, in the 78th year of his age. He was a member of the Institute of France, a councellor [*sic*] of state, and Knight of the Order of Vasa, of the Legion of Honor, and of the Order du Lys [Long obit] (*BPAT* 14 Aug 1817).

Durang (Durand?), Richard, merchant, was m. last Sat. eve. by Rev. Glendy, to Miss Margaret Connell, all of Baltimore (*FGBA* 29 July 1817; *BPAT* 29 July 1817 gives the groom's name as Durand).

Durham, Mrs. M., informs her friends and customers that she has recovered from her indisposition and will attend to business at her store 203½ Baltimore St. (*BPAT* 29 Dec 1819.

Dusis, Lewis, owes taxes for the year 1815, on 10 a., Lot 153 from Caton (*BPAT* 7 Jan 1819, 3 Aug 1819).

Dutton, Mr. John, and Miss Sarah Parks, all of Baltimore, were m. last Tues. eve. by Rev. Waugh (*BPAT* 9 June 1819).

DuVal, Mr. E. W., Esq., of Washington, was m. [date not given] at Philadelphia, to Miss Ellen Jones, dau. of Lloyd Jones of Philadelphia (*BPAT* 11 July 1817).

Duvall, Alex'r. J., and Miss Eliza Musgrove, dau. of Major Musgrove of Montgomery Co., were m. Thurs, 18th inst., by Rev. Nathaniel Hoskins (*FGBA* 23 March 1819; *BPAT* 23 March 1819).

Duvall, Edward B. of Prince George's Co., was m. last eve. [Wed.] by Rev. Richards. To Miss Augusta Caroline McCausland, of Baltimore (*BPAT* 7 Jan 1818).

Dwyer, William, and Miss Ann Susan Hughes, were m. last Sat. by Rev. Rev. Bartow (*FGBA* 7 April 1818; *BPAT* 7 April 1818).

Dykes, James, Esq., merchant of Norfolk, d. at Charlottesville, Va. (*BPAT* 14 Oct 1819).

Dysart, Mr. Moses A., of Baltimore, was m. last eve. [Mon.] to Miss Ann Goswick, of Baltimore Co. (*BPAT* 10 Nov 1818).

"E"

Eagan, Rev. John, and Miss Mary H. Phinnezy, were m. Wed., 1st inst., at the Glebe, Powhatan Co., by the Right Rev. Bishop Moore. Rev, Eagan had been admitted to Holy Orders in the Roman Catholic Church, and officiated for some time as pastor in Augusta, Ga., but prior to his marriage, expressed to Bishop Moore a wish o unite himself with the Protestant Episcopal Church and assured the Bishop that he should make a formal application for that purpose. From the *Rich. Comp.* (*BPAT* 13 Sep 1819).

Eagle, James, of Kent Co., was m. last Sun, by Dr. Roberts, to Miss Rachael Jeffers of Baltimore (*FGBA* 2 June 1818; *BPAT* 2 June 1818)

Eaverson, Joseph, was m. Thurs. eve. by Rev. Reis, to Mary Ann, dau. of William Cook, all of Baltimore (*BA* 27 Dec 1817; *BPAT* 26 Dec 1817).

Eccleston, Joseph, was m. last eve. [Tues.] by Rev. Fenwick, to Miss Jane Edward [*sic*], all of Baltimore (*BPAT* 7 Oct 1818).

Edgar, Mr. David, a native of Ireland and a respectable merchant of Baltimore, d. suddenly on Tues. afternoon, of an apoplexy, in his 37th year, leaving a widow and three children (*BPAT* 30 Oct 1819). HIs entire stock of groceries will be sold at his warehouse, at the corner of Howard and Franklin Sts. (*BPAT* 10 Nov 1819).

Edmondson, James, d. in Talbot Co. on 7th inst. (*BPAT* 15 Nov 1819).

Edmondson, Peter, Esq. d. Tues., 2nd inst., at Dover Bridge, aged sixty-six years (*BPAT* 15 Nov 1819).

Biographical Data from Baltimore Newspapers 1817-1819

Edmondson, William, son of William Edmondson, jeweler, late of Leeds, Yorkshire, England, dec., left England in 1812 as a sea apprentice on board the ship *Henry*, Captain Dryden, on a voyage to St. Croix, which ship was captured by the *Comet*, privateer, and was carried into Baltimore If the said William Edmondson will apply to Wm. Wilson and Sons of Baltimore, he will hear something to his advantage (*BPAT* 4 Jan 1817).

Edwards, Mr. Gouverneur, was m. Tues. eve. by Archbishop Marechal, to Mss Eugenia M. Chance, all of Baltimore (*BA* 29 Oct 1818; *BPAT* 29 Oct 1818).

Edwards, Capt. William, of Fells Point, has died. The guardian of the heirs of the late Capt. will auction a valuable three story brick house and lot of ground on Lancaster St. adjacent a lot which runs to Ann St. (*BPAT* 5 July 1817).

Eichelberger, Martin, of Baltimore Co. is an insolvent debtor (*BPAT* 14 Oct 1819).

Eicholtz, Mr. L., the celebrated self-taught limner of Lancaster, was m. at Columbia, Pa., last Thurs. by Rev. Mr. Andreas to Miss Catherine Trissler of the same place (*BPAT* 23 June 1818).

Eickler, C. T., died; Sarah Eickler, admx., advertises the sale of a lot of ground on the south side of Baltimore St. Extended, adjacent the property of John Matthews (*BPAT* 26 June 1818).

Elbert, William G., d. at Centreville, MD, aged about 30 (*BPAT* 18 Sep 1818).

Eldridge, William, was m. last Tues. by Rev. Bartow to Miss |Elizabeth Terry, all of Baltimore (*BPAT* 4 June 1819).

Elliott, Mr. Robert, was m. last Thurs. eve. by Rev, Dr. Inglis, to Mrs. Mary Coffin, all of Baltimore (*BA* 9 Aug 1817; *BPAT* 8 Aug 1817).

Elliott, Mr. William, was m. last eve. [Sun.] by Rev. Mr. Valliant, to Miss Elizabeth Steward (*BPAT* 17 March 1817; *BA* 19 March 1817).

Ellis, Mr. Rowland, merchant of James Creek, was m. 26th ult, [Thurs.] to Miss Julia Ann Wright, dau. of Major Edward Wright, all of Kent Co. (*BA* 11 July 1817).

Ellis, William, was m. last eve. [Thurs.] by Rev. Valiant to Miss Elizabeth Riley (*BPAT* 27 Nov 1818).

Elridge, William, and Miss Elizabeth Terry all of Baltimore, were m. last Tues. by Rev. Bartow (*Md. Gaz.* 1 June 1819).

Ely, Christian, of the 6th Dist., Baltimore Co., owes taxes for the years 1813, 1814, 1815, on 280 a. of *Campbell's Troubles*. (*BPAT* 7 Jan 1819).

Emberson, Charles, a black man, aged about 35, 5' 10 or 11" tall, formerly owned by Gassaway Rawlings, ran away from Samuel Maccubbin He has a wife at Mr. William Stewart's quarter, and another at Levy Stansbury's (*BPAT* 23 Sep 1818).

Ennes, Michael Lucas, a native of Ireland, by trade a carpenter, left his home in 1801 for Baltimore to meet his brother Thomas Ennes, who was settled there in the grocery line. If M. L. Ennes will apply in person or by letter to Pattison & Brother in Philadelphia, he will hear of something to his advantage (*BPAT* 3July 1817).

Ensey, William, was m. Tues., 9th inst., by Rev. Wells to Miss Julian Pierpoint of Baltimore Co. (*FGBA* 11 Feb 1819; *BPAT* 12 Feb 1819).

Ensor, John, on 28 June 1759 was sold part of *Cole's Harbor or Todd's Range* by Thomas Sligh, who also sold part of the tract to Thomas Bonfield (*BPAT* 24 Aug 1818).

Escaville, Joseph, was m. on Sun. eve. by Rev. Shane to Miss Sarah Pollard (*FGBA* 2 Feb 1819; *BPAT* 1 Feb 1819).

Evans, Andrew P., now dec., had purchased some land from the executors of Robert Montgomery, but died before he could obtain a patent for the said land. The land had been patented by William Hanby and had originally been thought to be in the state of Pennsylvania, but has since been found to be in the state of Maryland. Evans died and left the following heirs at law: John Evans, Robert Evans, James Evans, and Sarah Evans of Cecil Co. The heirs filed a bill of complaint against the heirs of a Jesse Reynolds (*BPAT* 8 March 1819).

Biographical Data from Baltimore Newspapers 1817-1819

Evans, Daniel, of the 7th Dist., Baltimore Co., owes taxes for the years 1813, 1814, 1815, on 35 a. *Golden Grove (BPAT* 7 Jan 1819).

Evans, Griffith, d. yesterday in his 57th year; he resided on Water St, *(BPAT* 10 Oct 1818). Griffith Evans, aged 56, was buried 10 Oct 1818 from St. Paul's Parish (ReamySP).

Evans, Henry and Miss Mary Ann Cook, all of Baltimore Co., were m. Thurs. eve., 7th inst., by Rev. Mr. Burch *(BPAT* 13 Oct 1819).

Evans, John, was m. last Sat. by Rev. Mr. Parks to Miss Sarah Daugherty, both lately from Europe *(BPAT* \ 19 Aug 1818).

Evans, John, of Baltimore Co. was m. last eve. [Mon.] by Rev. Jennings to Miss Susan Bartholomew, of Baltimore *(FGBA* 3 Feb 1819).

Evans, John K., was m. [date not given] at Georgetown to Miss Mary Ann Brush, dau. of John C. Brush, all of Georgetown *(FGBA* 13 May 1818; *BPAT* 12 May 1818).

Evans, Oliver, of Philadelphia, aged 64, d. last Thurs. at New York at the house of Elijah Ward *(BPM* 19 April 1819).

Evans, Thomas, was m. last Mon. by Rev. Bartow to Mrs. Elizabeth Fisher, all of Baltimore *(BA* 30 Oct 1818; *BPAT* 31 Oct 1818).

Everett, Thomas, d. yesterday. He resided at 221 Baltimore St. *(BA* 9 July 1817; *BPAT* 9 July 1817). For the will of Thomas Everett, filed in 1817, see BAWB 10:336.

Everett, William B. Esq., and Miss Emily Frazier of Kent Co., were m. 9th inst. [Thurs.] by Rev. Mr. Walker *(BPAT* 16 Dec 1819).

Everit, Thomas, of Baltimore Co., was m. last Thurs. by Rev. Joshua Wells, to Mrs. Elizabeth Burgess of Baltimore City *(BPAT* 7 Jan 1817).

Ewell, Maj. Charles, of Prince William Co., VA, was m. [date not given] at Washington to Mrs. Maria D. Craik of Alexandria *(BPAT* 7 Oct 1818).

Ewing, Mrs. Catherine, aged 104 years, d. at Greensburg, Pa., on the 5th last *(BPAT* 17 Dec 1819).

"F"

Fache, Mr. John, grocer, of Alisanna St., Fells Point, d. 13 inst. after a lingering illness, aged about 45 years. He will be buried from his late dwelling, in the Catholic Burying Ground *(BPAT* 14 Aug 1817).

Fagan, Mr. Andrew, formerly of Washington City, and for many years in the employment of the Ordnance Dept., d. at Augusta, Ga., in the 41st year of his age *(BPAT* 19 Oct 1819).

Fahnestock, Daniel F., of Baltimore, was m. to Miss Mary Fahnestock, dau. of Dr. S. Fahnestock, of Lancaster, PA, last Thurs. at York, PA, by Rev. Cathcart *(FGBA* 2 Aug 1819; *BPAT* 3 Aug 1819).

Fairall, Erasmus, was m. Thurs. by Rev. Mr. Hemphill, to Miss Harriet Woodward, all of Baltimore *(BPAT* 1 Feb 1817; *FGBA* 31 Jan 1817).

Fairbairn, James, of Baltimore, d. at Havana on 5th inst., in his 25th year, after an illness of five days *(BA* 23 June 1818; *BPAT* 23 June 1818).

Fairing, Augustus, was m. to Elizabeth Clous, all of Baltimore, on Tues. eve. by Dr. Kurtz *(BA* 10 Dec 1818; *BPAT* 10 Dec 1818 gives the bride's name as Ellen).

Falconer, Abraham H., was m. last eve. [Thurs.] by Rev. Mr. Duncan to Miss Catherine G. Cantwell, all of Baltimore *(BPAT* 16 Oct 1818; *BA* 16 Oct 1818).

Falconer, Mr. Peregrine, merchant of this city, d. Monday morning. He left a wife and five children *(BPAT* 26 Feb 1817; *FGBA* 25 Feb 1817). Peregrine Falconer, aged 41, was buried 24 Feb 1817 from St. Paul's Parish (ReamySP).

Farina, Mr., from Naples, having just arrived from Boston, intends opening an exhibition of famous, pure, and original paintings, from the best and immortal authors [sic] of Italy, viz.: Raphael, Titani, Guido Reini . . . , etc., and among these will be exhibited the superb extra large painting, the work of Spodaro of Naples, called "The Slaughter of the Innocents" *(BPAT* 19 Sep 1818).

Biographical Data from Baltimore Newspapers 1817-1819

Farnandis, Samuel, is an insolvent debtor in Baltimore Co. (*BPAT* 1 Dec 1818).

Farran, Mrs. Ann, of Baltimore, d. at Staten Island, N. Y. (*BPAT* 6 Oct 1819).

Farrell, James, d. 29th inst., in his 62nd year, long a resident of Fells Point; funeral from his dwelling in Bond St. (*BA* 31 Dec 1818). James Farrell of England, was naturalized on 13 November 1797 (Baltimore Co. Naturalization Docket 1:61). For his will, proved 1819, see BAWB 10:554.

Farrill, William, owes taxes for the year 1815, on ½ a. land from Thomas Gibbins in the 1st Dist. (*BPAT* 7 Jan 1819).

Farrin, Capt. Thomas, and Miss Eliza McClelland, all of Baltimore, were m. last Tues. by Rev. Glendy (*BA* 26 March 1818).

Fausbender, John, apprentice, aged about 16 years, ran away from Christopher Miller, French Lace Manufacturer, 64 s. Charles St. (*BPAT* 28 May 1818).

Feignahty, John, aged about 19 years, apprentice to the boot and shoemaking business, ran away from Edw. Hagthrop, Bond St., F. P. [Fell's Point], Baltimore. A reward of twelve and a half cents is offered (*BPAT* 11 June 1818).

Fennell, Caleb, was m. last eve. [Sun.] by Rev. Mr. Valiant, to Miss Eliz. Shaw, all of Baltimore (*BPAT* 24 Oct 1817; *BA* 24 Oct 1817).

Fenton, Thomas, a native of Great Britain, d. last Thurs., in his 63rd year (*BA* 24 March 1818; *BPAT* 24 March 1818).

Fenton, William C., d. Friday morning, after a painful illness of five weeks, aged 21 years and 11 mos. (*BPAT* 16 Dec 1817; *BA* 16 Dec 1817).

Fenwick, Col. Athanasius, of St. Mary's Co. was m. last eve. [or 30 Oct] at Philadelphia to Miss Susan Howell of that city (*BPAT* 3 Nov 1817; *BA* 7 Nov 1817).

Fenwick, Leo, and Miss Ann Eliza Childs, both of West River, were m. there Thurs. night by Rev. Orrell (*BA* 11 May 1819; *BPAT* 10 June 1819).

Ferguson, Flora, a Negro, d. at Smyrna, Del., on 19th ult., aged 130 years, a native of Guinea (*FGBA* 4 March 1819; *BPAT* 5 March 1819).

Fernan[?], Mr. John, was m. Thurs. eve. by the Rev. Mr. Glendy, to Miss Ann Waters (*BPAT* 23 Aug 1817).

Ferran, John, and Miss Ann Walker, all of Baltimore, were m. Thurs. eve. by Rev. Glendy (*BA* 23 Aug 1817).

Ferran, Mr. Thomas, was m. last eve. [Tues.] by Rev. Mr. Glendy to Miss Eliza McClennan, all of Baltimore (*BPAT* 25 March 1818; See Farrin, Thomas, above).

Ferris, Josiah, of New York, was m. Thurs. eve. by Rev. Mr. Bartow, to Miss Mary M'Kay, all of this city (*BPAT* 1 Feb 1817; *BA* 1 Feb 1817).

Fife, Mr. Andrew, was m. last Sat. eve. by the Rev. Mr. Healey, to Miss Eliza Ann Roberts, both of Baltimore (*BPAT* 29 Sep 1817).

Fincknaur, Henry, and Miss Margaretta, 2nd dau. of John Peter Maurer of Baltimore, were m. last eve. [Thurs.] by Rev. Kurtz (*FGBA* 28 May 1819). Henry Finchnaur or Finchmann, of the Grand Duchy of Hesse-Darmstadt, on 22 Sep 1824, filed his Declaration of Intent in Baltimore Co. Court Minutes, 1822-26, f. 217. His report and registration, filed 23 Sep 1824, stated he was aged 25, born in the town of Oderkeine, arrived in Philadelphia in Oct 1815, and resided in Baltimore. John Harryman and Maurice Shoemaker were witnesses: Baltimore Co. Court Naturalization Docket, 1:110).

Finlay, Mr. James P., a promising young man, lately from Westmoreland Co., Pa., d. at the house of Maj. Lewis in Baton Rouge, on the 22nd inst. (*BPAT* 22 Oct 1819).

Finley, E. L., Esq., and Miss Eliza W., youngest dau,. of the late John O'Donnell, of Baltimore, were m. Tues. eve. by Rev. Bishop Kemp (*FGBA* 2 Sep 1819; *BPAT* 2 Sep 1819).

Finley, Mrs. Mary, wife of Mr. John M. Finley of Baltimore, d. last Fri., after a tedious pulmonary indisposition, at the residence of her father. Matthew van Lear, Esq., near Williamsport (*BPAT* 11 June 1818; *FGBA* 11 June 1818).

Finn, William has lost all his tools in the late freshet, and asks anyone who has found them to return them (*BPAT* 25 Sep 1817).

Biographical Data from Baltimore Newspapers 1817-1819

Fishback, Philip, Sr., of Fauquier Co., Va., d. Monday, 31st May, after a painful illness, in his 90th year (*BPAT* 28 June 1819).

Fisher, Mrs. Ann Mary, d. last Sun., in her 67th year (*BA* 17 Nov 1818; *BPAT* 17 Nov 1818). Mrs. Ann Fisher was buried 15 Nov 1818 in the Cathedral Cemetery; she died of consumption (Grogaard).

Fisher, Basil, on Tues. eve., 19th inst. was m. by Rev. Helfenstein, to Miss Barbara Ewald, both of Baltimore (*BPAT* 21 Oct. 1819).

Fisher, Charles, some time previous to last August, resided at 17 S. Howard St.; anyone with information about him is asked to contact Frederick A. Sumner of Charlestown, New Hampshire (*BPAT* 5 Feb 1818).

Fisher, Mr. George, was m. last Fri. eve. by Rev. D. E. Reese to Miss Mary Wantland, both of Baltimore Co. (*BPAT* 22 Dec 1819).

Fisher, Henry, of Baltimore Co., was m. last Sun. by Rev. D. E. Reese, to Miss Henrietta Hupfield of Baltimore (*BA* 6 Aug 1817).

Fisher, Mr. James, d. last eve., after a lingering illness; in his 49th year; his funeral will be this eve. from his late dwelling, corner of Fleet and Wolf Sts., Fell's Point (*BPAT* 10 Aug 1819).

Fisher, Robert, from Baltimore, d. yesterday in his 28th year "Norfolk *Herald*" (*BA* 10 Sep 1817).

Fitch, Thomas, soldier of the corps of Artillery, deserted from Fort McHenry on 3rd inst. He was a paper hanger by trade and was born in the City of Baltimore, aged 29 years. He enlisted on the 11th of last month. His family resides in Baltimore, and he is supposed to be in or near the city. /s/ W. H. Nichols, Lieut., U.S. Corps of Artillery (*BPAT* 12 Dec 1817).

Fite, Mrs. Ann, wife of Jacob, d. 10 June, at her summer res., in her 46th year (*FGBA* 12 June 1819; *BPAT* 14 June 1819).

Fite, Conrad, was m. last Tues. eve. by Rev. Joshua Wells, to Miss Pamela, dau. of Cornelius H. Gist (*BPAT* 22 Dec 1819).

Fitzhugh, George, Jr., of Baltimore Co., is an insolvent debtor (*BPAT* 31 Dec 819).

Flaherty, Mrs. Catherine, consort of John R. Flaherty, d. Sat., 14th inst. (*FGBA* 16 Aug 1819). Catherine Flaherty died 14 Aug 1819 of a bilious fever, aged 25 years, and was buried 15 Aug 1819 in the Cathedral Cemetery (Grogaard).

Fletchall, Col. Thomas, d. 15th inst., of Montgomery Co., Md. (*BPAT* 20 Sep 1819).

Fletcher, William, aged about 19, apprentice to the cordwaining business, ran away from Alexander M'Mackon, 101 Bond St., Fell's Point; a reward of $20.00 is offered (*BPAT* 5 June 1818).

Floyd, William, and Miss Prudence Wright, both of Baltimore, were m. on Sun. by Rev. Glendy (*FGBA* 16 Feb 1819; *BPAT* 16 Feb 1819).

Focke, Capt. William, d. last night in his 22nd year. His funeral will be from the dwelling of John Bolte, in High St., Old Town, tomorrow morning at 10 o'clock (*BPAT* 1 April 1817; *FGBA* 1 April 1817).

Folsher. John, and Miss Mary Pendegrass, were m. last Thurs. by Rev, Bartow (*BA* 19 May 1818; *BPAT* 19 May 1818).

Foltz, William, died; his property at the southeast intersection of Pratt and Eutaw Sts., consisting of two brick houses, 3 stories high, will be sold (*BPAT* 27 May 1818).

Foltz, Mr. William, of Baltimore, d. 30 June in Frederick Town, in his 35th year, after a lingering illness (*BPAT* 7 July 1818). For his will, filed 1818, see BAWB 10:496.

Fonerden, Adam, Esq., d. yesterday morning, of a severe paralytic stroke, long a respectable inhabitant of this city. His interment is to take place this afternoon from his late dwelling, Baltimore St. (*BPAT* 27 Oct 1817; *BA* 27 Oct 1817; *FGBA* 27 Oct 1817). S. and J. Cole, auctioneers, will sell his property on Market St. (*BPAT* 12 May 1818). For his will, filed 1817, see BAWB 10:378.

Forbes, Mrs. Marianne Craik, wife of George Forbes, d. 23 March at Rose Hill, Charles Co., in her 20th year (*FGBA* 2 April 1818; *BPAT* 3 April 1818).

Biographical Data from Baltimore Newspapers 1817-1819

Forbes, William, dec; his heirs owe taxes for the years 1814 and 1815, on 6 lots of the Company's Lands, 280½ a., in the 1st Dist. (*BPAT* 7 Jan 1819).

Force, Mr. Peter, printer, was m. [date not given] in Alexandria to Miss Hannah Evans of that place (*BPAT* 2 or 5 Jan 1818).

Foreman, David, d. Thurs. morning, in his 73rd year, leaving a number of relatives (*BPAT* 25 July 1817; *FGBA* 24 July 1817 states he d. last Tues.).

Forman, Nelly, a Negro woman, ran away from P. A. Karthaus; her husband, Ezekiel Forman, lives at a Mr. Black's, Kent Co., and her mother at A. Boyd's, Esq.; she is about 30 years old (*BPAT* 28 Jan 1817)

Forney, Mr. Davis S., of Harrisburg, PA, was m. last Thurs. eve. by Rev. Mr. Henshaw to Miss Elizabeth Decker of Baltimore Co. (*BPAT* 3 March 1818); *BA* 3 March 1818).

Fornshil [?], John, was m. last eve. [Sun] by Rev. Dr. Glendy, to Miss Anne Davidson, all of Baltimore (*BPAT* 20 Dec 1819).

Forrest, Col. [-?-], of St. Mary's Co., and Miss Emily Jackson, were m. Tues., 2nd Feb, by Dr. Franklin (*FGBA* 16 Feb 1819; *BPAT* 12 Feb 1819).

Forrest, Mr. John, was m. Thurs. eve. by Rev. D. E. Reese, to Miss Mary Ratcliffe, all of Baltimore (*BPAT* 25 Oct 1817; *BA* 25 Oct 1817 states the bride was Miss Eliza Wright).

Forster, Capt. Francis, of Baltimore, was m. Sun. eve. by the Rev. Bishop Kemp, to Miss Barbara Ann Donaldson, of Harper's Ferry, VA (*BPAT* 30 June 1817).

Fosdick, Mr. John M., was m. Sun. eve., 26th inst. by Rev. Mr. Moranvilliers, to Miss Marie McDonald (*BPAT* 29 July 1818; *BA* 29 July 1818).

Foss, Charles, was m. Tues. eve. last, by Rev. D. E. Reese, to Miss Lydia Howard, all of Baltimore (*BPAT* 31 July 1819).

Fossbenner, Mr. Andrew, was m. to Mrs. Jane Wilson, both of Baltimore Co., on last Sun. eve. by Rev. D. E. Reese (*BPAT* 13 Dec 1817; *BA* 13 Dec 1817).

Fossbenner, John, in his 18th year, an apprentice to the Coach lace weaving business, ran away Christopher Miller, 64 South Charles St. This is the second time this month. It is supposed he may have gone to Philadelphia. The Philadelphia *Democratic Press* will please insert this notice for three times. A reward of six and a quarter cents is offered (*BPAT* 24 June 1818).

Foster, Charles, mariner, of Baltimore Co., has died. Conrad Switzer, admin. will settle the estate (*BPAT* 18 July 1817).

Foster, Capt. William, and Mrs. Hannah Schleicker, all of Baltimore, were m. last Mon. by Rev. Kurtz (*FGBA* 3 Feb 1819; *BPAT* 4 Feb 1819).

Fought, Thomas, a native of Carlisle, Pa., d. at Havana. 4th Feb. last (*BPAT* 26 March 1819).

Fouse, Mr. Henry, d. Mon. eve. last, in his 26th year. His remains will be interred with Masonic honors this evening. The funeral procession will start from his father's house in South Howard St. (*BPAT* 19 March 1817; *BA* 18 March 1817).

Fousz, Mr. Jacob, was m. last Tues. eve. by Rev. John Valiant to Miss Harriot Points, all of Baltimore (*BPAT* 7 March 1818; *BA* 9 March 1818).

Fowke, Mary, Catherine Elizabeth Fowke, William Augustus Fowke and **Virlinda Stone Fowke, infant** children of **Gerard Fowke,** and **Mary Bayne Fowke,** of Charles Co. will have an Act empowering the Justices of the Orphans' Court to appoint a guardian for certain purposes (*BPAT* 10 Feb 1817).

Fowler, Mr. David, was m. Wed., 4th inst. in Baltimore Co. by Rev. Mr. Grice, to Miss Catherine Morris, all of Baltimore (*BPAT* 7 March 1818; *BA* 7 March 1818).

Fowler, Mr. William, was m. on Sat., 2nd May, by Rev. Mr. Wells, to Mrs. Deborah Thompson, both of Baltimore (*BPAT* 4 May 1818).

Fowler, Mr. Wm., was married Tues., 289th inst. by Rev. John Hagerty, to Mrs. Willy Ann Jones, both of Baltimore (*BPAT* 30 Dec 1819).

Fox, Capt. Nathaniel, d. at his residence in Stafford Co., Va., 21st inst., in his 71st year; he was a soldier of the Revolutionary War (*BPAT* 30 Oct 1819).

Biographical Data from Baltimore Newspapers 1817-1819

Fox, Mr. S., d. at St. Germains on the 4th of Nov., a member of the Society of Friends (*BPAT* 3 Jan 1817).

Foy, Michael, was m. at Hagerstown, [date not given] to Miss Elizabeth Gilbert of that place (*BPAT* 19 Nov 1819).

Frailey, Philip, for many years a resident of Baltimore, d. last Sat. at Reading, PA, after a protracted illness of many years, aged 34 (*BPAT* 17 June 1819).

France, James, and Miss Margaretta Boyle, second dau. of Capt. Thomas Boyle, were m. last Thurs. eve. by Rev. Duncan (*FGBA* 13 Aug 1819; *BPAT* 13 Aug 1819).

France, John, and Miss Elizabeth Talbot, both of Baltimore, were m. on Thurs. by Rev. E. J. Reis (*BA* 23 April 1819; *BPAT* 17 April 1819).

Francisco, Mr. Samuel, was m. Mon. eve. last by Rev Dr. Roberts, to Miss Rebecca Pritchett, both of this city (*BPAT* 23 April 1817; *BA* 24 April 1817).

Frank, Ludwick, was m. last Sun. eve. by Rev. Mr. Merts to Miss Mary Rutter both of Baltimore (*BPAT* 121 July 1818; *FGBA* 22 July 1818).

Franklin, Jacob, Jr., d. 20th inst., at his father's residence, near West River, Anne Arundel Co., in his 38th year [long obit] (*FGBA* 3 Jan 1817).

Franklin, Capt. Samuel, of the Buenos Aires Navy, and Miss Louisa Moodie of Baltimore, were m. 13 Dec [Sun.] by Rev. Davis (*BA* 8 Jan 1819; *BPAT* 7 Jan 1819).

Franklin, Mr. Thomas, was m. last Thurs. eve. by Rev. Dr. Roberts, to Miss Eliza Cochran, both of Baltimore (*BPAT* 23 Oct 1819).

Franzone Signor Carlo, d. at Washington, D.C., suddenly on the morning of the 12th inst., in his 30th year, a native of Florence, Italy (*BPAT* 25 May 1819).

Fraser, John, and Miss Mary Ann Cheney, both of Baltimore, were m. last Thurs. by Rev. Hagerty (*BPAT* 28 April 1819; *FGBA* 26 April 1819).

Frazier, Dr. A., and Miss Rachel Pearce, all of Montgomery Co., were m. 8th inst. [Thurs.] by the Rev. Job Guest (*FGBA* 21 Jan 1818; *BPAT* 22 Jan 1818).

Frazier, Capt. Thomas, of Talbot Co., d. 12th inst., after a few weeks' indisposition (*BPAT* 20 Dec 1819).

Frederick, Mrs. Nancy, formerly of New London, Conn., d. 20th ult., at Baltimore (*BA* 22 April 1818; *BPAT* 22 April 1818).

Freeman, Mr. Charles, was m. last eve. [Thurs.] by Rev. Mr. Shane, to Miss Elvira Brown, both of Baltimore (*BPAT* 16 Oct 1818; *BA* 17 Oct 1818).

Freeman, Col. Isaac, of Kent Co., dec.; his real estate will be sold Monday, next 22 Nov,: *Mansion Farm*, 373¾ a., now occupied by Isaac Freeman; *Brick House Farm and ... Field*, 274 a. now occupied by Jesse Clark; *The Upper Farm*, 614¼ a., now occupied By James Fields; *The Farm or Plantation*, 60 a., now occupied by Mr. Mullen; the dower of Mrs. Martha Freeman is laid down on the above mentioned *Upper Farm*, and is subject to a life estate of 313 a. (*BPAT* 11 Nov 1819).

Freer, Mr. Peter J., was m. Tues. eve. by Rev. D. E. Reese to Miss Mary Goforth, all of Baltimore (*BPAT* 4 April 1818; *FGBA* 4 April 1818).

Frick, John, d. Thurs., 17th inst., in his 38th year. He was a native of Baltimore. The funeral will be from his late dwelling on N. Frederick (*BA* 19 Dec 1818; *BPAT* 27 Oct 1818).

Fricke, Henry C., d. 14 Oct, at Havana, in his 22nd year. He was a native of Penna., but for the last few months had resided in Baltimore. He leaves a mother (*BA* 15 Nov 1817; *BPAT* 15 Nov 1817).

Friend, John, printer, d. at Mobile, [date not given]; he was a native of Philadelphia (*BPAT* 27 Nov 1817).

Friendler, Mr. Andrew, of Franklin, Pa., was married at Hagerstown, [date not given] to Miss Catherine Postetru (*BPAT* 27 Nov 1819).

Frisbie, Mr. William, was m. [date not given] by Rev. Mr. Bartow to Miss Catherine Overe Ruth, all of Baltimore (*BPAT* 3 April 1818; *FGBA* 3 April 1818).

Frye, Nathaniel, Jr., was m. at the residence of George Boyd, Esq., Washington, to Mrs. Catherine Buchanan, late of Baltimore (*BPAT* 11 July 1817).
Furlong, Capt. William, dec.: S. & J. C., auctioneers, will sell a valuable lot of ground on Alisanna St., improved by a two story brick dwelling house, with extensive back buildings, and a spacious garden at the rear of the whole (*BPAT* 27 Nov 1818).
Fyatt, William, d. in Baltimore, in his 47th year (*BPAT* 17 Nov 1818).

"G"

Gaarde, P. J., d. when his boat upset on 30th ult. All are invited to his funeral from his late res. on Bond St. (*BA* 8 April 1819).
Galande, Mrs. Catharine, late consort of Mr. J. B. Galande of Baltimore, d. suddenly on Mon. night, in her 27th year (*BPAT* 12 March 1818). [See Garland below]. [John Baptist Gailand of France was naturalized on 1 Dec 1804 {Baltimore Co. Court: Naturalization Docket 1:133}].
Gale, Rasin, has died. E. F. Chambers, trustee, advertises the sale of 274 a. (*BPAT* 15 Nov 1817). Ezekiel F. Chambers, trustee, advertises the sale of 200 a. *Camble's Farm,* in Kent Co. Mrs. Martha Gale resides on the plantation. (*BPAT* 24 Dec 1819)
Gallaway, Jehu, was m. Thurs. eve. by Rev. Davis, to Miss Mary Little, all of this city (*FGBA* 14 July 1817; *FGBA* 12 July 1817).
Galloway, Ezekiel, dec.; His personal property will be sold at public auction tomorrow, 28th inst., at Lancaster St., Fell's Point, by Edward Quinn, auctioneer (*BPAT* 27 Aug 1819). His personal property in Lancaster St., will be sold by Edward Quinn, auctioneer (*BPAT* 27 Aug 1819).
Ganteume, Clementine, d. Fri., 19th inst., in her 18th year (*BPAT* 26 Feb 1819).
Gantt, Dr. Thomas, was m. Tues., 7th inst, by Rev. Mr. Bausman, to Miss Susan Gray, all of Calvert Co. (*BPAT* 15 Jan 1817).
Gantt, Thomas T., d. at Georgetown a few days ago, Cashier of the Central Bank, leaving a wife and family; formerly of Prince George's Co. (*FGBA* 11 May 1818; *BPAT* 11 May 1818).
Garden, William, printer, was m. in Philadelphia, to Miss Ann Sambourn [date not given] (*BPAT* 6 May 1817).
Gardner, Hezekiah B., was m. last Sun. by Rev. Davis, to Miss Ann Corwin, both of Baltimore (*FGBA* 28 Oct 1817; *BPAT* 28 Oct 1817 gives her name as Corum).
Gardner, Col. Robert, late Commissary of Prisoners for the U.S. in Canada, d. suddenly at Washington, on 10th inst., in his 55th year (*BPAT* 13 March 1818).
Garland, Mrs. Catherine, consort of J. B. Garland of Baltimore, d. on Mon., in her 27th year (*BA* 12 March 1818). [See Galande above].
Garrett, Jesse, d. Mon., 16th inst., aged 30 (*FGBA* 17 Feb 1818; *BPAT* 17 Feb 1818).
Garrett, Robert, of Washington Co., Pa., was m. Mon., 19th inst., by Rev. John M. Duncan, to Miss Elizabeth Stoufer of Baltimore (*BA* 20 May 1817; *BPAT* 20 May 1817).
Garrett, Thomas, d. Wed., 29th inst., aged 20 years (*FGBA* 30 April 1818).
Garrett, Thomas D., of Baltimore, d. last Wed., after a lingering illness (*BPAT* 2 May 1818).
Garrettson, Aquilla was m. to Miss Amelia George, all of Baltimore, last Tues. eve. by Rev. Mr. Wells (*BA* 25 Sep 1818; *BPAT* 24 Sep 1818; *FGBA* 25 Sep 1818 gives name as Rev. Hitselberger).
Gary, Everet, was m. to Miss Hannah Galloway, all of Baltimore, last eve. [Tues.] by the Rev. Mr. Hargrove (*BPAT* 2 June 1819).
Gassaway, Capt. Henry, an officer of the Revolution, died Tues., 10th inst., "Annapolis, 25 Feb." (*FGBA* 28 Feb 1818).
Gatchell, Major Samuel H., d. 16th inst., in his 61st year; for many years a resident of Fell's Point, after a distressing illness of two mos. (*BPAT* 19 Nov 1819).
Gate, William was m. to Mrs. Ellen Hills, both of Baltimore Co., last Wed. by Rev. Bartow (*BA* 19 Dec 1818; *BPAT* 1 Dec 1818).

Biographical Data from Baltimore Newspapers, 1817-1819

Geary, Mr. Matthew, and Miss Tabitha Whitaker, all of Baltimore, were m.. last Tues. eve. by Rev. Mr. Dashiell *(BPAT* 1 July 1819).

Gee. Cornelius, was m. to Miss Mary Start, all of Baltimore, on Sat. eve. by Rev. Mr. Force *(BA* 18 Nov 1818; *BPAT* 18 Nov 1818).

George, James B., was m. Thurs. eve. by Rev. Glendy, to Miss Mary Ellen Stewart *(BA* 23 Aug 1817; *BPAT* 23 Aug 1817).

Geiger, Rev. Jacob, of Manchester, was m. to Miss Catherine Seltzer of Baltimore, on Tues., 19th inst., by Rev. Dr. Becker *(Federal Gazette and Baltimore Daily Advertiser* 21 Feb 1818; *BPAT* 21 Feb 1818).

Gelder Mr. Van, d. in Piscataway, on 19th Feb., aged 117 years *(FGBA* 23 March 1818).

George, Jacob, about 17 years of age, apprentice to the brick-laying business, ran away from Jas. Hinds, Lombard St.; he is supposed to be in Philadelphia; a reward of five dollars is offered *(BPAT* 4 Nov 1817).

George, James, a taylor [sic] in the City of Pittsburgh, has absconded with the accounts, bills, and notes of the firm of James George and Co. All persons are warned not to take any assignment or pay any claims to the aid George. /s/ Rt. Christy and Thomas Liggett *(BPAT* 23 May 1818).

Gerachty, Capt. Peter, m. last (Thurs.) eve. at Fells Point by Rev. Mr. Bartow, Miss Mary Ann Despeaux *(FGBA* 30 May 1817; *BPAT* 31 May 1817). Peter Gerahty, aged 29, b. in Dublin, arrived in Baltimore in Nov 1815, where he resides. Report and registration were witnessed by John Purviance and Eli Despaux on 5 July 1819 (Baltimore Co. Court: Miscellaneous Court Papers: item 360). He filed his declaration of intent on 7 Sep 1824; same witnesses [Baltimore Co. Court: Naturalization Docket:102).

German, David, was m. to Miss Catherine Henderson, all of Baltimore, last Thurs. by Rev, D. E. Reese *(BA* 12 Dec 1818; *BPAT* 12 Dec 1818).

German, Jonathan, was m. to Miss Catherine Stansbury of Anne Arundel Co., on Thurs. eve. by Rev. Smith *(FGBA* 21 Sep 1818).

Gettings, Thomas Freeman, and Maria, dau. of Mashack Gettings, all of Charles Co. were m. there [date not given] *(BPAT* 19 June 1819).

Getty, Jacob, of Westminster, Md., was m. to Nancy Stuffelman of Baltimore on Thurs. eve. by Rev. Snyder *(BA* 11 Jan 1819; *BPAT* 11 Jan 1819).

Gettyer, George, aged 25, born in Baltimore, a blacksmith, supposed to have gone to York, Pa., deserted from the detachment under the command of Capt James Hook at Fort Covington *(BPAT* 13 April 1818).

Ghequiere, Charles, a native of Hamburg, and a resident of Baltimore for the last 36 years, merchant, President of the Baltimore Fire Insurance Co., died Wed., 12 Aug., aged 64 *(BA* 14 Aug 1818). Charles Ghequiere, age 60, d. 12 Aug 1818 of consumption, and was buried 13 Aug 1818 in the Cathedral Cemetery (Grogaard). For the will of Charles Ghequiere, filed in 1818, see BAWB 10:505.

Ghequiere, Henry Tiernan, d. Sat., 7th inst., after a long illness, in his 20th year *(BA* 13 Nov 1818; *BPAT* 13 Nov 1818). Tiernan Ghequiere, age 21, d. 7 Nov 1818 of consumption and was buried 8 Nov 1818 in the Cathedral Cemetery (Grogaard).

Gibbons, John, owes taxes for the years 1814 and 1815, on one-half a. of one lot of I. Carroll in the 1st Dist. *(BPAT* 7 Jan 1819).

Gibbons, John N., merchant of Norfolk, VA, was m. to Mss Martha Adeline Gray of Baltimore, last Wed. by Rev. Glendy *(BA* 18 Dec 1818; *BPAT* 18 Dec 1818).

Gibbs, Hannah, of Cecil Co., is an insolvent debtor *(BPAT* 30 Dec 1819).

Gibney, John Franklin, burgher and merchant of Baltimore, married Elizabeth Maillard, widow of Capt. Nicol Cochran of the Island of St. Bartholomew, and mother of Grace Cochran, who married Francis Pizany, Jr., burgher and merchant of this Island. Mrs. Elizabeth Gibney died in the United States in Aug 1816. Said Gibney is summoned to appear in court, either in person or by attorneys, to render an account of his wife's estate *(BPAT* 25 Nov 1817). (Mrs. Elizabeth Gibney, wife of John Gibney, and a native of St. Martin's, died Tuesday, 6 August 1916, aged 52 *(BA* 9 Aug 1816).

Biographical Data from Baltimore Newspapers, 1817-1819

Gibson, James, of Caroline Co., and Miss Jane Medford of Kent Co. were m. at St. Paul's Church, Kent Co., on 9th inst. [Tues.] (*BPAT* 10 Nov 819).

Gibson, John, Esq., d. at his seat near Magothy River, after a short but painful illness (*BPAT* 30 Dec 1819).

Gibson, Joshua, of Baltimore Co., is an insolvent debtor (*BPAT* 8 Nov 1819).

Gidney, Dr. Eleazer, informs those afflicted with Cancers, Schirrous, and Scrofulus complaints that he has just arrived in this city and will offer treatment. He will only be in his city for a few days (*BPAT* 16 Feb 1818).

Giesler, Mrs. Catherine, d. last eve. in her 78th year (*BPAT* 26 Feb 1817).

Giffin, John, died at Easton, MD (*BMC* 24 May 1819).

Gilbert, Jesse, of the Head of Chester, and Miss Eliza, only dau. of the Rev. John Forman of Del., were m. 23 Feb [Tues.], in Queen Anne's Co. (*FGBA* 20 April 1819; *BPAT* 21 April 1819).

Gilder, Capt. Reuben, of Baltimore, and Miss Eliza M. Hughes, of Baltimore Co. were m. Thurs. eve. last by Rev. Reis (*BPAT* 20 Feb 1819).

Giles, Jacob W., Esq., was m. at Woodlawn on the 15th inst. [Thurs.], by the Rev. Mr. Stevens, to Mrs. Ann Beacon, both of Harford Co. (*BPAT* 16 May 1817).

Gill, Edward, Sr. d. 7th inst., in his 75th year, at his late residence on the Western Run, Baltimore Co. (*BPAT* 9 Oct 1818; *BA* 9 Oct 1818). For the will of Edward Gill, filed in 1818, see BAWB 10:539.

Gill, John, aged about 18, apprentice to the blacksmithing business, on 27 April 1817 has runaway from Jesse Haslup (*BPAT* 28 April 1817).

Gill, Stephen G., and Miss Agnes M'Clain Gill, both of Baltimore Co., were m. last Thurs. by Rev. Dr. Glendy (*FGBA* 28 Aug 1819).

Gillespie, David, advertises he will open a new U.S. Lottery Office and an Exchange Office at No. 182 Market St. (*BPAT* 18 Nov 1819).

Gillingham, Mrs. Elizabeth, wife of James Gillingham, died this morning, The funeral will be tomorrow from her late residence (*FGBA* 22 Jan 1819, *BPAT* 22 Jan 1819).

Gilly, Mr. John, and Mrs. Sarah Clark, all of Baltimore, were m. last Thurs. eve. by Rev. Mr. Bartow (*BPAT* 22 Dec 1819).

Gist, William, and Miss Margaret Ann Kipp, dau. of John Kipp, all of Baltimore, were m. last eve. [Tues.] by Rev. Joshua Wells (*FGBA* 10 June 1818; *BPAT* 10 June 1818).

Gittens, Mr. J., d. at Easton, Md. (*BPAT* 2 Nov 1819).

Gittings, Mrs, Elizabeth, consort of Col. James Gittings, d. 24th inst. at Long Green in her 77th year (*BA* 29 Aug 1818; *BPAT* 29 Aug 1818).

Gladding, Mr. Samuel, was m. last Thurs. by the Rev. Mr. Jennings, to Miss Sarah Phillips, both of Baltimore (*BPAT* 11 Oct 1817).

Glandon, Francis, aged 18, born in Lower Canada, late of Montreal, enlisted 18 May 1817, deserted from the Barracks at Carlisle, Pa. /s/ James Pratt, Capt., 5th Infantry (*BPAT* 2 SEP 1817).

Glaspy, George, was m. last Sat. by Rev. Glendy, to Mrs. Jane Williams, all of Baltimore (*BA* 15 Nov 1817; *BPAT* 15 Nov 1817).

Glass, Mr. John, and Miss Theresa All, were m. last Thurs. by Rev. Dr. Glendy (*BPAT* 20 Dec 1819).

Glendy, Samuel, eld. son of Rev. Dr. Glendy, d. 14th on his passage from Havana to Baltimore, in his 21st year [Long obit is given] (*BA* 3 May 1818; *BPAT* 23 May 1818).

Goddard, Robert, aged 25 tears, a labourer, a private in Capt. Nath. N. Hall's Company, Corps of Artillery, deserted from Fort McHenry on 1st inst. (*BPAT* 6 June 1817).

Goddard, William, Esq., d. at Providence, R. I., last Tues. eve. [23 Dec] after a long illness. He was the first editor of the *Providence Gazette*, which he established in 1764. He published newspapers in New York, Philadelphia, and Baltimore. He had just completed his 77th year (*BPAT* 2 Jan 1818; *BA* 2 Jan 1818).

Godefroy, Miss Eliza Anderson, step-daughter of Maximilian Godefroy, Esq., and granddau. of the late Dr. John Crawford, d. 7th inst., in the 19th year of her age [A long obit gives details of her illness] (*BPAT* 1 Oct 1818).

Godfrey, Capt. Benjamin, was m. last Thurs. by Rev. Mr. Davis, to Miss Harriet Cooper, both of Baltimore (*FGBA* 28 Nov 1817; *BPAT* 29 Nov 1817).

Goff, Mr. Jacob, and Miss Ann Covington, both of Baltimore, were m. last Sun. eve, by Rev. D. E. Reese (*BPAT* 1 \July 1818; *BA* 1 July 1818; *FGBA* 1 July 1818 gives his name as Groff).

Gohagan, Capt. John, of Baltimore was m. to Miss Louisa Wilson of New London, Conn., last Thurs. by Rev. Mr. Waugh (*BPAT* 31 May 1819).

Goldsborough, Robert, a native of Annapolis, Md., d. on board the *Mars* at Port au Prince on 28 May (*FGBA* 14 July 1819).

Goldsborough, Mrs. Sarah, late wife of Charles Goldsborough of Talbot Co., Md., f. 26th ult., in Easton, in her 32nd year (*BPAT* 6 Dec 1819).

Goldthwaite, Mrs. Sarah, wife of Capt. Ezekiel Goldthwaite of Baltimore, d. last Sat., in her 23rd year (*FGBA* 5 Aug 1818; *BPAT* 5 Aug 1818).

Gooding, Sarah, and **James Gooding,** children of Richard Gooding of St. Mary's Co., will have an act passed for their benefit (*BPAT* 10- Feb 1817).

Goodrich, Walter, a boy from Baltimore, was lost at sea from the brig *Patriot* of Boston (*BPAT* 24 April 1819).

Goodwin, Mr. Caleb, and Miss Julia Ann Bell, all of Baltimore, were m. last eve. [Tues.] by Mr. Waugh (*BPAT* 22 Dec 1819).

Goodwin, Mr. John, of Boston, Mass., and Mrs. Elizabeth Thompson of Frederick Town, were m. at Charleston, S. C. [date not given] (*BPAT* 18 Aug 1819).

Goodwin, Oliver, owes taxes for the year 1815, on Land Office .... (*BPAT* 7 Jan 1819).

Gordon, John, dec.; A. MacDonald, Henry Payson, and Wm. Lorman, by virtue of a deed of mortgage given to them, will sell 4 a. of *David's Fancy*, near Howard's Branch, it being the Rope walk heretofore carried on by the said Gordon (*BPAT* 26 March 1818).

Gordon, Robert, of Baltimore Co., is an insolvent debtor (*BPAT* 25 Nov 1819).

Gore, Henry, was m. last Thurs. eve. by Rev. Styres, to Miss Evalina Whalen, both of Anne Arundel Co. (*BA* 5 March 1817; *BPAT* 5 March 1817).

Gorsuch, Charles, of Muskingum Co., Ohio, was m. last Thurs. by Rev. Grice, to Miss Rachel Bond of Baltimore Co. (*FGBA* 3 Nov 1817; *BPAT* 1 Nov 1817).

Gorsuch, Joseph, of Baltimore, was m. last Thurs. by Rev. James Smith, to Miss Elizabeth Merryman, dau. of John Merryman of Baltimore Co. (*BA* 5 Aug 1817).

Gorsuch, Robert, will have an act passed allowing him to complete his collection in Baltimore Co. (*BPAT* 10 Feb 1817).

Gorvin, Daniel, of Baltimore, and Miss Charity Baily of Harford Co., were m. last eve. [Tues.] by the Rev. Maybury Parks (*BPAT* 3 Nov 1819).

Gose, John D. was m. last Tues. by Rev. Jennings to Miss Suzanne H. Sitzler, both of Baltimore (*FGBA* 14 Feb 1818; *BPAT* 14 Feb 1818).

Gosse, Dennis, dec: his property, a valuable tract of land called *Hermitage,* at present occupied by Francis Mottu, situated about four miles from Baltimore, between the Falls and the Reisterstown Road, and adjoining the property of Owen Dorsey, will be sold at auction on Mon., 27th inst., by James Horton, auctioneer. The tract consists of 106 acres. [A detailed description of the property is given.] (*BPAT* 24 July 1818). For the will of a Dennis Goss, filed in 1805, see BAWB 7:413.

Goszler, George, and **Philip Goszler,** brothers, d. at St. Thomas in the West Indies, sons of Mr. John Goszler of Georgetown. Mr. George Goszler had recently been m. to a lady of the island, and his brother was on a visit to them, when the two were struck by the fever and died (*BPAT* 14 Nov 1817).

Gott, Henrallsia [sic], owes taxes for the years 1813, 1814, 1815, on 100 a, part if Lawson's tract in the 2nd Dist. (*BPAT* 7 Jan 1819).

Gott, Mrs. Ruth, wife of Richard Gott of Samuel, d. last Mon. night, 26 May, aged 57 years (*BPAT* 27 May 1819).

Gould, Alexander, was m. last Thurs. by Rev. Rossell, to Miss Catherine Rollins, both of Baltimore (*BA* 22 March 1817; *BPAT* 22 March 1817).

Gould, Mr. C. C., of Boston, was m. in Baltimore last Tues. eve. to Miss Susannah Jackson of Philadelphia , by Rev. Fenwick (*BA* 16 July 1818; *BPAT* 16 July 1818).

Biographical Data from Baltimore Newspapers, 1817-1819

Gould, Mr. James, of Baltimore, was m. at Beverly, Mass. to Miss Eliza Leach [date not given] (*BPAT* 16 Dec 1817).

Gould, Mr. James C., and Miss Jane White, all of Baltimore, were m. yesterday morning [Sun.], by Rev. Dr. Glendy (*BPAT* 30 Aug 1819).

Gould, James F., and Jane White, all of Baltimore, were m. yesterday [Sun.?] morning by Rev. Dr. Glendy (*FGBA* 30 Aug 1819).

Gould, Mr. John, was m. to Miss Caroline M'Ilvain, all of Baltimore, were m. last eve. [Wed.] by Rev. Bartow (*BPAT* 5 March 1818; *FGBA* 6 March 1818).

Gould, John, a Negro man,, aged about 24 years, ran away from Henry Myers, living on Pennsylvania Ave., near St. Mary's College, Baltimore. Gould was purchase from a Mr. Carman, living in or near Centreville; he is a butcher by trade, and may try to get to New Jersey of Philadelphia (*BPAT* 29 Dec 1819).

Grace, John, late of Baltimore, dec.; Thomas Armstrong will administer the estate (*BPAT* 19 May 1819). For the will of John Grace, filed in 1818, see BAWB 10:413.

Gracie, Mr. Henry, was m. last Wed., by Rev. John Glendy, to Mary M'Conkey, all of thus city (*BPAT* 28 Jan 1817 (*FGBA* 28 Jan 1817).

Graham, Mrs. Jane, d. at Washington, at a very advanced period of life, the relict of Richard Graham, late of Dumfries, VA, and the dau. of George Brent, Esq., of Woodstock, Stafford Co., VA (*BPAT* 6 Dec 1817).

Graham, Capt. William, of Baltimore was m. to Miss Lavinia Teackle of Accomac Co., Eastern Shore of VA [date not given] (*BPAT* 27 Oct 1818).

Graham, William, d. 19th inst., His funeral will be from his late dwelling, Bond and Wilkes St., Fells point (*BA* 20 Nov 1818).

Grammer, John A., of Annapolis, was m. last Sun. eve. at Buckingham House, Frederick Co., by Rev. Mr. Martin, to Miss Eliza, dau. of John Hasselbach (*BA* 11 June 1817; *BPAT* 11 June 1817).

Grant, Capt. Henry, and Mrs. Eliza Driscoll, both of Baltimore, were m. last Sun. by Rev. Mr. Moranville (*BPAT* 4 Nov 1819).

Grant, William, was m. last Sun. eve. by Rev. Mr. More, to Miss Mary Ann Burton, both of Baltimore (*BPAT* 27 March 1817; *BA* 27 March 1817).

Grapewine, Sally, a bound girl, ran away from Henry Working, who offered a reward of six cents and a needle full of thread (*BPAT* 25 Aug 1818).

Gray, Frederick Christian, has produced an exequatur signed by the President of the United States recognizing him as Vice Consul for the Free Hanseatic City of Hamburg for the City of Baltimore and the State of Maryland (*BPAT* 28 Dec 1819).

Gray, Capt. French S., of the U. S. Army, late from Amelia Island, d. Tues., 15h inst., at Gettysburg, Pa., on his way to visit friends in Ky. (*BPAT* 26 June 1819).

Gray, John, and Mrs. Frances H. Claiborn were m. in St. Mary's Co., [date not given] (*BPAT* 13 July 1819).

Graybill, Capt. Philip, d. this morning, aged 86. His funeral will be from his late dwelling , tomorrow morning (*BPAT* 22 Oct 1819; a long obit in the *BPAT* of 25 Oct 1819 tells of his career in the Revolutionary War).

Green, Benjamin, of Baltimore, d. 20 April, aged 29 years (*FGBA* 24 April 1819). For the will of Benjamin Green, filed in 1819, see BAWB 10:603.

Green, Charles R. of Baltimore, is an insolvent debtor (*BPAT* 29 March 1817).

Green, Mr. Isaiah, d. yesterday morning, aged 43 years (*BPAT* 5 May 1817; *BA* 5 May 1817). Isiah [sic] Green, aged 40 years, was buried 5 May 1817 from St. Paul's Parish (ReamySP).

Green, John, Jr., and Elizabeth Marking, both of Baltimore, were m. 17 Sep [Thurs.] by Rev. Wells (*BA* 19 Sep 1818; *BPAT* 18 Sep 1818).

Green, John N., was m. to Julia Ann Wooden on 17 June [Thurs.] 1819 by Rev. D. E. Reese (*BA* 19 June 1819).

Green, Levin B., of Dorchester Co., dec.; Elisha Bonner is the acting admin. (*BPAT* 26 May 1818).

Green, Oliver, of the ship *William* of Baltimore, d. at Amsterdam, last of May (*FGBA* 31 July 1818; *BPAT* 29 July 1818).

Green, William W., of Del., was m. to Mrs. Mary Ann Logan of Baltimore last Mon. by Rev, Glendy (*FGBA* 24 March 1819; *BPAT* 20 March 1819).

Greenfield, Amos, and Miss Ann King, all of Baltimore, were m. Sun. eve. by Rev. Montgomery (*BA* 23 Sep 1817).

Greenslaw, James, formerly of Baltimore, drowned off The Hook on 16th ult., having just started on an outward voyage (*FGBA* 24 Sep 1818; *BPAT* 23 Sep 1818).

Greenway, Edward M., was m. last Tues. eve. by Rev. Dr. Inglis to Miss Maria H. Taylor, dau. of William W. Taylor, all of Baltimore (*BPAT* 24 Jan 1817; *FGBA* 23 Jan 1817).

Grees, Lydia, d. 29th inst., in the 37th year of her age (*BPAT* 2 Dec 1817; *BA* 1 Dec 1817).

Greetham, William, merchant, d. last Fri., in his 46th year (*BPAT* 30 Nov 1818). William Gretham, aged 45 years, was buried 27 Nov 1818 from St. Paul's Parish (ReamySP).

Gregory, Lieut. Francis H., of the U. S. Navy, and Miss Elizabeth, dau. of Commodore John Shaw, were m. at Philadelphia, Tues. eve. last, by Right Rev, Bishop White (*BPAT* 25 Sep 1818; *FGBA* 26 Sep 1818; *BA* 26 Sep 1818).

Grehum, Mr. Frederick, Minister Resident of His Prussian Majesty, and Mlle. Virginie Bridon, of Paris, France, were m. at Kalorama, near Washington City, the residence of the Hon. H. Middleton, on last Sat morning, by Rev Mr. Matthews (*BPAT* 23 Nov 1819).

Gresham, Mrs. Margaret, of Kent Co. died possessed of a tract called *Gresham Hall*, which is now possessed by Thomas Wilkins of Kent Co. Lot No 1 is encumbered by the will of the late Richard M. Gresham, with payments to be made to Miss Elizabeth Wilkins and Miss Margaret Wilkins (*BPAT* 17 July 1818).

Grierson, Mr. Andrew, and Miss Ann T. Miller, both of Baltimore, were m. last Tues. eve. by Rev. Mr. Fry (*BPAT* 24 Sep 1818; *FGBA* 25 Sep 1818).

Griesley (Grisset?), Mr. William, was m. last Wed. eve. by Rev. D. E. Reese , to Miss Kesiah Roberts, all of Baltimore (*BPAT* 20 Sep 1817).

Griffin, William, and Miss Mary Blondie, both of Baltimore, were m. last Thurs. by Rev. Fenwick (*BA* 8 Aug 1818; *BPAT* 8 Aug 1818).

Griffith, Adam, was m. last Thurs., by Rev. Glendy, to Mrs. Bridget McM'Kirk (*BPAT* 17 April 1817; *BA* 15 April 1817 gives groom's name as David Adam Griffith).

Griffith, Edward, and Miss Hannah Emily Stump, were m. last Sun. at Mount .,, Harford Co., by Rev. .... (*FGBA* 20 Feb 1817).

Griffith, Mrs. Hannah E., wife of Edmund Griffith, and dau. of the late Herman Stump, after an illness of several weeks (*BPAT* 1 July 1817; *BA* 1 July 1817).

Griffith, Howard, Jr., merchant of Baltimore, was m. last Thurs. by Rev. Sneathen, to Miss Ruth Plummer, of Frederick Co. (*BPAT* 24 Nov 1817; *BA* 25 Nov 1817).

Griffiths, Richard Eli, and Muss Eliza Richardson, all of Baltimore, were m. last Sat. eve. by Rev. D. E. Reese (*BPAT* 16 Aug 1819).

Griggs, Mrs., was buried in Glendy's Burial Ground, some time after Sep 1817 (*MGSB* 30 (3) 293).

Groome, Mrs. Elizabeth, wife of Dr. John Groome, and eld. dau. of James Black, Esq., formerly Newcastle Co. [Del.], dec., d. at Elkton, Md. on the 7th inst., after a long and painful illness. In her 55th year. She was buried on the 9th. She leaves a husband and six children (*BPAT* 14 May 1817).

Groome, Miss Harriet Lucinda, dau. of Mr. Samuel Groome, d. at Easton, Md. (*BPAT* 29 Nov 1819).

Groome, William, and Miss Catherine Keplinger, both of Baltimore were m. last Thurs. eve. by Rev. Mr. Healey (*BPAT* 26 May 1818; *FGBA* 27 May 1818).

Gross, Abraham, d. last Wed. eve. in his 17th year, from "a most poignant affliction" (*BPAT* 26 Sep 1817; *BA* 27 Sep 1817).

Gross, Charles, a black man, aged about 22, ran away from George Herrack of Union Town, Frederick Co.; Gross is an excellent hostler (*BPAT* 14 Sep 1818).

Grosvenor, Thomas P., d. Wed. eve. last at Waterloo, the seat of Judge Hanson, in the 36th year of his age, His funeral will be from Belmont, the seat of A. C. Hanson *(BPAT* 26 April 1817; *FGBA* 25 April 1817).

Grove, Stephen, merchant of Baltimore, d. 20 Nov *(BPAT* 28 Nov 1818). For the will of Stephen Grove, filed in 1818, see BAWB 10:53.

Grundy, Miss Mary, dau. of George Grundy d. Tues., 17th inst. Funeral will be in St. Paul's Church yard *(BA* 19 Nov 1818; *BPAT* 19 Nov 1818). Mary Grundy, aged 30 years, was buried 19 Nov 1818 from St. Paul's Parish (ReamySP).

Gudgeon, Jesse, owes taxes for the 1815, on 324 a, *Adventure* etc., in the 2nd Dist. *(BPAT* 7 Jan 1819).

Guinand, Edward F. and Miss Cecilia M. Dean, were m. last Tues. eve. by Rev. Bubad *(FGBA* 11 Jan 1817).

Guthro, Joseph, dec.: two lots of ground, fronting 25 feet on the Washington Road, the schooner *Margha,* and other property, will be sold Tuesday at the auction room, head of Frederick St. Dock, by Van Wyck and Morgan, auctioneers *(BPAT* 5 Dec 1818). For the will of a Joseph Guthrot [sic], filed in 1811, see BAWB 9:129.

Guttry, Mrs. Eliza, aged 55 years, d. Sat., 17th inst. *(FGBA* 29 April 1819; *BPAT* 30 April 1819). Elizabeth Guttry, aged 54 years, was buried 17 April 1819 from St. Paul's Parish (ReamySP).

Guynn, Dr. John, was m. at Annapolis to Miss Louisa Ann Hobbs [date not given] *(BPAT* 10 Nov 1817; *BA* 11 Nov 1817).

Guyton, Mr. Thomas, and Miss Allender, both of Baltimore Co., were m. Thurs., 16th inst, by Rev. Mr. Greenfield *(BPAT* 25 Sep 1819).

Gwynn, Major William, d. last Fri., at Monkton Mills, in his 70th year; he was a native of Ireland, and became a resident of Pa. in 1772. In 1776 he joined the Revolutionary Army, and was appointed a Major under Gen. Mifflin. After the War he moved to Md., and for the last 30 years lived on his farm. He leaves a wife and other relatives *(BPAT* 4 Oct 1819). For the will of William Gwynn, filed in 1819, see BAWB 11:82.

"H"

Haddaway, Lieut. Edward, of the U. S. Navy, d. 15 June, of a pulmonary complaint, with which he had long been afflicted, at St. Michael's, on the Eastern Shore of Maryland *(BA* 23 June 1817; *BPAT* 23 June 1817).

Hagthorp, Thomas, was m. last Sun. eve. by the Rev. Mr. Moranville, to Miss Mary Donnell of Cecil Co. *(BA* 11 June 1817; *BPAT* 10 June 1817).

Haigh, David, and Miss Harriet Snyder, both of Baltimore, were m. last Thurs. eve. by Rev. Dr. Roberts *(BPAT* 11 Dec 1819).

Hale, Mrs. Jane, d. lately at a very advanced age; for fifty years of her life had kept a Toy, Fruit and Cake Table at the market near Gay St. She was born in Eng., and raised a family of children and grandchildren. She refused to remove to the Alms house, and lived in a wooden tenement which she held on a ground rent [a long obit follws] *(BPAT* 22 Nov 1819). Jane Hale, aged 92 years, was buried 6 Nov 1819 from St. Paul's Parish (ReamySP). For the will of Jane Haile, filed in 1820, see BAWB 11:126.

Hale, Nicholas, owes taxes for the years 1813, 1814, 1815, on six acres of *Part of Tracey's Park* in the 1st Dist. Of Baltimore Co. *(BPAT* 7 Jan 1819).

Hall, Andrew, merchant, and Miss Ann Giles Moore, dau. of Philip Moore of Baltimore, were m. Wed. morn, 23rd inst. by Rev. Mr. Waugh *(BPAT* 25 Sep 1819).

Hall, Carter A., merchant, was m. last eve. [Thurs.] by Rev. Dr. Duncan to Miss Ann M. Diffenderfer, dau. of Peter Diffenderfer *(BA* 18 Sep 1818; *BPAT* 18 Sep 1818).

Hall, Edward, is an insolvent debtor of Baltimore *(BPAT* 27 March 1817).

Hall, Elias, was m. 3rd inst. [Sun.] by Rev. Dr. Glendy, to Miss Margaret Maher, all of Baltimore *(BPAT* 7 Oct 1819).

Hall, Capt. Ezekiel, of Baltimore Co. died; Sophia Hall, admx., advertises she will settle the estate *(BPAT* 26 Feb 1818).
Hall, Mrs. Hannah, d. Friday, aged 22 years, after a painful illness *(BA* 4 Aug 1817; *BPAT* 4 Aug 1817). Hannah Hall, aged 22, was buried 1 Aug 1817 (ReamySP). Her death was also recorded in the records of the East Baltimore Station of the Methodist Church (PedenM)
Hall, Henry, was m. Sun. eve. by Rev. Valiant to Ann Blades, all of Baltimore *(BA* 23 Dec 1818; *BPAT* 21 Dec 1818).
Hall, Jacob, and Co., owe taxes for the years 1816 and 1817 on 10 a. *Mount Gilboa* in the 1st Dist. *(BPAT* 3 Aug 1819).
Hall, Jesse, of Baltimore, was m. last Wed. by Rev. Bartow to Mrs. Elizabeth Graham of Baltimore *(FGBA* 21 July 1819; *BPAT* 21 July 1819).
Hall, John, an apprentice to the piloting business, ran away from James Griggs last 6 April *(BPAT* 29 May 1818).
Hall, Mrs. Mary, consort of Benedict W. Hall, d. yesterday in her 25th year *(FGBA* 2 July 1818; *BPAT* 2 July 1818).
Hall, Mr. Nelson, was m. Thurs. eve. last, to Miss Emily Augusta Swan, all of Baltimore *(BPAT* 13 Dec 1819).
Hall, Shadrick, was m. 15th inst. [Sat.] by Rev. Hargrove, to Miss Mary Barrett *(BA* 18 March 1817; *BPAT* 19 March 1817).
Hall, William I., was m. at Annapolis, last Thurs. eve., to Miss Margaret Harwood, all of Anne Arundel Co. *(BPAT* 27 Nov 1819).
Hamilton, Eleanor, eld. dau. of Edward Hamilton, Esq., d. 26th ult. in Charles Co., in her 18th year *(BPAT* 7 Sep 1818).
Hamilton, James, Esq., of Philadelphia, d. suddenly, 20th inst., at Poughkeepsie, NY, in the 43rd year of his age *(BPAT* 26 July 1817).
Hamilton, James, was m. Tues. eve. by Rev. Glendy to Miss Mary Linton, all of Baltimore *(BA* 12 March 1818; *BPAT* 12 March 1818).
Hamilton, Hon. James, d. Sat. Morning, 13 Feb, aged about 67 years, after two days' illness, by a paralytic stroke, at his home in Carlisle, Pa. *(BPAT* 25 Feb 1819).
Hamilton, James B. of Baltimore, was m. on Thurs., 11th inst. by Rev, Valliant to Miss Aliceanna Fardon of Harford Co. *(FGBA* 16 Feb 1819; *BPAT* 15 Feb 1819).
Hamilton, John, 30 years of age, a farmer, born in Co. of Tyrone, Ireland, and enlisted in Philadelphia on 23 July 1818, deserted from the Camp near the Arsenal on 12 Aug 1818. /s/ James H. Hook, Capt., 4th Inf. *(BPAT* 18 Aug 1818).
Hamilton, Col. John, formerly Consul of His Britannic Majesty to the State of Virginia, d. at London, last 12th Dec at a very advanced age. He had been Consul at Virginia for over twenty years and was recalled in consequence of the late war *(BPAT* 12 March 1817).
Hamilton, Samuel S. was m. at Washington to Miss Elizabeth M. Hill of Prince George's Co. *(BPAT* 14 June 1819).
Hammer, Christian, d. this morning, aged 24, after suffering for several years of a consumption of the lungs. The funeral will be from the residence of his brother August Hammer, 173 Baltimore St. *(FGBA* 8 Aug 1818; *BPAT* 8 Aug 1818).
Hammer, Frederick, d. 18th inst., after a short illness, in his 55th year, leaving an only dau. and a brother *(BA* 19 March 1818; *BPAT*19 March 1818). August Hammer, of 173 Baltimore St., brother of Frederick, advertises a sale of Frederick's entire stock in trade, including glass, violins, coffee mills, pistols and gun locks *(BPAT* 16 Aug 1816).
Hammerton, James, servant to Wm. Cobbett, has been sent to Baltimore to sell seeds imported from England and books. He has taken a stand under the store of L. Holmes, Jr., in Lexington St., two doors from Paca St., opposite the New Market *(BPAT* 16 April 1819).
Hammon, Joseph, was m. 16th inst. [Thurs.], by Rev. Glendy, to Miss Catherine Cullen *(FGBA* 28 Jan 1817 [but see John Harrison below]).

Biographical Data from Baltimore Newspapers, 1817-1819

Hammond, John, of Baltimore Co., dec.; Robert Casey and his wife Elizabeth, extx. of John Hammond, advertise the sale of a number of ground rents (*BPAT* 19 Oct 1818).

Hammond, Dr. Matthias, d. at his residence in Anne Arundel Co., in the zenith of manhood (*BPAT* 13 Sep 1819). For the will of Matthias Hammond, filed in 1819, see AAWB JG-:52.

Hammond, Rezin, late of Anne Arundel Co., dec., made a will on 10 May 1808 manumitting a number of his Negroes, including a Negro named Allen. John Gassaway, Register of Wills, certified, on 2 Oct 1817, that the said Allen was raised at Elk Ridge, Anne Arundel Co., was f'5" tall, and had a scar on his right cheekbone near his eye. Andrew Warfield, at one time an acting Justice of the Peace in Anne Arundel Co., refutes the 'illiberal handbill' of George Howard [long notice giving the details of the case] (*BPAT* 29 July 1819). (For the will of Rezin Hammond, filed in 1809, see AAWB JG#2:513).

Hammond, Vachel, and Mrs. Priscilla Haff were m. at Fredericktown [date not given] (*BPAT* 15 Nov 1819).

Hand, Edward, d. in Havana on 25th ult., son of the late Gen. Hand of Lancaster, PA, and a partner of the House of Hugh Boyle and Co., Baltimore (*FGBA* 11 Feb 1818; *BPAT* 11 Feb 1818).

Handle, John, states that he married Mary Dawson, not knowing she had a husband living at the time (William Dawson, q.v.); he has discharged Mary from his abode, and will not be responsible for her debts (*BPAT* 27 Feb 1819).

Hands, Rose, aged 30, of Fells Point, was buried 3 Sep 1819 (*FBBA* 3 Sep 1819).

Handy, Miss Sarah Custis, dau. of John Handy, Esq., d. of a rapid decline, on 14th inst., at Snow Hill, Worcester Co., in her 18th year (*BPAT* 30 Sep 1819).

Handy, William, was m. Thurs. eve. by Rev. Dr. Roberts, to Miss Ann Button, both of Baltimore (*BA* 16 Aug 1817; *BPAT* 15 Aug 1817)

Hannaman, Jacob, was m. last Tues. eve. by Rev. D E. Reese, to Miss Sarah Griffith, both of Baltimore (*BA* 24 April 1817; *BPAT* 25 April 1817 gives the groom's name as Jacob Hennaman).

Hannaman, John, d. 26th inst., at his res. in Baltimore co., in his 64th year (*BA* 30 Dec 1817). [See John Hennaman below].

Hanson, Alexander C., U.S. Senator, d. 23rd April at Belmont, Md., in his 33rd year (*BA* 24 April 1819; *BPAT* 24 April 1819).

Hanson, Benedict H., will have his property, including his right, title, and interest in a tract called *Penny Come Quick,* 208 a., sold, by virtue of a writ of *venditioni exponas,* issued out of Harford Co. Court, at the suit of John Stump, John Johnson and Thomas Wilson. /s/ Jason Moore, Sheriff (*BPAT* 17 April 1817).

Hantzman, Mr. Henry, was m. last eve. [Wed.] by Rev. Dr. Jennings, to Miss Elizabeth Hackney, all of Baltimore (*BPAT* 25 Sep 1817).

Hardester, Isaac, son of Capt. Benjamin Hardester of Baltimore, d. 22nd inst., aged 11 years and 6 mos. (*BPAT* 27 April 1818).

Hardesty, Charles R., was m. last Sun, by Rev. Bartow to Miss Sarah L. Murray, all of Baltimore (*FGBA* 2 March 1819; *BPAT* 2 March 1819).

Harding, Lyman, Esq., Attorney General of the State of Mississippi, was m. [date not given] to Miss Elizabeth Abercrombie, dau. of Rev. James Abercrombie, D.D., of Philadelphia (*BPAT* 5 Oct 1818).

Hardinge, Mr. Samuel, comedian, d. in Wilmington, N. C., formerly of the Philadelphia and Charleston Theatres (*BPA* 31 March 1817).

Hardt, Peter, editor of the York *Recorder,* was m. On Thursday, 2nd ult., to Miss Catherine Sides of Hanover (*BPAT* 16 June 1819).

Hardy, Alexander, aged 20, b. in Chester, Chester Co., Pa., lately a resident of York Co., Pa., a cooper, enlisted 14 July, deserted 26 July from the Carlisle Barracks /s/ James Pratt, Capt., 5th Infantry (*BPAT* 2 Sep 1817).

Harent, Rev. Joseph, d. in Martinico last April, in his 63rd year, one of the members of St. Mary's College, Baltimore (*BA* 15 June 1818; *BPAT* 15 June 1818). For the will of Joseph Harent, filed in 1818, see BAWB 10:477.

Harkles, Thomas, a Negro man, aged 39 years and 5'7" tall, ran away from Hiram Jones, living near Rick Hall, Kent Co. (*BPAT* 29 Sep 1819).

Harmon, Mr. Zebulon, was m. last Thurs. eve. by Rev. Mr. Moore, to Miss Mary King, both of this city (*BPAT* 17 Feb 1817; *FGBA* 17 Feb 1817).

Harner, John, was m. last eve. [Tues.] by the Rev. Mr. Hargrove to Miss Sarah Knight of Baltimore Co. (*BA* 3 Sept 1818; *BPAT* 3 Sep 1818).

Harper, Mary Diana, eld. dau. of Gen. Harper, d. early in Feb, in her 15th year, at *La Bouteleye*, the seat of Dennis Fonlevy, Esq., near Poitiers in France (*BPAT* 16 April 1818).

Harr, Peter, was m. last Thurs. by Rev. Bartow to Miss Hannah Gordon (*BA* 10 Oct 1818; *BPAT* 10 Oct 1818).

Harrington, Peter, of Dorchester Co., dec.; William Jones will administer the estate (*BPAT* 4 Oct 1819).

Harris, Henry, a light colored Negro man, 25 years old, ran away from Joshua Barney. He was raised by the late Isaac Freeman, near Chestertown, Kent Co. and was purchased last Sep from Mr. Samuel M. Sutton, the attorney for Carvell and Martha Freeman, admins. of the said estate. He has been accustomed to working on board bay craft, and was last seen with his wife, who lives with Mr. Shaw in North Charles St. (*BPAT* 25 March 1818).

Harris, Nehemiah, was m. last Thurs. eve., by Rev. Dr. Roberts, to Miss Margaret Campbell, all of Baltimore (*BA* 29 Nov 1817; *BPAT* 29 Nov 1817).

Harris, Mrs. Ruth, consort of John P. Harris of Baltimore, d. Wed., 11th inst., in her 36th year, leaving a husband and five small children (*FGBA* 17 Aug 1819; *BPAT* 18 Aug 1819). Ruth Harris, died in July [sic] 1818 death was recorded in the class lists of the Baltimore City Station of the Methodist Church (PedenM)

Harris, Samuel, was m. last Thurs. by Rev. Force, to Miss Mary Ann Green, all of Baltimore (*FGBA* 27 March 1819; *BPAT* 27 March 1819).

Harris, Dr. Thomas, of the U. S. Navy, m. at Philadelphia, Miss Jane P. Hodgdon, dau, of Samuel Hodgdon of that city (*BPAT* 17 Dec 1819).

Harris, William C., was m. last eve. [Thurs.] by the Rev. Mr. Hargrove to Mehitable Hagger, dau. of Mr. B. K. Hagger, all of Baltimore (*BA* 8 May 1818; *BPAT* 8 May 1818).

Harris, William C., editor of the *York Gazette*, d. at York, Pa., in the 26th year of his age, leaving a wife and infant family (*BPAT* 14 Dec 1818).

Harrison, Mrs. Elizabeth, d. yesterday, after a long and painful illness, aged 22 years (*BA* 17 Nov 1818; *BPAT* 17 Nov 1818).

Harrison, Harry, Negro, ran away from Joshua Barney, who bought him from the estate of Col. Freeman of Kent Co.; he is about 24 years of age and a shoemaker by trade; he may be at or near, Port Deposit (*BPAT* 2 Sep 1818).

Harrison, Mr. John, was m. 16th inst. [Thurs.], by Rev. John Glendy, to Catharine Cullen (*BPAT* 28 Jan 1817; *BA* 28 Jan 1817 [but see Joseph Hammon, above]).

Harrison, Kensey, of Queen Anne's Co., was m. there on the 15th inst. [Tues.] to Mrs. Margaret Elizabeth Wright, also of that county (*BPAT* 21 June 1819).

Harrison, Jonathan N., was m. last Wed. eve., by Rev. Dr. Roberts, to Miss Susanna Roselba Green (*BPAT* 17 Feb 1817; *BA* 17 Feb 1817).

Harrison, Robert M., was m. at Washington, to Miss Susan A. Harkness, all of that City (*BPAT* 5 April 1817).

Harrison, Mr. Robert, of the House of Messrs, Ryan, Hampson and Co., d. at Alexandria, D. C., aged 34 years (*BPAT* 21 Dec 1819).

Harrison, Zebulon, was m. last Thurs. eve. by Rev. Mr. Moore, to Miss Mary King, all of this city (*BPAT* 15 Feb 1817; *BA* 15 Feb 1817).

Harry, George I., merchant, was m. at Hagerstown, on Tues., 15th inst., by Rev, J. H. Reily, to Miss Susan D. Bell, all of that place(*BPAT* 26 June 1819).

Hart, John, was m. on Sun, eve. by Rt. Rev. Bishop Kemp to Mrs. Eliza Dempsey, all of Baltimore (*BA* 9 Dec 1818; *BPAT* 9 Dec 1818).

Hartshorne, Mrs. Sarah, wife of P. S. Hartshorne, of Baltimore, d. last eve. (*FGBA* 31 Dec 1818; *BA* 1 Jan 1819; *BPAT* 1 Jan 1819).

Biographical Data from Baltimore Newspapers, 1817-1819

Harvey, Mr. James, was m. on Thurs. eve,. by Rev. Dr. Kurtz, to Miss Eliza, only dau. of Philip Uhler, Esq., all of Baltimore (*BPAT* 6 Sep 1819).

Harwood, Richard H., d. 21st ult. at Annapolis (*BMC* 29 May 1819).

Haskins, Henry, of Dorchester Co., dec.; H. P. Waggaman, admin., will settle the estate (*BPAT* 9 July 1818).

Haslet, Andrew, formerly of Baltimore, d. last 23 July at Natchez (M.T.), after an illness of three weeks (*FGBA* 22 Aug 1817; *BPAT* 18 Aug 1817)).

Hasselbach, Miss Catherine, eld. dau. of John Hasselbach, d. last Mon. at Buckingham House, Frederick Co., after a long and painful indisposition (*BA* 6 Feb 1818; *BPAT* 6 Feb 1818).

Hatcher, Dr. Hardaway, d. at Powhatan, Va., in his 30th year (*BPAT* 9 Nov 1819).

Hathaway, Ebenezer, of Baltimore Co., was m. at Portsmouth, N. H., on 9th inst., by Rev. Mr. Putnam, to Miss Sarah Ann Penhallow, dau. of John Penhallow, Esq., of Portsmouth (*BPAT* 14 Aug 1819).

Hathaway, Capt. John, of Baltimore, was m. 17th May [Sun.] in Lexington, Ky., to Miss Tabitha Ann S. Jackson of Alexandria (*FGBA* 9 June 1818; *BPAT* 10 June 1818).

Haubert, Frederick, d. Wed., in his 49th year, long a resident of Baltimore, he lived on Lombard St. (*BA* 23 April 1818; *BPAT* 22 April 1818). For the will of Frederick Haubert, filed in 1818, see BAWB 10:460.

Haveland, Cornelius, son of James Haveland, d. yesterday; he resided at York and Lloyd Sts. (*BPAT* 23 Jan 1818).

Haven, Mrs. Elizabeth, d. yesterday afternoon, in her 76th year; she was long a resident of Baltimore (*BPAT* 7 Aug 1817).

Hawkins, William, d. Sat., 16th inst., in his 64th year (*FGBA* 21 May 1818; *BPAT* 22 May 1818). For the will of William Hawkins, filed in 1818, see BAWB 10:480.

Hawkins, William, aged 30, d. at the Hospital, and was buried 2 Sep 1819 (*FGBA* 3 Sep 1819).

Hawkins, William, and Miss Mary Brown, all of Baltimore Co., were m. Tues. eve. last by Rev. D. E. Reese (*BPAT* 4 Sep 1819).

Hayden, Clement Whitfield, was m. last Thurs. by Rev. Glendy to Miss Hannah Stacey, all of Baltimore (*BPAT* 6 July 1818).

Hayden, Dennis E., was m. last Thurs. by Archbishop Marechal to Miss Rachel M. Fowler, all of Baltimore (*FGBA* 8 Aug 1818; *BPAT* 8 Aug 1818).

Hayes, Mrs. Belinda, wife of John Hayes of Baltimore, d. 28th inst.; aged 38, leaving a husband and three children (*FGBA* 10 April 1818; *BPAT* 9 April 1818). She is buried in Westminster Presbyterian Churchyard, Baltimore (HaywardW).

Hayes (or Hays), William, was m. Thurs. eve by Rev. Richards to Miss Jane Moren of Baltimore (*BA* 24 Oct 1818; *BPAT* 23 Oct 1818 gives bride's name as Jane Moran).

Hayward, John L., of Baltimore, was m. last Thurs. eve. by Rev. Anderson to Miss Esther Longstreth, youngest dau. of John Longstreth of Groveville, Burlington Co., N. J. (*BA* 21 May 1818; *BPAT* 6 May 1818).

Hazard, Ebenezer, formerly Post Master General of the United States, d. last Friday in his 73rd year, at Philadelphia, of which he was a native and long an inhabitant (*BPAT* 19 June 1817).

Headly, Joseph, aged about 19, apprentice to the house carpenter trade, ran away last Sat. eve. from Charles Farquharson (*BPAT* 14 May 1818).

Heard, Samuel, of Baltimore, d. 8th inst., after a lingering illness, in his 36th year (*FGBA* 10 Aug 1818; *BPAT* 10 Aug 1818).

Heath, John P., late a Captain in the U. S. Marine Corps, was m. at Bladensburg to Miss Elizabeth Deakins, dau. of Col. Deakins, at Bladensburg (*BPAT* 30 March 1819; *American Farmer* 2 April 1819).

Hebbelwhite, Benjamin, born in England, a farmer, deserted from the Rendezvous, Light St., about the 15th of December. /s/ James H. Hook, Captain, 4th Infantry (*BPAT* 9 Jan 1818).

Hedrick, Thomas, was m. to Mrs. Mary Tupper, both of Baltimore, on Tues. by Rev. Duncan (*FGBA* 9 July 1818; *BPAT* 8 July 1818).

Heister, Mrs. Barbary Ann, d. yesterday, aged 103 years (*BPAT* 10 April 1818).

Hellias, Mr. John, and Miss Amelia Armstrong, all of Baltimore, were m. Thurs., 8th inst. by Rev. Dr. Jennings *(BPAT* 16 Oct 1819).

Helm, Mr. Leonard, was m. Thurs. eve. by Rev. D. E. Reese to Miss Isabella Oliver, all of Baltimore *(BPAT* 12 May 1817).

Helsby, Mrs. Mary, d. at Trappe on the Eastern Shore *(BPAT* 29 Nov 1819).

Henderson, Frisby, was m. to Mrs. Mary H. Gilpin, at Elkton, MD, by Rev. Mr. Bell *(FGBA* 5 April 1819).

Henderson, John, merchant of Philadelphia, was m. last eve. [Mon.] by Rev. Dr. Glendy, to Miss Charlotte Cochran Irvine, granddau. of Alexander Irvine of this place *(BPAT* 1 June 1819, 9 June 1819).

Henderson, Lieut. John, of the U.S. Navy, late of Petersburg, drowned in the James River on 9th inst. *(BPAT* 31 July 1819).

Henderson, Dr. Josiah, d. Thurs., 21st inst., in his 24th year, another victim to the destructive calamity which raged in the eastern section of Baltimore. He was a resident of Clarksburg, Va., and left his comfortable home to aid in the relief of suffering humanity *(BPAT* 25 Oct 1819).

Hendrick, Manuel, was m. Mon. eve. by Rev. Moore, to Miss Emeline (or Emily) Gafford, both of Baltimore *(BA* 8 May 1817; *BPAT* 7 May 1817).

Henisy, Mrs., arrived in the ship *Thomas Gibbons* from Corn, is asked to leave a line in the post office, addressed to H. B.; she will hear something to her advantage *(BPAT* 17 Sep 1819).

Hennaman, Mr. John, d. 26th inst. at his residence in Baltimore Co., in his 64th year, formerly a respectable inhabitant of Baltimore *BPAT* 30 Dec 1817). [See John Hannaman above].

Henning, George, d. last Sat., after a short but painful illness, eld. son of Benjamin Henning of Baltimore *(FGBA* 4 March 1818; *BPAT* 4 March 1818)

Henry, Lieut. Henry, of the U. S. Navy, was m. at the Navy Yard, Gosport, to the truly amiable and accomplished Miss Mary Ann Cassin, niece of Commodore Cassin, commandant of this station *(BPAT* 5 Oct 1817).

Henry, Robert J., was m. to Susannah Brotherton, all of Baltimore, last Thurs. by Rev. Rev. Bartow *(BA* 19 Dec 1818; *BPAT* 19 Dec 1818).

Hensel, Mr. William, Jr., of Lancaster, Pa., was m. Thurs. eve. last by Rev. Dr. Roberts, to Miss Mary Norton of Harford Co. *(BPAT* 26 July 1819).

Henwood, Joshua, aged 34, b. in Annapolis, Anne Arundel Co., Md. 5th Regt., U,. S. Infantry, ran away from Carlisle Barracks on 8th Inst. *(BPAT* 2 Aug 1817).

Hepburn, John M., of Georgetown, D. C., was m. to Miss Eliza S. Johnston, dau. of Christopher Johnston of Baltimore, last eve. [Tues.] by Rev. Dr. Inglis *FGBA* 15 April 1818; *BPAT* 16 April 1818).

Herbert, William, Sr., President of the Bank of Alexandria, one of the oldest and most respectable inhabitants of that town, d. Wed., after a lingering illness *(BPAT* 27 Feb 1819).

Herd, Mr. James, was m. last Tues. by Dr. Jennings, to Miss Nancy Carter, all of Baltimore Co. *(BPAT* 15 Oct 1819).

Herford, Mr. Henry, of Washington City, d. at Augusta, Ga., on 30th ult. He had been on a tour of the southern states for benefit of his health, and was seized with a fever at Augusta *(BPAT* 13 Aug 1817).

Heron, Alexander, merchant, was m. to Miss Ann Heck of Lancaster, PA, on Thurs. eve. by Rev, Duncan *(BA* 21 Nov 1818; *FGBA* 21 Nov 1818 gives his name as Herring; *BPAT* 21 Nov 1818).

Herring, Mr. David, and Miss Julian Kalbfus, all of Baltimore, were m. last Tues eve,. by Rev. Dr. Jennings *(BPAT* 4 Nov 1819).

Herring, Ludwig, d. yesterday, in his 55th year. The funeral will be from his late dwelling, 72 Albemarle St. *(FGBA* 8 Jan 1817). Jacob Graflin, trustee, advertises the sale of 170 a. of prime land *(BPAT* 21 Aug 1817). Elizabeth Herring, admx., advertises that her son Henry Herring has declined the agency of her affairs, and she had appointed Jacob Grafflin as her sole agent *(BPAT* 21 March 1818). His dwelling house on Albemarle St., next door to the corner of Queen or Pratt Sts., will be sold 27 Nov inst. by Jacob Grafflin, trustee *(BPAT* 16 Nov 1818).

Heslip, Mrs. Elizabeth, consort of John Heslip, d. Mon. 26th inst., in her 65th year *(BA* 27 May 1817; *BPAT* 27 May 1817).

Hewes, Capt. Daniel, of Louisville, Ky., was m. to Miss Mary Jones of Baltimore last Monday by Rev. Inglis *(BPAT* 15 April 1819).

Hewes, Mrs. Eunice, wife of Daniel Hewes, late of Baltimore, d. at Louisville, Ky., on 22nd ult. *(BPAT* 15 Jan 1819).

Hewett, Mr. Elmer, was m. on 8th inst. [Tues.] by Rev. John Glendy, to Mrs. Grace McDermett *(BPAT* 17 April 1817; *BA* 15 April 1817).

Hickman, Henry, was m. to Mary Jane Clark, both of Baltimore, last eve. [Tues.] by Rev. Valiant *(BA* 26 Aug 1818; *BPAT* 26 Aug 1818).

Hickman, Dr. Joshua, was m. to Miss Elizabeth Perry, dau. of Erasmus Perry, Esq., all of Montgomery Co. *(BPAT* 11 Feb 1817).

Hicks, Mr. George, of Baltimore, and Mrs. Mary Hilliard of Georgetown, D. C., were m. at the latter place on Sun. morning last, by Dr. Allison *(BPAT* 25 June 1819).

Higgins, Mrs. Harriet, wife of Mr. Solomon Higgins, merchant, of Cambridge, Dorchester Co., d. there after a long and lingering illness, in her 26th year *(BPAT* 15 Nov 1819).

Higinbotham, Delozier, midshipman, and a native of Baltimore, aged 20, d. 15 Oct on board the U.S.S. *Independence,* after an illness of three days *(BA* 22 Oct 1817; *BPAT* 21 Oct 1817).

Hignat, John, was m. to Miss Caroline Pritchett, all of Baltimore, on 11th inst. [Thurs.] by Rev. Mr. Waugh *(FGBA* 24 Feb 1819; *BPAT* 25 Feb 1819).

Hill, Mrs. Margaret, consort of Charles Hill, Esq., of Prince George's Co., Md., d. last Saturday in her 21st year, after a short but painful illness *(BPAT* 29 March 1817).

Hill, Mrs. Rebecca, aged 30, wife of Capt. John Hill, d. yesterday morning *(FGBA* 10 April 1819; *BPAT* 3 April 1819).

Hill, Mr. Richard, aged 38 years, who is supposed to have lived in Baltimore, died at Hingham, Mass., on 10 Oct on his passage from Baltimore, to Pembroke, his native place *(BPAT* 10 Nov 1817).

Hill, Mr. Thomas H., d. last evening, aged about 29 years, late one of the proprietors of the *Baltimore Telegraphe (BPAT* 16 Sep 1819).

Hillard, Mr. John, was m. Thurs. eve. to Miss Thomazine Craft, both of this place by Rev. Rev. Bartow *(BPAT* 26 July 1817; *BA* 26 July 1817).

Hilleary, Capt. Clement T., of Frederick Co., was m. to Miss Henrietta B. Mullikin, of Prince George's Co., last Mon. eve. by Rev. Armstrong *(BPAT* 4 Dec 1818).

Hillen, John, offers $20.00 reward for the return of a trunk stolen from behind a carriage at the door the previous evening. Hillen states that the practice of robbing carriages has become so prevalent that all constables, watchmen, and others are requested to keep a look out *(BPAT* 6 Oct 1817).

Hillen, John, President of the Friendship Fire Co,, advertises for the return of a large two story ladder, from the place where it was deposited for safe-keeping, under the projection of the west side of the Centre Market House *(BPAT* 22 Aug 1818).

Hindes, Wm., of the Eastern Shore of Md., was m. last Tues. eve., by the Rev. Dr. Roberts, to Miss Elizabeth Burgess of this city *(BPAT* 31 March 1817; *BA* 31 March 1817).

Hines, John, and Miss Catherine Simms, both of Baltimore, were m. on Sun., 21st ins. by Rev. Dr. Roberts *(FGBA* 22 Feb 1819; *BPAT* 22 Feb 1819).

Hines, Samuel, was m. to Miss Keziah Howard, both of Baltimore, last eve. [Tues.] by Rev. D. E. Reese *(FGBA* 27 May 1818).

Hiss, Jacob, Jr., and Miss Susan R. Hurst, both of Baltimore, were m. last eve. [Thurs.] by Rev. Mr. Burch *(BPAT* 3 Dec 1819).

Hiss, Joseph, was m. to Elizabeth G. Buck, of Baltimore, on Thurs. eve. by Dr. Jennings *(BA* 22 Dec 1818; *FGBA* 22 Dec 1818; *BPAT* 22 Dec 1818).

Hitchcock, Caleb, was m. to Miss Elizabeth Marshall, both of Baltimore Co., on Thurs., 1st inst., by Rev. Rockhold *(FGBA* 9 Jan 1818; *BPAT* 9 Jan 1818).

Hizer, Robert, aged 20 years and 8 mos., apprentice to the sailmaking business, ran away from Benjamin Buck, No. 81 Smith's Wharf, six cents reward is offered (*BPAT* 10 May 1817_).

Hobbs, Charles, of Queen Anne's Co., has died. Anne Hobbs and Nicholas M. Hobbs, admins., have been directed by the Queen Anne's Co. Orphans Court to give notice to creditors of Charles Hobbs to exhibit their claims (*BPAT* 19 April 1817).

Hodges, James, d. 3rd inst. at his res. near Rock Hall, Kent Co., aged 86 years (*BPAT* 14 Feb 1818).

Hoffman, Ann McKean, infant dau. of David Hoffman, d. this morning (*FGBA* 3 March 1819; *BPAT* 4 March 1819). Ann M. Hoffman, aged 8 mos., was buried 3 March 1819 from St. Paul's Parish (ReamySP).

Hoffman, George, was m. to Mary Smith, dau. of the late Job Smith, all of Baltimore, were m. last eve. [Tues.] by Rev. John Snyder (*FGBA* 5 May 1819; *BPAT* 5 May 1819).

Hoffman, Henry, a yellow boy, apprentice, ran away from Arthur Jones, of Ann St., Fells Point; a reward of six cents is offered (*BPAT* 31 Dec 1817)

Hogdstin, James, of Harford Co. will have an Act of the Assembly for his benefit (*BPAT* 10 Feb 1817).

Hohn, John, a Patriot of the Revolution, d. 9th inst., in his 78th year, leaving a widow (*BA* 13 Jan 1818).

Holbrook, Jacob, and Miss Jane Hyatt, both of Baltimore, were m. last Thurs. eve. by Rev. James Reed (*BA* 19 May 1818; *BPAT* 18 May 1818).

Holland, George L., apprentice to the blacksmith business, ran away from Salem Willard (*BPAT* 10 Nov 1818).

Holland, Mr. James, and Miss Ann Fuller, all of Baltimore, were m. last eve. [Sun.] by Rev. Dr. George Roberts (*BPAT* 28 Sep 1818).

Holland, Mrs. Mary, d. 3rd inst. at her residence in Cumberland Co., Va., aged one hundred and seven (*BPAT* 26 July 1819).

Hollingsworth, Edward Ireland, of Baltimore Co. will have an Act to alter and change his name (*BPAT* 10 Feb 1817).

Hollingsworth, Horatio D., and Miss Emily Caroline Ridgely, dau. of the late Judge Henry Ridgely, were m. yesterday [Thurs.] by Rev. Wyatt (*FGBA* 2 Jan 1818).

Hollingsworth, Jona., has died. Hannah Hollingsworth, extx., advertises a sale of 207 a. of land south of Winchester, Frederick Co. (*BPAT* 14 Nov 1817; and again on 9 March 1818).

Hollingsworth, Mrs. Rachel Lyde, widow of Jesse Hollingsworth, died 6 March in her 71st year (*BA* 9 March 1819; *FGBA* 8 March 1819; *BPAT* 9 March 1819). Her death on 4 March 1819 death was recorded in the class lists of the Baltimore City Station of the Methodist Church (PedenM). For the will of Rachel L. Hollingsworth, filed in 1819, see BAWB 10:581)

Hollingsworth, Capt. William (of Henry), d. Sat., 19th of April last, d. at Elkton, MD, of a pulmonary complaint, with which he had been afflicted for any years, formerly, a member of the Senate of MD, in his 45th year (*BPAT* 14 May 1817).

Hollins, Jesse, and Miss Lucinda Delavetic, all of Baltimore Co., were m. last Thurs. eve. by Rev. Dr. Johnson (*FGBA* 9 Feb 1818; *BPAT* 10 Feb 1818).

Holly, Mr. John, was m. by the Rev. Mr. Parks, to Miss Lydia Harrod, all of this city (*BPAT* 3 Sep 1817; *BA* 3 Sep 1817).

Holmes, Mr. [Armoran or Almoran], late of Wiscassel, in Maine, was m. yesterday [Thurs.], by the Rev. Mr. Hargrove, to Miss Adelia Reynolds of this city (*BPAT* 23 May 1817; *BA* 23 May 1817).

Holmes, Juliana, d. this morning, on her 19th birthday, of consumption, last child, and 3rd dau. of John Holmes, Esq. (*BPAT* 16 Sep 1817; *BA* 17 Sep 1817).

Holmes, Dr. Oliver, of Baltimore, and Miss Christine Fahnestock, were m. at Carlisle, PA, by Rev. Mr. Keller (*FGBA* 31 July 1819; *BPAT* 30 July 1819).

Holston, Mr. Hamilton B., was m. Thurs. eve. last by Rev. Mr. Inglis, to Miss Sarah Walker, all of Baltimore (*BPAT* 25 June 1817; *BA* 25 June 1817).

Hontsberger, Mrs. Kitty, widow of Peter Hontsberger, d. Fri., 13th inst., at Greensburg, Pa., leaving six small orphan children; a long obit gives details of her death from the bite of a rattlesnake *(BPAT* 27 Aug 1819_.

Hood, Rachel Howard, 2nd dau. of Col. Thomas Hood of Anne Arundel Co., d. 5th inst., in her 15th year, a member of the Methodist Society *(BPAT* 26 April 1819).

Hook, Thomas, and Miss Mary Blufford, all of Baltimore Co., were m. last Thurs. eve. by Rev. Parson Grice *(FGBA* 15 Feb 1819 *BPAT* 16 Feb 1819).

Hooper, John, dec.; James Gaines and Ann Gaines, admx., advertise the sale of a one-story house (nearly new and in tolerable order) and lot on Ross St. *(BPAT* 23 Aug 1819).

Hopkins, Mr. Greenbury, was m. last Thurs. eve. by Rev. Mr. Glendy to Miss Elizabeth Palmer, all of Baltimore *(BPAT* 22 Dec 1817; *BA 20 Dec 1817, 22 Dec 1817).*

Hopkins, Dr. Joel, of Elkridge, was m. last eve. [Thurs.], by Rev, Mr. Hargrove, to Mrs. Harriet H. Beard, dau. of the Rev. Mr. Hargrove *(BPAT* 31 Oct 1817; *Bl* 31 Oct 1817),

Hopkins, John, d. 22nd inst. at his res. near Baltimore, aged 72, after a short illness caused by a paralytic stroke. Interment was in the family burying ground *(FGBA* 26 Feb 1818; *BPAT* 22 Feb 1818). For the will of John Hopkins, filed in 1818, see BAWB 10:430.

Hopkins, John, was m. to Rebecca C. James, at Friends' Meeting House in Lombard St., yesterday morning [Wed.] *(BPAT* 11 June 1818; *BA* 10 June 1818).

Hopkins, Mr. Nicholas, was m. Tues. eve. last by Rev. Mr. Richards, to Miss Magaretta Morrison, all of Baltimore *(BPAT* 10 Oct 1817; *BA* 9 Oct 1817).

Hopkins, Mr. Richard, was m. Thurs. eve. last by Rev. Dr. Roberts to Miss Mary Ann Gover, both of Baltimore *(BPAT* 22 Nov 1817; *FGBA* 24 Nov 1817).

Hopkins, Solomon, Baltimore merchant, and Miss Maria H. Coates, eld. dau. of John Coates, were m. at Boston on 25th inst. [Thurs.] by Rev. William E. Channing *(FGBA* 1 March 1819).

Hoppe, Frederick, son of Mr. Justus Hoppe, of Baltimore, d. Thurs., 12th inst., aged one year and eight days *(FGBA* 16 Aug 1819; *BPAT* 17 Aug 1819).

Horn, Mr. John, d. Fri. eve. last in his 78th year, a distinguished revolutionary patriot. He leaves an aged widow *(BPAT* 12 Jan 1818).

Horn, Mrs. Mary, wife of Mr. J. S. Horn, formerly of this city, d. 16th inst. *(BPAT* 20 Dec 1819).

Horner, Mr. Abel, and Miss Keziah Patterson, all of Baltimore, were m. last Thurs. eve. by Rev. D. E. Reese *(BPAT* 19 May 1818; *BA* 19 May 1818).

Horner, Elizabeth, dau of Job Horner, left the house of Mr. Rogers in Market St., Philadelphia last Feb, saying she was going to her father's house, residing near New Egypt, Monmouth Co., N. J. She never arrived and two months ago, her parents received a letter stating she was then in Baltimore with a Mr. and Mrs, Davis, and would be at her father's house in July. She is about 20 years old *(BPAT* 24 Aug 1818).

Horsey, Morris, merchant, and Miss Ellen Legrande, eld. dau. of S. D. Legrande, all of Baltimore, were m. last Mon. at Philadelphia *(BPAT* 8 May 1819).

Horsey, Smith, of Worcester Co. has been murdered, and Gov. Samuel Sprigg has offered a reward of $200.00 *(BPAT* 30 Dec 1819).

Horton, Lewis, informs his friends that he has resumed his former situation at the corner of Baltimore and Calvert Sts., where he keeps the usual variety of mineral waters. He offers these salubrious waters to the afflicted poor, when prescribed by a physician gratuitously. His brother, A. Horton, has opened an establishment nearly opposite the Fountain Inn, Light St. Magnesia Water may be obtained at either place *(BPAT* 21 May 1818).

Horton, Nicholas F. was m. last Sun. eve. by Rev. Dr. Jennings, to Miss Lavinia Cady, all of Baltimore *(BPAT* 18 Nov 1817).

Horze, Mr. William, was m. last eve. [Thurs.] by the Rev. Mr. Kurtz, to Miss Rebecca Hertzog, both of Baltimore *(BPAT* 25 July 1817; *BA* 26 July 1817).

Horton, Nicholas F., and Miss Lavinia Cady, all of Baltimore, were m. last Sun. eve. by Rev. Dr. Jennings (*BA* 19 Nov 1817).

Horton, William, in addition to his old establishment at the corner of Baltimore and Gay Sts., has opened one at his dwelling, 15 York St. where mineral waters are prepared with chemical accuracy (*BPAT* 26 April 1819).

Hose, Mr. Elias, was m. last Thurs. eve. by Rev. Dr. Roberts, to Miss Eliza Williams, all of Baltimore (*BPAT* 5 Sep 1818; *BA* 5 Sep 1818).

Hoskins, Richard, d. yesterday of a pulmonary consumption of two years, in his 23rd year (*BPAT* 30 Nov 1819). Richard Hoskins d. 29 Nov 1819, aged 23, of consumption, and was buried 30 Nov 1819 in the Cathedral Cemetery (Grogaard).

Hough, Mr. William, merchant, was m. last eve. [Thurs.] by Rev, Dr. Roberts, to Miss Mary Ann Chalmers, of this city (*BPAT* 17 Jan 1817; *BACDA* 18 Jan 1817 gives this name as Haugh).

Houston, Hon. James, District Judge of the U.S., for the District of Md., died at Chestertown, Md. (*FGBA* 10 June 1819).

How, Mr. John, merchant, was m. to Miss Susan Gates, all of Baltimore, on Thurs. eve. by Rev. Mr. Glendy (*BPAT* 27 Dec 1817; *BA* 27 Dec 1817).

Howard, Benjamin C., was m. Tues. eve. by Rev. Dr. Inglis, to Jane, eld. dau. of William Gilmor, Esq. (*BPAT* 26 Feb 1818; *BA* 27 Feb 1818; *FGBA* 25 Feb 1818).

Howard, Mrs. Elizabeth, wife of Joshua Howard of Frederick Co., d. 17th inst, aged 70, leaving a husband, eight children, and many grandchildren (*FGBA* 23 April 1817).

Howard, Dr. Henry, d. 17 July, at Cornelius Howard's, in his 44th year. His funeral will be from his late residence on Lombard St. (*BA* 21 July 1817). Rebecca Howard, extx., advertised she would settle the estate (*BPAT* 12 Dec 1817). For the will of Henry Howard, filed in 1817, see BAWB 10:342.

Howard, Mr. John, of Baltimore, was m. last Tues. eve. by Rev. Mr. Reynolds, to Miss Juliet, eld. dau. of Alexander Warfield, of Frederick Co. (*BPAT* 24 Jan 1818; *FGBA* 24 Jan 1818).

Howard, Mrs. Sarah, wife of Robert Howard of Baltimore, d. 5th inst., leaving a husband and one child (*BPAT* 12 Feb 1819).

Howard, Thomas W., of Montgomery Co., dec.; Elizabeth R. Howard of Rockville, admx., will settle the estate (*BPAT* 31 Oct 1818).

Howard, Thomas, aged 14 or 15, 4' 5 or 6" tall, apprentice, ran away from Alex. Beard (*BPAT* 6 April 1819).

Howe, Capt. Edward, Jr., has died. One-third of the Brig *Hider Ally*, belonging to his estate, will be sold (*BPAT* 5 Dec 1817).

Howell, John Brown, and Miss Susan E. Miles, all of Baltimore, were m. last eve. [Tues.] by Rev. M. Reis (*BPAT* 5 May 1819).

Hoyland, John, and Mrs. Martha McCormick, both of Baltimore, were m. last Thurs. by Rev. Glendy (*BA* 27 April 1819; *BPAT* 26 April 1819).

Hoyt, Richard C., of Alexandria, was m. last Thurs. eve. by Rev. Mr. Wyatt, to Miss Sophronia Stephens, of Baltimore (*BPAT* 17 Aug 1818; *BA* 17 Aug 1818).

Hudson, Henry, a free black man, aged 20 or 21, was kidnapped from a field near Germantown. He was a native of Kent Co., Delaware. A reward of $100.00 is offered by Reuben Haines, No. 300, Chestnut St., Philadelphia (*BPAT* 7 May 1819).

Hubbell, Capt. Josiah, of Baltimore, was m. at Salisbury, E.S., [Eastern Shore] on Thurs., 26th ult., to Miss Leah Dashiell, of Somerset Co. (*BPAT* 6 March 1818; *BA* 7 March 1818).

Hughes, Mr. Hugh C. T., was m. on Sun. eve. by Rev. Mr. Moranville, to Miss Mary Ledevidge, all of Baltimore (*BPAT* 6 Oct 1818; *FGBA* 6 Oct 1818; *BA* 6 Oct 1818).

Hughes, James, merchant, was m. Thurs. eve., 13th inst., by Rev. George Brice, to Miss Elizabeth, dau. of Mr. Isaac Green of Baltimore Co. (*BPAT* 15 Feb 1817).

Hughes, Jehu, and Elizabeth, dau. of Isaac Green of Baltimore Co., were m. Thurs., 13th inst. by Rev. George Grice (*FGBA* 15 Feb 1817).

Hughes, John, aged about 20, apprentice to the shoemaking trade, ran away 1st inst., from Alexander McMackan; a reward of six cents is offered (*BPAT* 14 April 1818).

Hughes, John, dec.; his heirs owe taxes for the years 1813, 1814, 1815, on a six-acre lot on Mill Run, and a three-acre lot on Gallows Hill, both in the 5h Dist. (*BPAT* 7 Jan 1819).

Hughes, Mr. Richardson, d. 19th inst., late of Philadelphia, of a short but painful illness, aged 43 years (*BPAT* 22 Nov 1817; *FGBA* 21 Nov 1817). Richard [*sic*] Hughes, aged 43, was buried 17 Oct 1817 from St. Paul's Parish (ReamySP).

Hulett, William, aged about 15 years, apprentice to the printing business, ran away from Richard Williams of the office of the *Farmer's Repository:* a reward of one hundred cents is offered (*BPAT* 17 June 1817).

Hulse, Mr. John, was m. last Tues. eve. by Rev. Mr. Healey, to Miss Elizabeth Ann Barton, all of Baltimore (*BPAT* 20 Oct 1817; *FGBA* 21 Oct 1817; *BA* 21 Oct 1817).

Humphreys, Charles, was m. Fri. eve. by Rev. Glendy to Miss Margaret Fitzpatrick (*BPAT* 24 Oct 1818; *BA* 24 Oct 1818).

Hunt, Capt. Henry, and Miss Elizabeth Standiford, all of Baltimore, were m. Tues. eve. by Rev. McJilton (*BPAT* 14 Oct 1819).

Hunt, William T., and Miss Elizabeth Hutton, were m. Sun. night by Rev. Dr. Canback (*BPAT* 27 Dec 1819).

Hunter, James, and Miss Mary Miller, were m. last Thurs. at Annapolis (*BMC* 24 May 1819; *BPAT* 24 May 1819).

Hunter, Mrs. Jane, d. last Wed., 28th Jan., at an advanced age, relict of Capt. George Hunter, long a respectable inhabitant of Baltimore. Interment was in the Western Cemetery of First Presbyterian Church (*BPAT* 31 Jan 1818; *FGBA* 30 Jan 1818). She is buried in Lot # 147 in the Westminster Presbyterian Churchyard, Baltimore (HaywardW).

Hurley, Thomas, d. in Philadelphia, on Sat. morning, in his 59th year (*FGBA* 27 Jan 1817).

Hurst, Thomas, aged 21, b. in Norfolk, Va., 5th Regt., U. S. Infantry, ran away from Carlisle Barracks on 8th Inst. (*BPAT* 2 Aug 1817).

Hurtt, John D., of Baltimore, and Miss Elizabeth C. Armstrong, of Kent Co., were m. Thurs. eve. last near Chestertown by Rev. Mr. Dodson (*BPAT* 20 Dec 1819).

Husband, William, a worthy member of the Society of Friends, d. 24th inst., in his 44th year (*BPAT* 25 Sep 1818; *FGBA* 24 Sep 1818; *BA* 26 Sep 1818).

Huschwadel, Christian David, who was born at Kircheim in the Kingdom of Wurtemburg, went from that place about 22 years ago, when he was about 42 years old, and was employed as a merchant's clerk; his parents gave never heard anything from him, and he is wanted to return home to take possession of his father's estate; the father died 20 years ago. Any information should be sent to C. W. Karthaus, of Baltimore (*BPAT* 8 Nov 1818).

Hust, Mr., was m. last Tues. eve. by Rev. Mr. Montgomery, to Miss Blanche Gudgeon, all of Baltimore (*BPAT* 24 Oct 1817; *BA* 24 Oct 1817).

Hutchins, Mr. John, of New York, was m. last eve. [Thurs.] by Rev. Mr. Davis, to Miss Sarah Ellis, of Baltimore (*BPAT* 30 Oct 1818).

Hutchinson, Mrs. Mary, consort of Joseph Hutchinson, d. at Snow Hill, Worcester Co., on the 6th inst., in her 19th year (*BPAT* 20 July 1818).

Hutton, Samuel, coachmaker, aged 32 years, formerly of Baltimore, d. last Sun. night at Alexandria (*BPAT* 19 Sep 1818).

Hutton, Samuel, owes taxes for the year 815, on 25 a. *Piccabelly Hill* in the 5th Dist. (*BPAT* 7 Jan 1819).

Huxthal, Lewis, d. 20th inst, aged two years, 2nd son of Lewis Huxthal (*BPAT* 22 April 1819).

Hyatt, Henry, aged near 16 years, apprentice to the house painting and glazing business, ran away from Jacob Sigler, opposite the Mechanics bank; a reward of six cents is offered (*BPAT* 24 May 1817).

Hyatt, John, and Miss Ann Roberts, both of Baltimore, were m. Thurs. eve. by Rev. Mr. Force (*FGBA* 6 Feb 1819; *BPAT* 5 Feb 1819).

Hyatt, Richard, of Baltimore Co., is an insolvent debtor (*BPAT* 14 Oct 1819).

Hyde, Thomas W., of Georgetown, was m. at Washington City, [date not given], to Emily, dau. of Capt. John Wales of Montgomery Co. (*BPAT* 11 Nov 1819).
Hyland, Mr. Horatio, d. at Hagerstown, aged 25 years (*BPAT* 25 Oct 1819).
Hyland, Lambert, d. 6th inst., in his 67th year at his farm *Peach Blossom,* near Princess Ann. He leaves a wife and four children (*FGBA* 20 Aug 1819; *BPAT* 18 Aug 1819).
Hynson, Amos, a black man, aged about 22, ran away on 27 Dec last, from Howard Miller on Hawkins Point, on the west side of the Patapsco River, Anne Arundel Co., has a brother living in Annapolis (*BPAT* 20 Jan 1818).
Hynson, Robert C., being about to move out of state, offers for sale, two properties: a farm in Kent Co. called *Jamaica,* about one mile from Chestertown, containing 240 to 250 a., 40 a. of which are in woodland, and adjoining the properties of William Barroll and James M'Clean; the other is a lot in Chestertown, adjoining that of William Harris (*BPAT* 23 April 1818).

"I"

Inglis, Mr. George, was m. Tues. eve. last, by Rev. D. E. Reese, to Miss Elizabeth Divers, all of this city (*BPAT* 5 Feb 1817).
Inglis, Rev. James, D.D., of the First Presbyterian Church, died 15 Aug 1819 (*FGBA* 16 Aug 1819). He is buried in Lot # 70 of Westminster Presbyterian Churchyard, Baltimore (HaywardW). All persons who have in their possession books belonging to the estate of the late Rev. Dr. Inglis are requested to return them without delay to the dwelling, 13 Conewago St. (*BPAT* 6 Sep 1819). James Mosher, Jr., admin., advertises a sale of household furniture including an elegant dining sideboard, breakfast tables, fancy sophas [*sic*], common chairs, and one Parisian timepiece (other items listed also) (*BPAT* 16 Oct 1819).
Inglis, Mr. John, was m. last Thurs. eve. by Rev. Mr. Bartow, to Miss Rebecca Neville (*BPAT* 26 Dec 1818; *BA* 28 Dec 1818; *FGBA* 28 Dec 1818).
Inloes, George, a decent looking young man, about five-feet-ten-inches tall, apprentice to the Morocco Business, ran away from Lewis Kalbfus, living one mile from Baltimore on the Reister's town road (*BPAT* 24 June 1817). (His name was given a George Anloes in the *BPAT* of 20 June 1817).
Innes, Mr. John, d. Wed., 19th Feb., after a short illness, aged 43 years. He came from Guernsey, Eng., which was also the place of residence of the celebrated poet Cowper (*BPAT* 26 Feb 1817). For the will of John Innis, filed in 1817, see BAWB 10:291.
Innis, Mrs. Mary, formerly of Baltimore, d. at her residence in Baltimore Co., on 8th inst., in her 50th year. For many years she had been a member of the Church of Christ (*BA* 11 Sep 1818; *BPAT* 11 Sep 1818).
Ireland, Edward, Esq., and Miss Deborah Owings, eld. dau. of Thomas Moale, Esq., were m. [date not given] by Rev. Mr. Wyatt at Walnut Grove (*FGBA* 19 Aug 1819; *BPAT* 20 Aug 1819).
Ireson, Richard M., and Miss Mary Divers, both of Baltimore, were m. last Thurs. eve. by Rev. Bartow (*BA* 2 June 1817).
Irvine, Alexander, will not pay the debts of his wife Mary Ann, who as eloped from his bed and board without his consent (*BPAT* 7 Jan 1817).
Irvine, John, died Sat. eve., for many years a Baltimore merchant (*FGBA* 5 April 1819). John Irvin [*sic*], aged 36 years, was buried 5 April 1819 from St. Paul's Parish (ReamySP).
Irving, Thomas Pitt, Principal of the Hagerstown Academy, d. 16 Jan. He was a husband and father (*BA* 27 Jan 1818).
Irwin, Jared, d. at Old Providence on 20 Sep., formerly a representative in Congress, who joined General M'Gregor's standard at Amelia Island, and has since been attached to the command of Com. Aury (*BPAT* 4 Feb 1819 /
Irwin, Samuel, and Miss Hush, both of Baltimore, were m. last Wed., by Rev. Hagerty (*BPAT* 21 Aug 1818).

Biographical Data from Baltimore Newspapers, 1817-1819

Isley, Matthew, will not be responsible for the debts of his wife Eliza, who has been a very imprudent woman (*BPAT* 24 April 1819).

"J"

(60)Jackson, Major [-?-], of Baltimore, was m. last Thurs., by Rev. Mr. Hagerty, to Mary F. Stansbury, of Baltimore Co. (*FGBA* 4 Aug 1817).

Jackson, G., d. Sat., aged 34. Funeral from the res. of his bro. James Jackson in Conway St., two doors from Sharp St. (*BA* 16 June 1817; *BPAT* 16 June 1817). For the will of Gilbert Jackson, filed in 1817, see BAWB 10:327.

Jackson. Henry, d. in Baltimore yesterday, in his 75th year, formerly of Dublin. He was a native of Ireland and the father-in-law of Oliver Bond, who was a martyr to liberty in Dublin [long obit] (*BA* 1 July 1817, 10 July 1817; *BPAT* 1 July 1817). Harrison and Sterett, auctioneers, advertise the sale of his two-story brick house on Lombard St., opposite the Friends Meeting house (*BPAT* 25 July 1817). For the will of Henry Jackson, filed in 1817, see BAWB 10:334.

Jackson, Holton, was m. Mon. eve. by Rev. Dr. Inglis, to Miss Frances Jane Grant, of Baltimore (*BA* 19 Nov 1817).

Jackson, Mr. Major, of Baltimore, was m. last Thurs. eve. by Rev. Mr. Hagerty, to Miss Mary F. Stansbury of Baltimore Co. (*BPAT* 4 Aug 1817).

Jackson, Nathaniel, dec.: Van Wyck & Morgan, auctioneers, advertise the sale of a two story brick house and lot at the corner of Fleet St. and Argyle Alley, property of the said Jackson (*BPAT* 30 Sep 1818).

Jacobs, Philip, Esq., aged 80, was m. last eve. [Mon.] by the Rev. Mr. Schaeffer, to the amiable Miss Eliza Brown, all of Baltimore (*BPAT* 25 Feb 1817).

Jacobs, Samuel, was m. last Tues., by Rev. S. Williams, to Miss Deborah Peters (*BA* 18 Sep 1817; *BPAT* 18 Sep 1817 gives the groom's name as Samuel Jacob).

James, Henry, d. Fri., 6th inst, at his residence near Baltimore leaving a wife and eight children (*FGBA* 9 March 1818). For the will of Henry James, filed in 1818, see BAWB 10:442.

James, Mrs. Rachel, wife of George James of Baltimore, d. yesterday in her 84th year (*FGBA* 11 Feb 1817; *BPAT* 12 Feb 1817).

James, Samuel, will have his property, including 66 a. *Johnson's Range,* will be sold at a Sheriff's Sale, to pay and satisfy a writ of *fieri facas* issued out of Harford Co. Court at the suit of Thomas Hayes, for the use of Stevenson Archer. /s/ Jason Moore, Sheriff (*BPAT* 20 Feb 1817).

James, William, Esq., d. at Annapolis on Sat., 18th inst, aged 77 (*BPAT* 24 April 1818).

Jamieson, John, was m. last Sun., by Rev. Mr. Moore, to Miss Ann Stevenson, both of Baltimore (*FGBA* 4 April 1817; *BPAT* 5 April 1817).

Jamison, Cecilius C., merchant of Baltimore, was m. Tues. eve. last, at Annloslin [Anacostia?], D.C., the seat of Gen. John Mason, to Miss Ann E. M. Johnson (*BACDA* 24 May 1817; *BPAT* 23 May 1817).

Jamison, Lieut. William, of the U. S. Navy, was m. at Norfolk [date not given] to Miss Catherine Rose, eldest dau. of Mrs. Mary Rose (*BPAT* 23 Oct 1819).

Janiewar, Jacob, of Baltimore Co. is an insolvent debtor (*BPAT* 13 Dec 1819).

Janney, Abijah, of Alexandria, was m. yesterday [Wed,] at Friends Meeting House in Lombard St., to Mary J. Ellicott of Baltimore (*FGBA* 17 April 1817; *BPAT* 18 April 1817).

Janney, Israel, Jr., of Alexandria, D. C., was m. 3rd inst., [Mon.] at Friends Meeting House in Philadelphia, to Elizabeth, dau. of John Warder of Philadelphia (*BPAT* 11 Nov 1818).

Janson, Mr. Raphael, of Frederick Co., d. Mon. morning last (*BPAT* 25 Jan 1817).

Janvier, John, was m. 21st inst. [Tues.], by Rev. John Barton, to Miss Susanna Biddle, all of Newcastle Co., DE (*BA* 29 Jan 1817; *BPAT* 29 Jan 1817).

Biographical Data from Baltimore Newspapers, 1817-1819

Janvier, Peregrine, was m. last Thurs. eve. by Rev. Jennings, to Miss Catherine Howell, 2nd dau. of William Howell, merchant of Baltimore (*FGBA* 7 Feb 1818; *BPAT* 7 Feb 1818).

Janvier, Mrs. Sarah, d. 16 Nov., of a consumption, in the 56th year of her age, consort of Mr. Joseph Janvier of this city (*BPAT* 17 Nov 1819).

Janvier, William B., of Newcastle, was m. last Thurs. by Rev. Glendy, to Miss Jane W. Clopper of Baltimore (*FGBA* 22 Feb 1819; *BPAT* 22 Feb 1819).

Jarrett, Abraham, was m. last Thurs. in Harford Co. by Rev. Bend, to Miss Elizabeth Hays, dau. of Archer Hays (*BA* 22 Oct 1817; *BPAT* 22 Oct 1817).

Jay, Samuel, of Harford Co., d. Sat, 12th inst., a husband and father (*FGBA* 16 Sep 1818; *BPAT* 18 Sep 1818).

Jefferies, Samuel, a Baltimore bookseller, d. 7th inst., in his 33rd year, leaving a wife and two children. His residence was at Sharp St., adjacent the African Meeting House (*FGBA* 9 Feb 1818; *BPAT* 10 Feb 1818).

Jefferies, Thomas, was m. Thurs., March 18, by Rev. Kurtz, to Miss Elizabeth Hemmel (*FGBA* 20 March 1819; *BPAT* 20 March 1819; *BA* 20 March 1819 gives the groom's name as Jeffries).

Jeffers, James H., was m. last Thurs., by Rev. Dr. Roberts, to Miss Louisa C. Browning, both of Baltimore (FGBA 2 Sep 1818; *BPAT* 3 Sep 1818).

Jeffray, James, a native of Scotland, and for many years a merchant of Baltimore, d. 12th inst., in his 72nd year (*FGBA* 21 April 1818; *BPAT* 22 April 1819).

Jenkins, Mrs. Ann, wife of Henry Jenkins, d. yesterday morning of consumption (*BA* 15 Sep 1817; *BPAT* 15 Sep 1817). Ann Harrison Jenkins, wife of Henry Neale Jenkins, d. 14 Sep 1817 age c30, of consumption; she was buried 15 Sep 1817 in the Cathedral Cemetery (Grogaard).

Jenkins, Benedict, was m. last eve. [Wed.] by Rev. Mr. Fenwick, to Miss Adeline Murphy, all of this city (*BPAT* 16 Jan 1817; *BA* 17 Jan 1817).

Jenkins, Custis, of Somerset Co. has died. Thomas Jenkins will settle the estate (*BPAT* 30 June 1817).

Jennings, Nathan, of New York, was m. last Thurs. eve. by Rev. Mr. Duncan, to Miss Sarah Lee Sleppy, dau. of Mr. Jacob Sleppy of this city (*BPAT* 17 Jan 1817; *BA* 17 Jan 1817).

Jennings, Nathan, formerly of New York, lately a resident of Baltimore, d. 22nd ult., in his 26th year (*FGBA* 8 Oct 1818).

Jeremiah, John, was m. Thurs. eve. by Rev. Rozzell, to Miss Effy McCrellen (*BA* 25 Oct 1817; *BPAT* 25 Oct 1817).

Jeys, Thomas, Esq., was m. [date not given], at Kingston, Jamaica, by Rev. Francis Humberstone, to Miss Eliza M. Edgar, formerly of Baltimore (*BPAT* 24 Nov 1819).

John, Amblius, formerly of Baltimore, d. at New Orleans of the prevailing fever (*BPAT* 3 Dec 1819).

Johns, Aquila, for 53 years a respectable inhabitant of Fells Point, d. Wed., 2nd inst., in his 87th year, after a short but painful illness (*BA* 7 Nov 1817; *BPAT* 7 Nov 1817). For the will of Aquila Johns, filed in 1817, see BAWB 10:379.

Johns, Mrs. Hannah, relict of the late Aquila Johns, d. Tues., 14th inst., in her 84th year, leaving numerous descendants, relatives, and friends (*BA* 18 July 1818; *BPAT* 18 July 1818; *BPAT* 18 July 1818). Her death was recorded in the class lists of the Baltimore City Station, Methodist Church (PedenM). For the will of Hannah Johns, filed in 1818, see BAWB 10:509.

Johns, Capt. Richard, of Baltimore, aged 60 years, long a respectable inhabitant of this town, d. 28th Aug in Chargress[?] (*BPAT* 28 Oct 1819).

Johns, William, d. yesterday afternoon, aged 25 years; his residence was at the corner of Ann and Aliceanna Sts., Fells Point (*BA* 10 April 1817; *BPAT* 10 April 1817). William Johns was buried 8 April 1817 from St. Paul's Parish (ReamySP).

Biographical Data from Baltimore Newspapers, 1817-1819

Johnson, Betsey, a Negro woman, commonly called Betsey, about 50 years of age, raised by Mr. Sellman, near Gray's Gardens, Western Precincts, ran away from William Myers (*BPAT* 23 Dec 1819).

Johnson, Charles Henry, was m. last Sun. eve. by Rev. Bartow, to Miss Eliza Green, all of Baltimore (*FGBA* 16 March 1819; *BPAT* 13 March 1819).

Johnson, David, was m. last Thurs. eve. by Rev. Dr. Jennings, to Miss Abigail Lyon Armitage, all of Baltimore (*BA* 3 Sep 1818; *BPAT* 2 Sep 1818).

Johnson, David, a naval hero of the Revolution, aged 70, was m. in Fairfax Co., Va., on 23rd inst. [Sun.], to Mrs. Sarah Mollihorn, a lady much admired for her virtues (*BPAT* 29 May 1819).

Johnson, Elijah, Jr., was m. last eve. [Tues.] by Rev. Shane, to Miss Hannah Barnett of Baltimore Co. (*FGBA* 28 April 1819).

Johnson, Fayette, of Baltimore Co., was m. at Fredericktown on 18th inst. [Thurs.], by Rev. Mr. Westerman, to Miss Catherine Johnson, dau. of the late John Johnson of Frederick Co. (*FGBA* 24 Feb 1819; *BPAT* 25 Feb 1819).

Johnson, Francis, of Calvert Co. was m. last Thurs. eve. by Rev. Mr. Shane, to Miss Martha Howard of Baltimore (*BEP* 27 April 1818; *BPAT* 27 April 1818).

Johnson, Mr. Henry, was m. last Tues. by Rev. Moranville, to Miss Phebe Hall, all of Baltimore (*BA* 31 July 1818; *BPAT* 31 July 1818).

Johnson, Henry Mackubin, eld. son of Edward Johnson, d. Thurs., in his 15th year, of a rheumatism of the heart (*BA* 24 May 1817; *BPAT* 23 May 1817). Henry Mackubin Johnson, aged 15 years, was buried 22 May 1817 from St. Paul's Parish (Reamy SP).

Johnson, Isaac, 24 years old, b. in Salem, N.J., deserted from Carlisle Barracks on 8th inst. (*BPAT* 2 Aug 1817).

Johnson, Jacob, of Philadelphia, was a member of the Society of Friends. For many years a respectable bookseller, he d. at Lexington, Ky., on 7th inst. (*BPAT* 29 Sep 1819).

Johnson, James, owes taxes for the year 1815, on 25 a. *Mount Royal* in the 2nd Dist. (*BPAT* 7 Jan 1819).

Johnson, John, was m. last Thurs. by Rev. Duncan, to Miss Elizabeth Mecleve, both of Baltimore (*BPAT* 12 Dec 1818).

Johnson, Miss Mary Ann, eld. dau. of the late Horatio Johnson, d. 4th inst. at Rockland, Baltimore Co., the residence of Dr. Thomas Johnson. She was buried in the family vault at Chantilla (*BPAT* 6 Nov 1819).

Johnson, Reverdy, Esq., of Baltimore was m. last Tues. eve. at Mount Willow, near Queen Anne, to Miss Mary M. Bowie, of Prince George's Co. (*BPAT* 19 Nov 1819).

Johnson, Mrs. Susanna, a native of Pennsylvania, d. 15th inst., at Fells Point, aged 89 years. In the early part of her life resided near Hanover, Pa. (*BPAT* 19 Jan 1818).

Johnson, Thomas, was m. last Friday, by Rev. Glendy, to Miss Catherine Spears, both of Baltimore (*FGBA* 12 Jan 1819; *BPAT* 12 Jan 1819).

Johnson, Thomas, Esq., first Governor of Md., d. at Fredericktown, aged 88 years (*BPAT* 29 Oct 1819).

Johnson, Thomas Rinaldo, of Calvert Co., was m. 8 Sep [Mon.] by Rev. Brady, to Miss Sarah Ann Mason of St. Mary's Co. (*BPAT* 17 Sep 1818).

Johnston, Christopher, d. last Sat. in his 69th year. He was a native of Scotland, who came to this country some years before the beginning of the Revolutionary War (*FBBA* 9 March 1819; the *FGBA* of 8 March says he was in his 72nd year; *BPAT* 8 March 1819). For the will of Christopher Johnson [or Johnston], filed in 1819, see BAWB 10:586.

Johnston, Isaac, was m. 20th inst. [Thurs.] by Rev. Bare, to Miss Agnes Howard (*FGBA* 22 May 1819; *BPAT* 21 May 1819 gives the minister's name as Glendy).

Jolly (or Jolley), William, d. 7th inst., at his residence in Harford Co., in his 50th year (*FGBA* 14 Jan 1818; *BPAT* 14 Jan 1818).

Biographical Data from Baltimore Newspapers, 1817-1819

Jones, Rev. Absolom, of the African Episcopal Church of St. Thomas, Philadelphia, d. Fri., in his 72nd year (*BPAT* 17 Feb 1818).

Jones, Awbrey, d. last Sat., in his 58th year, a soldier in the struggle for our independence in 1776 (*BA* 15 June 1818; *BPAT* 15 June 1818). Aubray [sic] Jones died 12 June 1818, aged 60 years, and was buried 13 June 1818 in the Cathedral Cemetery (Grogaard).

Jones, C. L., was m. Mon. eve. by Rev. Mr. Parks, to Miss Ann Johnson (*BA* 3 Sep 1817; *BPAT* 3 Sep 1817).

Jones, Capt. Daniel, of Louisville, KY, was m. last Mon. by Rev. Dr. Inglis, to Miss Mary Jones of this place (*BMC* 14 April 1819).

Jones, David, owes taxes for the year 1815, on 12 a. leased from Caton in the 1st Dist. (*BPAT* 7 Jan 1819).

Jones, Mr. Edgar S., of Philadelphia, d. 26 Sep at Sullivan's Island, near Charleston, in his 22nd year (*BA* 10 Oct 1817; *BPAT* 10 Oct 1817 gives his name as Edward S. Jones).

Jones, Ellis, owes taxes for the years 1814 and 1815, on 161 a. *Plains of Peram* [*Plains of Paran*] in the 6th Dist. (*BPAT* 7 Jan 1819).

Jones, Capt. Jacob, U. S. Navy, was m. at Colchester, Kent Co., on 28th ult. [Sat.], by Rev. Mr. Davis, to Miss Ruth Lusby of Cecil Co. (*BPAT* 14 Sep 1819).

Jones, John, owes taxes for the year 1815, on 7 a. *Harrison* in the 7th Dist. (*BPAT* 7 Jan 1819).

Jones, Capt. John N., was m. last Thurs. eve. by Rev. Bartow, to Miss Mary Ann Eliza Griffen, all of Baltimore (*FGBA* 16 Jan 1819; *BPAT* 16 Jan 1819).

Jones, Lewis, living four doors from the corner of Calvert and Bank Sts., offers a reward for the return of his discharge as a private soldier in the 38th Regt,, U.S. infantry, which he put into the possession of a certain Joseph Cary then residing on Fell's Point. The discharge was signed by Capt. John Rothrock of the said regt. (*BPAT* 28 Jan 1818).

Jones, Mahlon, was m. Thurs. eve. by Rev. Stephen G. Rossell, to Mrs. Ann Marriott, all of Baltimore (*FGBA* 6 Nov 1817; *BPAT* 5 Nov 1817).

Jones, Rasin, advertises he will sell 200 a. of land in Kent Co. near the upper end of Worton; information can be supplied by himself or by Mr. Daniel Jones, 21 Market St., Fells Point, Baltimore (*BPAT* 2 Jan 1819).

Jones, Richard, was m. last Thurs. eve. by Rev. D. E. Reese, to Miss Ann Phelps, both of Baltimore (*BPAT* 4 Jan 1817).

Jones, Col. Roger, of the U. S. Army, and Mary Ann, eldest dau. of William Byrd Page, dec., of Frederick Co., VA, were m. Wed., 2nd Dec, by the Rev. William Meade (*BPAT* 8 Dec 1818).

Jones, Thomas A., merchant, was m. yesterday [Thurs.] by Rev. Hargrove, to Catherine Smith, dau. of George C. Smith, of the House of Frick and Smith (*BA* 30 Oct 1818; *BPAT* 30 Oct 1818).

Jones, William, age 29, born in Amsterdam, a barber, deserted from my Rendezvous, Light St., about 13 Nov last. /s/ James H. Hook, Captain, 3th Infantry (*BPAT* 9 Jan 1818).s

Jones, William, of St. Mary's Co., was m. Tues. eve. by Rev. Rev. Bartow, to Mrs. Margaret White of Baltimore (*BA* 13 Nov 1818; *BPAT* 13 Nov 1818).

Jordan, Mrs. Christiana, d. this morning in her 48th year, leaving five children. Her funeral went from Goodman St., near Hill St., Federal Hill (*FGBA* 25 Jan 1819; *BPAT* 26 Jan 1819).

Jordan, Fred., owes taxes for the year 1817 on 50 a. part of *Wells Manor* in the 1st Dist. (*BPAT* 3 Aug 1819).

Jordan, John, was m. last Mon. by Rev. Valiant, to Miss Elizabeth Keith, all of Baltimore (*FGBA* 3 March 1819; *BPAT* 4 March 1819)

Biographical Data from Baltimore Newspapers, 1817-1819

Joy, Edward, an apprentice to the bell hanging business. ran away from John Allen, 41 North Gay St; he may have gone to sea, or to St. Mary's, Western Shore of Md. A reward of 15 dollars was offered (*BPAT* 17 Aug 1818).

Junge, William H., of Baltimore Co., an insolvent debtor: his creditors will have a first hearing on 2 Aug to nominate some person as a trustee (*BPAT* 10 June 1817).

"K"

Karr, Thomas, apprentice to the bricklaying business, aged 19 years, ran away from Felix Gildea in Paca St. (*BPAT* 28 July 1819).

Kauffman, John, d. last Sat. eve. in his 30th year (*BPAT* 15 July 1818).

Kean, Robert, d. at Philadelphia, on Mon. one day after his 43rd year of age. He was an exile from Ireland, who rendered many services to emigrants from Ireland (*BA* 26 Feb 1818; *BPAT* 25 Feb 1818).

Kearsley, John, Esq., of Shepherdstown, W. Va., d. in Philadelphia, of *cholera morbus;* obit gives details of his illness (*BPAT* 26 July 1819).

Keaver, Samuel, owes taxes for the years 1814 and 1815, on 2 a. part *Orange* in the 4th Dist. (*BPAT* 7 Jan 1819).

Keavin, Samuel, a native of Londonderry, Ireland, and long a resident of Baltimore, d. Tues. morning (*BPAT* 31 March 1819).

Keefer, Jacob, was m. at Hagerstown [date not given] to Miss Jane M. Herberd (*BPAT* 19 June 1819).

Keene, James, Sheriff of Caroline Co., was empowered by an act of the Legislature to complete his collections (*BPAT* 10 Feb 1817).

Keene, Col. Richard, d. 1 Sep at his residence on Long Marsh, E.S.; in the toils of '76 he shared and continued to be esteemed as a genuine lover of Independence (*BPAT* 15 Sep 1819).

Keene, Samuel, of Dorchester Co. was m. last Tues. by Rev. Mr. Whitefield to Miss Elizabeth Roberts of Harford Co. (*BPAT* 26 Dec 1818),

Keener, Christian, was m. last eve. [Tues.] by Rev. Jennings to Miss Mary Clare Brice, eld. dau. of John Brice, Jr., all of Baltimore (*FGBA* 28 Jan 1818; *BPAT* 29 Jan 1818).

Keener, Mr. Jacob, d. Tues. morning, after a severe illness of six days, in his 44th year (*BPAT* 23 Dec 1819). For the will of Jacob Keener, filed in 1820, see BAWB 11:100.

Keener, Melchor, d. 4th inst., in his 34th year (*BPAT* 7 May 1819). He was buried 5 May 1819 from St. Paul's Parish (ReamySP). For the will of Melchor Keener, filed in 1819, see BAWB 10:609.

Keeports, Geo. P. an old officer of the Revolutionary War and resident of Baltimore, d. last Sun., in his 65th year (*BA* 5 Sep 1817; *BPAT* 4 Sep 1817).

Keho, John, was m. to Miss Ann Timon, all of Baltimore on Sat., 24th inst., by Rev. Fenwick (*BA* 27 May 1817).

Keilholtz, John, aged about 16, apprentice to Levin Taylor, wheel-wright on Market St. extended, opposite Mrs. Booth's Gardens, ran away on 29th ult. A reward of six cents was offered (*BPAT* 10 Aug 1818.

Kell, Miss Juliet, second dau. of Thomas Kell, d. Fri., 22nd inst., after a long and painful illness, in her 16th year (*BA* 23 Aug 1817, *BPAT* 23 Aug 1817).

Keller, Rev. Isaac, was m. to Miss Margaret Schnebley, at Hagerstown (*BMC* 17 May 1819).

Kelly, Bartholomew, states his wife has left his bed and board and he will not pay her debts (*BPAT* 14 Oct 1819).

Kelly, James, constable, d. yesterday of a tedious illness. He leaves a wife (*BPAT* 25 Jan 1819). James Kelley, aged c45 years, died of consumption, and was buried 25 Jan

1819 in the Cathedral Cemetery (Grogaard). For the will of James Kelley, filed in 1819, see BAWB 10:563 or 11:1

Kelly, James, d. 4th inst. at York, PA, for 37 years a lawyer and a member of Congress (*BPAT* 15 Feb 1819).

Kelly, James, and Miss Jane Graham, all of Baltimore, were m. Thurs. eve. by Rev. Mr. Duncan (*BPAT* 4 Dec 1819).

Kelmeyer, Dawrence [Lawrence?], owes taxes for the year 1815, on ¾ a. lot on the Turnpike Road in the 1st Dist. (*BPAT* 7 Jan 1819).

Kelsey, Eli, was m. to Miss Sarah Hitchcock, all of Baltimore, last evening [Fri.] by Rev. Valliant (*BPAT* 15 July 1818).

Kennard, Thomas J., of the Eastern Shore, was m. to Miss Mary Ann Tanner of Baltimore, last Thurs. by Rev. Davis (*BA* 19 Dec 1818; *BPAT* 19 Dec 1818).

Kennedy, William, of Baltimore, was granted a discharge as an insolvent debtor (*BPAT* 30 Oct 1817).

Kennier, Frederick R., was m. to Mrs. Frances McKeldin, last Thurs. by Rev. E. J. Reis (*BA* 3 Sep 1818; see Kimmer below).

Kent, Emanuel, d. this morning in his 69th year. Funeral will be from Eutaw St. (*FGBA* 25 May 1818; *BPAT* 25 May 1818). For the will of Emanuel Kent, filed in 1818, see BAWB 10:470.

Kent, Emanuel, was m. to Miss Eliza B. Edwards in Baltimore by Dr. Jennings (*BA* 13 Aug 1818).

Kerns, John, d. Sat evening, in the 56th year of his age (*BPAT* 29 June 1819).

Kerr, Robert, and others of Harford Co.. were the subjects of an Act of the Legislature passed for their benefit (*BPAT* 10 Feb 1817).

Keys, Bayly, was m. to Miss Priscilla Taylor, eld. dau. of Joseph Taylor, all of Baltimore, last eve. by Rev. Dr. Inglis (*FGBA* 2 July 1818).

Keyser, Mrs. Elizabeth, d. last eve. [Wed.] consort of Major George Keyser (*FGBA* 8 Feb 1817).

Keyser, William W., merchant, was m. to Mss Elizabeth Fort of Baltimore Co. last eve. [Thurs.] by Rev. Frey (*FGBA* 10 July 1818).

Kidd, Mrs. Pamela A., wife of Samuel Kidd of Cincinnati, and dau. of the Rev. Mr. Hargrove of Baltimore, d. at the former place on 16th inst., aged 33 (*BA* 26 April 1817; *BPAT* 26 April 1817).

Kidwell, Robert.C., was m. last eve. [Fri.] by the Rev. Mr. Healey, to Mrs. Lucinda Fullington, all of this city (*BPAT* 7 Feb 1817; *BA* 8 Feb 1817).

Kieffer, Rev. Daniel H., was m. to Miss Elizabeth Storm, all of Baltimore, last Thurs. eve. by Rev. Dr. C. L. Becker (*FGBA* 13 April 1818; *BPAT* 11 April 1818).

Kiersted, Mrs. Emily, d. yesterday morning, in her 31st year (*BPAT* 27 Nov 1817).

Kilgour, Charles J., of Rockville, Montgomery Co., was m. to Miss Louisa McIlhenny of VA, in Washington last Tues. (*FGBA* 24 June 1818).

Killmary, Henry, 22 years, born in Ireland, a laborer, deserted from the 5th Regiment, Carlisle Barracks, /s/ James Pratt, Captain of Superintendent Recruiting Services, 5th Regiment (*BPAT* 2 Sep 1817).

Kimmel, Mr. Anthony, Sr., aged 72 years, d. yesterday morning, after a long and painful illness, long a respectable merchant of Baltimore. He resided at 64 Lexington St. (*BA* 17 May 1817; *BPAT* 17 May 1817). For the will of Anthony Kimmel, filed in 1817, see BAWB 10:318.

Kimmer, Mr. Frederick H., painter, was m. to Mrs. Frances M'Keldin [date not given], by Rev. E. J. Reis (*BPAT* 2 Sep 1818; see Kennier above).

King, George Wilson, and Miss Mary Ann Gormely, all of Baltimore, were m last Sat, eve. by Rev. Mr. Birch (*BPAT* 27 Dec 1819).

King, Isaiah, aged about 18, apprentice to the coach-making business, eloped from Wm. Comegys, Coach-Maker, No. 15, Commerce St. a reward of 50 dollars was offered (*BPAT* 26 Nov 1817).

Biographical Data from Baltimore Newspapers, 1817-1819

King, John, was m. to Miss Hester Stouffer, dau. of Henry Stouffer, of Baltimore, on Thurs. eve. by Rev. George Roberts (*FGBA* 4 April 1818; *BPAT* 4 April 1818).

King, John S., of this city, was m. last Thurs. eve. by Rev. Dr. Roberts, to Miss Elizabeth Reinhart of Anne Arundel Co. (*BPAT* 12 July 1817; *BA* 14 July 1817).

King, Joseph, Jr., was m. last Wed. at Friends Meeting House on Lombard St. to Tacy, dau. of Elias Ellicott, all of this city (*BPAT* 23 Dec 1817; *BA* 23 Dec 1817).

King, Josias Wilson, was m. in Washington on Thurs. eve. by Rev. Mr. Addison, to Miss Catherine Whetcroft, both of that city (*BPAT* 24 Feb 1817; *BA* 25 Feb 1817).

King, Upthout, d. [in Somerset Co.?] in his 70th tear (*BPAT* 30 Sep 1819).

King, William, d. 1st inst., leaving a widow and three children (*FGBA* 7 Jan 1817).He was 38 years old and was buried 2 Jan 1817 from St. Paul's Parish (ReamySP). For the will of William King, filed in 1817, see BAWB 10:265.

Kingsmore, Mr. John, was m. last Thurs. eve. by Rev. D. E. Reese to Miss Mary Spear, both of Baltimore Co. (*BPAT* 10 July 1819).

Kirk, Aquila W., of York, PA, was m. to Sarah Needles of Baltimore last Wed. at the Friends Meeting House on Lombard St. (*FGBA* 1 June 1818; *BPAT* 2 June 1818).

Kirk, Samuel, was m. last eve. [Tues.] by Rev. Mr. Kurtz, to Miss Albina Powell, all of Baltimore (*BPAT* 19 March 1817; *BA* 19 March 1817).

Kirke, Mr. Mahlon, was m. by Rev. Glendy on Thurs. eve. to Miss Elizabeth Brown, all of Baltimore (*BAPT* 21 June 1817).

Kirkland, David, was m. to Miss Eliza, dau. of Jacob Workinger, all of Baltimore on Tuesday eve. by Rev. Dashiell (*BMC* 27 May 1819; *BPAT* 26 May 1819).

Kirkland, James, was m. to Miss Eliza Josephine Pilch, both of Baltimore, last Tues. by Rev, Moranville (*FGBA* 10 April 1818).

Kirwain, Capt. Matthias, of Dorchester Co., Eastern Shore of Md., master of the schooner *Sally,* took on board a cargo on the Rappahannock River last 10 Sep., and since then has not been heard from (*BPAT* 16 Oct 1818).

Kline, Mr. Jacob, was m. last Thurs. eve. by Rev. Dr. Baker, to Miss Catherine Hedinger, all of this city (*BPAT* 20 March 1817).

Klocke, Mrs. Engel Christian, born in Gotting, Germany, late a resident of Baltimore. d. last Sat. (*FGBA* 17 Feb 1818; *BPAT* 17 Feb 1818).

Knight, Ignatius, was m. to Miss Eliza Twist, both of Baltimore Co., last Monday by Rev. John Allen (*BA* 4 Sep 1817).

Knox, James, was m. to Miss Sarah Hayes, all of Baltimore, last Sun. by Rev. Dr. Roberts (*BPAT* 22 Dec 1818).

Kohne, H. W., native of Germany, d. 9th inst., in his 24th year. The funeral will be from the house of Mrs. Williams, No. 40, Albemarle St. (*BA* 10 Sep 1817).

Kolb, Miss Rebecca, dau. of George Kolb. Esq., d. in Fredericktown last Tues. morning (*BPAT* 8 Nov 1819).

Kolb, Mrs. Sarah, wife of Michael Kolb, died 18th inst., in Frederick Town (*BMC* 22 May 1819).

Konig, C. S. Esq., has produced an exequator [*sic*] signed by the President of the United States, appointing him Consul of His Majesty, King of the Netherlands for the Port of Baltimore (*BPAT* 24 Dec 1819).

Koons, Jacob, was m. to Mrs. Mary Hammer, both of Baltimore on Sun. eve. by Rev. Force (*BA* 27 Nov 1818; *BPAT* 27 Nov 1818).

Kraft, Christian, an "indebted" [*sic*] German servant man, aged about 27 years, ran away from Leinhart Zigler, butcher, at the corner of Howard and Conway Sts. (*BPAT* 28 May 1817).

Kreps, George, late of Hagerstown, was m. to Miss Evelina Ball, dau. of Capt. William Ball of Winchester, VA, at the latter place (*BPAT* 27 Nov 1818).

Krick, George, 24 years old, born in Hanover, York Co., Pa. a hatter, a recruit of the 5th Regt., deserted from the Barracks on 22 inst. /s/ James Pratt, Capt. Superintending the Recruiting Service, 5th Infantry, Carlisle Barracks (*BPAT* 3 Sep 1817).

Biographical Data from Baltimore Newspapers, 1817-1819

Kuenstler, Mr. A., was m. last Thurs. by Rev. Mr. Davis, to Mrs. Sally Fenner, all of this city (*BPAT* 29 March 1817l *BA* 29 March 1817).

Kuntz, Jacob, dec.: Henry Kuntz, admin., will sell one lot of ground at the corner of Barnet St. and Forrest Lane, and the improvements including two dwelling houses (*BPAT* 6 April 1819).

"L"

Lacey, John, of Georgetown, was m. [date not given] at Rockville, Md., to Miss Emily M. Lodge of the former place (*BPAT* 25 April 1817).

Lacock, Cadet Dryden, of Pittsburgh, d. at the Military Academy in West Point, 15th inst., in his 19th year (*BPAT* 27 Oct 1818).

Lafitte, John, Jr., was m. last Thurs. eve, by Archbishop Marechal, to Miss Theresa Leduc (*BA* 2 Nov 1818).

Lallemand, Gen. Henry, was m. on 28th Oct. by the Rev. Mr. Carr, at the residence of Stephen Girard, Philadelphia, to Miss Harriet Girard, niece of Stephen Girard, Esq. Those in attendance were Messrs. Ct. de Survilliers, Marshal de Grouchy, and son, Generals Vandamme and Charles Lalellmand, Sr., and a large company of the friends and families of the happy couple (*BPAT* 5 Nov 1817; *BA* 6 Nov 1817).

Lambert, J. B., left Baltimore the beginning of last January, leaving a wife and two children. In February he was in Augusta, Savannah, and Charleston Georgia, since which time he has not been hard from. Any information will be gratefully received at the offices of the Baltimore *American* (*BPAT* 12 June 1819).

Lamborn, Daniel, will have his right, title, and interest in a lot of land sold, by virtues of five writs of *fieri fiacas* issued out of Harford Co. Court at the suit of Buckler Bond; Lamborn lives in the said land, which is comprised of parts of the following tracts, part of *Joshua's Meadows*, part of *Joshua's Meadows Enlarged*, part of *Poplar Neck*, and part of *Clacksons Purchase*, cont. 30 a. /s/ Jason Moore, Sheriff (*BPAT* 5 April 1817). Another notice of a trustee's sale was published in Jan 1818 (*BPAT* 15 Jan 1818).

Lambert, J. B., went away from Baltimore in the beginning of last January, leaving a wife and two children. His wife has since died, and the children are very much in want of him. Last February he was in Augusta, Ga., Savannah, and Charleston. Since then he has not been heard from (*BPAT* 11 June 1819).

Lammot, Daniel, Esq., was m. at Philadelphia on Thurs. eve. by Rev. Dr. Janeway, to Miss Ann P., dau. of Robert Smith, all of that city (*BPAT* 4 Dec 1819).

Lammot(te), Mrs. Susan P., d. at Philadelphia, wife of Daniel Lamotte, dau. of Paul Beck, and a mother "The *Philadelphia Gazette*" (*BPAT* 3 JAN 1818, 8 Jan 1818).

Landrom, Moses, owes taxes for the years 1813, 1814, 1815, on 3 a. of *Cubb's Hill* in the 2nd Dist. (*BPAT* 7 Jan 1819).

Lane, John, of Baltimore Co., was m. [date not given] to Mrs. Barbara Fout of Frederick Co. (*BPAT* 11 June 1819).

Lane, Presley Carr, Jr., d. at his father's residence near Shelbyville, Ky., on 1st inst., late of Fairfax Co., Va., in the 23rd year of his age (*BPAT* 31 July 1819).

Lane, Mr. Thomas, d. 1st inst., aged 107. he was born within five miles of the place in which he died—Friendship, Anne Arundel Co. (*BPAT* 30 Dec 1819).

Langley, Hezekiah, of Washington City, was m. at Washington on Mon., 9th inst., by Rev. Mr. Angier to Miss Catherine S. Jameson, dau. of R. Jameson of Charles Co. (*BPAT* 13 March 1818).

Langley, Capt. Philip, was m. Tues., 6th inst. by Rev. Carbury to Miss Mary Thomas, both of St. Mary's Co. (*BPAT* 14 Oct 1818).

Lankford, Jesse, about 19 years old, 5', 5 or 6" tall, light hair, light complexion, and blue eyes, apprentice to the sail-making business, ran away from Thomas Hedrick of Baltimore (*BPAT* 28 May 1819).

Biographical Data from Baltimore Newspapers, 1817-1819

Lansdale, Mary, late of Washington Co., dec.: John Harris, admin., has obtained letters of administration (*BPAT* 15 Sep 1818).

Large, James, of Philadelphia, was m. last Wed. at Friends Mtg. to Miss Elizabeth, dau. of Thomas Poultney of Baltimore (*FGBA* 17 Jan 1817).

Laroque, Francis, was m. last eve. by the Rev. Mr. Hargrove to Mrs. Sophia Le Gendre, all of Baltimore (*BA* 18 March 1817).

Laroque, Mr. J. M., was m. on 23rd inst. by Rev. Babade to Miss Alexandra Leroy (*BA* 29 Dec 1817; *BPAT* 29 Dec 1817).

Lasquar, Mr. John, of Baltimore Co., was m. last Thurs. eve. by the Rev. Mr. Jennings, to Miss Sarah Riston of this city (*BPAT* 11 Oct 1817).

Lastly, John, was m. last Thurs. by Rev. Bartow to Miss Mary Ann Dorman, all of Baltimore (*FGBA* 16 Jan 1819; *BPAT* 16 Jan 1819).

Latimer, James B., of Baltimore, was m. on Tues., [20 May] by Rev. Dr. Inglis to Catherine H., dau. of Major Robert Lyon of Baltimore Co. (*FGBA* 21 May 1817).

Latour, J., of Baltimore Co., is an insolvent debtor; P. A. Guestier has been appointed trustee (*BPAT* 20 Oct 1817). John Latour of France was naturalized 13 May 1806 (Baltimore Co. Naturalization Docket 1:32).

Lawrence, James, was m. on Sun. 23rd inst., to Miss Margaret James, both of Baltimore (*BA* 29 Nov 1817; *BPAT* 29 Nov 1817).

Lawrence, John M., of Baltimore, was m. at Cumberland, Allegany Co., by Rev Sigler to Miss Eliza Pollard of the latter place (*BA* 24 Feb 1817).

Lawrenson, Mrs. Elizabeth, consort of the late Capt. James Lawrenson, d. last Tues., after an illness of six weeks, aged 49 years, leaving three children, two of whom are helpless (*BPAT* 2 Sep 1819).

Lawson, Diana, wife of the late Richard Lawson, d. 19 Nov 1818 (*BA* 24 Nov 1818). Diana Lowson [sic], aged 48 years, was buried 20 Nov 1818 from St. Paul's Parish (ReamySP).

Lawson, Mrs. Elizabeth, d. at Alexandria, after a short illness, in the 85th year of her age (*BPAT* 14 July 1819).

Lawson, Henry, was m. yesterday eve. by Rev. Dr. Glendy, to Miss Isabelle Freeman, all of Baltimore (*FGBA* 7 May 1818; *BPAT* 7 May 1819 gives the groom's name as Henry Lamson [sic]).

Lawson, Robert, and Mrs. Sarah Warner, both of this city, were m. last Thurs., 16th inst. by Rev. John Hargrove (*BPAT* 21 July 1818; *FGBA* 22 July 1818).

Layman, Jacob, and Miss Keturah Moke, both of Baltimore Co., were m. yesterday morning [Mon.] by Rev. Shane (*BPAT* 7 June 1819).

League, Nathaniel, aged 28, a shoemaker, ran away from the detachment under my command at Fort Covington on 3rd March. /s/ Capt. James H. Cook (*BPAT* 13 April 1818).

Leche, David, merchant of Baltimore, and Miss Jane Weakly of York, Pa., were m. at York last Tues. by Rev. Dr. Cathcart (*FGBA* 11 Jan 1819; *BPAT* 12 Jan 1819).

Lecouet, Thomas, of N. Y., was m. [date not given] to Miss Sarah Wonderley of Philadelphia (from the Philadelphia *Union*). (*BPAT* 24 Sep 1819).

Lecoumpt, Philip, formerly an apprentice to William Walker, sail maker, has conducted himself in so unbecoming a manner, that Walker has turned him away, and warns all persons not to trust him (*BPAT* 18 March 1817).

Lee, George S., was m. last Thurs. eve., by Rev. John Glendy, to Miss Mary Jones, all of this city (*BPAT* 29 March 1817; *BA* 29 March 1817).

Lee, Maj. Henry, late of the U. S. Army, was m. at Pope's Creek in Westmoreland Co., VA, to Miss Ann R. McCarty, dau. of Fontaine Maury, Esq., of Fredericksburg (*BPAT* 9 April 1817).

Lee, James H. and Miss Maria Cooke, all of Baltimore, were m. 2 Oct [Fri.] by Rev. Mr. Shane (*FGBA* 19 Oct 1818).

Lee, Mrs. Mary H., aged 30 years, wife of William Lee, Esq., and youngest dau. of the late John Robert Holliday, Esq., of Baltimore Co., d. 10th ult., at the residence of the Hon. Outerbridge Horsey in Wilmington, Del., leaving a husband and five children (*BPAT* 7 Sep 1818).

Lee, Thomas Sim, d. 9th inst., at Needwood, Frederick Co., in his 75th year; he bore a conspicuous part in the struggle for independence, and was the second Governor of Md., succeeding the late Gov. Johnson (*BPAT* 15 Nov 1819).

Lee, Lieut. William Arthur, U.S.N., son of the late Charles Lee of Va., d 9 July at Bladensburg, last Wed. morning, as a result of a duel (*BPAT* 15 July 1817; *FGBA* 14 July 1817).

LeFevre, John Brutus, a native of Havre de Grace, France, and Miss Ann Thompson, a native of the Island of Guernsey, were m. in Baltimore last sat. by Dr. Kemp (*BPAT* 5 Jan 1819).

Legrand, Mrs. Elenor, wife of Capt. Samuel D. Legrand, d. Mon. last in her 37th year, leaving a husband and nine children, the youngest only one hour old (*BPAT* 17 Jan 1818; *FGBA* 16 Jan 1818).

Lehmann, Godfrey Daniel, of the French military service, d. on board the *Regulator en route* from Philadelphia to Boston. He was a native of Cothens near the Rhine and was aged 35 (*BA* 16 June 1817).

Lemmon, Geo., and Miss Margaret Miles, all of Baltimore Co., were m. last eve.[Wed.] by Rev. Mr. Stansbury (*BPAT* 21 Oct 1819).

Lemmon, Moses, owes taxes for the years 1813, 1814, 1815, on 24 a. *Bond's Meadows* in the 6th Dist. (*BPAT* 7 Jan 1819).

Lemmon, Richard, and Miss Sarah Ann Stevenson, eld. dau. of the late Capt. William Stevenson, were m. Thurs. eve. by Rev. George Lemmon (*FGBA* 13 March 1819; *BPAT* 13 March 1819).

Lemmon, Dr. Robert, of Salisbury, Somerset Co., dec.; Richard Lemmon, exec., will settle the estate (*BPAT* 26 Aug 1817).

Lenox, Mr. James, Jr., d. 22nd inst., aged 34 years (*BPAT* 23 July 1818; *BA* 24 July 1818).

Leonard, Mrs. Elizabeth, consort of Mr. Joseph Leonard, d. in Talbot Co. on 28th inst., in the 59th year of her age (*BPAT* 6 Dec 1819).

Leonard, Joseph, and Mrs. Eleanor Reed, all of Baltimore, were m. last Mon. eve. by Rev. Glendy (*BA* 31 Dec 1817; *BPAT* 31 Dec 1817).

Lerew, Abraham, d. yesterday, at 11 o'clock. A funeral procession will be formed at Concordia Lodge (*BPAT* 11 July 1817; *BA* 11 July 1817). James Horton, auctioneer, advertises a sale of household furniture at the deceased's late residence, Eutaw St. between Market and Pratt Sts. In addition to the household goods, an extensive collection of valuable books will be sold, including: 14 vols. of *Encyclopedia*, 8 vols. of *Corey's Atlas*, and Marshall's *Life of Washington* (*BPAT* 24 July 1817).

Lervingston [Livingston?], James, and Miss Elizabeth Proctor, all of Baltimore, were m. last Thurs. eve. by Rev. D. E. Reese (*FGBA* 6 Nov 1818; *BPAT* 5 Nov 1818).

Lester, Thomas, of Baltimore Co., dec.; Achsah Lester and Charles Timanus advertise the sale of a two story frame house on the Baltimore and Frederick Town Turnpike, two miles from the former place near the first toll gate (*BPAT* 8 April 1817).

Lete, Mr., just arrived in this city, informs the public that he mends Hand Organs of every description; persons who would honor him with their custom can inquire of him at Mr. Gerard's, 3 Second St. (*BPAT* 6 Jan 1817).

Levely, George, d. by March 1819, leaving a house and lot at 140 Market St., next door to Littig's Brush Manufactory. The "very valuable" property is being sold by Susannah Louisa Weise, extx. of Augustus Weise, dec. (*BPAT* 10 March 1818).

Levely, Mr. William, d. 17th inst., in his 38th year (*BPAT* 23 July 1818; *FGBA* 23 July 1818).

Levely, Mr. William, of Baltimore, and Mrs. Mary Holtzman of Georgetown, were m. at Washington Thurs., 13th Aug (*BPAT* 20 Aug 1818; *FGBA* 19 Aug 1818; *BA* 20 Aug 1818).

Biographical Data from Baltimore Newspapers, 1817-1819

Levy, Miss Maria, d. 3 Feb., in her 37th year (*FGBA* 6 Feb 1819). Mary Levy, aged 39 [sic] years, was buried 4 Feb 1819 from St. Paul's Parish (ReamySP).

Lewis, Mr. A. J., of Baltimore, was m. at Friendship, Harford Co., on 15th inst., by the Rev. Mr. Stephenson, to Miss Ann Maria Stump (*BPAT* 20 May 1817; *BA* 21 May 1817).

Lewis, Mr. James, was m. by Rev. D. E. Reese on last Sun. eve. to Miss Catherine Jeffery, all of Baltimore (*BPAT* 31 Dec 1818; *BA* 31 Dec 1818).

Lewis, James B., aged about 19 years, an apprentice to the shoemaking business, ran away from William Bandel on Union St., in Old Town. He may have gone to the Eastern Shore, to Centreville, or Chestertown, where he was raised, but he has a grandmother in Georgetown, D.C. (*BPAT* 13 May 1817).

Lewis, Jane, of Irish Town, at the head of Charles St., offers a reward for the recovery of articles stolen from her house including china, a large looking glass, brassware, and a red Cashmere shawl with a black border and Merino Trimming (*BPAT* 5 May 1817).

Lewis, Mr. Simeon H., and Miss Matilda Keys, all of Baltimore, were m. last eve by Rev. D. E Reise (*BPAT* 22 May 1818; *BA* 23 May 1818).

Liddle, Mr. Michael, was m. last Sun. eve. by Rev. Mr. Moranville, to Miss Matilda Myers, dau. of Capt. Nicholas Myers of Baltimore (*BPAT* 14 Oct 1817; *BA* 14 Oct 1817).

Light, Jacob, and Miss Nancy Austin, dau. of Thomas Austin of Sharpsburg, were m. [date not given] at Hagerstown (*BPAT* 16 April 1819).

Lily, James H., and Miss Harriet Rose, were m. in Norfolk, [date not given] "Sweet Couple!" (*BPAT* 1 Dec 1818).

Linderman, John, of Va., was m. Sun. 9th inst., by Rev. John Hagerty, to Miss Sarah Ourstler of Baltimore Co. (*BPAT* 12 Feb 1817; *BA* 12 Feb 1817).

Lindsey, John, d. by May 1818 when Samuel Young, Clerk, advertised that commissioners would meet to establish the division lines between the properties of Elizabeth Lindsey, extx. of John Lindsey, Peter Bond, Elizabeth Edwards, Timothy Richards, Lewis Miller, John Amos, Lambert Thomas, and R. Kenter (*BPAT* 25 May 1818).

Lindsey, Mr. John G., and Miss Mary Barnes, dau. of President Basil Barnes [sic], of Swan-Creek Neck, all of Prince George's Co., were m. 4th inst. [Tues.] (*BPAT* 13 Aug 1818).

Lineberger, Mr. William, of Petersburg, Va,. was m. Tues. eve. by Rev. Dr. Roberts, to Miss Catherine Ann Redman, of this city (*BPAT* 7 Aug 1817; *BA* 7 Aug 1817).

Ling, Joseph, and Miss Mary Goodall, all of Baltimore, were m. last Monday morning by Rev. Bartow (*FGBA* 21 July 1819).

Linvill, Mr. James, d. Sat, evening last, after a short illness, aged 25 years (*BPAT* 18 Feb 1817; *BA* 18 Feb 1817).

Lipscomb, Mr. Overton P., of Richmond, was m. last Tues. eve. in Washington City, by Rev. Mr. Matthews, to Miss Mary Ann Dillon, of the former place (*BPAT* 21 Feb 1817).

Little, Charles, sailed from the port of Baltimore last summer with the intention of coming to Philadelphia, since which time his friends have had not intelligence of him. Any information will be thankfully received by his wife at 163 Chestnut St., Philadelphia (*BPAT* 17 Aug 1819).

Little, Capt. George, and Miss Ann T. Jacquett, both of Baltimore, were m. last Thurs. eve. by Rev. Davis (*BPAT* 8 Aug 1818; *BA* 10 Aug 1818).

Little, Mrs. Hannah, a member of the Society of Friends, d. yesterday morning, in her 60th year. The funeral will be from the dwelling house of Jesse Talbot, in Fayette St. (*BPAT* 7 Nov 1817; *BA* 7 Nov 1817).

Little, James, was m. last Thurs. eve. by Rev. Mr. Wells, to Miss Catherine Wallace, both of this city (*BPAT* 6 Jan 1817; *FGBA* 7 Jan 1817 gives the bride's name as Catherine Woller).

Biographical Data from Baltimore Newspapers, 1817-1819

Little, Capt. Thomas, a native of Philadelphia, d. at sea on board his Schooner *Freemason*, after an illness of six days (*BPAT* 20 June 1817).

Little, William, and Miss Dorcas Fennell, all of Baltimore, were m. last Tues. by Rev. Fennell (*FGBA* 14 April 1818).

Littleton, Thomas, of Ohio, was m. Sun. eve. by Rev. Dr. Jennings, to Mrs. Elizabeth Dillon of Baltimore Co. (*BPAT* 6 Sep 1819)

Logan, Neal, d. yesterday, 22nd Oct. in his 49th year. His funeral will be this afternoon from his late dwelling in Mill St., near the jail (*BPAT* 23 Oct 1818; *FGBA* 23 Oct 1818).

Logan, Miss Sarah, dau. of the late David Logan of Huntingdon Twp., Pa., d. Mon., 25th Dec., in her 24th year "Greensburgh (Penna.) 25 Jan" (*FGBA* 18 Feb 1817).

Logan, William, of Carlisle, Pa., and Miss Caroline Henry, of Baltimore,. were m. at Cincinnati on Christmas Eve. by Rev. Trueman Bishop (*FGBA* 12 Feb 1819).

Lohr, Mrs., d. Fri., 9th ult., in Rockingham Co., Va., aged 103 years (*BPAT* 9 Oct 1818).

Long, Archibald, and Miss Juliana Hunt, all of Baltimore, were m. last eve. [Thurs.] by Rev. Dr. Roberts (*BPAT* 19 Nov 1819).

Long, Samuel, d. this morning in his 45th year; funeral from his late residence, Bridge St., O. T. (*FGBA* 29 Jan 1817). For the will of Samuel Long, filed in 1817, see BAWB 10:279.

Loose, John, owes taxes for the years 1813, 1814, 1815, on 22 a. *Peace and Good Neighborhood* in the 1st Dist. (*BPAT* 7 Jan 1819).

Lord, Mr. Joseph L., was m. last Sun. eve. to Mrs. Fanny Douglass, both of Baltimore (*BPAT* 1 April 1818).

Lough, John, aged 38, of the firm of Lough and McKee of Baltimore, a native of Ireland, d. [date not given]. He had been in Baltimore for only a year (*FGBA* 23 Aug 1819; *BPAT* 23 Aug 1819).).

Love, Dr. John, was m. on Thurs. last by Rev. Dr. Fenwick to Mrs. Ann Legg, all of Baltimore (*BPAT* 22 Nov 1819).

Lovering, Francis, dec.; John Wane and Geo. Elliott, administrators, will sell a neat two-story dwelling, located on Duke St., on a lot 20' by 100' (*BPAT* 31 Dec 1818).

Low, Mrs. Rebecca, consort of Mr. H. P. Low, d. Thurs., 4th inst., in her 31st year, leaving a husband and six small children (*BPAT* 6 June 1818; *BA* 6 June 1818). Her death was recorded in the class lists of the Baltimore City Station of the Methodist Church (PedenM)

Lowe, Master James, son of the late John Lowe, d. at Easton, Md. (*BPAT* 5 July 1819).

Lowry, James, d. at Port Deposit on Sunday, 14th inst., after a severe illness; he was a husband and father (*BPAT* 1 Jan 1818).

Lowry, Robert, Esq., was m. to Miss Elizabeth S. Armistead, both of Elizabeth City Co., VA (*BPAT* 5 May 1817).

Lucas, Rev. Thomas, d. 11 Jan. in Baltimore Co., in his [86th?] year; for many years he was an itinerant preacher of the M. E. Church (*FGBA* 12 Jan 1819; *BPAT* 13 Jan 1819). (For the will of Thomas Lucas, filed in 1819, see BAWB 11:63)

Luneberg, John, d. yesterday, in his 45th year (*BA* 6 Aug 1817).

Lunlay, Mr. John, of Doylestown Twp., Pa., aged 67 years, was m. [date not given] to Miss Elizabeth Care, aged 64, of Philadelphia . This couple had courted 45 years ago, but something intervened and they were separated for 39 years (*BPAT* 26 Nov 1819).

Lyles, David C., and Miss Juliet Ann Dunbar? [Dunlap?], were m. last Tues. eve,. by Rev. Roberts (*BA* 11 Dec 1817; *BPAT* 11 Dec 1817).

Lyeth, Samuel, Sr., d. yesterday, in his 72nd year, after an illness of three days, caused by a paralytic stroke, an old inhabitant of Baltimore (*BPAT* 7 April 1817; *BA* 7 April 1817). For the will of Samuel Lyeth, filed in 1817, see BAWB 10"309)

Lynch, James, aged about 18, an apprentice to the coopering business, ran away from Morris Leahy (*BPAT* 13 May 1817).

Lynch, Mr. Thomas, was m. last eve. by Rev. Dr. Roberts, to Miss Mary B. Moore, dau. of the Rev. Mr. Moore, all of this city (*BPAT* 28 March 1817).

Lyon, Rev. Mr. [-?-], was last Sun. by the Rev. Mr. Parks, to Mrs. Ann Linch, both of this city (*BPAT* 17 June 1817, *BA* 17 June 1817).

Lyon, Mrs. Mary, d. in Baltimore, in her 56th year, consort of the late John Lyon; funeral from her late dwelling in Concord St. (*BPAT* 8 July 1818; *BA* 8 July 1818).

Lyon, Stephen, was m. 1st inst., in S. C., to Miss Rebecca Lamb (*BPAT* 12 Feb 1817).

Lyons, Mrs. Mary, d. at the residence of her dau. in Talbot Co., on the 9th inst., in her 63rd year (*BPAT* 12 or 21 Sep 1819).

Lysles [Lyles], Mr. Dennis, of Prince George's Co., was m. to Miss Elzie W. Seaton of Alexandria (*BPAT* 17 Nov 1817).

Lytle, Mr. Thomas, of Baltimore Co., was m. last Thurs. eve. by Rev. Mr. Roszel, to Miss Charity McComas of Baltimore (*BPAT* 26 April 1817; *BA* 26 April 1817).

Lyvet, Louis Hyppolite, was m. last eve. by Rev. Mr. Hargrove, to Miss Amelia Deschamps, all of this city (*BPAT* 28 March 1817; *BA* 28 March 1817).

"M"

McAllister, Richard, was m. Mon., 16th inst., to Miss Jane Barry, dau. of Col. Standish Barry, all of Baltimore (*FGBA* 18 Aug 1819; *BPAT* 18 Aug 1819).

M'Arthur, Mr. Arthur, of Philadelphia, d. in Baltimore on Monday, after a short illness, which he attributed to sleeping in a damp bed (*BA* 12 June 1817; *BPAT* 11 June 1817).

M'Caffer, John, of Baltimore, d. yesterday aged 55. He resided at High and French Sts. (*BA* 2 Jan 1818).

Macarty, Charles, cooper, formerly of Philadelphia, d. at New Orleans (*BPAT* 17 Nov 1819).

M'Carty. George, 24 years of age, born in Old Chester, Pa/. deserted July 1817 from Super'g recruiting service, for 5th Regt. Infantry, Carlisle Barracks. /s/ M. Marston, Major (*BPAT* 2 Aug 1817).

M'Cawley, Samuel, aged about 20, ran away from the Clifton Factory, St. Mary's Co., on 18 March 1817. He may go to Baltimore, where he had worked, or to Connellsville, Fayette Co., Pa., where he has an acquaintance named George Stacey, a fuller. /s/ Peter Gough & Co. (*BPAT* 11 April 1817).

McCleary, Mr. Henry, d. in Fredericktown in the 78th year of his age (*BPAT* 29 Nov 1819).

McCleish, Archibald, of Alexandria, was m. last Thurs. by Rev. Bartow, to Miss Catherine Green, of Baltimore (*FGBA* 13 March 1819; *BPAT* 13 March 1819).

McClish, Mr. William, of Baltimore, was m. at Washington, by Rev. Amery, to Mrs. Elizabeth Osburn of that place (*BPAT* 1 June 1819).

McColley, Zedekiah Fletcher, d. 22nd inst., aged 11 years and nine mos., of an inflammation of the brain occasioned by *bathing in cold water while in a state of perspiration* (*BPAT* 5 July 1829).

McCombs, John, owes taxes for the years 1813, 1814, 1815, on 1 lot of Rogers' land in the 1st Dist. (*BPAT* 1 Jan 1819).

McConkey, William, of James, was m. last Tues. by Rev. Mr. Waugh, to Miss Tabitha Morsel, all of Baltimore (*BA* 26 Nov 1818; *BPAT* 26 Nov 1818).

McConnell, Mrs. Priscilla, dec.; her personal property will be sold by order of the Honorable Orphans' Court of Baltimore Co. (*BPAT* 8 Dec 1819).

McCorkhill, James Douglas, age 28 years, born in Chester, Pa., deserted July 1817 from Super'g recruiting service, for 5th Regt. Infantry, Carlisle Barracks. /s/ M. Marston, Major (*BPAT* 2 Aug 1817).

McCormick, James, was m. last Tues. by Rev. Dr. Glendy, to Miss Margaret H. Cross, both of Baltimore (*FGBA* 23 July 1819; *BPAT* 23 July 1819).

Biographical Data from Baltimore Newspapers, 1817-1819

McCormick, Mrs. Jane, aged 56, relict of the late James McCormick, d. 19th inst., at her late residence near Baltimore (*BPAT* 24 July 1818).

McCormick, William, stone-cutter, died. His property, which had been conveyed by the late John O'Donnell to Christian Kraus, is to be sold. It consists of a lot on South Frederick St., improved by a two-story frame house, with a two story brick back building, with a hydrant of water in the yard (*BPAT* 12 May 1818).

McCornisky, Mary, owes taxes for the years 1813, 1814, 1815, on 100 a. *Bosley's Enclosure* in the 3rd Dist. (*BPAT* 1 Jan 1819).

McCoy, Henry, d. at Elk Ridge on 3 Oct. in his 54th year (*BPAT* 6 Oct 1817; *BA* 7 Oct 1817). Joseph A. Wallace, admin., will settle the estate (*BPAT* 29 Nov 1817). A later notice advertised the sale of a number of servants (*BPAT* 25 Feb 1818). Henry McCoy, born 23 Sep 1761, died 3 Oct 1817, is buried in Lot # 75 Westminster Presbyterian Churchyard, Baltimore (HaywardW).

McCoy, Isaac, merchant, d. last Thurs., after a severe illness, in his 27th year (*BPAT* 8 Nov 1819).

McCoy, James, of Baltimore, and Miss Eliza Waters of Philadelphia, were m. last Thurs. eve. by Rev. Dr. Roberts (*BPAT* 6 Dec 1819).

M'Coy, Capt. John, was m. last Sun. eve. by Rev. Mr. Rev. Bartow, to Miss Jane [Wescote?]. all of Baltimore (*BPAT* 2 Dec 1819_.

McCristle, Mrs. Mary, wife of John McCristle, d. yesterday, aged 32 years. She resided at George St., Fells Point (*BPAT* 8 May 1819).

McCubbin, William, aged 19, son of Moses McCubbin, of Baltimore, was murdered (*BA* 27 Oct 1817). His father, Moses McCubbin offers a reward for the apprehension and conviction of the murderer (*BPAT* 4 Nov 1817).

McCubbin, William H., owes taxes for the years 1814, 1815, on Land Office Return in the 4th Dist. (*BPAT* 1 Jan 1819).

McCulloh, Dr. James H., was m. Tues. eve. by the Rev. Mr. Wyatt, to Susan W. Latimer, of Baltimore (*FGBA* 31 Dec 1818; *BA* 1 Jan 1819; *BPAT* 1 Jan 1819).

M'Daniel, Walter, was m. in Washington, to Miss Sarah Cannon (*BPAT* 11 Feb 1817).

McDonald, Eliza, aged 16, threw herself into the North River, near Duane St. The inquest was held yesterday (*BA* 17 April 1818).

M'Donald, Isabella, d. yesterday in her 22nd year. Her funeral was from her father's residence, corner of Ann and Albemarle Sts. (*FGBA* 16 Jan 1818). Lines on her death were published (*BPAT* 17 Jan 1818).

McDonaugh, John, of Baltimore Co., is an insolvent debtor (*BPAT* 14 Oct 1819).

M'Dougal. James, a native of Scotland, arrived in this country some time ago. He will hear of something to his advantage by writing to F. S., head of Bond St., Fell's Point (*BPAT* 8 April 1818).

McElderry, Mrs. Elizabeth, d. 20th int., in her 50th year, consort of the late Thomas McElderry, after a long and painful illness (*BPAT* 23 Oct 1819). For the will of Elizabeth McElderry, filed in 1819, see BAWB 11:61.

McElderry, Mr. James, of Baltimore, d. 31st ult., at the Sweet Springs, of a decline, in the 19th year of his age (*BPAT* 13 Sep 1819).

M'Entire, John, was m. last Tues. eve. by Rev. Mr. Davis to Jane Ligget, both of Baltimore (*BPAT* 23 Sep 1818; *BA* 24 Sep 1818).

M'Fadden, Capt. James, d. last Fri. in his 28th year [long obit] (*BA* 29 Aug 1817; *BPAT* 28 Aug 1817).

M'Fadon, Mrs. Ann, consort of William M'Fadon, d. (*BPAT* 3 April 1819).

McFadon, Edward, was m. last Thurs. by Rev. Valiant to Miss Elizabeth Pilchard, all of Baltimore (*FGBA* 30 Nov 1818; *BPAT* 27 Nov 1818).

M'Fadon, Samuel, of Chester Co., PA, was m. Thurs. by Rev. Duncan to Miss Eliza King of Philadelphia (*BA* 23 May 1818; *BPAT* 23 May 1818).

M'Farland, Francis Frederick, the celebrated Hibernian vocalist and member of the Philadelphia Theatre, d. at Philadelphia on 24th Feb (*FGBA* 26 Feb 1819; *BPAT* 26 Feb 1819).

Biographical Data from Baltimore Newspapers, 1817-1819

M'Farland, John, a resident of Baltimore, d. at his brother's residence near Pittsburgh, aged about 43 years (*BA* 27 April 1818; *BPAT* 27 April 1818).

M'Ferlan (McFerran?) John, Jr., of Baltimore, was m. last Thurs. by Rev. William Paxton to Miss Eliza W. Moore of Adams Co., PA (*BA* 11 June 1817; *BPAT* 11 June 1817).

McGay, John, of Baltimore Co., will have an Act of the Legislature for his benefit (*BPAT* 10 Feb 1817).

M'Gowan, Lieut. James, of the U.S. Navy, was m. Mon. eve. by Rev. Roberts, to Miss Eliza Brown, dau. of Mr. J. Brown of Baltimore (*BPAT* 21 March 1817).

McHaffie, Mr. James, late postmaster and President of the Bank of Westminster, d. 3rd inst., in Frederick Co. in his 39th year (*BA* 10 Jan 1818; *BPAT* 2 Jan 1818).

McHenry, Dennis, has had Charles S. Sewell appointed trustee of his personal estate for the use of his creditors (*BPAT* 9 Nov 1818).

McHenry, Francis D., Esq. of Baltimore was m. last Thurs. eve. at Willow Cottage by the Rev. Mr. Duncan to Miss Milcah Owings, dau. of the late Caleb Owings (*BPAT* 22 Nov 1817; *BA* 22 Nov 1817).

M'Intosh, Mr. Samuel, d. yesterday morning, formerly a merchant of Cadiz, but for the last ten years a resident of Baltimore (*BPAT* 22 Sep 1819).

M'Kay, Mr. Benjamin, was m. 21st inst., [Thurs.] by the Rev. Rev. Bartow, to Miss Susan [Rine?], both of Alexandria, D.C. (*BPAT* 23 Aug 1817).

McKean, Samuel M., was m. at Washington, [Tues.] 19 May by Rev. Hawley to Miss Mary Frances King, dau. of Josias W. King of the latter city (*BA* 22 May 1818).

M'Kean, Miss Sophia Dorothea, d. at Philadelphia, early last Mon. morning, youngest dau. of the late Gov. Thomas M'Kean (*BPAT* 31 Dec 1819).

McKean, Thomas, Gov. of PA, and Chief Justice of Pa., d. 24 June at Philadelphia (*BA* 27 June 1817. He had been a member of Congress from Del. from 1774 to 1790 (*BPAT* 27 June 1817).

M'Kee, Cornelius, was m. Thurs. eve. by Rev. Mr. Fenwick, to Miss Mary Hanley, all of Baltimore (*BPAT* 10 Nov 1817; *BA* 10 Nov 1817).

McKenzie, Edward K., a journeyman pressman, ran away from William Hamilton of Lancaster, Pa., without paying his debts; he may intend to join the sea service (*BPAT* 25 June 1817).

McKim, John, merchant, an aged and respectable inhabitant of Baltimore, a member of the Society of Friends, d. 1 May 1819. His funeral took place from his late dwelling on the York Road (*BPAT* 3 May 1819; *FGBA* 4 May 1819). For the will of John McKim, filed in 1819, see BAWB 10:606.

McKim, Robert, an aged inhabitant of Baltimore, d. last Thurs. eve. (*FGBA* 16 Jan 1819). For the will of Robert McKim, filed in 1819, see BAWB 10:563.

McKinley, John, late a captain in the U.S. Army, was killed in Baltimore on 22 July by lightning. He was a merchant in New York, and was in his 43rd year. He left children (*BA* 14 July 1817; *BPAT* 24 July 1817). John McKinley, a native of Ireland, d. 22 July 1817, aged c. 43 years, killed by a sudden streak of lightning. He was buried 23 July 1817 in the Cathedral Cemetery (Grogaard).

McKowan, James B. was m. to Miss Bathia P. Donaldson last Thurs. eve, by Rev. Dr. Jennings; they were both of Baltimore (*FGBA* 13 Dec 1817; *BPAT* 13 Dec 1817).

M'Lanahan, James J., of New Orleans, was m. last eve, [Wed.] to Miss Eliza Tennant, dau. of Col. Tenant of this city, by Bishop Kemp (*BPAT* 10 Sep 1818).

McLaughlin, Mrs. Mary, consort of Peter McLaughlin, of Baltimore, d. Fri., 3rd inst., in her 26th year, leaving a husband and two children (*FGBA* 7 April 1818; *BPAT* 7 April 1818). Mary McLaughlin, aged 25 years, died 3 April 1818 in childbirth. She was buried 4 April 1818 in the Cathedral Cemetery (Grogaard).

McLean, Adam, of Baltimore Co., dec.; Demarius McLean and John McLean, administrators, will sell a lot of ground facing 27 feet on the west side of South St., with three two-story brick houses, next 3 Dec (*BPAT* 24 Nov 1818).

Biographical Data from Baltimore Newspapers, 1817-1819

McMackin, Silas, aged about 16, indented apprentice to the copper-smith business, ran away from Hugh Bonner (*BPAT* 10 June 1817).

M'Nantz, Miss Emily, third dau. of the late Charles M'Nantz of Washington City, d. at the Ladies' Seminary in Georgetown last Sun. morning, after a long protracted illness, in the 14th year of her age (*BPAT* 2 Dec 1819).

McNeal, John, and Miss Mary K. Allan, all of Baltimore were m. last Tues. eve. by Rev. Bartow (*FGBA* 25 June 1819; *BPAT* 24 June 1819).

McNulty, John, d. 21 Dec 1818 in his 46th year (*BA* 22 Dec 1818; *BPAT* 22 Dec 1818). John McNulty, aged 45, d. 20 Dec 1818 of consumption. He was buried 21 Dec 1818 in the Cathedral Cemetery (Grogaard).

M'Pherson, John, of Baltimore Co., was m. last Thurs. eve. by the Rev. Mr. Duncan, to Miss Mary Waters (*BPAT* 18 Oct 1817; *BA* 18 Oct 1817).

McReding, Mrs. Margaret, wife of Edward McReding, and dau. of Mr. Anthony Otheman, of Boston, d. in this city, aged 22 years (*BPAT* 6 March 1817).

M'Remick, Mr. J. O., formerly of Mass., d. in Frederick Town, aged 25 years (*BPAT* 13 April 1818).

Mace, Dr. Charles R., of Baltimore Co., was m. to Miss Sophia C., dau. of Hezekiah and granddau., of Col. William Viers of Montgomery Co., on Thurs., 22nd, inst., by Rev. Healey Viers (*BA* 24 May 1817; *BPAT* 24 May 1818).

MacGill, Mr. Thomas, was m. last Tues. eve. by the Right Rev. Bishop Kemp, to Miss Elizabeth Simmonds, all of Baltimore (*BPAT* 27 Feb 1817).

Mackelfresh, John, merchant, d. Fri., 9th inst., at Reisterstown in his 50th years (*BA* 13 Jan 1818).

Mackenheimer, John, Jr., was m. last Thurs, by Rev. Glendy to Miss Jane Crozier (*FGBA* 14 Sep 1818; *BPAT* 14 Sep 1818).

Mackey, Benjamin, was m. last Wed. by Rev. Bartow to Miss Susan Rinker (*BA* 26 Aug 1817).

Mackey, Mr. John, Jr., was m. Mon. eve. last, by Rev. Mr. Whitfield, to Miss Ann M'Henry, both of Baltimore (*BPAT* 1 July 1819).

Maddigan (Maddigain), Paul, who resided at Pratt near Commerce Sts., d. yesterday morning, aged 39 years, after a tedious illness (*BA* 20 Feb 1818; *BPAT* 20 Feb 1818).

Madelaine, Mrs. Mary, d. Tues., aged 65 years "Philadelphia, 20 March" (*FGBA* 21 March 1817).

Magers, William, 26 years of age, born in Baltimore, Md., deserted July 1817 from the Super's recruiting service, for 5th Regt. Infantry, Carlisle Barracks. /s/ M. Marston, Major (*BPAT* 2 Aug 1817).

Magill, Basil, of Baltimore, was m. to Miss Amelia D. Griffith, of Montgomery Co. on Thurs., 25th inst. in the latter place by Rev. Mr. Wheaton (*FGBA* 28 March 1819; *BPAT* 29 March 1819).

Magill, Mrs. Christiana, wife of Samuel Magill, d. 31st ult., in Cumberland, Allegany Co., after a painful illness (*BPAT* 12 Jan 1818).

Magill, Thomas, Jr., was m. to Miss Elizabeth Simmonds, all of Baltimore, last Tues. by Bishop Kemp (*FGBA* 27 Feb 1817).

Magness, Mr. James M., and Miss Elizabeth Sheridan, both of Harford Co., were m. last Wed. by Rev. D. E. Reese (*BPAT* 4 Oct 1819).

Magnien, Col. Bernard, a distinguished officer of the Revolutionary army, d. at Portsmouth, Va. (*BPAT* 9 Nov 1819).

Magruder, Dennis, Esq., was m. Sun. eve., 5th inst., by Rev. Mr. Kohlman, to Miss Frances Fitzgerald, both of Prince George's Co. (*BPAT* 10 Oct 1817).

Magruder, Mrs. Frances, d. 1st inst. in Prince George's Co. (*BPAT* 15 Jan 1819).

Magruder, Henry W., was m. to Miss Susan Guttry, all of Baltimore, last Tues. eve. by Rev. Wyatt (*BA* 22 Oct 1818; *BPAT* 22 Oct 1818).

Magruder, John M., of Calvert Co., d. 1st inst., as a result of a stab with a dirk given by Michael Taney, Sr. (*FGBA* 14 July 1819; *BPAT* 14 July 1819).

Biographical Data from Baltimore Newspapers, 1817-1819

Magruder, Thomas W., U.S.N., d. Wed., 16th inst., in his 27th year, at his father's residence in S. Charles St. (*FGBA* 17 April 1817).

Mahanna, Thomas, 19 year old apprentice to the block making business, ran away from Anthony Helmling whose shop was at the head of the Bason [Basin] (*BPAT* 6 Jan 1817).

Maitland, Alexander, d., aged about 24 years, lately from New York, a native of Scotland (*BPAT* 15 Oct 1819),

Mallory, Carlos L. a native of Woodbury, Litchfield Co., Conn., then resident with David Woodward of that place, as an apprentice to the tanning, currying and shoemaking business, left his home in 1814, and has not been heard of since. If now living, he would be 24 years old. Anyone with information should contact Mr. Nathaniel F. Mallory, Newtown, Fairfield Co., Conn. (*BPAT* 11 Jan 1819).

Mallory, Capt. John, was m. Thurs. eve. by the Rev. Mr. Rev. Bartow, to Miss Elizabeth Lockerman, all of this city (*BPAT* 26 July 1817; *BA* 26 July 1817).

Mangels, John, was m. to Miss Catherine Schianeman, both of Baltimore, on Thurs. eve. by Rev. Davis (*FGBA* 17 Jan 1818).

Manigault, Major G. H., of the U. S. Army, was m. at Charleston, to Miss Ann Heyward, all of that city (*BPAT* 19 April 1817).

Mann, Mrs. Catherine, consort of James Mann, and dau. of Mr. Zachariah Keene of Baltimore, d. Wed., 21st inst., in her 21st year (*FGBA* 6 March 1818; *BPAT* 5 March 1818). Catherine Mann, aged 21 years, was buried 4 March 1818 from St. Paul's Parish (ReamySP).

Mannery, Mr. was m. at Alexandria, [date not given], to Mrs. Mary Dixon, both of that place (*BPAT* 19 June 1819_.

Manning, Mr. Dennis, was m. last Thurs. by Rev. John Glendy, to Miss Margaret Rider (*BPAT* 17 April 1817; *BA* 15 April 1817).

Maranna, Thomas, aged 19 last Aug., almost five-feet-four inches tall, apprentice to the block making business, ran away from Anthony Helmling (*BPAT* 6 Jan 1817).

Marcher, George H., was m. to Miss Elizabeth Wilson, all of Baltimore, last Thurs. eve. by Rev. Richards (*FGBA* 12 June 1819; *BPAT* 12 June 1819).

Marean, Thomas, of Baltimore, is an insolvent debtor (*BPAT* 19 Oct 1819).

Maris, George, was m. to Mrs. Mary Dagan, all of Baltimore, on Tues. eve,. by Rev. Mr. Henshaw (*BA* 28 Aug 1818; *BPAT* 27 Aug 1818).

Markland, Mr. James, was m. last Thurs. eve. by the Rev. Mr. Rossell, to Miss Ann Mosher, both of Baltimore (*BPAT* 13 June 1817; *BA* 13 June 1817).).

Marr, William, owes taxes for the year 1815, on a Lot from Twist in the 1st Dist. (*BPAT* 1 Jan 1819).

Marrast, Dr. John, was m. Wed. night, 14th inst., by the Rev. Stephen G. Rozzel to Miss Ann Jennings, dau. of Dr. Samuel K. Jennings, all of Baltimore (*BPAT* 16 May 1817; *FGBA* 15 May 1817).

Marriott, Joshua, of Thomas, and Miss Henrietta Warfield, of Anne Arundel Co., were m. last Thurs. by Dr. Roberts (*BPAT* 2 May 1818).

Marriott, Lemuel H., and Miss Ann Catherine Hyde, were m. by Rev. D. E. Reese on Thurs. eve. (*BPAT* 4 Dec 1819).

Marrow, Mr. Isaac, and Miss Margaret F. Wheelwright, both of Boston were m. last eve. [Sun.] by Rev. Robbins (*BPAT* 29 Dec 1817).

Marsh, G., of Baltimore, drowned on the outward passage (*BPAT* 20 April 1819).

Marshall, John, and Mrs. Tracy Fro. [or Tebo], both of Baltimore, were m. last Thurs. by Rev. Bartow (*BA* 10 Oct 1818; *BPAT* 10 Oct 1818).

Marshall, Dr. William, of Prince George's Co. was m. at Alexandria to Mrs. Eleanor Benson of Charles Co. (*BPAT* 19 Nov 1817).

Martin, Jacob, was m. at Hagerstown, [date not given], to Miss Barbary Negley (*BPAT* 27 Nov 1819).

Biographical Data from Baltimore Newspapers, 1817-1819

Martin, James, was m. last Thurs. eve. by Rev. Mr. Duncan to Miss Delia Walter, both of Baltimore (*BPAT* 7 Oct 1817; *FGBA* 6 Oct 1817 gives the bride's name as Delia Wattles).

Martin, Simeon, of Providence, has died. His ship *George Washington,* will be sold at the auction rooms of Van Wyck & Morgan (*BPAT* 8 Nov 1819).

Martin, Mr. Thomas, was m. last Thurs. eve. by the Rev. Mr. Roberts to Miss Ann Rice, both of this city (*BPAT* 3 Sep 1817).

Mask, Isaac Green, aged between 16 and 17, apprentice boy to the tailoring business, ran away from William Lusby, 100½ Market St. The following papers are asked to publish the notice four times and send their bills to the subscriber: *National Intelligencer, Alexandria Herald, Fredericktown Examiner, Hagerstown Gazette, Lancaster Journal, York Gazette, and Democratic Press,* Philadelphia (*BPAT* 7 April 1818).

Mason, Gen Armistead T., was m. at Dr. Charles Cocke's in Albemarle (Va.), to Miss Charlotte Eliza Taylor, youngest dau. of the late John Taylor, Esq., of Southampton (*BPAT* 10 May 1817).

Mason, Gen. Armistead T., of Loudon Co., Va., was killed in a duel near Bladensburg, on Sat. morning. He was 33 years old. He had been a Representative from Va. in the Senate of the U.S. He leaves a mother, wife and child (*BPAT* 8 Feb 1819).

Mason, George, Jr., owes taxes for the year 1815, on a transfer of land in the 1sr Dist. (*BPAT* 1 Jan 1819).

Mason, Joseph, a student of medicine, d. in Queen Anne's Co., Md., after a short illness (*BPAT* 30 Aug 1819).

Mason, Thomson, of Loudon Co., VA, and Miss Ann, dau. of William Thomas of St. Mary's Co., MD, were m. [date not given] at Brentfield, Charles Co. (*BPAT* 25 Nov 1818).

Massey, Miss Elizabeth H., dau. of the late Joseph Massey of Baltimore, d. 14th inst., in her 23rd year (*BPAT* 19 Nov 1819). Eliz. H. Massey, aged 22 years, was buried 15 Nov 1819 from St. Paul's Parish (ReamySP).

Matthews, Mr. Leonard, was m. last eve.[Mon.] by Rev. E. J. Reis to Miss Jane Wilson Levering, all of Baltimore (*BPAT* 21 Oct 1817; *BA* 30 Oct 1817).

Matthes, Priscilla, d. in Somerset Co. on the 14th inst., in the [96th?] year of her age (*BPAT* 30 Sep 1819).

Matthews, Samuel P., and Miss Anne Maria Camper, all of Baltimore, were m. last eve. [Tues.] by Rev. Valiant (*BA* 21 Oct 1818; *BPAT* 21 Oct 1818).

Matthews. Mrs. Sarah, wife of John Matthews, a native of Belfast. Ireland, d. last Thurs. eve. in her 31st year, of lingering consumption. She leaves a husband and five children (*BPAT* 6 July 1818).

Matthews, William, and Miss Emily Rose, were m. last Thurs. by Rev. Force (*FGBA* 29 March 1819; *BPAT* 29 March 1819).

Matthews, Mr. William, Esq., d. this morning, long a respectable merchant of Baltimore (*BPAT* 23 Nov 1819). William Matthews, b. March 1753, d. 25 Nov 1819, merchant, is buried in Lot # 89, in the Westminster Presbyterian Churchyard, Baltimore (HaywardW). For the will of William Matthews, filed in 1819, see BAWB 11:76, 78.

Mattison, Daniel Jones, aged 11, youngest son of Mrs. S. Mattison, d. Sunday, 17th inst. (*BA* 25 Aug 1817).

Mattison, James, aged 18, eldest son of Mrs. Sarah Mattison, of Baltimore, d. 14th July on his passage from West Indies to Baltimore (*BA* 25 Aug 1817).

Mattison, William, aged 18, d. at Hospital, and was buried 2 Sep 1819 (*FGBA* 3 sep 1819).

Maund, Mrs. Harriet Lucy, d. 6th inst. at her residence, Nominy Hall, Westmoreland Co, Va., in the 32nd year of her age (*BPAT* 13 Sep 1819).

Maund, John J., d. 6th Sep in Westmoreland Co., Va., in his 26th year (*FGBA* 14 Sep 1818; *BPAT* 18 Aug 1818).

Biographical Data from Baltimore Newspapers, 1817-1819

Maund, Miss Julia C., of Westmoreland Co., Va., d. 5th inst, in Baltimore, in her 17th year (*BPAT* 8 Oct 1818).

Maurice, Capt. Theodore W.. of the U. S. Army Corps of Engineers, was m. Tues. eve. last at *Mouth Airy*, Prince George's Co., to Miss Margaret Matilda Edelen, dau. of Joseph Edelen, Esq. (*BPAT* 27 July 1819).

Maury, Lieut. John M., of the U. S. Navy, was m. Thurs. at the residence of Thomas Strachan, Esq., by the Rev. Mr. Wilson to Miss Eliza Maury, dau. of Fontaine Maury, Esq., of Fredericksburg (*BPAT* 9 April 1817).

Maydwell, James, and Miss Harriet George, all of Baltimore, were m. Mon. eve. by Rev. Mr. Valiant (*FGBA* 2 Feb 1819; *BPAT* 2 Feb 1819).

Mayer, Mr. Charles F., of Baltimore, and Miss Susan T. Pratt of Philadelphia, were m. at that city by Rev. Dr. Abercrombie [date not given] (*BPAT* 11 Dec 1819)

Mayer, Mr. Lewis, of Baltimore, was m. last Tues. eve. by the Rev. Mr. Rozzell to Miss Ann Maria Croney, all of Baltimore (*BPAT* 3 Nov 1817; *BA* 3 Nov 1817).

Meade, Capt. Joseph, and Mrs. Elizabeth Ridgely, all of Baltimore Co., were m. last eve. [Fri.], by Rev. Henshaw (*BPAT* 2 Oct 1819).

Mearess, Jacob, and Miss Louisa Keppard, both of Baltimore, were m. Sun., 20th inst. in Georgetown by Rev. Mr. Keith (*BA* 28 Dec 1818; *BPAT* 26 Dec 1818).

Medcalf, Mrs. Jemima, wife of Abraham Medcalf, d. yesterday evening; the funeral will be from her late dwelling on Loudenslager's Hill (*FGBA* 18 Jan 1817; *BPAT* 18 Jan 1817).

Meeks, James C., dec.; Levi James urges all creditors to come forward to receive their dividends of the assets in hand on or before next 1 June (*BPAT* 20 March 1819).

Meetch, Daniel, is requested, "in the name of your afflicted Mother, to give her some information how and where you are. Your total silence since you left home has been productive of serious consequences. Your absence . . . may be termed . . . in the highest degree criminal. Your mother is recovering from a spell of sickness, in which her life was despaired of. Your promptitude in complying with her present request will evince your disposition to atone." /s/ Your brother, J. B. Meech, Harrisburg, Pa. (*BPAT* 15 Oct 1819).

Meigs, Samuel, Esq., of Washington, d. 16th inst. at Baltimore (*BA* 24 July 1818; *BPAT* 23 July 1818).

Melish, John, Esq., geographer and map publisher, was m. in Philadelphia [date not given] to Miss Jane Pattinson, dau. of the late Mr. William Pattinson of Whitehaven, Eng. (*BPAT* 6 May 1818).

Mellen, Mr. Henry Orlando, and Miss Ann S. Parker, all of Baltimore, were m. last eve. [Tues.] by Rev. Mr. Duncan (*BPAT* 17 Nov 1819).

Melvin, James, Jr., was m. at Georgetown, [date not given] to Miss Margaret C. Swett, of Newburyport, Mass. (*BPAT* 20 Dec 1817).

Melvin, Mr. James, an old and respectable inhabitant of Georgetown, d. at Williamsport, Md. (*BPAT* 10 Aug 1818).

Menzies, James, Jr., formerly of Boston, and Miss Sarah Teacle [Teackle?] of Baltimore, were m. last eve. [Sat.] by the Rev. Roszel (*BA* 13 Dec 1817; *BPAT* 12 Dec 1817).

Mercer, Mrs. Elizabeth, consort of James Mercer of Cecil Co., d. at Mr. Gadsby's estate in Baltimore Co. on Wed., 3rd inst., after a short but painful illness, in her 28th year. She leaves a husband and two children (*BPAT* 9 Nov 1819).

Mercer, Col. John, d. recently in the upper country [near?] Fredericksburg, Va.], son of Gen. Mercer who fell in the fields of Princeton, in the cause of American liberty (*BPAT* 27 Nov 1817).

Mercer, Mr. John, Esq., of West River, Md., was m. 25th inst. [Thurs.], at Alexandria, to Mary Swann, dau. of Thomas Swann of the latter place (*FGBA* 29 June 1818; *BPAT* 30 June 1818).

Mercer, Sally, aged about 18, mulatto, ran away, with her child, from Nath'l Driggs (*BPAT* 5 Aug 1818).

Meredith, Samuel, d. at Belmont, his seat Wayne Co., Pa., on the 40th inst., after a painful illness, aged 76. He was formerly Treasurer of the United States (*BPAT* 24 Feb 1817).
Merrick, Mary, d. Sat., 27th inst., at her son's residence; a member of the Society of Friends (*BPAT* 31 March 1819).
Merryman, Mrs. Ann, consort of Mr. John Merryman, d. Tues. night in her 57th year, leaving a husband and two children (*BPAT* 20 Sep 1817; *FGBA* 19 Sep 1817).
Merryman, Job, and Miss Catherine Lavely, all of Baltimore, were m. last Thurs. eve. by Rev. George Roberts (*FGBA* 2 April 1819; *BPM* 3 April 1819 gives the bride's name as Margaret Lavely).
Merryman, Mr. John B., of Baltimore Co., was m. last Tues. eve. by Rev. Bishop Kemp to Miss Mary Ann Shortt of Baltimore (*BPAT* 25 Nov 1819).
Merryman, Dr. Moses, d. last eve. at his father's residence in Baltimore Co. (*BPAT* 24 Nov 1819).
Mettee, Martin, was m. last Thurs. eve. by Rev, Mr. Sheaffer of PA, to Miss Elizabeth Howard, both of Baltimore (*BPAT* 10 Oct 1818: *BA* 10 Oct 1818).
Meyer, John James, son of Capt. James Meyer, of Newburyport, d. in Baltimore on Sun., 7th inst. (*BPAT* 9 March 1819).
Meyers, Christian, d. 29th inst., in his 17th year; his death was caused by the accidental firing of a gun. His funeral was from his mother's dwelling, No. 7, Union St., Old Town (*FGBA* 31 March 1819; *BPAT* 2 April 1819).
Meyers, Capt. Daniel, and Miss Maria Thomas, were m. last Sun. by Rev. Dr. Elbert (*FGBA* 27 March 1819; *BPAT* 27 March 1819).
Meyers, Mr. Jacob, was m. last eve. [Tues.] by Rev. Mr. Kurtz, to Miss Rachel Daughaday [Daughaday?], all of this city (*BPAT* 23 April 1817; *FGBA* 24 April 1817).
Mick, Charles, was m. last Thurs. by Rev. Davis, to Miss Eliza Boyce, both of Baltimore (*BPAT* 21 Sep 1818; *BA* 21 Sep 1818).
Middleton, Dr. James, d. 15 Dec 1818 in his 28th year (*BA* 17 Dec 1818; *BPAT* 17 Dec 1818).
Middleton, Mrs. Mary Elizabeth, consort of Gilbert Middleton, and mother of the late Dr. Middleton, d. Thurs., 18th inst., in her 69th year (*BPAT* 22 Feb 1819).
Milborn, York, a Negro man, about 25 years of age, ran away from Wm. M. Coe, 9 S. Calvert St. (*BPAT* 25 May 1818).
Mileron, Mr. Jacob, was m. by the Rev. Mr. Kurtz, to Mrs. Mary Brensinger, both of this city (*BPAT* 15 Sep 1817; *BA* 15 Sep 1817).
Millar, Horatio S., d. Sun. last, at the residence of his mother in Charles Co., in his 30th year (*BPAT* 11 Feb 1818; *FGBA* 11 Feb 1818).
Miller, Adeline F., d. last night, aged 13 years and 6 mos. (*FGBA* 5 Feb 1818).
Miller, Mr. George, d. Fri. eve. last, in his 59th year, after several years indisposition (*BPAT* 13 Oct 1817; *BA* 14 Oct 1817). For the will of George Miller, filed in 1817, see BAWB 10:377.
Miller, Henry D., of Elkton, and Miss Ann Dowerty of Philadelphia, were m. at the residence of Tobias Rudulph last Wed. eve. by Rev. William Duke (*BPAT* 6 Nov 1819).
Miller, James D., of the House of Disney & Miller, merchants of Baltimore, was m. Thurs., 22nd inst., by the Rev. Mark Moore to Miss Emily Evans, of the same place (*BPAT* 26 May 1817; *BA* 27 May 1817).
Miller, Miss Laura [or Louisa], d. 29 Sep after a short but painful illness, in her 13th year, only child of Alexander Miller of Baltimore (*BPAT* 4 Oct 1817; *BA* 4 Oct 1817 gives her name as Louisa).
Miller, Capt. Michael, and Miss Isabella Geise, all of Fells Point, were m. last eve. [Sun.] by Rev. Mr. Davis (*BPAT* 12 Nov 1818).
Miller, Mrs. Phebe, wife of Peter Miller of Richmond, Va., and for many years a resident of Baltimore, d. Friday, in her 58th year (*BA* 27 Oct 1818; *BPAT* 2 Oct

1818). "Philey" [sic] Miller aged 57, was buried 23 Oct 1818 from St. Paul's Parish (ReamySP).
Miller, Reuben C., and Miss Attantick [Atlantgick?] Ocean Walton were m. [date not given] in VA *(BPAT* 14 Jan 1818).
Miller, Capt. Robert, d. at his residence near Baltimore, aged 73. He was a native of Scotland, but for the last 40 years had lived in Baltimore. He leaves a wife and children *(BPAT* 19 Sep 1818). He may be the Robert Miller of Great Britain who was naturalized on 15 March 1796 (Baltimore Co. Court Naturalization Docket 1: 1, #3).
Miller, Susan, a Yellow Girl, was free-born in March 1808, the dau. of Francis and Ruth Miller. Like James Bayard (q.v.), she was born in Appoquinnock Hundred, New Castle Hundred, Del. She was missing some 8 or 9 mos., and Mingo Bayard went to Baltimore, where he learned she and his son James may have been kidnapped and sold into slavery. He is seeking information on their whereabouts *(BPAT .*
Miller, Mr. Wm. P., and Miss Mary Ann Elliott, all of Baltimore, were m. last Thurs, eve. by Rev. Mr. Wyatt *(BPAT* 15 Nov 1819).
Millet, Mr. Charles, of Boston, was m. last eve. [Thurs.] by Rev. Mr. Moranville, to Miss Augusta Richard of Baltimore *(BPAT* 31 July 1817).
Milliron [or Milliror], Jacob, who resided in Paca St. Extended, d. yesterday morning *(BPAT* 5 June 1818; *BA* 5 June 1818). For the will of Jacob Milleron [sic], filed in 1818, see BAWB 10:488.
Mills, Benjamin, 19 years old, apprentice to the boot and shoe-making business, ran away from Barton Harris of Rockville, Montgomery Co. *(BPAT* 5 Feb 1819)\.
Mills, Henry, about 20 years of age, fond of string drink, apprentice to the baking business, ran away from J. P. Winchell, 59, South St., Baltimore; may have gone to Alexandria, where he had relatives *(BPAT* 22 July 1817).
Mills, Capt. James, d. at Annapolis last Sun., on board his schooner, *The Tantamount* *(BPAT* 6 Aug 1819).
Minicks, John, and Miss Fredericka [?] Aikenbrode, all of Baltimore, were m. Sun, eve. *(BA* 18 May 1819; *BPAT* 17 May 1819).
Minskey, Samuel, formerly of Baltimore, d. 14th inst. in Anne Arundel Co., leaving a wife and three children *(BPAT* 31 March 1819).
Mitchel, Edward, aged about 11, apprentice to the trunk making business, ran away from Jas. Jackson, 44 Calvert St.*(BPAT* 5 March 1818).
Mitchell, Mr. Alexander, d. at Annapolis, after a short, thought distressing illness, in the 23rd year of his age *(BPAT* 29 Oct 1819).
Mitchell, Maj.-Gen. David, d. 15 May 1818 in his 77th year, at his residence in Juniata Twp., Cumberland Co., Pa. "Another Revolutionary Patriot gone!" [long obit] *(BPAT* 10 June 1818; *FGBA* 10 June 1818).
Mitchell, John, and Miss Frances Sweatman, all of Baltimore, were m. last Thurs. by Rev, Hargrove *(FGBA* 27 July 1819; *BPAT* 27 July 1819).
Mitchell, Mrs. Margaret, d. Sat. eve. last, in her 61st year; her funeral will be from her late residence in S. Calvert St. *(FGBA* 24 March 1817; *BPAT* 24 March 1817).
Mitchell, Mrs. Mary Ann, wife of Capt. John I. Mitchell, d. 30th ult., in her 33rd year *(BPAT* 2 Feb 1819).
Mitchell, Precilla, (as one of the heirs of Robert Carter?) owes taxes for the years 1813, 1814, 1815, on 523 ¾ a. or two lots in the 1st Dist. *(BPAT* 1 Jan 1819).
Moffett, Mr. James, and Mrs. Ann Roach, all of Baltimore, were m. last eve. [Thurs.] by Rev. Wyatt *(FGBA* 23 Jan 1818; *BPAT* w23 Jan 1818).
Moffit, Mr. John, was m. last Thurs. by the Rev. John Glendy, to Miss Ellen Eager, all of this city *(BPAT* 19 Aug 1817; *BA* 20 Aug 1817).
Mohler, Peter, he or his heirs owe taxes for the years 1813, 1814, 1815, on 6 a. Back of Hookstown in the 1st Dist. *(BPAT* 1 Jan 1819).
Molleston, Del. Henry, Governor Elect of the State of Delaware, d. at his seat in Kent Co. [Del.] *(BPAT* 18 Nov 1819).

Mondel, William, has been missing since last Sunday eve., and his wife and children fear he may have met with some distressing accident, or is wandering about the country, or he Town. He is 47 years old. Anyone with information is asked to contact his wife or children, or Jno Sykes & Son, Baltimore (*BPAT* 27 Feb 1819). For the will of William Mondel, filed in 1819, see BAWB 10:600.

Monjef, Mr. Samuel, d. 16th inst., at the advanced age of 86 years. He was a resident of Baltimore since 1756. He leaves two daus. and several grandchildren (*BPAT* 21 sep 1819).

Monk [or Mork], Lieut. James, formerly of the U.S.N., d. at St. Mary's, suddenly, on 21st inst., aged about 35 years (*FGBA* 6 Nov 1818; *BA* 6 Nov 1818; *BPAT* 5 Nov 1818).

Monks, Francis E., of Harford Co. is an insolvent debtor. James G. L. Presbury has been appointed his trustee (*BPAT* 24 July 1818).

Monro, Dr. George, d. last Mon., nearly 60 years old, very suddenly, in Wilmington, Del., where he was First Burgess, a constant friend of the poor (*BPAT* 15 Oct 1819).

Montgomery, James, of Frederick Co., and Miss Caroline Eliza, eld. dau. of John Sedwic of Calvert Co., were m. Thurs., 31 Dec, by Rev. Mr. Bausman (*BPAT* 14 Jan 1819).

Moore, Aaron, and Miss Martha Wright, were m. last eve. [Sun.] by Rev. Mr. Valiant (*BPAT* 21 Dec 1818; *BA* 23 Dec 1818).

Moore, George, Esq., of the house of Higgins, Moore, and Co., of Baltimore, was m. there on 8 Feb. [Sat.] to Miss Sally Nicholson of Baltimore (*BPAT* 6 May 1817; *BA* 6 May 1817).

Moore, Jason, of Harford Co.; his property will be sold at public sale, to wit: part of *Joshua's Meadows*, part of *Joshua's Meadows Enlarged*, part of *Bond's Addition to Joshua's Meadows Enlarged*, and Part of *Clarkson's Purchase*; in all 30 a.; also part of *Clarkson's Purchase*, 312 a.; also two half-acre lots in the town of Bell-Air where Jason Moore now resides, and other property (*BPAT* 15 June 1818).

Moore, John, merchant, and Miss Catherine Blunt, were m. [date not given] at Portsmouth (*BPAT* 10 Jan 1818).

Moore, Robert Scott, d. Thurs. last, 2nd, inst., in his 25th year, younger bro. of Col.. Samuel Moore, of S. Charles St. (*FGBA* 6 Jan 1817; *BPAT* 6 Jan 1817).

Moore, Mr. William P., was m. on Sun. eve. by Rev. Mr. Glendy, to Miss Ann Maria King, all of this city (*BPAT* 5 Aug 1817; *BA* 5 Aug 1817, 20 Aug 1817).

Moran, Mr. Gabriel, and Miss Maria Krebs, both of Baltimore, were m. last Thurs. eve. by Rev. Dr. Roberts (*BPAT* 25 July 1818)

Moran, Thomas, and Miss Rebecca Bowler, both of Baltimore Co., were m. last Thurs. by Rev. D. E. Reese (*BPAT* 7 Jan 1818).

Moran, William, of Baltimore Co. is an insolvent debtor (*BPAT* 14 Oct 1819).

Morehead, Mr. Lewis, of Fauquier Co., Va., was m. Tues., 20th inst., by the Rev. Mr. Davis, to Miss Susan Worthington, dau. of Samuel Worthington, dec., of Baltimore Co. (*BPAT* 26 May 1817; *BA* 26 May 1817).

Morgan, Augusta, dau. of Robert C. Morgan, formerly of Preston, Conn., d. in Baltimore on 6th inst. (*BPAT* 8 My 1819).

Morgan, John, was m. on 19th inst. [Thurs.] by Rev. D. E. Reese to Miss Eliza Willey (*BPAT* 30 March 1818; *BA* 30 March 1818 gives day as Friday).

Morgan, Robert, a native of Harford Co., d. 24th inst., in his 50th year (*BPAT* 27 March 1819).

Morgan, Miss Sarah Ann, formerly of Caroline Co., d. Sat., 7 Aug (*FGBA* 11 Aug 1819; *BPAT* 11 Aug 1819).

Morland, Elisha, aged 21, a bricklayer, b. in Morris Town, N. J., deserted from my Recruiting Rendezvous on 19th inst. /s/ J. H. Hook, Capt., 4th Inf. (*BPAT* 3 Oct 1817).

Biographical Data from Baltimore Newspapers, 1817-1819

Morris, John B., was m. last eve. [Fri.] by the Right Rev. Bishop Kemp, to Miss Ann Maria Hollingsworth, all of Baltimore (*BPAT* 22 March 1817; *BA* 22 March 1817).

Morrison, Mrs. Ann, wife of David Morrison, Esq., late of Newcastle, Del., d. 3rd inst., after a lingering illness one year and seven mos., leaving a husband and five small children (*BPAT* 5 July 1819).

Morrison, John, aged 13 mos., was buried 2 Sep 1819 (*FGBA* 3 Sep 1819). John Morrison, aged 13 mos., was buried 2 Sep 1819 from St. Paul's Parish (ReamySP).

Morrison, Murdoch, native of Scotland, d. in Philadelphia, on the 15th inst., in his 104th year (*FGBA* 18 Feb 1819).

Morton, John A., Jr., of Baltimore, is an insolvent debtor (*BPAT* 19 Oct 1819).

Mory, Capt. Lewis, of Philadelphia, d. 13th inst. at St. Mary's (*BPAT* 29 Aug 1818; *BA* 29 Aug 1818).

Mosart, John G., aged 22, by occupation a labourer, deserted from Capt. Nath. N. Hall's Co., Artillery Corps at Fort McHenry (*BPAT* 6 June 1817).

Moses, Mr. James, was m. on 10th inst. [Fri.] by Rev. D. E. Reese to Miss Margaret Crothers of Baltimore (*BPAT* 21 April 1818; *FGBA* 21 April 818).

Mosher, James, Esq., was m. Sun. eve. by Rev. Dr. Inglis, to Mrs. Elizabeth Nickerson, relict of Capt. Lewis Nickerson, all of Baltimore (*BPAT* 1 July 1817; *BA* 1 July 1817).

Mosher, James, Jr., Esq., of Baltimore Co., was m. 8th inst. [Wed.], at Georgetown, by Rev. Dr. Atkinson, to Eliza M., dau. of Dr. Magruder of Georgetown (*BPAT* 10 Dec 1819).

Mosher, William, and Elizabeth, second dau. of Col. Thomas Sheppard, all of Baltimore, were m. last eve. by Rev. Glendy (*BA* 7 Jan 1819).

Mountgarret, Thomas, owes taxes for the years 1813, 1814, 1815, on 1 lot of Carroll's land in the 1st Dist. (*BPAT* 1 Jan 1819).

Mull, Jacob, aged about 15 years, fair hair and light complexion, apprentice to the sail-making business, ran away from Peregrine Ward (*BPAT* 5 Jan 1819).

Mullen, Henry, born in Fontaneu, Co. Tyrone, Ireland, lately from Va., aged 32 years, a Recruit of the 8th infantry, deserted from the 2nd Plank Co., 5th Infantry. /s/ James Pratt (*BPAT* 4 June 1817).

Muller, Mrs. Theresa, wife of George Henry Muller, and dau. of Capt. Otto Muller, formerly a resident of Baltimore, d. at Havana on 9 June (*FGBA* 2 July 1819; *BPAT* 2 July 1819).

Mullikin, Belt, of Anne Arundel Co., has died, leaving two valuable tracts of land in Anne Arundel Co. to be sold: 337 a. *Simpson's Choice*, and 300 a. *Worthington's Beginning*. /s/ Basil D. Mullikin, trustee (*BPAT* 24 June 1817).

Mullikin, Mr. Edward, was m. on Tues. eve. by Rev. Mr. Valiant, to Miss Sarah Hitchcock, all of Baltimore (*BPAT* 15 July 1818; *FGBA* 15 July 1818 states that he married Miss Mary B. Hall, of Baltimore).

Mullikin, Richard D., d. owning two lots of ground on the east side of North Charles St., near St. Paul's Church. William Wilson, Jr., and Baruch Mullikin, executors, advertise the sale or lease of the lots (*BPAT* 6 March 1818). For the will of Richard D. Mullikin, filed in 1815, see BAWB 10:93.

Mummey, Mr. Joshua, was m. last Mon. eve., by the Rev. Mr. Wells, to Miss Maria C. Warking, both of Baltimore (*BPAT* 14 Oct 1817).

Mummey, Samuel, Sr., d. Sat afternoon in his 78th tear (*BA* 16 Nov 1818).

Munn, Mrs. Ann, consort of the late Mr. Lindsey Munn, d. yesterday morning, after an indisposition of four days (*BPAT* 26 Oct 1819).

Munn, Mr. Lindsey, formerly of Philadelphia, d. at New Orleans on the 14th ult., after a short illness, leaving a wife and four children (*BPAT* 26 Oct 1819).

Munro, Mrs. Catherine, arrived in Baltimore from Charleston S.C., and is at the Fountain Inn; she is seeking her son Robert, who arrived here a short time since, after a long voyage (*BPAT* 3 Aug 1819).

Biographical Data from Baltimore Newspapers, 1817-1819

Munro, Robert, Esq., of Georgetown, D.C., and Miss Catherine H. Crawford, dau. of Edward Crawford, Esq., of Chambersburg, PA, were m. in the latter place on Mon., 24th ult. (*BPAT* 5 Dec 1817).

Munroe, George Marshall, youngest child of Mr. Nathaniel Munroe, formerly of Concord, Mass., d. last Sat. eve. (*BPAT* 14 Sep 1818).

Munroe, John, d. at Annapolis on the 17th inst., an old citizen of Annapolis, and long the Postmaster of that city (*BPAT* 21 Nov 1817). For the will of John Munroe, filed in 1817, see AAWB JG#3:208.

Murdoch, George W., d. at Frederick Town (*BMC* 31 May 1819).

Murdoch, Miss Lavinia, dau. of the late Patrick Murdoch, d. at Cumberland, Allegany Co., on 21st inst., in her 24th year. She was a member of the New Jerusalem Church (*FGBA* 5 Nov 1817).

Murduck [Murdock?], Mr. James and Miss Hannah Clouse, all of Baltimore, were m. Tues. eve. by Rev. Mr. Fenwick (*BPAT* 21 May 1818; *BA* 21 May 1818).

Murphey, Terry, lately arrived from Ireland and worked for a few weeks in Washington, is anxiously sought by his wife, who arrived in Baltimore on Thurs. week, and is staying at Mr. James Martin's (*BPAT* 23 July 1819).

Murphy, Benjamin, d. Sat, eve., 21st Aug., in his 21st year (*FGBA* 23 Aug 1819; *BPAT* 24 Aug 1819)

Murphy, John, and Miss Ophelia Berry, all of Baltimore, were m. by Rev. D. E. Reese on Thurs. eve, last (*BA* 10 April 1819; *BMC* 10 April 1819; *BPAT* 9 April 1819).

Murphy, John, and Miss Sarah Miller, all of Baltimore, were m. last eve. [Mon.] by Rev. Dr. Roberts (*FGBA* 13 May 1819; *BPAT* 24 April 1819).

Murphy, Mrs. Mary, consort of Capt. Isaac Murphy of Baltimore, d. 19th inst., in her 65th year (*BPAT* 29 April 1817; *BA* 29 April 1817).

Murphy, Mr. Patrick, of St. Johns, N.B., was m. [date not given] in that city TO Miss Sarah Ellek of Philadelphia (*BPAT* 23 Nov 1819).

Murray, Elizabeth, d. in Harford Co. prior to May 1817. A decree of the High Court of Chancery directed the sale of all of the deceased's estate, right, title, and interest in 205 a. of *Arabia Petrea* (*BPAT* 6 May 1817).

Murray, Mr. James, was m. to Mrs. Ann McLaughlin by Rev. Dr. Glendy on 26th ult. [Sun] (*BPAT* 1 May 1818; *BA* 1 May 1818).

Murray, Samuel, of Baltimore Co., is an insolvent debtor (*BPAT* 23 June 1818).

Murray, Capt. Thomas Gist., native of Maryland, of highly respectable parents and connections, d. on board the ship *Tennessee,* on her voyage from New Orleans to Philadelphia. He commanded a division at Fort Plaquemine, during the memorable siege of New Orleans [Long obit] (*BPAT* 2 Oct 1817).

Musket, Mr. John, of Fells Point, d. Tues. morning last, aged 39 years (*BPAT* 4 Sep 1817; *BA* 5 Sep 1817 states he was in his 39th year). He was buried in Glendy's Burial Ground (*Maryland Genealogical Society Bulletin* 30 (3) 298).

Myer, Mr. Thomas, was m. Tues. eve. last by Rt. Rev. Bishop Kemp to Miss Ann Ringgold, all of Baltimore (*BPAT* 26 March 1818; *BA* 26 March 1818).

Myers, Christopher, and Miss Margaret Brown, were m. at Frederick Town (*BMC* 31 May 1819).

"N"

Nabb, John, was m. last eve. [Mon.] by Rev. Valiant, to Miss Elizabeth Onion, both of Baltimore (*BA* 21 June 1817; *BPAT* 21 June 1817).

Nagle, David, d. 20 Feb at Havana in his 72nd year, a native of Ireland and a merchant of Baltimore (*BPAT* March 1819).

Nagle, Mr. Henry, d. suddenly, Sun. morning, in his 59th year; for the last eleven years he had suffered from an affliction that deprived him of the use of his limbs (*BPAT* 27 Dec 1819). For the will of Henry Nagle, filed in 1820, see BAWB 11:97.

Biographical Data from Baltimore Newspapers, 1817-1819

Nancarrow, John, was m. 11th inst. [Tues.] by Rev. Jennings, to Miss Charlotte Walters, both of Baltimore (*BA* 1 May 1819; *BPAT* 13 May 1819).

Nancarrow, John, a member of the Society of Friends, aged 34, d. Thurs. eve. last, after a short but painful illness (*BPAT* 21 Aug 1819).

Nanca..v[?], John, d. last Thurs. He had been married only two months (*FGBA* 24 Aug 1819).

Nantz, John, was m. Thurs. eve. by Rev. Davis, to Margaretta Bowyer, all of Baltimore (*BA* 14 March 1818; *BPAT* 14 March 1818).

Nantz, Capt. John, was m. last Thurs. eve. by Rev. Richards, to Miss Ann Evans, all of Baltimore (*FGBA* 13 Feb 1819; *BPAT* 15 Feb 1819).

Nantz, Mrs. Sarah, wife of Capt. John Nantz, d. yesterday in her 47th year. She resided on Gough St., near Bond (*FGBA* 24 Jan 1818; *BPAT* 24 Jan 1818 gives her name as Nants).

Nathanham, George, was m. last Sun. by Rev. Parks, to Miss Rebecca Ruth, all of Fells Point (*BA* 17 June 1817; *BPAT* 17 June 1817).

Nathstine, Leonard, born in Northampton Co., Va., aged 26 years, employed at some factory in Baltimore, enlisted on 23rd inst., and deserted on 24th inst. from the Recruiting Rendevous for the 4th Infantry. /s/ J. H. Hook, Captain. (*BPAT* 3 Oct 1817).

Neale, Most Rev, Leonard, Archbishop of Baltimore, died Wed., 18th inst., in the 71st year, after a short and painful illness of only 36 hours. He succeeded Dr. John Carroll in the Archepiscopal See. His remains were conveyed yesterday from Trinity Church to the Cemetery of the Convent. The obituary contains an account of the funeral procession (*BPAT* 20 June 1817; see also *FGBA* 20 June 1817).

Neely, Mrs. Susanna, relict of John Neely, Sr., d. 2nd, inst. in Adams Co., Pa., in her 99th year (*FGBA* 13 Feb 1819; *BPAT* 15 Feb 1819).

Neill, Hugh, of Baltimore Co., was m. last Thurs. eve. by Rev. Mr. Stephenson, to Miss Rachel Stephenson of Harford Co. (*BPAT* 23 Oct 1817).

Neilson [Nelson?], James, d. 20th Aug. in his 36th year, after a severe illness (*BA* 22 Aug 1817; *BPAT* 22 Aug 1817). For the will of James Nelson [*sic*], filed in 1817, see BAWB 10:345.

Neilson, Nathaniel, d. 6th inst., cashier of the Bank at Port Gibson (Miss. Territory) and formerly of this place (*BPAT* 30 Oct 1819).

Nelson, Jacob, was m. last Thurs., by Rev. Glendy, to Miss Anna Benson, all of Baltimore (*BA* 14 June 1819; *BPAT* 14 June 1819).

Nelson, Chancellor Robert, d. in Williamsburg, Va., on 9 July, aged 40 (*BA* 21 July 1818; *BPAT* 18 July 1818, 20 July 1818).

Nelson, Mr. Thomas, and Miss Elizabeth White, all of Baltimore, were m. Mon., 5th inst., by Rev. D. E. Reese (*BPAT* 10 July 1819).

Neltner, John, an indented German, aged about 23 years, ran away from Mary Seltzer on Tues. last. (*BPAT* 14 Feb 1818).

Nes, Samuel, of York, was m. Thurs., 20th inst., by Rev. Kurtz, Miss Elizabeth Small of Baltimore (*FGBA* 29 Aug 1818; *BPAT* 31 Aug 1818).

Nesbit, Moses, of Dorchester Co., dec.; Francis Higgins, admin. *de bonis non*, will settle the estate (*BPAT* 24 Feb 1819).

Nesbit, Wilson, Esq., late a Representative in Congress from South Carolina, was m. Tues. eve. last, at the residence of E. W. Duvall, by the Rev. Dr. Hunter, to Miss Susan T. Duvall (*American Farmer* 9 July 1819).

Nester, Major Peter, an old and distinguished revolutionary office, d. at Norfolk, Va. [date not given] (*BPAT* 5 May 1817).

Neville, Mr. Samuel, and Mrs. Elizabeth Rawlings, both of Centreville, Md., were m. Thurs., 9th inst., by Rev. Mr. Martindale (*BPAT* 20 Dec 1819).

Newell, John, born in Milton, Mass., aged 33 enlisted on 10 Dec 1817, deserted from Fort Covington on 10 Jan 1818. /s/ Jas. H. Hook, Capt., 4th Infantry. (*BPAT* 24 Jan 1818).

Newman, Col. Francis, d. in Charles Co., on 5 March, after a long and painful illness (*FGBA* 14 March 1818; *BPAT* 12 March 1818).
Newman, George, was m. [date not given] in Queen Anne's Co. to Miss Mary Thompson (*BPAT* 29 Nov 1819).
Newnam, Joseph, of Kent Co., has died. The Commissioners will sell a 226 a. farm lying within one mile of New Market (*BPAT* 4 June 1817).
Newton, Mr. Nimrod, was m. last Tues., to Temperance Hynson, both of Baltimore (*BA* 18 Aug 1818).
Nicholson, Joseph Hopper, Chief Judge of the Sixth Judicial Circuit, and a Judge of the Court of Appeals, d. 4 March 1817, aged 47, after a short illness, leaving a wife and children (Long obit follows) (*FGBA* 5 March 1817; *BPAT* 5 March 1817). By a decree of the Court of Chancery, the trustees of Judge Nicholson will sell various tracts of land situated on Elk Ridge, in Anne Arundel Co., adjoining the lands of Col. Charles Sterrett Ridgely, and containing a total of 500 a. (*BPAT* 12 April 1817).
Nicholson, Miss Rebecca S., d. Fri., 5th inst. in Talbot Co., Eastern Shore, after a long and tedious indisposition (*BA* 22 June 1818; *BPAT* 22 June 1818).
Nickson, Edward, was m. last Wed. eve. by Rev. Hargrove, to Mrs. Catherine Burns (*BA* 27 June 1817; *BPAT* 27 June 1817).
Nicodemus, John, owes taxes for the years 1816 and 1817 on 6 a. *Nancy's Fancy,* in the 1st Dist. (*BPAT* 3 Aug 1819).
Nicol, William H., aide de camp to Major Gen. Riley, was m. 6th inst. [Wed.]at Washington City, to Miss Harriet V. Conway of Northumberland Co., Va. (*FGBA* 13 May 1818; *BPAT* 12 May 1818).
Nicols, Hugh, of Baltimore, was m. Thurs. eve. by Rev. Stephenson, to Miss Rachel Stephenson of Harford Co. (*BA* 21 Oct 1817; *BOPAT* 20 Oct 1817).
Nicols, Samuel, Jr., of Baltimore, merchant, was m. 6th inst. [Tues.] by Rev. Blayne, to Miss Ann Coursey of Queen Anne's Co. (*BA* 10 Oct 1817; *BPAT* 10 Oct 1817).
Nimmo, William R., was m. by Rev. Rev. Bartow, to Miss Sidney E. Thornton, all of Baltimore (*BA* 28 Dec 1818; *BPAT* 26 Dec 1818).
Noble, Alexander, is an insolvent debtor in Baltimore Co. (*BPAT* 21 Nov 1818).
Nones, Mr. Solomon B., d. at Norfolk, after an illness of three days, of the House of Marks, Nones, and Co. (*BPAT* 18 Aug 1819).
Norris, Bazil, merchant, was m. at Frederick Town, [date not given], to Miss Elizabeth Charlton (*BPAT* 7 Sep 1819).
Norris, Edward, is an insolvent debtor in Baltimore City (*BPAT* 13 Dec 1819).
Norris, Mrs. Eliza, formerly of Baltimore, d. at Easton on 21 June (*FGBA* 6 July 1819; *BPAT* 6 July 1819, 7 July 1819).
Norris, John, Jr., was m. Thurs., 25th inst., by Rev. Matthew Johnson, to Miss Sophia McComas of Harford Co. (*BA* 31 Dec 1817).
Norris, Mr. S. C., was m. Wed. by Rev. Mr. Wyatt, to Miss Eliza March, both of Baltimore (*FGBA* 5 May 1817; *BPAT* 5 May 1817).
Norris, William, Jr., d. Mon., 11th inst., in his 36th year, leaving a wife and six children (*FGBA* 14 Jan 1819; *BPAT* 15 Jan 1819). On 29 March 1819 various property of his will be sold at his dwelling house, 30 Hanover St. (*BPAT* 24 March 1819). For the will of William Norris, Jr., filed in 1819, see BAWB 10:552.
Norton, Stephen, was m. Thurs. eve. by Rev. Kurtz, to Miss Mary Ann McDaniel, all of Baltimore (*BA* 19 Sep 1818; *BPAT* 18 Sep 1818).
Norwood, John, of Miss., was m. 15th Oct. [Thurs.] at Long Green, by Rev. Johnson, to Elizabeth Smith, all of Baltimore Co. (*BA* 24 Oct 1818; *BPAT* 24 Oct 1818).
Norwood, Thomas, of Baltimore Co., was m. 5 March [Thurs.], by Rev. Welsh, to Henrietta H. Linthicum of Anne Arundel Co. (*BA* 6 March 1818; *BPAT* 6 March 1818).
Nowland, John C., was m. last Sun. by Rev. D. E. Reese to Mrs. Elizabeth Gibbs, all of Baltimore (*BA* 30 Oct 1817; *BPAT* 30 Oct 1817).

Biographical Data from Baltimore Newspapers, 1817-1819

Noyes, John P., was m. Tues. eve. by Rev. J. M. Duncan, to Miss Mary Ann Adair, both of Baltimore (*BPAT* 5 Feb 1818).

Nuttall, Christopher, machinist d. last 28 Dec. at the Warren Factory, Gunpowder Falls, in his 59th year. He was a native of Lancashire, Eng. (*FGBA* 17 Jan 1818).

"O"

Ocherman, John, a German redemptioner, aged about 26 years, employed in the baking business, ran away from John Freeburger, who offers a reward of $10.00 if taken in the State, or $20.00 if taken out (*BPAT* 4 Dec 1817).

O'Connor, Mrs. Honora, d. 20th inst., in her 65th year, after an illness of three days; long a respected inhabitant of Baltimore (*BPAT* 21 Sep 1819).

O'Connor, Mr. James, publisher of the *Norfolk Herald,* d. last Sat., aged 60 years, in Norfolk, Va. (*BPAT* 9 July 1819).

O'Connor, Dr. John, of Fell's Point, d. of the prevailing disease, in the prime of life, leaving a widow and a sister; their mother had died only a few days previously (*BPAT* 5 Oct 1819). For the will of John O'Connor, filed in 1819, see BAWB 11:57.

Oerstedt, Capt. John, a native of Sweden, d. last Thurs., supposed to be about 40 years of age. He left several papers which may be of interest to others, who, if interested, may apply to Thomas Warner, No. 9, East St. (*BPAT* 23 Dec 1817).

Ogden, Col. John Wesley, of Ky., was m. last Thurs. by Rev. Duncan, at Strawberry Hill, the residence of Amos Ogden, to Miss Nancy Ogden, of Baltimore Co. (*BA* 27 Dec 1817; *BPAT* 27 Dec 1817).

Ogilvie, James, a native of Keith, in the north of Scotland, is asked, if he is in this town, to call at the Post Office for some letters sent to him by a friend in New York, or upon Capt. Samuel W. Turner, of the schooner *Leonidas,* now lying ay Smith's Wharf; he will hear of something to his advantage (*BPAT* 13 Feb 1819).

Ogle, John, was m. at Frederick Town [date not given] to Miss Susan Thomas (*BPAT* 2 Nov 1819).

Okely, John, owes taxes for the year 1815, on a lot in the Eastern Precincts and a lot in the Western Precincts (*BPAT* 7 Jan 1819).

Oldfield, Granville S., merchant of Eng., was m. 5th inst. [Wed.], by Rt. Rev. Bishop Kemp, to Ann, eld. dau. of Ralph Higinbotham, Esq., of Baltimore (*FGBA* 6 Aug 1819; *BPAT* 6 Aug 1819). Granville S. Oldfield was born at Lambeth, Surrey, Eng., filed his declaration of intent at New York on 26 April 1817. John S. Tyson and Ebenezer L. Finly were witnesses [when he was naturalized on 23 May 1822] (Baltimore Co. Court: Naturalization Docket, 1796-1851, p. 57).

Olems, Thomas, owes taxes for the year 1815, on land in 1st Dist. leased from N. Rogers (*BPAT* 7 Jan 1819).

Onderburg, Mr. Adrian, was m. at Dumfries, Va., last Sat. eve. by the Rev. Mr. Luck, to Miss Harriet Steel, both of this city (*BPAT* 3 Sep 1817).

O'Neale, Capt. Henry, d. at his residence in Montgomery Co. on Sun., 19th inst., in his 32nd year. He was a captain of a company in the regular army during the late war. In the service he contracted an inflammatory rheumatism which led to his death. He has left handsome legacies to the church of which he was a member (*BPAT* 24 Oct 1817).

Onis, Dona Frederica de Merklein y, consort to the Chevalier de Onis, H.C.M. Envoy Extraordinary and Minister Plenipotentiary to the United States, d. at Washington, on Wed. afternoon, after an illness of ten months (*BPAT* 26 May 1817).

Orem, Thomas, was m. at Easton, [date not given], to Miss Rebecca Bartlett (*BPAT* 15 Nov 1819).

Orem, William, of Dorchester Co. died. William Craft, *admin. de bonis non,* will settle the estate (*BPAT* 27 June 1818).

Orthoff, Andrew, silversmith, formerly of Baltimore, d. 8th inst. in Pittsburgh *(BA* 19 May 1815; *BPAT* of 8 May 1818 gives his name as Andrew Osthoff).
Osburn, William, was m. last Thurs. eve. by Rev. Dr. Inglis, to Mrs. Elizabeth Coler, all of Baltimore *(BA* 2 June 1817; *BPAT* 2 June 1817).
Overfeld, Martin, distiller, absconded from the employ of Owen Allen. Overfeld is about 38 years of age, and has recently married a common strumpet whose maiden name was Roney; he has said he would go to South America, but may be on his way to Virginia or Canada *(BPAT* 12 Dec 1818).
Owen, Kennedy, d. Wed. night, aged 43, a respectable merchant *(BACDA* 28 March 1817). Kennedy Owen, aged 43 years, was buried 27 March 1817 from St. Paul's Parish (ReamySP).
Owens, Edward, was m. Tues. eve. by Rev. Morse, to Miss Sally Thomas, all of Baltimore *(FGBA* 11 April 1818; *BPAT* 10 April 1818).
Owens, Isaac: his property as advertised by Thomas L. Emory. Esq., trustee, will be sold by Samuel Cole, auctioneer *(BPAT* 5 June 1818).
Owings, Jesse, owes taxes for the years 1813, 1814, 1815, on 283 a. *Bachelor's Refuge,* etc., in the 6th Dist. *(BPAT* 7 Jan 1819)_.
Owings, Richard, d. yesterday at his farm in Elk Ridge, in his 70th year *(BPAT* 26 Jan 1819). For the will of Richard Owings, filed in 1819, see AAWB JG-:17.

"P"

Pain, Nathaniel, was m. last Thurs. by Rev. Healey to Charity Wright, all of Baltimore Co. *(BA* 12 Dec 1818; *BPAT* 10 Dec 1818).
Palmer, Mr. A. R., of Baltimore, was m. at Christiana, Del., on 7th inst. [Sat.] to Miss Rachel Bines of Wilmington, Del. *(BPAT* 26 Nov 1818).
Pampilion, William J., of Baltimore, was m. Tues., 4th inst., at Trap, near Oxford on the Eastern Shore of MD, by Rev. Orem, to Miss Mary E. Dreams, of Trap *(BA* 10 May 1819; *BPAT* 10 May 1819).
Parham, Hannah, widow of the late John Parham of Haddonfield, N. J., d. at Philadelphia, on Monday last, in the 70th year of her age *(BPAT* 10 Dec 1817).
Parish, John, owes taxes for the years 1813 and 1814 on 2 a. *Soldier's Delight* in the 7th Dist. *(BPAT* 7 Jan 1819).
Parish, Mr. Mark, was m. to Miss Jane Latimer, both of Elizabeth City Co. *(BPAT* 5 May 1817).
Parisot [*sic*], John B., and Miss Eliza W. Boetefuerr, both of Baltimore, were m. Tues. eve. last by Rev. Mr. Helfenstein *(BPAT* 26 July 1819).
Park, Mr. Mungo, the celebrated British traveler, died in the interior of Africa when his boat struck some rocks in the rapids of the river, sank, and he was frowned *(BPAT* 6 May 1819).
Parker, Charles, printer of Baltimore, d. last night in his 27th year, leaving a wife and three small children *(FGBA* 30 July 1819; *BPAT* 30 July 1819).
Parker, Brig.-Gen. Daniel, Adjutant and Inspector General of the U.S. Army, was m. at Washington last June, by Rev. Mr. McCormick to Miss Ann Collins, dau. of Zacheus Collins of this city *(FGBA* 24 Jan 1818).
Parker, Mr. Ezra, d. yesterday, in his 28th year *(BA* 2 Sep 1817; *BPAT* 2 Sep 1817).
Parker, John, born in New London, aged 23 years, by profession , deserted on the 19th inst. from the Recruiting Rendezvous of J. H. Hook, Capt., 4th Infantry *(BPAT* 3 Oct 1817).
Parker, Peter, d. yesterday, in his 36th year, after a long and painful illness, leaving a widow and numerous relatives *(BA* 5 Nov 1818; *BPAT* 5 Nov 1818). For the will of Peter Parker, filed in 1818, see BAWB 10:534.
Parker, Mr. William, d. at Concordia, La., of the prevailing fever, aged 18. He had but just arrived from Baltimore *(BPAT* 16 Oct 1819).

Biographical Data from Baltimore Newspapers, 1817-1819

Pamelee, Pvt. John, of the 4th Regt. Infantry, 27 years old, a carpenter, born in the City of New York and enlisted in Baltimore on 16 July 1818, deserted from the Camp near the Arsenal on 7 Aug 1818. /s/ James H. Hook, Capt. of the 4th Inf. (*BPAT* 18 Aug 1818).

Parrott, Mrs. Eliza, d. at Easton, Md., consort of Mr. Joseph Parrott of that town (*BPAT* 4 Oct 1819).

Parrott, James, was m. [date not given] at Easton, Md., to Miss Eliza D. Littleton of Easton Point (*BPAT* 25 Jan 1819).

Parsons, John D., was m. last Tues. by Rev. Mr. Kurtz, to Miss Margaret Etchberger, all of this city (*BPAT* 9 Jan 1817; *FGBA* 8 Jan 1817).

Pascault, Francis, Esq., of Baltimore, was m. last Thurs. at Oakland, by Rev. Mr. Whitfield, to Miss Catherine D., dau. of Col. Thomas Hood of Anne Arundel Co. (*BA* 23 Dec 1817; *BPAT* 22 Dec 1817).

Patterson, Mr. Adolphus, merchant, formerly of Baltimore, was m. 14th ult. [Tues.], in Mifflin Co., PA, to Miss Elizabeth Anderson, youngest dau. of Col. Enoch Anderson of said county (*BPAT* 3 Feb 1817; *BA* 3 Feb 1817).

Patterson, Mrs. Averilla, relict of John Patterson, d. 16th inst., in Harford Co. in her 63rd year (*FGBA* 25 Jan 1819; *BPAT* 26 Jan 1819).

Patterson, James, an apprentice to the boot and shoe making business, ran away from Wm. Rogers. A reward of six cents was offered (*BPAT* 19 Aug 1818).

Patterson, Joseph W., was m. last Tues. night by Rev. Kemp to Miss Charlotte Nicols, dau. of James Nicols, all of Baltimore (*BPAT* 2 Jan 1818; *BA* 2 Jan 1818).

Pattison, Mr. [-?-], was m. 20th inst. [Thurs.] by Rev. Bare to Miss Martha Ward, both of Baltimore (*FGBA* 22 May 1819; *BPAT* 24 May 1819 gives the groom's name as Mr. Patterson).

Payson, John, was m. on 14th Sep [Mon.] by Mr. Willis to Miss Ann Shawen, all of Loudon Co., VA (*BA* 19 Oct 1818).

Pearce, Thomas, a black boy, absconded from John Williams, boot black, a poor unfortunate cripple at the corner of Thames and Bond Sts., Fell's Point (*BPAT* 1 May 1819).

Pearce, William, was m. 21st inst. [Fri.] by Rev. John Glendy to Susan Nelson (*FGBA* 28 Nov 1817; *BPAT* 28 Nov 1817).

Pearce, Wm. W., of Baltimore Co., was m. last Tues. by Rev. E. J. Reis to Miss Ann M. Britton also of Baltimore Co. (*FGBA* 3 April 1818; *BPAT* 3 April 1818).

Pease, Seth, aged 56, late one of the Assistants of the Post Master General, d. at Philadelphia, after a painful illness of eight days (*BPAT* 3 Sep 1819).

Peck, I., dec.: his heirs owe taxes for the years 1813, 1814, 1815, on 307 a. Company's Lands Transferred in the 1st Dist. (*BPAT* 7 Jan 1819).

Peck, John, dec.; his heirs owe taxes for the years 1816 and 1817 for 122 a. of the Baltimore Company's Land (*BPAT* 3 Aug 1819).

Peck, John S., d. Tues. evening, a native of England and member of the Society of Friends, aged 45 years. He died in the presence of his wife and her brothers (*FGBA* 16 April 1818; *BPAT* 16 April 1818). For the will of John S. Peck, filed in 1818, see BAWB 1:459.

Pendleton, Daniel, and **Frederick Jenkins**, of Baltimore, will have an Act, relative to a tobacco note, passed for their benefit (*BPAT* 10 Feb 1817).

Pendleton, Joseph Jenkins, only child of Daniel Pendleton of Baltimore, d. 6th inst., aged two years and two months (*BPAT* 9 May 1818).

Penniman, William, and Miss Henrietta Griffith of Montgomery Co., were m. this [Sat.] morning by Rev. Sparks (*FGBA* 10 July 1819; *BPAT* 10 July 1819).

Penniman, William, of Baltimore Co., is an insolvent debtor (*BPAT* 14 Oct 1819).

Pennington, Capt. Charles, one of the gallant defenders of Fort McHenry, drowned on his passage from Baltimore to New Orleans on 9 Dec 1817; he was not married (*BA* 4 May 1818; *BPAT* 3 May 1818).

Biographical Data from Baltimore Newspapers, 1817-1819

Pennock, Lewis, d. 4th last month, at his residence in East Marlborough Twp., Chester Co., Pa., aged 92 years, a member of the Society of Friends, leaving a wife to whom he had been married for more than three score years (*BPAT* 22 March 1817).

Penquite, Mrs. Mary, aged 98 years, 9 mos., and 6 days, d. lately in Fauquier Co., Va., at the residence of her son, William Penquite, Esq. (*BPAT* 29 Aug 1818; *FGBA* 4 Sep 1818).

Pentland, Brevet Major John, d. at Pittsburgh, 17th inst., late of the 22nd Regt., U.S. Infantry. He was at the taking of York and Fort George; other details of his military career are given (*BPAT* 7 Oct 1818).

Peoples, Walter Thomas, late of Litterkenny, Ireland, a member of the Royal College of Surgeons, d. Wed., 30th ult., in his 19th year (*BA* 5 Jan 1819; *BPAT* 5 Jan 1819).

Peregoy, Mr. Caleb, was m. 28 Oct [Tues.] by Rev. Rozzell, to Maria Croney, both of Baltimore (*FGBA* 3 Nov 1817; *BPAT* 1 Nov 1817, 3 Nov 1817).

Peregoy, Charles, and Sarah Tschudy, both of Baltimore Co., were m. 23rd Feb [Tues.] by Rev. Tidings (*FGBA* 26 Fen 1819; *BPAT* 27 Feb 1819).

Peregoy [Perrigo], Capt. Joseph, was m. last Sun. by Rev. Mr. Davis to Miss Rebecca Briggs, all of Baltimore (*FGBA* 18 Aug 1817; *BPAT* 18 Aug 1817).

Peregoy, Robert, was m. 24 July [Thurs.] by Rev. Roberts, to Miss Ruth Peregoy, both of Baltimore (*BA* 5 Aug 1817; *FGBA* 5 Aug 1817; *BPAT* 5 Aug 1817).

Peren, John, was m. last Sun eve. by Rev. Mr. Parks, to Miss Sarah Merchant (*BA* 17 June 1817; *BPAT* 17 June 1817).

Perine, Mr. David M., was m. last eve. [Sun.] by Rt. Rev. Bishop Kemp to Miss Mary Glenn, dau. of Elias Glenn, Esq., all of Baltimore (*BPAT* 2 March 1818; *BA* 3 March 1818).

Perkins, Benjamin, of Baltimore, and Mary P. Tuck, second dau. of Samuel Tuck, formerly of Boston, were m. at Allen's Mills, Baltimore Co. on Mon. by Rev. Tidings (*FGBA* 4 Feb 1819; *BPAT* 5 Feb 1819).

Perkins, Daniel, of Kent Co., dec.; by a decree of the Court of Chancery, several properties in Kent Co. will be sold. /s/ George W. Thomas trustee (*BPAT* 25 March 1817).

Perkins, Thomas, and Miss Catherine Rhode, all of Baltimore, were m. last Thurs. by Rev. Glendy (*FGBA* 27 Feb 1819; *BPAT* 27 Feb 1819).

Perrigo. See Peregoy.

Peterkin, Sarah Jane, d. Wed., 1 Sep. Her sister died recently (*FGBA* 3 Sep 1819; *BPAT* 3 Sep 1819). Sarah Jane Peterkin, aged 15 years, was buried 18 Sep 1819 from St. Paul's Parish, and Mary Jane Peterkin, aged 13 years, was buried 15 Sep 1819 (ReamySP).

Peterson, John, of Baltimore Co., dec.: Margaret Peterson, admx., has obtained letters of administration (*BPAT* 25 Sep 1818).

Pettecord, Mr. John, and Miss Catherine Wilson, all of Baltimore, were m. last Wed. eve. by Rev. D. E. Reese (*BPAT* 12 June 1818; *BA* 12 June 1818).

Pettigill (or Petti Gill), John, apprentice, aged 17, ran away from James Griggs; a reward of six cents was offered (*BPAT* 17 March 1817).

Peyton, John S., Esq., of Winchester, VA, was m. Thurs. eve., 9th inst., by Rev. Mr. Fenwick, to Miss Mary Carrere, second dau. of John Carrere, Esq., of this city (*BPAT* 15 Jan 1817; *FGBBA* 15 Jan 1817).

Pfeiffer, Mr. Henry H., and Miss Dorothy S. Bausman, were m. last eve. [Thurs.] by the Rev. John P. Bausman (*BPAT* 5 Nov 1818).

Pfeiffer, Margaret, an indented German Redemptioner, ran away from Mary Seltzer. She is now in Baltimore, secreted at the house of Abraham Bowers (*BPAT* 23 June 1818).

Phelan, Elizabeth, of Baltimore Co., dec.: Luke Tiernan, admin., has obtained letters of administration (*BPAT* 10 Sep 1818).

Phillips, Mrs. Bathia, d. Wed., 16th inst., in her 73rd year, having been sorely afflicted for the past eight years (*BPAT* 25 Sep 1818; *BA* 26 Sep 1818; *FGBA* 24 Sep 1818).

Phillips, Isaac, of Baltimore Co., is an insolvent debtor (*BPAT* 19 Oct 1819).

Biographical Data from Baltimore Newspapers, 1817-1819

Phillips, Isaac, Jr., was m. last eve. [Tues.] by Rev. John Mason Duncan, to Miss Ann B. Sweeting, all of Baltimore (*FGBA* 14 May 1817; *BPAT* 14 May 1817).

Phillips, James, of Baltimore Co., was m. at Bristol, R.I., [date not given], to Miss Lucy Waldron of Bristol (*BPAT* 11 Aug 1819).

Phillips, John, d. last eve. [Thurs.], in his 32nd year. The funeral will be from his brother William's residence in Dutch Alley (*FGBA* 29 Jan 1819; *BPAT* 30 Jan 1819).

Phillips, William, owes taxes for the years 1813, 1814, 1815, on 1 lot on the Turnpike (*BPAT* 7 Jan 1819).

Pic, Mr. Francis, d. at Washington City, aged 63 years (*BPAT* 24 Dec 1819).

Pickett, Mrs. Ann, consort of George Pickett, d. Mon. eve., 11th inst.; in her 52nd year; she was a faithful member of the Methodist Episcopal Church, leaving a husband and three children (*BPAT* 13 Oct 1819).

Pidgeon, Mr. Christopher, d. at Philadelphia, on Sun. eve., 28th inst., in his 51st year, long a respectable inhabitant of that city (*BPAT* 4 Dec 1819).

Pierce, Miss Caroline, dau. of Israel Pierce, d. Wed., 12th inst., aged 16 years. (Long obit follows) (*BA* 18 Nov 1817; *BPAT* 18 Nov 1817). Her funeral sermon will be preached next Sun. afternoon by Rev. Samuel Jennings at Eutaw Church (*BA* 29 Nov 1817).

Pierpoint, Amos, dec.; his heirs owe taxes for the years 1813, 1814, 1815, on 50 a. Cannon's Lot in the 1st Dist. (*BPAT* 7 Jan 1819).

Pierpoint, Samuel, owes taxes for the year 1817 on a lot in Journey Cake Town [Johnny Cake Town?] in the 1st Dist. (*BPAT* 3 Aug 1819).

Pierpoint, Thomas, dec,; his heirs owe taxes for the years 1813 and 1815 on 50 a. Cannon's Lot in the 1st Dist. (*BPAT* 7 Jan 1819).

Pindell, John, and Miss Sarah Fisher, all of Baltimore, were m. 11th inst. [Sun.] by Rev. Glendy (*FGBA* 14 July 1819; *BPAT* 14 July 1819).

Pinnell, F. A., advertises a reward for capture and bringing to trial of the three ruffians who robbed him last Thurs. night while he was on his way from Baltimore to Washington (*BPAT* 29 Sep 1817).

Pitman, Rev. Hipkins, aged 74, was m. in Va., [date not given] to Miss Phebe Adams, aged 72. The mother of the lady is still living and enjoys excellent health. She was married to Mr. James Bates about 1725 and now has about 80 living descendants (*BPAT* 19 June 1819).

Pizany, Francis, Jr., burgher, merchant, and inhabitant of the island of St. Bartholomew's, married Grace Cochran, dau. of Capt. Nichol Cochran and Elizabeth Maillard, who later married John Francis Gibney, burgher and merchant of St. Bartholomew's but now residing in Baltimore. Elizabeth Gibney died, and Gibney has never told Pizany or his wife about said Elizabeth's death (*BPAT* 25 Nov 1817). [Mrs. Elizabeth Gibney, wife of John Gibney, a native of St. Martin's, died Tues., 6th inst., aged 52 (*Baltimore American* 9 Aug 1816)],

Placide, Mrs. Louisa, d. last Sat night, after a long and painful illness (*BPAT* 22 Sep 1818; *BA* 22 Sep 1818). Louise Placide d. 19 Sep 1818, age 40, of consumption. She was buried 20 Sep 1818 in the Cathedral Cemetery (Grogaard).

Plains, Mr. George, and Miss Isabella Prints, all of Baltimore, were m. last Thurs. eve. by Rev. D. E. Reese (*BPAT* 28 March 1818; *BA* 28 March 1818).

Plater, John Rousby, eldest son of Judge Plater, and Miss Ann Elizabeth Plater, all of St. Mary's Co., were m. Tues., 3rd inst., at Bloomsbury, Leonardtown, St. Mary's Co., by Rev. Mr. Brady (*BPAT* 10 Nov 1818; *BA* 10 Nov 1818).

Plummer, Joseph P., of Baltimore, was m. 10 Sep [Fri.] by John Beadle, Esq., to Lydia Husband of Washington, Dutchess Co., N.Y. (*BPAT* 20 Sep 819).

Plummer, Priscilla, d. 23rd inst., in her 97th year, at her seat in Prince George's Co. Born in Prince George's Co., on 7th d., 1st mo., 1722 o.s., she was married at age 16, and of nine children, those living are: John, 78, William, 76, Yate, 74, Susannah, 60, Thomas, 58, and James 56. Her father, John Lamar, died at age 82. She leaves 25 grandchildren and 18 great-grandchildren (*FB BA* 30 July 1818).

Biographical Data from Baltimore Newspapers, 1817-1819

Plummer, Thomas, d. 19th inst., in his 59th year, at his farm in Anne Arundel Co. (*FGBA* 30 Oct 1818; *BPAT* 31 Oct 1818). For the will of Thomas Plummer, filed in 1818, see AAWB JG#3:235.

Pochon, Mrs. Harriet, wife of Charles F. Pochon, d. 12th ult., in her 21st year, leaving a husband and two infant daus. (*FGBA* 18 Feb 1818). Harriet Pochon, consort of Charles F. Pochon, d. 12 Jan 1818, age 22, of a bilious complaint. She was buried 13 Jan 1818 in the Cathedral Cemetery (Grogaard).

Pogue, John G., and Miss Mary Jones, dau. of William Jones, all of Baltimore, were m. last eve. [Thurs.] by Rev. Duncan (*FGBA* 15 Jan 1819; *BPAT* 16 Jan 1819).

Polley, Mr. Henry, of Baltimore, was m. [date not given], at Portsmouth to Miss Ann Nichols of the latter place (*BPAT* 2 Dec 1819).

Pollock, John, Esq., d. at Col. Young's, Albemarle Co., Va., last Sat., 26th April, in his 34th year. Mr. Pollock reached our shores about 16 months ago, on a visit to his brother, who survived his arrival only one month. Less than two months after that his father died, and three months after that his mother died, making four deaths in the same family in 15 months (*BPAT* 5 May 1817).

Poole[?], Mr. Edward, of Edwardsville, Ill., was m. [date not given], to Miss Lucina E. Snow, late of Baltimore (*BPAT* 13 Sep 1819).

Poor, Moses, of Baltimore Co., is an insolvent debtor (*BPAT* 14 Oct 1819)

Pope, Abner, of Baltimore, and Maria Perkins of Alexandria, were m. 30th ult. [Thurs.] at the Friends Meeting House in the latter place (*FGBA* 13 May 1818; *BPAT* 12 May 1818).

Pope, Mr. Joseph, was m. 2nd inst. [Tues.] to Miss Mary Marshall, both of Prince George's Co., MD (*BPAT* 5 Dec 1817).

Porter, Mr. John, and Miss Susan Wilson, all of Baltimore, were m. Thurs. eve. last by Rev. D. E. Reese (*BPAT* 30 Oct 1818; *FGBA* 3 Oct 1818; *BA* 3 Oct 1818).

Potter, Stephen, of Baltimore Co., and a native of New England, aged 57, d. 6th inst. (*BPAT* 16 Sep 1819).

Potter, Thomas, and Charlotte Wilson, all of Baltimore Co., were m. Sun., 22nd inst., by Rev. D. E. Reese (*BA* 27 Nov 1818; *BOPM* 27 Nov 1818).

Potts, William, d. 18th inst., in his 76th year. (From the Frederick Town *Herald*) (*FGBA* 25 Jan 1817; *BPAT* 25 Jan 1817).

Potts, Dr. William, d. 13th inst., aged 32 years and a few days. [Long obit follows]. (From the *Frederick Herald*) (*FGBA* 24 April 1818).

Pouder, Mrs. Mary, consort of George Pouder, and dau. of Peter Fowble, d. Sat., in her 22nd year, leaving a husband and two small children (*BA* 28 Dec 1818; *BPAT* 28 Dec 1818).

Powell, Thomas, is supposed to have arrived here with his family, from England, last summer or fall, will find a letter waiting for him at the office of the *Federal Gazette* (*BPAT* 16 Feb 1818).

Power, Mrs. Eliza, a native of the County of Waterford, Ireland, d. Tues. at her residence at 11 Pratt St. (*BA* 24 April 1818; *BPAT* 23 April 1818).

Power, Mr. Michael, and Miss Eliza Hannah, all of Baltimore, were m. last eve. [Fri.] by Rev. Moranville (*BPAT* 7 Nov 1818; *BA* 7 Nov 1818).

Powers, Richard, about 16 or 17 years old, apprentice to the shoemaking business, ran away from Joseph Fefel, 100 Pratt St. (*BPAT* 8 June 1819).

Powley, George, apprentice, has taken goods from several persons in his master's name and without his orders; all persons are warned not to let him have anything without a special order from John Curlet (*BPAT* 14 March 1817).

Presbury, George, Esq., of Harford Co., and Miss Ann Stiles of Baltimore were m. last Tues. by Rev. Glendy (*BPAT* 1 Dec 1819).

Prestman, George, d. 17th Aug. in his 81st year. His funeral will be from his residence in Goodman St. (*FGBA* 18 Aug 1819; *BPAT* 18 Aug 1819). For the will of George Prestman, filed in 1819, see BAWB 11:35.

Biographical Data from Baltimore Newspapers, 1817-1819

Preston, Benjamin B., born in Belle Air, Md., aged 32, a carpenter, deserted from the detachment under the command of James H. Cook, Capt. of Infantry at Fort Covington, on 4 March (*BPAT* 13 April 1819).

Preston, Miss Letitia, a native of Md., d. 28th inst., aged 27 years, at Philadelphia (*BPAT* 2 Sep 1818; *FGBA* 3 Sep 1818).

Preston, William, and Miss Laurena Darcus, both of Baltimore, were m. last Thurs. eve. by Rev. Dr. Roberts (*BPAT* 7 Feb 1818; *FGAB* 6 Feb 1818).

Prevost, Col. Andrew M., of Philadelphia, was m. last eve. [Tues.] by Rev. John Glendy to Miss Hannah Coulter, dau. of Dr. Coulter of Baltimore (*BA* 17 Dec 1817; *BPAT* 17 Dec 1817).

Price, Andrew, of Baltimore Co., is an insolvent debtor (*BPAT* 17 March 1818).

Price, Rev. Jonathan, from Philadelphia, and Miss Mary Pearse of Baltimore Co. were m. last Wed. at Mount Pleasant by the Rev. Thomas Poteet (*BPAT* 2 Dec 1819).

Price, Nehemiah, d. Fri., 14th inst., in his 36th year (*FGBA* 20 Aug 1818; *BPAT* 18 Aug 1818). Thomas Price, exec., advertises the sale of a three story house, unfinished, and lot, 21' x 70', on the east side of N. Charles St., near Franklin St. (*BPAT* 19 April 1819). Charles Peregay [Peregoy], agent for Thomas Price, exec., urges all persons indebted to the estate of Nehemiah Price to settle their accounts, or have their debts be placed in the hands of officers of collection, without respect to persons (*BPAT* 12 Oct 1818). For the will of Nehemiah Price, filed in 1818, see BAWB 10:503).

Price, Mr. Thomas, and Miss Elizabeth Keigler, all of Baltimore, were m. last eve. [Thurs.] by Right Rev. Bishop Kemp (*BPAT* 31 July 1818; *BA* 31 July 1818).

Price, William, d. Sat., 8th inst., at Woodbine, his estate in Baltimore Co., in his 70th year (*BA* 13 May 1819; *BPAT* 12 May 1819). For the will of William Price, filed in 1819, see BAWB 11:7.

Prince, William, of Ky., and Miss Everline [sic] Dorsey of Montgomery Co., were m. [date not given] (*BPAT* 29 Aug 1818).

Pringle, Mark, merchant, of Baltimore, d. Wed. morning at his seat near Havre-de-Grace; long a respectable merchant of Baltimore (*BA* 11 Jan 1819; *BPAT* 11 Jan 1819).

Proebsting, Mrs. Frances, wife of Theodore C. Proebsting, d. last night, aged 23 years, 8 mos., and 6 days. She resided at 260 Market St. (*FGBA* 4 Aug 1819; *BPAT* 4 Aug 1819).

Pullen, Robert, and Miss Eliza Walton, all of Baltimore, were m. last Wed. eve. by Glendy (*BA* 31 Oct 1818; *BPAT* 31 Oct 1818).

Pullin, Everet R., apprentice to the boot making business, from Va., with friends in or near Battletown, aged about 18, ran away from Rezin Pool, No. 43 South St. (*BPAT* 7 June 1817).

Purdon, Mr. Joseph, printer, formerly of Baltimore, d. at New Orleans (*BPAT* 15 Oct 1819).

Purdy, Mr. John, merchant, was m. last Thurs. eve. by Rev. Henshaw to Miss Caroline Pickersgill, all of Baltimore (*BPAT* 5 Dec 1817).

"Q"

Quigley, James, owes taxes for the year 1815 on 153 a. *Hooker's Meadows* in the 7th Dist. (*BPAT* 7 Jan 1819).

Quinlan, Marcus, aged 26, born in Ireland, lately a resident of New Holland, a shoemaker, enlisted 21 June 1817 and deserted 4 Aug from the Carlisle Barracks /s/ James Pratt, Capt., 5th Infantry (*BPAT* 2 Sep 1817).

Quinn, Thomas, died yesterday. His funeral will be from the house of his brother Edward Quinn, Bond St., Fells Point (*BA* 12 Dec 1817; *BPAT* 12 Dec 1817).

Biographical Data from Baltimore Newspapers, 1817-1819

"R"

Raborg, Christopher, of Baltimore Co., dec.; his real estate, consisting of two two-story brick houses on Lovely Lane, and one three-story brick house at 13 Water St., will be sold by Harrison & Sterett, Auctioneers. (*BPAT* 11 March 1819).
Raborg, George W., son of the late Mr. Christopher Raborg, died last Sat., in his 30th year (*FGBA* 13 Jan 1817). **N.B.**: George William Raborg, son of John Henry and Catherine Raborg, died in 1817 aged 30. He was originally buried in St,. Peter's Church, but in 1870 his tomb was moved to where he is now buried in Lot #49 in Westminster Presbyterian Churchyard, Baltimore (HaywardW). For the will of George W. Raborg, filed in 1817, see BAWB 10:273.
Ramsay, Mary Jane, dau. of David Ramsay, printer, d. this morning, aged 4 mos., and 3 weeks (*FGBA* 13 May 1819; *BPAT* 13 May 1819).
Ramsay, Thomas, d. last eve., after a lingering illness, in the 38th year of his age. The funeral will be this afternoon at 2 o'clock, from his late dwelling, Fleet St., Fells Point (*BPAT* 5 Dec 1817). For the will of Thomas Ramsay, filed in 1817, see BAWB 10:391.
Ramsey, Col. Nathaniel, of Baltimore, d. 24 Oct 1817, an officer in the Rev. War, and a Naval officer of this port (*FGBA* 27 Oct 1817; *BA* 27 Oct 1817; *BPAT* 25 Oct 1817). His sarcophagus reads "Col. Nathaniel Ramsay who departed this life October 23rd 1817 aged 76 years, 7 months and 27 days." He is buried in Lot # 118 of Westminster Presbyterian Churchyard, Baltimore (HaywardW). For the will of Nathaniel Ramsey, filed in 1817, see BAWB 10:375.
Randall, John, dec.; his property, consisting of four lots on Hanover St., adjoining the property of William Paterson, Esq., and opposite the dwellings of Messrs Stump and Mr. Wilmer, will be sold at auction (*BPAT* 24 March 1818). For the will of John C. Randall, filed in 1817, see BAWB 10:395.
Randall, Jonathan, owes taxes for the year 1817 on a 1½ a. lot in the 1st Dist., leased from [-?-] Payson (*BPAT* 3 Aug 1819).
Randolph, William Elston, d. Mon. night, after a short illness. His funeral will take place his evening from Mrs. Messersmith's, Washington Square, at 6 o'clock (*BA* 18 June 1817; *BPAT* 17 June 1817).
Rankin, Henry, owes taxes for the years 1813, 1814, 1815, on 1 a. *Broad's Improvement* in the 2nd Dist (*BPAT* 1 Jan 1819).
Rasin, Capt. Samuel, late of the U. S. Army, was m. Thurs., 4th inst. by Rev. Dr. Roberts, to Miss Mary S. Stevens, of Baltimore (*BA* 16 Nov 1818; *BPAT* 13 Nov 1818).
Rasin, Capt. Thomas, of Still Pond, Kent Co., d. Fri., 12 Nov., in about the 49th year of his age, leaving an amiable wife and five small children (*BPAT* 19 Nov 1819).
Rawlings, Gassaway, dec.; Samuel Maccubbin advertises for the return of his black man named Charles (*BPAT* 21 Oct 1818).
Rawlings, Stephen, of Queen Anne's Co., dec.; William Chambers, admin., will settle the estate (*BPAT* 19 March 1819).
Rawson, F., Land Agent for this city, has died. E. Gillespy, at 19 N. Frederick St., will investigate land titles in the Western States (*BPAT* 1 Nov 1819).
Ray, Miles, owes taxes for the years 1813, 1814, 1815, on a lot on Green St. (*BPAT* 7 Jan 1819). [See also Miles Ray Kelly].
Read, William, was m. last Mon. eve. by Rev. Dr. Inglis, to Miss Lydia Maria Fenn (*FGBA* 20 Jan 1819; *BPAT* 19 Jan 181).
Reardon, Mr. Thomas, was m. at Chestertown to Miss Charlotte Garey [date not given] (*BPAT* 17 Nov 1817).
Redgrave, Mr. John, was m. last Thurs. eve. by Rev. Dr. Inglis, to Miss Elizabeth Hoffman, all of Baltimore (*BPAT* 2 May 1817; *BA* 3 May 1817).
Reding, Mrs. Margaret, wife of Edward M. Reding, and dau. of Anthony Otheman of Boston, d. in Baltimore, aged 22 years (*FGBA* 5 March 1817).

Biographical Data from Baltimore Newspapers, 1817-1819

Reed, Capt. James, of the U. S. Army, Commandant at Fort Mifflin, d. at Philadelphia (*BPAT* 13 Aug 1819).

Reed, John, aged about 17 years old, 5' 3 or 4" tall, middling stout, dark complected, pock marked, with a scar across the upper joint of his left thumb, apprentice to the oak coopering business, ran away from William Holland, 99 Saratoga St. The Philadelphia *Gazette* is asked to carry this advertisement for three times (*BPAT* 2 Nov 1818).

Reeves, John, was m. last Thurs. by Rev. John Davis, to Miss Ann Grace, all of Fells Point (*BA* 27 June 1818; *BPAT* 26 June 1818).

Regester, Samuel, was m. Thurs., 23rd inst. at Friends Meeting House, Old Town, to Elizabeth Amos, both of Baltimore (*BPAT* 30 Oct 1817; *FGBA* 30 Oct 1817).

Reily, Clagon, late a doctor in the 8th U.S. Infantry, U.S. Army, d. last Thurs at Washington in his 26th year (*BPAT* 28 Feb 1818).

Relf, Samuel, d. at St. Louis, near New Orleans in the 15th year of his age, second son of Samuel Relf, editor of the *Philadelphia Gazette;* of the malignant fever (*BPAT* 19 Oct 1819).

Rennell, John N., a native of England, but for the last 21 years, a resident of Baltimore, d. this morning, aged 44 years (*FGBA* 5 Dec 1818). His library of over 500 books, and other valuable property, will be sold at auction by S. & J. Cole, auctioneers (*BPAT* 21 Jan 1819). For the will of John N. Rennells, filed in 1818, see BAWB 10:542.

Rennalds, Caesar, a Negro boy, aged about 22, a butcher by trade, ran away from John Maxfield, butcher, who asks that the *York Gazette, Lancaster Journal,* the Philadelphia *Franklin Gazette,* and the New York *Mercantile Advertiser* insert the above notice (*BPAT* 15 April 1818). (In the *BPAT* of 19 Oct 1818, the runaway's name is give as Caesar Runnells, and the butcher is James Maxwell}.

Rennous, John, was m. 25th inst., [Thurs.] by Mr. Choate to Miss Susannah Grice (*FGBA* 31 March 1819; *BPAT* 2 April 1819).

Renshaw, Thomas, of Chillicothe, Ohio, was m. to Miss Elizabeth C. Corwin of Baltimore last eve. [Fri.] by Rev. Mr. Fry (*BPAT* 26 Nov 1818).

Reteu, William, was m. to Miss Rebecca Mahana, all of Baltimore, last Thurs. by Rev. Sparks (*BMC* 17 May 1819; *BPAT* 15 May 1819).

Revell, John, printer, d. yesterday in his 30th year; he resided in Commerce St. *BA* 22 April 1818; *BPAT* 21 April 1818).

Reynolds, Jesse, purchased some land In Nottingham Township, formerly believed to be in Pennsylvania, but later found to be in Maryland from the Intendant of Maryland. Reynolds died leaving a widow Sarah and the following heirs: Levi Reynolds, Mary Reynolds, William Reynolds, Samuel Johnson and wife Lydia, James Cox and wife Rebecca, Henry Reynolds, Leonard Reynolds, Olivia Reynolds, John Fough and wife Elizabeth, John Hallowell and wife Sarah, Jesse Reynolds, Elisha Reynolds, Immer Reynolds, John Brown and wife Sarah, Nathan Brown and wife Rachel, Elisha Reynolds, Elizabeth Reynolds, and Mary Reynolds. The widow and the heirs are being sued in Cecil Co. Court by the heirs of Andrew P. Evans (see above). The bill of complaint states that Levi Reynolds, John Fough and wife Elizabeth, John Hallowell and wife Sarah, Jesse Reynolds, Immer Reynolds, John Brown and wife Sarah, Nathan Brown and wife Rachel, Elisha Reynolds and Elizabeth Reynolds all reside without the state of Maryland (*BPAT* 6 March 1819).

Reynolds, John, was m. to Miss Barbara Forney, all of Baltimore, last Tues. eve. by Rev. Mr. Inglis (*BPAT* 25 June 1818).

Reynolds, John, was m. to Mrs. Mary Skelton last eve. [Thurs.] by Rev. Healy (*BPAT* 30 April 1819).

Reynolds, Dr. John, was m. to Miss Maria Sprigg at Hagerstown (BMC or *Maryland Gazette or Baltimore General Advertiser* 17 May 1819).

Reynolds, William, of Baltimore Co., dec.: Susanna Reynolds, admx., will settle the estate (*BPAT* 19 Jan 1819). For the will of William Reynolds, filed in 1819, see BAWB 10:548.

Biographical Data from Baltimore Newspapers, 1817-1819

Rhodes, Zachariah, and Miss Lucy Churchill, both of Baltimore Co., were m. Sun., 6th inst., at Avalon, by Rev. English *(FGBA* 9 June 1818; *BPAT* 10 June 1819).

Ricaud, Thomas P., will sell at public auction on 1 March 1817, the house and lot at 106 Market St. now occupied by him as a Fancy Dry Goods Store *(BPAT* 20 Feb 1817). He is an insolvent debtor *(BPAT* 16 Nov 1818).

Rice, Mr. John, was m. at Washington, [date not given], by the Rev. Dr. Elliott, Chaplain of the U.S. Army, to Miss Betsey Weysell *(BPAT* 21 May 1817; *BA* 22 May 1817).

Rice, Mr. Lewis, was m. Friday, 21st inst., by Rev. D. E. Reese to Miss Susannah Dickson, all of Baltimore *(BPAT* 28 Nov 1817; *BA* 28 Nov 1817).

Richards, John A., and Miss Sarah Hook, both of Baltimore Co. were m. 12 Feb [Thurs.] by Rev. Smith *(BA* 18 Feb 1818; *BPAT* 18 Feb 1818).

Richards, William, Jr., watchmaker, of Philadelphia, d. at Cincinnati, Ohio, in the 36th year of his age *(BPAT* 9 July 1819).

Richardson, Dr. Charles, and Miss Juliana Smith, dau. of Samuel R. Smith, all of Baltimore, were m. last Tues. by Rev. Mr. Reid *(FGBA* 22 Jan 1819; *BPAT* 22 Jan 1819).

Richardson, Daniel P., of Caroline Co., and Miss Catherine Medcalfe, of Talbot Co. were m. [date not given] *(BPAT* 25 Jan 1819).

Richardson, Mrs. Ricey, consort of James Richardson of Baltimore, died last eve,. in her 50th year *(BPAT* 27 June 1818).

Richardson, Major Samuel, Register of Wills for Harford Co., died 27 Feb in that county *(BA* 11 March 1818; *BPAT* 11 March 1818).

Richmond, Mr. James C., was m. Tues. eve. by Rev. Mr. Sewell, to Miss Ann E. G. Stanly, eld. dau. of the late Capt. Robert Stanly of Baltimore *(BPAT* 20 March 1817; *BA* 20 March 1817).

Rico, Lewis, was m. on Fri., 21st inst., by Rev. D. E. Reese, to Miss Susannah Dickson, all of Baltimore *(BPAT* 28 Nov 1817).

Riddle, Capt. Edward, d. last Sat., aged 36 years *(BPAT* 6 July 1818).

Rider, Mr. Edward, was m. last Sat. eve. by Rev. Mr. Healey, to Miss Rachel Gorsuch, both of Baltimore Co. *(BPAT* 6 March 1817). For the will of Edward Rider, filed in 1817, see BAWB 10:217.

Rider, Frederick, was m. [date not given] in Baltimore to Miss Leonora Rabb *(American Farmer* 2 April 1819).

Ridgaway, James, of Caroline Co., will have an act passed for his benefit *(BPAT* 10 Feb 1817).

Ridgaway, Mr. William C., of Cambridge, Dorchester Co., was m. [date not given], to Miss Henrietta Scott of Queen Anne's Co. *(BPAT* 21 April 1817).

Ridgely, Charles, Jr., of "Hampton," d. last Sat., in his 36th year *(BA* 22 June 1819; the *BPAT* of 21 June 1819 states he d. Sun. eve., and that he was the eldest son of the late Gov. of Maryland). For the will of Charles Ridgely, Jr., filed in 1819, see BAWB 11:22.

Ridgely, Charles, of John, dec.; Joseph Young and wife Elizabeth petitioned the court that some of the representatives are absent or reside out of the estate *(BPAT* 4 Jan 1817).

Ridgely, David, of Annapolis, was m. to Maria Sellman of Baltimore on Tues. eve. by Rev. Dr. Jennings *(BA* 17 Dec 1818; *BPAT* 17 Dec 1818).

Ridgely, John W., of Pomona Grove, was m. Tues., 17th inst., by Rev. Force to Isabella Folger, of Baltimore Co. *(BA* 20 Nov 1818; *BPAT* 20 Nov 1818).

Ridgely, N. H., and Miss Jane O., eldest dau. of Samuel Vincent, all of Baltimore, were m. last Thurs. by Rev. Greenbury Ridgely *(BA* 14 June 1819; *BPAT* 15 June 1819).

Ridgely, Richard, owes taxes for the years 1813, 1814, 1815, on 465¼ a. of various tracts in the 1st Dist. *(BPAT* 7 Jan 1819).

Ridgely, Mr. Richard, and Miss Mary Jane, dau. of Nicholas Brewer, of Annapolis, were m. there on Tues. eve. by Rev. Mr. Guest *(BPAT* 17 Dec 1819).

Biographical Data from Baltimore Newspapers, 1817-1819

Riggs, Mrs. Eliza, consort of George W. Riggs, d. 5th inst., in her 39th year (*BPAT* 8 May 1819).

Riley, Mr. Michael, and Miss Martha J. W. Kreider, both of Baltimore, were m. Sat. eve. 21st inst., by Rev. Mr. Fenwick, P.P. (*BPAT* 25 Aug 1819).

Rind, William Alexander, Jr., editor of the *National Messenger,* was m. last 7 May [Thurs.] to Miss Susan Maria Bruff, all of Columbia District (*BPAT* 25 Nov 1818).

Ringler, Mr. George, and Miss Ann Gardner, all of Baltimore, were m. last Tues. eve. by Rev. Mr. Dashields (*BPAT* 17 Sep 1819).

Ringgold, James W., and Miss Anna W. Comegys, were m. Tues. eve. last at Chestertown (*BA* 9 Nov 1818; *BPAT* 7 Nov 1818).

Riston, Abraham, d. 6 Feb in Baltimore Co., aged 53 years. His eldest and youngest sons died within eight days of him (*BA* 12 March 1818; *BPAT* 11 March 1818).

Riston, Jesse, of Baltimore, d. last Sun., in his 20th year in Baltimore Co., at the residence of Daniel Hughes, and was the youngest son of Abraham Riston (*BA* 10 March and 12 March 1818).

Riston, John, aged 27 years at his residence in Baltimore Co., on 28 Feb., the eldest son of Abraham Riston (*BA* 12 March 1818; *BPAT* 11 March 1818).

Ritchie, Mr. Abner, was m. at Georgetown, D. C., [date not given], to Miss Harriet Semms, dau. of Benjamin Semms, Esq., of Charles Co. (*BPAT* 24 July 1817).

Ritchie, Mrs. Frances, d. at Fredericktown, aged 63 (*BPAT* 23 Aug 1819).

Roach, John, a native of Maryland, d. in Richmond on the 9th inst., in the 20th year of his age; by profession a slater (*BPAT* 15 Sep 1817; *BA* 15 sep 1817).

Robbins, John L., of New York, and Miss Ellen Brown of Baltimore, were m. last Monday by Rev. Richards (*FGBA* 14 Jan 1818).

Roberts, Capt. John, a respectable merchant of Baltimore, d. yesterday (*BA* 21 Oct 1818; *FGBA* 21 Oct 1818; *BPAT* 21 Oct 1818). John Roberts, aged 47 years, was buried 18 Oct 1818 from St. Paul's Parish (ReamySP).

Roberts, Jonah, was m. Thurs. eve. by Rev. Bartow to Mrs. Ellen M. Quillon, all of Baltimore (*BPAT* 12 June 1819).

Roberts, Joseph, a native of France, was m. last Thurs. by Rev. Mr. Davis, to Miss Elizabeth Hammond (*BMC* 10 April 1819; *BPAT* 9 April 1819).

Roberts, Mr. St. George E., was m. Mon. eve. by Rev. John Glendy, to Mrs. Eliza Ranton, both of Philadelphia (*BPAT* 17 April 1817).

Robertson, John, son of George Robertson, d. 28th ult., leaving a mother, father, and sisters (*BPAT* 6 Oct 1818). John Alexander Robertson, aged 22 years, was buried 28 Sep 1818 from St. Paul's Parish (ReamySP).

Robeson, Capt. William [L.?], of the U. S. Army, was m. at Cragfont, Tenn., on 17th June [Tues.], to Miss Selima Winchester, dau. of Gen. James Winchester (*BPAT* 26 July 1817).

Robey, Townley, late Sheriff and Collector of Charles Co. is to have an Act of the Assembly to allow him to complete his collections (*BPAT* 10 Feb 1817).

Robins, Mrs. Elizabeth, wife of James B. Robbins of Worcester Co., d. last Mon. [long obit] (*BA* 6 Aug 1817). Eliza Robbins [sic]. aged 38 years, was buried 4 Aug 1817 from St. Paul's Parish (ReamySP).

Robinson, Charlotte, youngest dau. of Alexander Robinson, d. Sat., 10th inst., in her 15th year (*BA* 13 April 1819; *FGBA* 17 April 1819; *BPAT* 12 April 1819).

Robinson, Elijah, aged 16 or 17, an "indebted" apprentice to the cordwaining business, ran away from Thomas Bryne (*BPAT* 1 Dec 1818).

Robinson, Mr. James S., was m. last eve. [Wed.] by Rev. Mr. Waugh, to Mary, dau. of Jacob Rogers, all of Baltimore (*BPAT* 20 Aug 1818; *BA* 20 Aug 1818).

Robinson, Joshua D., d. 23rd inst., at Denton, Md., aged 25 years (*BPAT* 1 Feb 1817).

Robison, Jesse, d. yesterday morning, in his 26th year; his funeral will be from his mother's dwelling, North Howard St. (*BPAT* 12 Nov 1817; *BA* 12 Nov 1817). He is buried in Lot # 61 in Westminster Presbyterian Churchyard, Baltimore (HaywardW).

Biographical Data from Baltimore Newspapers, 1817-1819

Roche, John, of Alice Anne St., Fells Point, d. Wed., 13th inst., aged about 45 years. He was interred in the R.C. burying ground (*BA* 14 Aug 1817). For the will of John Roche, filed in 1817, see BAWB 10:346.

Rodney, Mr. John, eldest surviving son of Caesar A. Rodney, Esq., of Del., d. in his 19th year, cut off by a fever of great malignity. He was a Midshipman in the U. S. Navy, and when first attacked was on board the *Ontario.* He was taken to New York City, where he died on the 14th inst. (*BPAT* 27 Aug 1817).

Rogers, Lloyd N., Esq., was m. at Washington on Sat. by Rev. McCormick to Miss Eliza Law, dau. of Thomas Law, Esq. (*BPAT* 9 April 1817; *FBA* 8 April 1817).

Rogers, Mrs. Rebecca, wife of Philip, d. Monday afternoon, after a short illness (*BPAT* 22 Oct 1818).

Rogers, Mr. William, of Richmond, Va., and Miss Mary Sweetser of Baltimore, were m. last eve. [Thurs.] by Rev. Mr. Waugh (*BPAT* 24 April 1818; *BA* 24 April 1818 states they were m. on Wed. morning).

Rogers, William C., of Baltimore Co., is an insolvent debtor (*BPAT* 28 Nov 1818).

Rogge, Mr. Charles, was m. last Sun. eve. by Rev. Mr. Fenwick, to Miss Mary Magdalen Eisler, all of Baltimore (*BPAT* 28 Oct 1817; *BA* 28 Oct 1817).

Roiston, Mr. Robert, of Baltimore Co., was m. last Thurs. eve. by Rev. Dr. Roberts, to Miss Sarah M. Bowen of Baltimore (*BPAT* 22 Nov 1817; *BA* 22 Nov 1817).

Rook, John A., and Miss Ransell, both of Baltimore, were m. last Tues. by Rev. Glendy (*FGBA* 16 Feb 1819; *BPAT* 16 Feb 1819).

Rooker, Rev. James, late of Baltimore, and Miss Smart of Germantown, were m. there last Thurs. by Rev. Charles Dupuy (*FGBA* 25 Jan 1819; *BPAT* 25 Jan 1819).

Rooker, Mr. James C., son of Rev. James Rooker, late of Baltimore, d. at New Orleans on 4 Sep, after an illness of four days (*BPAT* 5 Oct 1819).

Root, William, was m. by Rev. Glendy, on 5th inst. [Sun], to Miss Sarah Mumma, all of Baltimore (*BPAT* 8 Oct 1817; *BA* 9 Oct 1817).

Rosensteel, Mr. Henry, was m. last Sun. eve. by the Rev. Mr. Fenwick, to Miss Margaret Ryland of this city (*BPAT* 11 Feb 1817; *BA* 11 Feb 1817).

Ross, David, Esq., d. at Richmond, after a long indisposition. He was more than 80 years of age and had long been a resident of that city. As a commercial agent, he greatly befriended the commonwealth during the struggles of the Revolution, a time when we most needed assistance. Though for a long time deaf, he was an interesting and intelligent companion. From the *Enquirer* (*BPAT* 10 May 1817).

Ross, Mrs. Elizabeth, d. at Philadelphia, last Thurs., aged 105 years and 3 mos., a native of Ireland (*FGBA* 23 Sep 1818; *BPAT* 24 Sep 1818).

Ross, Sandy, a Negro man, about 22 years old, ran away from Osborn Belt, living near Vanesville, Prince George's Co. (*BPAT* 10 Sep 1818).

Ross, Mr. William, was m. last Thurs. eve. by Rev. Mr. Fenwick, to Miss Mary F. Heuisler, all of Baltimore (*BPAT* 18 April 1818; *FGBA* 18 April 1818).

Rothrock, Mr. Jacob, d. yesterday afternoon, in the 76th year of his age, for many years, a respectable inhabitant of this city. The funeral will be from his late dwelling, corner of Howard and German Sts. this afternoon at half-past 3 o'clock (*BPAT* 7 Jan 1817; *FGBA* 7 Jan 1817).

Rothrock, Mr. Jacob, native of Md., and formerly a citizen of Baltimore, d. 7th Oct ult., at New Alexandria, Red River, La., after an illness of twelve days of the yellow fever (*BPAT* 17 Nov 1819).

Rowan, Mr. George H., and Miss Barbary Ann Dickinson, all of Baltimore, were m. Tues. eve. last by Rev. Mr. Hagerty (*BPAT* 26 Feb 1818); *FGBA* 25 Feb 1818)..

Rowe, Mrs. Elizabeth, consort of Capt. John K. Rowe of Baltimore, died Sunday, 19th inst., aged 44 years (*BPAT* 3 Aug 1818; *FGBA* 1 Aug 1818).

Rowe, Elizabeth Ann, eld. dau. of Capt. John K. Rowe of Baltimore, died last Sat. morning, aged 21 years (*BPAT* 16 July 1817; *FGBA* 15 July 1817).

Rowles, William, owes taxes for the years 1816 and 1817 on 1½ a. from Chamberlain in the 1st Dist. (*BPAT* 3 Aug 1819).

Biographical Data from Baltimore Newspapers, 1817-1819

Rozenberry, Peter, aged 17, stout for his age, apprentice, ran away from Nathaniel Duvall. Peter may have gone towards Harford Co. A reward of 5 dollars was offered *(BPAT* 17 June 1818)

Rubenthal, John, apprentice to the printing business, aged between 18 and 19, about 5' 7 "or 9" tall, ran away from William Hamilton *(BPAT* 25 June 1817).

Ruckle, Samuel, merchant, was m. Tues. Eve. last by Rev. Dr. Jennings to Miss Elizabeth Foltz, all of this city *(BPAT* 23 Oct 1818).

Ruckle, William, d. Friday night about 6 o'clock. His funeral will be from his late residence, opposite St. Paul's Cemetery in German St. *(BPAT* 24 July 1818; *FGBA* 25 July 1818).

Rudulph, Zebulon, of Elkton, Md., and Mary Ann, only dau. of Capt. Edward Wallington of Philadelphia, were m. in that city on 1st inst. [Fri.], by Rev. Dr. Kemper *(FGBA* 13 Jan 1819; *BPAT* 13 Jan 1819).

Rush, Mrs. Catherine, d. Fri. last at Philadelphia, aged 110 years and 11 months *(BPAT* 6 May 1817.

Russell, Alexander, was m. last Thurs. eve. by Rev. Mr. Force to Mrs. Ann DeGroff, of Baltimore *(BA* 9 Jan 1819; *BPAT* 7 Jan 1819).

Russell, Mr. Philip, and Miss Ann Maria Coleman, all of Baltimore Co., were m. Sun. eve. by Rev. Henshaw *(BPAT* 10 Aug 1819).

Russell, William, was m. last Thurs. eve. by Rev. Mr. Rossell, to Miss Mary Bowers, both of Baltimore *(BPAT* 22 July 1817; *BA* 22 July 1817).

Russell, William M., was m. 8th inst., [Wed.] by Rev. Mr. Kurtz, to Miss Mary Ann Curry, both of Baltimore *(BPAT* 11 Dec 1819).

Rutter, Thomas, Esq., Marshal of Maryland, d. yesterday about 2 o'clock, after a short illness, in the 50th year of his age His funeral will take place tomorrow and carriages will be waiting at Washington Square to proceed to his late dwelling *(BPAT* 6 Oct 1817; *FGBA* 6 Oct 1817).

Ryan, James, of Montgomery Co. will have an act passed to make valid a deed to him *(BPAT* 10 Feb 1817),

Ryder, Frederick, was m. last eve. [Thurs.] by Rev. Davis to Miss Leonora Ward, all of Baltimore *(FGBA* 26 March 1819; *BPAT* 27 March 1819 which gives the bride's name as Leonora Rabb).

Rynd, Bryan, dec.; his brick house on Wilks St., on the Causeway, and a commodious brick house at 77 Fleet St., owned by Capt. Stenon, will be leased by Christopher Rynd *(BPAT* 22 Dec 1818).

"S"

Sadler, Mr. Henry, was m. Wed., 8th inst., at St. Mary's, by Rev. Mr. Bell, to Miss Catherine A., eld. dau,. of J. H. McIntosh, Esq., all of the former place *(BPAT* 27 Dec 1819).

Sadler, Mr. Thomas, of Dorchester Co., E. S., was m. Sun. eve., 19th inst., by Rev. Dr. Roberts, to Miss Ann Maria Forest of Baltimore *(BPAT* 21 Dec 1819).

St. Clair, Mrs., relict of the late Major General Arthur St. Clair, d. 18th inst. at Chesnut Ridge, near Greensburgh, Pa. *(BPAT* 29 Sep 1818).

Salenave, James, was m. last eve. [Fri.] by Rev. Mr. Moranville, to Miss Annette Prevatori, both of Baltimore *(BPAT* 4 Dec 1819).

Salgues (Salges), Mr. John J. (or B.), was m. last Tues. eve. by the Rev. Dr. Fenwick to Miss Margaret Burbine, both of Baltimore *(BPAT* 25 Sep 1817; *BA* 25 Sep 1817).

Salmon, Valentine, emigrated from King's Co., Ireland and landed at New York last July. He settled near Marshaltown, Chester Co., Pa., last Oct., and last March left his wife and child in search of employment at Baltimore; he has not been heard from since. Any information sent to H. Niles, editor of the *Weekly Gazette* will be forwarded to the gentlemen who have kindly interested themselves in behalf of the helpless female stranger *(BPAT* 15 May 1819).

Biographical Data from Baltimore Newspapers, 1817-1819

Sanders, Benedict I., was m. last Thurs. eve. by Rev. Kurtz to Miss Sarah Schorr, all of Baltimore (*BPAT* 5 March 1819).

Sanderson, Joseph M., and William H. Ward, of Baltimore Co., are insolvent debtors (*BPAT* 6 Oct 1819).

Sands, Samuel, was m. last eve. [Thurs.] by Rev. Mr. Richards, to Miss Sarah B. Innes (*BA* 23 April 1819; *BPAT* 24 April 1819).

Sanfer, Mr. John, was m. Thurs., 3rd inst., by Rev. Mr. Parks, to Miss Coleste [Celeste?] Young, both of Baltimore (*BPAT* 5 April 1817; *BA* 5 April 1817).

Sankey, William, was m. last Thurs. by Rev. Dr. Roberts, to Mrs. Bridget Horner, all of Baltimore (*FGBA* 23 May 1818; *BPAT* 23 May 1818).

Sargent, Samuel, of Baltimore, was m. last Sunday in Anne Arundel Co. by Rev. Maybury Parks, to Miss Sarah Fountain, of the latter place (*BA* 15 May 1818; *BPAT* 15 May 1818).

Sauner, Mr. John G., and Miss Elizabeth Keilholtz, both of Baltimore, were m. last Thurs. eve. by Rev. Dr. Kurtz (*BPAT* 7 Oct 1819).

Saunders, Robert B., aged about 20, apprentice to the boot making business, ran away from Rezin Pool, No. 43, South St. (*BPAT* 7 June 1817).

Saunders, Samuel, d. Fri., 27 Dec 1816, aged 56, a native of Williamsburg, VA, but for several years a respectable inhabitant of this place. He leaves a widow and four small children (*FGBA* 3 Jan 1817).

Saubere, Samuel, of Baltimore Co., is an insolvent debtor (*BPAT* 28 July 1818). On 12 Nov 1818 he advertised the opening of an academy for young gentlemen at No. 20 North Gay St. He stated that in no instance would corporal punishment be resorted to (*BPAT* 12 Nov 1818).

Savage, Mrs., wife of P. Savage, H. B. M. Consul at Norfolk, died there (*BPAT* 14 Jan 1818).

Savage, Mr. John, m. 12th inst. [Fri.], by Rev. Courtney, Mrs. Moody of Henrico Co., Va. She is the fourth lady he has married; the other three are still living. His third wife, Margaret, has abandoned the name of Savage (*BPAT* 22 June 1818).

Savage, Patrick, Esq., H.B.M. Consul for Va., and lately a resident of Norfolk, d. Monday last at Philadelphia, where he had gone for his health (*BPAT* 11 Aug 1818).

Sayer, Stephen, died 27 Sep last, in his 85th year, at the residence of his son, in Va.; on the very next day his wife died (*BPAT* 5 Dec 1815).

Schaeffer, Mr. C. A., of Baltimore, was m. at Philadelphia on Monday morning last, by Rev. Mr. Myer, to Miss Ellen, dau. of John R. Baker, Esq., of Philadelphia (*BPAT* 22 Dec 1819).

Schaeffer, George B., was m. last eve. [Tues.] by Rev. Dr. Jennings to Miss Frances M., second dau. of the late John Hawkins (*BA* 26 May 1819; *BPAT* 26 May 1819).

Schley, Mr. David, of Frederick Town, was m. last Tues. eve. by Rev. Mr. Phinney, to Miss Anna Mary, dau. of Mr. Peter Hoke of Harford Co. (*BPAT* 16 Dec 1819).

Schley, Henry, merchant, was m. Tues. eve. by Rev. Dr. Henshaw, to Miss Sarah Maria Worrell, all of Baltimore (*BA* 30 Oct 1817; *BPAT* 30 Oct 1817).

Schley, Jacob, merchant of Baltimore, was m. yesterday [Fri.] at Walnut Grove by Rev. Mr. Inglis, to Miss Ann B. Jones, dau. of the late Judge Jones of Baltimore Co. (*FGBA* 5 June 1818; *BPAT* 6 June 1818).

Schliecker, Peter Jasper, native of Altonia, Duchy of Holstein, d. 10th inst., in his 33rd year. He resided in Bank St. (*BA* 12 March 1818).

Schraer, Louis, a native of Westphalia, Germany, 5'5" tall, 19 or 20 years old, took merchandise worth $600.00 from the subscriber, and may attempt to sell it and pocket the proceeds. He left Fredericktown for Pittsburgh and may head to New Orleans. /s/ Mark Killion of Baltimore (*BPAT* 25 Feb 1818).

Schulte, Mr. J. E. C., a native of Magdeburg, Germany, and long a merchant of Baltimore, d. last Thurs. morning (*BA* 16 Feb 1818; *BPAT* 16 Feb 1818). For the will of J. E. C. Schultze, filed in 1818, see BAWB 10:419.

Biographical Data from Baltimore Newspapers, 1817-1819

Schumacher, Maurice, a German Redemptioner, aged about 30, who arrived here last November, absconded from Jo. K. Stapleton, brushmaker, 159 Baltimore St. He is a good German scholar, a catholic by profession, and understands a little French and Latin; he speaks English perfectly. He may have gone with two other German servants, one, a baker by trade, belonging to Joseph Worley, innkeeper, and the other to Mr. Edmondson, and had driven a cart (*BPAT* 8 April 1817). He may be the Maurice Schumacher, born in the canton of Luzerne, Switzerland who filed his Decl. of Intent in Baltimore Co. Court in Sep 1822, and was naturalized on 25 Oct 1824. George Savage and Edward N. Sweeny were witnesses (Baltimore Co. Court Naturalization Docket 1:86).

Schunck, John, Jr., d. this morning in his 34th year (*FGBA* 15 Jan 1818; *BPAT* 16 Jan 1818).

Schwartz, Conrad, aged 76, was m. last Sun. at Lancaster, Pa., by Rev. Endress to Mrs. Eliza Shawler, aged 58 (*FGBA* 19 March 1819; *BPAT* 20 March 1819).

Schwarz, Mr. J. E., merchant, was m. at Ridge retreat, near Philadelphia, [date not given], to Catherine, dau. of Abraham Sheridan (*BPAT* 16 Sep 1819).

Schwartzaur, Philip, of Baltimore, dec.; Joseph Sumwalt, clerk, announces that commissioners will meet to determine the boundaries of his property located on the road to Fort McHenry, and adjacent to the Fort (*BPAT* 13 May 1817).

Schwartze, August J., of Baltimore Co., is an insolvent debtor (*BPAT* 13 Oct 1819). August J. Schwartze of Great Britain, was naturalized 8 Dec 1796 (Baltimore Co. Court Naturalization Docket 1:59).

Schweitzer, Mr. Michael, was m. last Sun. eve. by the Rev. Dr. C. L. Becker, to Miss Sophia Bishop, both of Baltimore (*BPAT* 16 Sep 1817; *BA* 16 Sep 1817 gives the bride's name as Britton).

Scott, Mrs. Elizabeth, venerable relict of the late Dr. Scott, d. at Annapolis last Tues. night at an advanced age (*BPAT* 13 Sep 1819). For the will of Elizabeth Scott, filed in 1819, see AAWB JG-:50.

Scott, Henry, of the firm of William and Henry Scott, d. 5th inst., in his 32nd year (*FGBA* 10 Sep 1817). Henry Scott, aged 33 years, was buried 4 Sep 1817 from St. Paul's Parish (ReamySP).

Scott, John, was m. last Thurs. by Rev. Glendy, to Miss Mary Ann Beard, all of Baltimore (*BA* 29 Nov 1817; *BPAT* 28 Nov 1817).

Scott, Dr. John, of Kent Co. has died. By an order of the Kent Co. Court, there will be a sale of his real estate: a farm lying on the main branch of Langford's Bay, containing between 300 and 400 a. of land, about five miles from Chestertown, and a messuage and lot in town (*BPAT* 3 May 1817).

Scott, Mrs. Louisa, relict of the late Henry Scott, d. last Friday in her 34th year, after a lingering illness (*FGBA* 17 June 1818; *BPAT* 18 June 1818). Louisa Scott was buried 13 June 1818 from St. Paul's Parish (ReamySP). For the will of Louisa Scott, filed in 1818, see BAWB 10:486.

Scott, Mrs. Margaret, relict of David Scott, formerly of Armagh, Ireland, d. 10th inst., in her 28th year, leaving a husband and three children; she resided near Owings and Sulphur Springs (*BA* 22 May 1818; *BPAT* 22 May 1818).

Scott, Lieut. R. I., of the U.S. Artillery, was m. at Washington last Tues. eve. by Rev. Wilmer, to Miss Mary Ann Lewis, dau. of Henry Lewis of Hagerstown, Md. (*FGBA* 26 Sep 1818; *BPAT* 28 Sep 1818).

Scott, Mr. Sabrett, merchant of Georgetown, was m. at Alexandria, to Miss Maria Mandeville (*BPAT* 24 July 1817).

Scott, Samuel, was m. by Rev. Glendy on 5th inst. [Sat.] to Miss Eliza Embry, all of Baltimore (*BA* 12 July 1817).

Scott, William, merchant, was m. Thurs., 22nd inst. by Rev. Dr. Jennings, to Mrs. Margaret Baxley, all of Baltimore (*BA* 24 Oct 1818; *BPAT* 24 Oct 1818).

Scott, Gen. Winfield, of the Army, was m. 11th inst. [Tues.], at Belville, Va., to Miss Maria D. Mayo, eld. dau. of Col. Mayo of that place (*BPAT* 17 March 1817; *BA* 18 March 1817).

Biographical Data from Baltimore Newspapers, 1817-1819

Scrooby, Amos, was m. 16th Jan [Thurs.] by Rev. Mr. Mines, to Miss Ann Phillips, all of Loudon Co., Va. (*BPAT* 14 Feb 1817).

Scrote, Mathias, was m. last Sat. by Rev. Shane, to Miss Evelina Davidson, all of Baltimore (*BPAT* 29 June 1818).

Searl, Mr. James, of Philadelphia, was m. on 31 March [Mon.] by Rev. Mr. McCormick to Miss Eliza Ann Parry of Washington (*BPAT* 9 April 1817; *BA* 8 April 1817).

Sears, James F., was m. on 3 Dec [Thurs.] by Rev. Kemp to Maria C. Coe, both of Baltimore (*BA* 7 Dec 1818; *BPAT* 4 Dec 1818).

Sears, Richard, a youth of about 18 years, accidentally fell overboard from the steam boat *Surprise* last evening; Amos A. Williams will pay anyone who returns his body to his disconsolate family (*BPAT* 10 Nov 1817).

Seavers, Christiene, an indented servant girl, about 13 years of age, dau. of a man who lives in Hanover, Pa., ran away from L. Zigler (*BPAT* 18 Sep 1818).

Seche, Mr. Joseph, was m. last Thurs. eve. by Rev. Dr. Glendy, to Miss Adeline Gosse, all of this city (*BPAT* 27 Sep 1817; *BA* 29 Sep 1817).

Sedden, Thomas, was m. last eve. [Tues.] by the Rev. Mr. Hargrove to Miss Jane Geddis, all of Baltimore (*FGBA* 9 Jan 1818; *BPAT* 8 Jan 1818).

Seed, Capt. James, formerly of Portland, d. this morning, at 4 o'clock (*BPAT* 6 Dec 1817).

Seegar, Thomas, d. Fri., 24 July at his res. in Queen Anne's Co. in his 68th year [long obit] (*BPAT* 30 July 1818).

Seguin, Claude, was m. Tues., 17th inst., by Rev. Mr. Barbad to Miss Rachel C. Jones, all of Baltimore (*BPAT* 25 Nov 1818).

Sellman, Johnzee, long an inhabitant of Baltimore, d. 1st inst., in his 65th year (*FGBA* 6 May 1818). [The Commissioners of Baltimore were to meet on 16 June 1818 to establish the lines of several of Johnzee Sellman's properties which his executors had leased to Peter Henderson, James B. M'Kowan, Geo. A. Hughes, E. T. Bayley, Jr., Amos Ryan and Charles Griffith, respectively (*BPAT* 12 June 1818)]. John C. [sic] Sellman, aged 54 years, was buried 2 May 1818 from St. Paul's Parish (ReamySP). For the will of Johnzee Sellman, filed in 1818, see BAWB 10:461.

Sellman, Jonathan, d. last Mon., in the 66th year of his age, long an inhabitant of Baltimore, after a long and painful illness (*BPAT* 25 Sep 1817). Jonathan Selman [sic], aged 66, was buried 22 Sep 1817 from St. Paul's Parish (ReamySP).

Sellman, Vachel, d. 8 Oct., a husband and a father (*FGBA* 13 Oct 1818; *BPAT* 14 Oct 1818).

Sergeant, Alling, of Baltimore Co., is an insolvent debtor (*BPAT* 14 Oct 1819).

Sergeant, Private William, aged 21 years, a farmer, deserted from Fort McHenry on the night of the 1st inst. /s/ Nathaniel N. Hall, Capt. U.S. Army (*BPAT* 6 June 1817).

Servant, Richard B., Lieut.-Col. Commandant of the 115th Regt., V.M., d. last Sat., at his residence in Hampton, leaving a wife and six children; a long obit gives details of his military career (*BPAT* 28 Feb 1818).

Seth, John, d. at Hillsborough, Caroline Co., after a short illness (*BPAT* 15 Nov 1819).

Seton, John, born in Ireland, aged between 16 and 17, apprentice to the printing business, ran away from William McCorkle, editor of the *Freemans Journal*, Philadelphia. He is believed to have gone to New York. A reward of ten dollars is offered (*BPAT* 22 June 1818).

Sewell, Benjamin, of Annapolis, and Mary, dau. of John Smith of Baltimore, were m. last eve. [Fri.] by Rev. Thomas Burch (*FGBA* 22 May 1819; *BPAT* 25 May 1819).

Sewell, George, d. 1 Sep, at Havana, on board the ship *Unicorn*, in his 16th year, of yellow fever (*BA* 7 Nov 1818; *BPAT* 7 Nov 1818).

Sewell, James H., of Baltimore Co., is an insolvent debtor (*BPAT* 16 July 1817).

Seymour, Mrs. Sally, formerly of Talbot Co., d. last sat., in her 35th year (*BPAT* 10 Nov 1817).

Shade, Philip, 19 years old, about five-feet-four inches high, apprentice to the saddler's business; has brothers residing in Baltimore; ran away from John Geyer at the

Biographical Data from Baltimore Newspapers, 1817-1819

White House on the Frederick and Baltimore Turnpike Road, near Lisbon in Anne Arundel Co. (*BPAT* 28 Jan 1817).

Shamberg, John, and Miss Jane Montgomery, both of Baltimore, were m. last Tues. eve. by Rev. Jennings (*BPAT* 3 June 1819).

Shaw, Lieut. John A., of the U. S. Navy, d. at Philadelphia (*BPAT* 10 Aug 1819).

Shaw, Mr. Joshua, of Baltimore Co., was m. last Thurs. eve. by the Rev. Mr. Davis, to Miss Margaret Smith of Baltimore (*BPAT* 10 June 1817).

Shaw, Mrs. Mary, d. Mon., 15th inst., in her 76th year (*FGBA* 17 Feb 1819; *BPAT* 17 Feb 1819).

Shaw, Mr. William C., was m. last Thurs. eve. by the Right Rev. Bishop Kemp, to Miss Ann Maria Usher (*BPAT* 10 May 1817; *FGBA* 9 May 1817).

Shawen, Mr. David, merchant, and Miss Frances Ann Fox of Waterford, VA, were m. 17th inst. [Tues.] at Harper's Ferry, by the Rev. William Gilmor (*BPAT* 26 Nov 1818).

Shed. Capt. James, of Baltimore Co. d. by Jan 1818. Jona. Winship, admin., advertised he would settle the estate (*BPAT* 31 Jan 1818).

Sheetz, John, d. at Bedford, Pa., last Sat., aged 30, leaving a wife and three children. *Bedford Gazette* (*FGBA* 15 July 1817; *BPAT* 16 July 1817).

Sheffield, William Robinson, was m. Thurs., 14th inst., by Rev. Dr. Glendy, to Miss Elizabeth Hopkins, all of Baltimore (*BPAT* 22 Oct 1819).

Shellman, Mr. William, of Md., was m. at Philadelphia ([date not given], to Miss Susan, dau. of George Krebs of that city (*BPAT* 23 Oct 1819).

Sherlock, Miss Louisa, eld dau. of the late John Sherlock, d. yesterday at her grandfather's (R. Gilmor), in her 19th year (*FGBA* 30 Sep 1818; *BA* 1 Oct 1818; *BPAT* 1 Oct 1818). Louis [sic] Sherlock, aged 18 years, was bur. 30 sep 1818 from St. Paul's Parish (ReamySP). For the will of Louisa Sherlock, filed in 1818, see BAWB 10:516.

Shields, Mr. James, was m. [date not given] at Washington, to Miss Sarah Varden, both of that City (*BPAT* 19 April 1817).

Shilliber, Jonathan, merchant of Alexandria, and Elizabeth Foster of Salem, Mass., were m. in Baltimore on 9 Dec [Wed.] by Rev. Abner Neal (*BA* 10 Dec 1818; *BPAT* 10 Dec 1818).

Shilling, Mr. Henry, d. at Funkstown, in his 24th year (*BPAT* 6 Aug 1819).

Shipley, Joseph, aged about 19 years, 5'6" tall, stoop shouldered, dark eyes, apprentice to the shoe and boot making business, ran away from John Davis, Bridge St., Old Town, Baltimore (*BPAT* 12 Nov 1818).

Shipley. Richard, living at the corner of Saratoga and Eutaw St., advertises for the return of a horse and gig, stolen from his stable last night (*BPAT* 23 Oct 1817).

Shoemaker, Mr. David, was m. [date not given] in Washington to Mrs. Tacy Bunson, both of that city (*BPAT* 3 Nov 1817).

Shoemaker, Samuel E., and Miss Sarah Falls of Baltimore Co., were m. Tues. eve., 13th int., by Rev. Dr. Sinclair, at the house of Moor Falls, Esq. (*BA* 16 Oct 1818, *BPAT* 18 Oct 1818).

Short, Tom, Negro man, 5 feet, 7 or 9 inches tall, between 35 and 40 years, ran away from Sarah Pumphrey, living near the head of Marley Creek, Anne Arundel Co., Md. (*BPAT* 1 Oct 1819).

Shortt, John, of Baltimore Co. is an insolvent debtor (*BPAT* 14 Oct 1819).

Shrim, Capt. John, d. yesterday, in his 57th year; the regiment would hold a parade n respect of his memory; the officers of the 3rd and 14th Brigades are respectfully invited to attend in uniform and they will be assigned a place in the funeral procession (*FGBA* 16 July 1819; *BPAT* 16 July 1819).

Silverthorn, Henry, was m. last Thurs. eve. by Rev. Dr. Roberts, to Miss Julian Norris, both of Baltimore (*BPAT* 11 Dec 1819).

Simkins, Eli, of the House of Simkins and Usher, d. yesterday morning, aged 29 years. His remains will be conveyed from Mr. Joshua Tevis', Eutaw St., and will be deposited in the family burying ground of Robert N. Carnan, Esq., Garrison Forest

Biographical Data from Baltimore Newspapers, 1817-1819

(*FGBA* 15 May 1817; *BPAT* 16 May 1817). Joshua Tevis, exec., advertised a sale of furniture and half a pew belonging to Eli Simkins, in Mr. Duncan's Church (*BPAT* 24 June 1817 and again in *BPAT* 1 May 1818). For the will of Eli Simkins, filed in 1817, see BAWB 10:321.

Simms, Col. Charles, Collector of Customs for the district of Alexandria and an early, gallant distinguished officer of the Revolutionary Army, d. at Alexandria in his 68th year (*BPAT* 3 Sep 1819).

Simms (Sims), Joseph, and Eliza Fite, both of Baltimore, were m. last Sun. eve. by Rev. Dr. Roberts (*BPAT* 24 May 1819; *FGBA* 22 May 1819).

Simms, Massey, Esq., Surveyor of the Port of Nanjemoy and Postmaster, d. at his seat in Nanjemoy, Charles Co., in his 49th year (*BPAT* 5 Dec 1817).

Simons, Ebenezer, citizen of Baltimore, d. in Philadelphia, on 23rd ult., in his 28th year (*BPAT* 3 May 1819).

Sims, Joseph. See Joseph Simms, above.

Sims, Robert, and Miss Elizabeth Brown, all of Baltimore, were m. last Tues. eve. by Rev. Mr. Davis (*FGBA* 27 Jan 1819; *BPAT* 22 Jan 1819).

Singleton, Thomas S., of Baltimore Co., d. at Alexandria, D.C., on 25 Sep of the prevailing fever, in his 22nd year (*BPAT* 3 Nov 1819).

Sinners, Mrs. Mary, d. Tuesday evening of the prevailing disease, which she contracted at the lower end of Fell's Point, in her 23rd year (*BPAT* 9 Sep 1819).

Skinner, Dr. Henry, late a surgeon in the U. S. Army, d. 23 June 1819 at Edgeville, Ky., in his 34th year, leaving a widow and two children. He was a native of Calvert Co., the eldest son of Frederick Skinner, and the elder bro. of the Post Master of Baltimore (*FGBA* 28 July 1819; *BPAT* 30 July 1819).

Skinner, Zebulon, merchant of Centreville, was m. in Talbot Co. [date not given], to Miss Mary Ann Farland, dau. of Capt. Joseph Farland (*BPAT* 15 Nov 1819).

Sinsner, Jesse, and Margaret Burgoyne, all of Baltimore, were m. last Thurs. eve. by Rev. Lewis Richards (*BPAT* 9 Dec 1817).

Skipper[?], Mr. David, and Miss Sarah Dusford, were m. by Dr. Glendy on 19th? inst. [Wed.?] (*BPAT* 21 May 1819).

Skelton, Mr. John, schoolmaster, d. Tues., in his 48th year (*BA* 10 Dec 1818).

Skenett, Ruth, aged 72, was bur 5 March 1817 from St. Paul's Parish (ReamySP). [See Mrs. Skerett below].

Skerett, Mrs., d. this morning, aged 73; the funeral will be from her late residence in Market St., Fells Point (*FGBA* 5 March 1817; *BPAT* 6 March 1817). [See Ruth Skenett above].

Slaytor, John, and Miss Mary Dougherty, were m. last eve. [Tues.] by Rev. Fenwick (*BA* 8 Jan 1817).

Sloan, James, Jr., of Baltimore, d. 31 March. He was the author of *Rambles in Italy* (*FGBA* 6 April 1819).

Sloan, William J., of Carlisle, and Miss Margaret Newman of Baltimore, were m. last eve. [Sun.] by Rev. Force (*FGBA* 8 March 1819; *BPAT* 6 March 1819).

Sloan, William, M. D., d. Wed., 7th inst., aged 28, eldest son of James Sloan, and one of the attending physicians at the Baltimore Alms House. He studied with Drs. Littlejohn and Donaldson of this city and graduated in Philadelphia in 1811. He was appointed Surgeon of the 14th Regiment of U. S. Infantry at the commencement of the war and continued on the Northern Frontier until the peace. Soon after his return he was appointed Attending Physician of the Alms House of this county (*BPAT* 12 April 1819).

Sloey, Thomas, baker, a native of Ireland, d. yesterday, leaving a wife and three children (*BA* 29 April 1819). Thomas Sloey, aged 40, d. 28 April 1819 of consumption, and was buried 29 April in the Cathedral Cemetery (Grogaard).

Smiley, John, d. 24th inst., in his 90th year (*FGBA* 27 July 1818). John Smiley, aged 97 years, was buried 25 July 1818 from St. Paul's Parish (ReamySP).

Smith, Miss Ann, youngest dau of Gen. Samuel Smith of Baltimore, d. yesterday, aged 18 years, after a lingering illness (*BPAT* 9 May 1817; *FGBA* 10 May 1817).

Biographical Data from Baltimore Newspapers, 1817-1819

Smith, Dr. Anthony W., was m. last Sat, by Rev. Glendy, to Miss Elizabeth E. B. Wheeler, all of Baltimore (*BPAT* 3 Nov 1818; *FGBA* 4 Nov 1818).

Smith, Rev. Armistead, of Matthews, Va., d. Friday, 12th inst., in his 63rd year; at Toddsbury, the seat of Philip Todd, Esq., in Gloucester Co., Va. (*BPAT* 24 Sep 1817).

Smith, Caleb, died, and his representatives had leased part of Lot 65, on Bridge St., between High and Green Sts., to David H. Thompson. A commission will be held to establish the lines of the lot (*BPAT* 21 July 1818).

Smith, Capt. Charles Henry, of Baltimore, was m. 14th inst. [Tues.] at New York by Rev. Dr. Schaeffer, to Miss Louisa Charlotte Stansfield (*BPAT* 18 Dec 1819)

Smith, Daniel, d. at Hagerstown (*BPAT* 24 Dec 1819).

Smith, Mr. Elie, and Miss Mary Peck, all of Baltimore were m. last eve. [Tues.] by Rev. Dr. Roberts (*FGBA* 10 March 1819; *BPAT* 12 March 1819).

Smith, Mrs. Elizabeth, consort of the late Capt. Joseph Smith, d. last Mon., in her 35th year (*BPAT* 2 July 1818). For the will of Elizabeth Smith, filed in 1818, see BAWB 10:485. Jesse L. Hiss, exec., has obtained letters of admin. (*BPAT* 15 Sep 1819).

Smith, Ferdinand, owes taxes for the year 1817 on 6 a. part of *Smith's Forest* in the 7th Dist. (*BPAT* 7 Jan 1819).

Smith, Mrs. Harriet, consort of Henry Smith, d. 24th inst., aged 24 years, three mos., and seven days; a wife and mother; long obit (*BPAT* 27 Aug 1819).

Smith, Mr. Jacob, d. Sun. eve. last, after a lingering illness, in his 63rd year; long a respectable inhabitant of Baltimore, residing at the corner of Franklin and Paca Sts. (*BPAT* 22 June 1818; *BA* 22 June 1818). For the will of Jacob Smith, filed in 1818, see BAWB 10:479.

Smith. James, d. yesterday morning, in his 22nd year (*BPAT* 3 Sep 1817). James Smith, aged 22 years, was buried 4 Sep 1817 from St. Paul's Parish (ReamySP).

Smith, James, son of George Smith of Baltimore, d. yesterday morning, after a long illness, in his 21st year (*BPAT* 11 Feb 1818; *FGBA* 11 Feb 1818). James Smith, aged 20, was buried 11 Feb 1818 from St. Paul's Parish (ReamySP).

Smith, James, came from Philadelphia, last winter, by profession a farmer and a gardener, is said to have a wife but no children in Baltimore; he is said to be employed somewhere between Annapolis and Baltimore; if he will call on Daniel Larrabe he may hear something to his advantage (*BPAT* 28 Oct 1819).

Smith, James V., left a small vessel lying opposite Fell's Point last Sunday and proceeded on the ice to Whetstone Point. He was last seen about 100 yards from the shore, and has not been heard from since. It is feared he has drowned. Anyone who finds him will be handsomely rewarded by Mrs. Latitia Hall at 75 S. Charles St. (*BPAT* 21 Jan 1819). (For the will of James V. Smith, filed in 1819, see BAWB 11:42).

Smith, John, aged 27, born in Drumore, Co. Armagh, a labourer, deserted from the Carlisle Barracks (for the second time), on 23 inst. /s/ Capt. James Pratt, Superintending Recruiting Service 5th Infantry (*BPAT* 3 Sep 1817).

Smith, John, and Miss Mary Mitchell [or Mary Michel], all of Baltimore, were m. last Tues. by Rev. Davis (*BPAT* 6 Feb 1819).

Smith, Capt. John, d. at Savannah in the 32nd year of his age; a native of Va., but for many years a resident of Charleston, S. C. (*BPAT* 11 June 1817).

Smith, Corporal John, aged 23, a chymist, deserted from Fort McHenry on the night of the 1st inst. /s/ Nathaniel N. Hall, Capt. U.S. Army (*BPAT* 6 June 1817).

Smith, Mr. John, Principal of the Academy at Hagerstown, d. at that place (*BPAT* 26 July 1819).

Smith, Capt. Joseph, of Baltimore Co., has died. Elizabeth Smith, admx., advertises she will settle the estate (*BPAT* 24 July 1817). For the will of Joseph Smith, filed in 1817, see BAWB 10:273. Tobias E. Stansbury and Jesse L. Hiss, admins., have obtained letters of administration (*BPAT* 15 Sep 1818).

Smith, Joseph, Esq., of Staunton, Va., and Miss Ann Price of Baltimore, were m. at the former place on 19th inst. [Wed.], by Rev. Mr. King (*BPAT* 29 Nov 1817).

Smith, Capt. Joseph F., and Miss Dorcas Franklin, all of Baltimore, were m. last eve. [Thurs.] by Rev. Williamson (*FGBA* 3 Sep 1819; *BPAT* 3 Sep 1819).
Smith, Mr. Madison, was m. to Miss Matilda Delpey of Alexandria (*BPAT* 17 Nov 1817).
Smith, Mrs. Miranda, d. last Mon. morning, aged 16, leaving a disconsolate husband (*BPAT* 17 Sep 1817).
Smith, Mrs. Polly, widow of Walter Smith, d. at Snow Hill, Worcester Co., in her 75th year, leaving children (*BPAT* 22 July 1818).
Smith, Mr. Robert S., was m. Thurs. last, by Rev. John Glendy, to Miss Keziah Poteet, all of this city (*BPAT* 15 March 1817; *BA* 15 March 1817).
Smith, Samuel, Esq., Postmaster of Cumberland, Md., d. there (*BPAT* 24 Dec 1819).
Smith, Capt. Shipley Francis, was m. last Mon. eve. by Rev. Mr. Healey, to Miss Johanna Voorhis, formerly of N. Y. (*BPAT* 17 April 1818; *FGBA* 15 April 1818).
Smith, Thomas, and Mary Smith, both of Baltimore, were m. Thurs. eve. by Rev. D. E. Reese (*FGBA* 2 April 1819; the *FGBA* of 3 April 1819 and *BPAT* 3 April 1819 state that the bride's maiden name was Baker).
Smith, Thomas, one of the proprietors and editors of the *Philadelphia Union*, d. Tues. eve. last (*BPAT* 4 Feb 1819).
Smith, Thomas, d. 28th ult., at his seat in Kent Co., in his 89th year. He helped form the Maryland Constitution of 1776 (*BPAT* 6 April 1819).
Smith, W. D., merchant, and Miss Sarah Coleman, dau. of John Coleman, all of Baltimore, were m. Thurs. eve. [17 Dec.] by Rev. Dr. Roberts (*BPAT* 19 Dec 1818; *BA* 19 Dec 1818).
Smith, William, of Adam, owes taxes for the years 1813, 1814, 1815 and 1817, on 35 a., part of *Wells Manor* in the 1st District of Baltimore Co. (*BPAT* 1 Jan 1819).
Smith, Col. William, of Talbot Co., and Miss Isabella Thornburg of Baltimore, were m. Tues. by Rev. Dr. Roberts (*BA* 31 Dec 1817; *BPAT* 31 Dec 1817).
Smith, Col. William B., d. at *Perry Hall*, his late residence in Talbot Co., on 14th inst., after a short and violent indisposition, in his 48th year, leaving a widow and two infant children (*BPAT* 27 Dec 1819).
Smith, William M., a resident of North Howard St., d. Mon. (*BA* 1 April 1818; *BPAT* 1 April 1818). William M. Smith, aged 39 years, was buried 31 March 1818 from St. Paul's Parish (ReamySP). For the will of William M. Smith, filed in 1818, see BAWB 10:464.
Smith, Major Wm. R., d. 10th inst., in his 44th year (*FGBA* 10 June 1818; *BPAT* 11 June 1818). William R. Smith, aged 44 years, was buried 10 June 1818 from St. Paul's Parish (ReamySP).
Smith, Winston D., of Baltimore Co. is an insolvent debtor (*BPAT* 19 Oct 1819).
Smoot, James H., Esq., of Alexandria, was m. at Prospect Hill, Charles Co., Md., last Sun. morning, by Rev. William H. Wilmer, to Miss Barbara Mackall, second dau. of the late Edward Briscoe, of Charles Co, (*BPAT* 2 Sep 1819).
Smother, Daniel, a Negro, aged about 25 years old, left Baltimore on 27 March in company with Richard Sparks (see below), and may be in the neighborhood of Havre de Grace; ran away from Nehemiah Birckhead, living near Friendship, Anne Arundel Co. (*BPAT* 23 June 1818).
Smyth, Dr. James, physician of Baltimore who resided on North Frederick St., d. this morning (*FGBA* 3 March 1819; *BPAT* 4 March 1819). Dr. Smyth, aged 31 years, was buried 2 March 1819 from St. Paul's Parish (ReamySP).
Snow, William, aged 9, son of Capt. Freeman, d. last Sun. (*BPAT* 4 March 1818).
Snowden, Mrs. Eliza, late consort of Richard Snowden, d. last Sat. at *Oakland*, the seat of Richard Snowden, in her 36th year; she left a husband and six children (*BPAT* 29 July 1817; *FGBA* 28 July 1817).
Snowden, Richard, and Miss Victoria Louise Warfield, dau. of the late Charles Alexander Warfield, were m. Mon. last at *Oakland*, Prince George's Co., by the Rev. Oliver Norris (*BPAT* 22 May 1818; *BA* 22 May 1818).

Biographical Data from Baltimore Newspapers, 1817-1819

Snyder, Philip Frederick Antes, the fourth son of Simon Snyder, Esq., d. at Selin's Grove, on the 13th inst., in the 19th year of his age (*BPAT* 20 Sep 1819).

Snyder, Simon, Esq., late Governor of Pa., d. at his residence, Selin's Grove, Northumberland Co, Pa.; obit gives details of his political career (*BPAT* 13 Nov 1819).

Solomon, Mr. William, was m. last Wed. eve. by Rev. Mr. Bartow, to Miss Ann Simmons, both of Baltimore (*BPAT* 15 Oct 1819).

Sourhoof, G., aged 17 mos., who lived West of the Falls, was buried 3 Sep 1819 (*FGBA* 3 Sep 1819).

Southcomb, Mr. Cary, was m. last Tues. by Rev. Mr. Davis, to Miss Alice Anna C. Ford, all of Baltimore (*BPAT* 2 July 1818; *FGBA* 1 July 1818).

Spalding, Thomas, Esq., d. at his farm, near Leonardtown, Md., and old and respected inhabitant (*BPAT* 1 Dec 1819).

Sparks, Richard, a black man, left Baltimore on 27 March, in company with Daniel Smother (see above), may have gone to the Fisheries (*BPAT* 23 June 1818).

Spear, William, of Baltimore Co. d. by June 1794. His heirs, John Spear, and others, conv. a lot of ground on the East side of Board St. between Bank and Wilk Sts., to Mary Anderson. The Commissioners of Baltimore were to meet to establish the boundary lines of the land (*BPAT* 11 May 1818).

Speck, Mr. William A., was m. last Tues. eve. by Rev. Mr. Moranville, to Miss Cecelia Peak, all of Baltimore (*BPAT* 11 March 1818).

Spedden, Mr. Edward, and Miss Eleanor Reese , all of this city, were m. last Sun. eve. by Rev. Dr. Roberts (*BPAT* 19 May 1818; *BA* 19 May 1818).

Spedden, Lieut. R., of the U.S. Navy, was m. Tues. eve. by the Rev. Mr. Bartow, to Miss Mary Ann Thompson, of Baltimore (*BPAT* 10 Sep 1817; *BA* 10 Sep 1817).

Spencer, Mrs. Elizabeth, consort of Robert Spencer of Baltimore Co., d. the morning of the 13th inst. (*BPAT* 24 Nov 1819).

Spencer, Richard, Esq., of Easton, Md., was m. last Tues. eve. by Rev. Nelson Reed to Miss Anna, dau. of the late William Baker of Baltimore (*BPAT* 21 Oct 1819).

Sperry, John, Esq., of Philadelphia, and Miss Augusta Fox of Baltimore, were m. Last Tues. eve. by the Rt. Rev. Bishop Kemp (*BPAT* 29 Oct 1818; *BA* 30 Oct 1818).

Spicknall, Charles M., of Baltimore Co., d. by Feb 1818. Daniel Kent, admin., advertised he would settle the estate (*BPAT* 10 Feb 1818).

Spickner, Mr. Nicholas, d. at Hagerstown, an old and respectable inhabitant of that county (*BPAT* 30 Aug 1819).

Spilman, Thomas F., and Miss Hannah Barrickman, both of Baltimore, were m. Tues. eve. by Rev. Mr. Fenwick (*BPAT* 25 May 1818; *FGBA* 23 May 1818).

Sponsler, Joseph, a mulatto boy between 21 and 22 years old, can speak English and German, ran away from John Strayer of Dover Twp., York Co., Pa. (*BPAT* 13 April 1818).

Spurrier, Mr. James, a native of Md., d. at Buenos Ayres (*BPAT* 5 July 1819).

Stambaugh, Mr. S. C., editor of the *Free Press*, was m. at Newholand on Sun. eve., 23rd ult. to Miss Ann Wielder of Lancaster. "Well done Brother Typo! (*BPAT* 16 June 1819). [Newspaper publishers faithfully reported the marriages and deaths of fellow newspapermen].

Stammen, Mr. Ulrick B., was m. last Tues. eve. by the Rev. Mr. Bartow, to Miss Maria Hughes (*BPAT* 17 June 1817; *BA* 17 June 1817). He is probably the U. B. Stamnig of Germany who was naturalized in Aug 1792 by subscribing to the Oath required by Act of Congress (Baltimore Co. Court Minutes, 1792-1797, f. 36).

Standley, George, Esq. was m. Sunday, 1st inst., at the Chapel, Head of Bohemia, by Rev. John Henry, to Mrs. Elizabeth O'Donald, [he] being only her fifth husband (*BPAT* 5 Feb 1818; *FGBA* 5 Feb 1818).

Stanes, Mr. John, was m. last Tues. eve, by Rev. D. E. Reese , to Miss Harriet Ann Lee, all of Baltimore (*BPAT* 7 Aug 1819).

Biographical Data from Baltimore Newspapers, 1817-1819

Stansbury, Mr. Elijah, was m. last Tues. eve., by the Rev. John Glendy, to Miss Eliza Eckel, dau. of Mr. Philip Eckel, all of Baltimore (*BPAT* 25 July 1817; *FGBA* 26 July 1817).

Stansbury, Mrs. Ellen Kent, who resided on High St., Old Town, wife of William Stansbury, d. 9 Nov, aged 26 years, 10 mos. (*BA* 12 Nov 1817).

Stansbury, Capt. James, and Miss Mary Dawes, both of Baltimore, were m. last Thurs. eve. by Rev. Dr. Jennings (*BPAT* 27 Dec 1817; *FGBA* 29 Dec 1817).

Stansbury, Mr. John, and Miss Sarah S. Pearce, both of Baltimore Co., were m. Thurs. eve. by Rev. Mr. Davis (*BPAT* 19 Sep 1818; *FGBA* 21 Sep 1818).

Stansbury, John E., and Mrs. Frances Abbott, both of Baltimore, were m. 10 June [Thurs.] 1819 by Rev. Bartow (*BA* 12 June 1819; *BPAT* 12 June 1819).

Stansbury, Capt. Robert D., and Miss Ann Kerr, both of Baltimore, were m. last Tues. eve. by Rev. Bartow (*FGBA* 14 Jan 1819; *BPAT* 14 Jan 1819).

Stansbury, Mr. William, d. Tues. eve. last at his res. in Baltimore Co., aged about 58 years (*BPAT* 25 June 1818). William Bosley, administrator, advertises he will settle the estate (*BPAT* 22 Sep 1819).

Stansbury, William, and Ann Ellender, all of Baltimore, were m. last Sun. by Rev. D. E. Reese (*FGBA* 26 March 1819; *BPAT* 26 March 1819).

Stansbury, William S., of La., and Miss Maria Norwood, of Baltimore, were m. last Thurs. eve. by Rev. Duncan (*BPAT* 19 March 1819).

Stansbury, Mrs. Winifred, consort of Nicholas Stansbury of Baltimore, d. last Friday, in her 29th year, leaving a husband and six children (*BPAT* 9 Feb 1819).

Starr, William, d. Sun., 4th inst., in his 41st year, leaving a widow and seven children (*FGBA* 7 July 1819; *BPAT* 7 July 1819). For the will of William Starr, filed in 1819, see BAWB 11:23.

Stattlemeyer, Mr. John, was m, at Hagerstown, [date not given], to Miss Susannah Wolf (*BPAT* 17 Nov 1819).

Staylor, Mr. Henry, and Miss Ellen Rilke, all of Baltimore Co., were m. last Sun. eve. by Rev. Mertz (*BPAT* 3 Feb 1818; *BA* 3 Feb 1818).

Steel, John, and Miss Maria V. H. Hinchman, were m. last Sun, eve. by Rev. Moranville (*FGBA* 15 April 1819; *BPAT* 15 April 1819).

Steele, John N., of Annapolis, and Miss Ann O. Buchanan, dau. of the Hon. Thomas Buchanan, were m. [date not given] at Hagerstown (*BPAT* 8 Oct 1819).

Steele, Ofle, about 17 years old, stout made, apprentice to the cordwaining business, ran away from Thomas Bryne (*BPAT* 3 June 1819).

Steer, Jacob, and Miss Peggy Wolf, all of York, Pa., were m. there on the 16th inst. [Sat.] (*BPAT* 25 May 1818).

Steger, Mr. Joseph, of Strasburg, Shenandoah Co., Va., d. yesterday at the Fountain Inn (*BPAT* 23 Nov 1819).

Steiger, Peter, aged 43, long a resident of Baltimore, d. 29th ult., in Frederick Co., after a short illness (*BPAT* 3 July 1818; *FGBA* 6 July 1818).

Steinhauer, Rev. Henry, d. Wed., 22nd inst., at Bethlehem, Pa., Principal of the Young Lady's Academy, leaving a wife and a brother (*FGBA* 30 July 1818).

Stephens, Mr. William, of New York, was m. Sun. eve. by Rev. Jennings, to Mrs. Rebecca Green of Baltimore (*BPAT* 6 Sep 1819).

Stephenson, Rev. Sater, d. last Tues., at his farm in Baltimore Co., last Tues., 2nd inst., aged 77 years and one month. He was a preacher in the Methodist Society and started preaching before the Revolutionary War (*BPAT* 5 Dec 1817; *FGBA* 5 Dec 1817; *BA* 5 Dec 1817).

Sterett, Mrs. Margaret, wife of Benjamin Sterett, merchant of this city, d. yesterday morning, aged 41 years (*BPAT* 24 Oct 1817; *BA* 24 Oct 1817).

Stevens, Dolly, a black girl, ran away from Benj. Collins and is supposed to be in the city and may try to make her way to Philadelphia. She took her 15 month old child who is of a much lighter complexion than mulatto children usually are (*BPAT* 8 July 1817).

Biographical Data from Baltimore Newspapers, 1817-1819

Stevenson, Mr. Alexander, was m. last Sun. eve. by Rev. Dr. Jennings to Miss Ann Evans, all of Baltimore (*BPAT* 10 March 1818; *BA* 10 March 1818).

Stevenson, Mrs. Ann, d. 13th inst, in her 19th year, consort of Alexander Stevenson, of Baltimore (*FGBA* 17 May 1819). Ann Stevenson, aged 21 years, was buried 14 May 1819 from St. Paul's Parish (ReamySP).

Stevenson, Maj. George P., late merchant of Baltimore, d. 11th June at Havana, aged 29, leaving a widow and children. He was buried in the burial ground of the First Presbyterian Church. He had severed as a major at the Battle of North Point in the War of 1812 (*FGBA* 28 June 1819; *BPAT* 26 June 1819; long obits in BPAT 13 July 1819, 19 July 1819). He is buried in Lot # 88 of Westminster Presbyterian Churchyard, Baltimore (HaywardW).

Stevenson, Mr. Henry, of Worcester Co., was m. Thurs. eve., 25 Sep, by the Rev. Dr. Roberts, to Miss Mary B. Waters, of Baltimore (*BPAT* 26 Sep 1817; *BA* 26 Sep 1817).

Stewart, David, d. last eve., aged 71, President of the Marine Insurance Co., and a respectable citizen of Baltimore; his funeral will be this morning from his late dwelling in Gay St. (*BPAT* 19 June 1817; *FGBA* 19 June 1817). For the will of David Stewart, filed in 1817, see BAWB 10:356.

Stewart, David C., d. 25th Oct, after a severe illness of a few days, in his 44th year (*BA* 27 Oct 1818; *BPAT* 27 Oct 1818).

Stewart, Godfrey, of Kilmarnock, Scotland, and Miss Elizabeth Watts, of Baltimore, were m. last Thurs. eve. by Rev. Mr. Wyatt (*BA* 9 Dec 1817).

Stewart, Mrs. Ellen, consort of Capt. John Stewart, d. Mon. 17th inst. (*BA* 24 March 1817).

Stewart, John, d. 21st inst., aged 58 years (*BPAT* 25 April 1817; *FGBA* 24 April 1817). John Stewart, aged 58 as buried 21 April 1817 from St. Paul's Parish (ReamySP).

Stewart, Col. John, d. 12th inst., at his seat in Westmoreland Co., Va., aged 52 years (*BPAT* 20 Dec 1819).

Stewart, Mrs. Sarah, d. 5th inst., at Furley, the residence of Wm. L. Bowly, in her 79th year, one of the oldest inhabitants of Baltimore (*FGBA* 8 Aug 1817; *BPAT* 4 Aug 1817). Sarah Stewart, aged 79, was buried 6 Aug from St. Paul's Parish (ReamySP).

Stewart, Thomas, a saddler from Airshire [sic], Scotland, arrived here last February and lodged with Mr. White, a locksmith in Baltimore; if he will call or send to this office, he will hear of something to his advantage (*BPAT* 8 Nov 1817).

Stewart, William, of the Philadelphia and Baltimore Theatres, d. at Westminster, MD, on Mon. last, leaving a widow (*BPAT* 29 Dec 1817; *BA* 30 Dec 1817 gives his name as William Steward).

Stiles, Mr. Edward, d. yesterday, after a long and painful illness, aged 49 (*BPAT* 28 Oct 1817; *BA* 29 Oct 1817).

Stiles, George, late Mayor of Baltimore, d. 16th June, in his 59th year (*FGBA* 17 June 1819). For the will of George Stiles, filed in 1819, see BAWB 11:12. A sale of household and kitchen furniture and Pew No. 37, in the middle aisle of Dr. Glendy's Church, will be sold next Thurs., 1 July (*BPAT* 30 June 1819).

Stiles, Mr. William, was m. last eve. [Thurs.] by Rev. Mr. Davis, to Miss Margaret Taylor, of Fells Point (*BPAT* 10 April 1818; *FGBA* 11 April 1818).

Stirling, Mrs. Elizabeth, wife of James Stirling of Baltimore Co., d. 30 Aug in her 53rd year (*BA* 3 Sep 1817; *BPAT* 3 Sep 1817).

Stinchcomb, Eliza, d. 25th inst., at Ceresville, Frederick Co., in her 25th year, leaving a husband and an 8 day old inf. (*BA* 2 March 1818).

Stith, Mr. Griffith, was m. last Thurs. eve. by the Rev. Mr. Wyatt, to Miss Mary Ann Wilmer (*BPAT* 28 June 1817; *FGBA* 27 June 1817).

Stockett, Mrs. Barbara, of Baltimore Co, has died. Frederick Shaffer and Owen Dorsey, execs., advertise a sale of a three story brick house on Bond St., Fells point, and a two story brick house and lot on Ann St,, late the property of Capt. Henry Stockett and Barbara Stockett his wife (*BPAT* 16 May 1817). For the will of Barbara Stockett, filed in 1817, see BAWB 10:313.

Stockett, Capt. William, d. at sea last 16 April, a worthy inhabitant of this city, leaving a wife [Long obit] (*BPAT* 6 June 1818; *FGBA* 9 June 1818). For the will of Capt. William S. Stockett, filed in 1818, see BAWB 10:504.

Stockton, Mrs. Arabella, wife of Francis B. Stockton, of Blakeley, Alabama Territory, and a dau. of Amos Loney of Baltimore, d. at the former place on 29 Aug in her 26th year (*BA* 27 Oct 1818; *BPAT* 24 Oct 1818).

Stockton, Francis B., Esq., of Philadelphia., was m. on 17th inst. [Mon.] by Rt. Rev. Bishop Kemp to Miss Frances Arabella Loney, dau. of Amos Loney, Esq., of Baltimore (*BPAT* 19 Nov 1817; *BA* 19 Nov 1817).

Stone, Mr. James, Jr., merchant, was m. on Mon eve., 3rd inst., at St. John's Church, by Rev. George Dashiell, to Miss Mary Ward, all of Baltimore (*BPAT* 12 June 1818; *BA* 5 Aug 1818).

Stone, John, aged 21 years, born in Petersburg, Va., deserted from Carlisle Barracks on 8th inst. /s/ Major M. Marston, Super'g recruiting service for the 5th Regt. Infantry (*BPAT* 2 Aug 1817).

Stone, John, Jr., about 19 or 20 years old, apprentice to the shoemaking business, ran away from Richard H. Jones, living near Elk Ridge Landing, Anne Arundel Co. (*BPAT* 1 Oct 1819).

Stone, John, Jr., aged about 19 or 20 years of age, apprentice to the shoemaking business, ran away from Richard H. Jones, living in Anne Arundel Co., near elk Ridge Landing. A reward of six cents is offered (*BPAT* 26 Sep 1818).

Storm, Mr. James, merchant, was m. at Emmetsburg on Tues, 31st inst., by the Rev. Mr. Duhamel, to Miss Sarah Gilllmeyer, all of Frederick Co. (*BPAT* 13 June 1817; *BA* 13 June 1817).

Storrow, Samuel Appleton, Esq., an officer in the U. S. Army, was m. at Farley, Culpepper Co., Va., last Thurs. eve., by Rev. Mr. Woodville, to Miss Eliza Hill Carter, only dau. of William Champe Carter. Esq. (*BPAT* 28 May 1819)

Stouffer, Margaret, infant dau, of Mr. John Stouffer, d. last night after a short illness, aged one year and three mos. (*BPAT* 6 June 1817).

Strause, Mr. Henry, d. at Montgomery Co., aged 52 (*BPAT* 6 Aug 1819).

Street, William, and Miss Eliza Crook, eld. dau. of Walter Crook, all of Baltimore, were m. last Thurs. by Dr. Jennings (*BPAT* 16 April 1819; *BPAT* 15 April 1819).

Streiby, Adam, d. at Philadelphia, aged about 60 years, on 27 Feb. Pittsburgh and Cincinnati papers are requested to copy the above (*BPAT* 3 March 1818).

Stringer, Dr. Samuel, d. 11 July, at Albany, in his 83rd year, a native of the State of Maryland. [A long obit gives details of his medical education and career during the French and Indian and Revolutionary Wars] (*BPAT* 26 July 1817; *FGBA* 22 July 1817).

Stroud, Reece P., of Christiana, Del., was m. last sat eve. by Rev. Mr. Bird, to Miss Rebecca Richards of Baltimore Co. (*BPAT* 2 Aug 1819).

Stuart, Mr. John, and Miss Eliza Miller, all of Baltimore, were m. Thurs. eve. by Rev. Valiant (*BPAT* 19 Sep 1818).

Stubbs, Mr. Joseph, and Miss Sarah Sumwalt, all of Baltimore, were m. Thurs. eve. by Rev. Mr. Rozsel (*BPAT* 6 Dec 1817; *BA* 6 Dec 1817).

Sugars, Edward, owes taxes for the year 1817 on 5¾ a. part of *Stout*, and 2½ a. *Banicker* in the 1st Dist. (*BPAT* 3 Aug 1819).

Sugars, Joseph, age 21, absconded from his security, who is bound for him in the sum of $400.00. A reward of $30.00 is offered. /s/ Edward Sugars and Sam'l Brown (*BPAT* 3 Aug 1818).

Suhr, Jacob, d. Wed., 4th inst., a native of Hamburg, aged 30 years (*FGBA* 12 Aug 1819; *BPAT* 12 Aug 1819). Jacob Suhr, aged 30 years, was buried 4 Aug 1819 from St. Paul's Parish (ReamySP).

Sumner, Mr. Henry Payson, and Miss Frances Allenby Steel, were m. Mon eve., the 29th inst., by Rev. Wyatt (*BPAT* 1 July 1818; *FGBA* 30 June 1818).

Biographical Data from Baltimore Newspapers, 1817-1819

Swan, Mr. Henry B., was m. last Thurs. eve. by the Rev. John Allen, to Miss Elizabeth Davis, both of Baltimore (*BPAT* 13 Aug 1817; *BA* 13 Aug 1817).

Swan, Mr. James, and Elizabeth, eldest dau of John Donnell, all of Baltimore, were m. last Tues. by Bishop Kemp (*BPAT* 2 Nov 1818; *BA* 3 Nov 1818).

Swan, Mr. William, a native of Baltimore d. at Savannah, aged 26 years (*BPAT* 11 Nov 1819).

Swann, Mr. Thomas, merchant, of Alexandria, was m. [date not given] at Rich Hill, Charles Co., to Miss Sarah Cox of the latter place (*BPAT* 12 June 1817).

Sweadner, Daniel, and Rebecca Etzler, 2nd, dau. of Andrew Etzler, all of Liberty Town, were m. last Thurs. by Rev. Rozel (*FGBA* 2 Feb 1819; *BPAT* 1 Feb 1819).

Swearingen, Col. Charles, d. 27th ult., at his residence in Washington Co., Md., in his 83rd year (*BPAT* 8 July 1818).

Sweatnam, Willis, d. 29th inst., in his 45th year. His relatives and friends, and particularly his Masonic Brethren are requested to attend his funeral opposite the Friends Meeting House, Old Town (*BPAT* 30 April 1819).

Sweeny, James, aged 21 years, born in Chester Co., Pa., lately resided in Lacock, Lancaster Co., laborer, enlisted on 14 June, deserted from the Carlisle Barracks /s/ James Pratt, Captain of Superintendent Recruiting Services, 5th Regiment (*BPAT* 2 Sep 1817).

Sweeting, John, of Baltimore Co., was m. last Thurs. eve. by Rev. Dr. Roberts, to Miss Rebecca Spicer of Baltimore (*BPAT* 23 Dec 1819).

Swell [Sewell?], Henry, owes taxes for the year 1815, on 1 lot in the 7th Dist. of Baltimore Co. (*BPAT* 7 Jan 1819).

Swift, George Washington, d. this morning, aged 19, son of Jonathan Swift of Alexandria (*FGBA* 6 Aug 1819; *BPAT* 7 Aug 1819).

"T"

Tagg, Stephen, was m. last Thurs. by Rev. Reid to Mrs. Smothers, both of Baltimore Co. (*BA* 24 June 1818; *BPAT* 24 June 1818).

Tailor, William, aged about 30 years, deserted from the U. S. Ship *Alert*, lying in the navy yard in this city [Washington] on Fri., 19th inst. /s/ Edmund P. Kennedy, Commander (*BPAT* 26 Feb 1817).

Talbot, Hon. Isham, U. S. Senator from Ky., was m. [date not given] in Washington City to Miss Adelaide Thomason (*BPAT* 31 March 1817).

Talbot, Joshua F. C., was m. last Thurs. eve. by Mr. Brice to Miss Eliza Denmead, all of Baltimore (*BA* 5 Aug 1818).

Talbott, Vincent, Sr., d. Sat. morning, 26th ult., in his 68th year, at his residence in Baltimore Co., after a short illness (*BPAT* 26 Nov 1819). For the will of Vincent Talbott, filed in 1820, see BAWB 11:92.

Tall, Mr. William, and Miss Elizabeth Todd, both of Baltimore, were m. last Sun. eve. by Rev. Dr. Roberts (*BPAT* 1 Dec 1818).

Taney, Octavius C., M.D., was m. [date not given] by Rev. Mr. Edelen, to Miss Jane Gray, both of Calvert Co., at the res. of Thomas H. Wilkinson, Esq. (*BA* 28 Dec 1818; *BPAT* 26 Dec 1818).

Tansfield, Zachariah, long an inhabitant of Baltimore, d. last eve. in his 56th year; he resided on Light St. (*FGBA* 2 Feb 1819; *BPAT* 3 Feb 1819).

Tarlton, Richard, d. Thurs. morning at Towson's Hotel, a respectable and worthy citizen of St. Mary's Co. (*BPAT* 26 Nov 1819).

Tarr, Eli, d. 19 March, at his residence near Snow Hill, Worcester Co. in his 76th year; for many years a member of the Methodist Church of that place, and "another veteran of '76" (*FGBA* 6 April 1819; *BPAT* 6 April 1819).

Taylor, Coleman, was m. last Thurs. by Rev. Glendy to Miss Sarah M. Collins, all of Baltimore (*FGBA* 9 June 1819; *BPAT* 9 June 1819).

Taylor, David, was m. last Tues. eve. by Rev. Davis, to Miss Harriet Van Horn, all of Baltimore (*FGBA* 11 Feb 1818; *BPM* 13 Feb 1818 gives the groom's name as John).
Taylor, Dilah, of Calvert Co., has d. leaving the following heirs: Alexander, Peregrine, and Frances Taylor, James Smith and wife Martha, and Mary Taylor. The heirs were subject to a bill of complaint in Chancery by Joseph Wilkinson. Alexander, Frances, and Mary Taylor do not reside in the State of Maryland. "Calvert County Chancery" (*BPAT* 9 April 1817).
Taylor, Mrs. Elizabeth, consort of Robert Taylor, d. this morning in her 32nd year. Her funeral will be from her late dwelling in Queen St., near the Lower Bridge (*FGBA* 31 July 1819; *BPAT* 31 July 1819).
Taylor, Mr. George, was m. last eve. [Thurs.] by Rev. Mr. Davis to Miss Margaret Hopkins, both of Baltimore (*BPAT* 22 Aug 1817).
Taylor, Capt. Humphrey, d. 16 Dec, aged about 78, a native of Edinburgh, Scotland, and for a long time a respectable inhabitant of this city (*BPAT* 30 Dec 1819).
Taylor, Mr. John and Miss Harriet Vanhorn, all of Baltimore, were m. Thurs., 5th inst., by Rev. John Davis (*BPAT* 13 Feb 1818).
Taylor, John, 16 years old, apprentice to the cordwaining business, ran away from Chas. F. Popp, in Waggon Alley (*BPAT* 8 May 1817).
Taylor, Capt. John, of Salisbury, late master of the Brig *Phebe* of Newburyport, d. 9th June at Cape Henry, Haiti (*BA* 1 Aug 1817).
Taylor, Col. John, of the State of Alabama, was m. at *John's and Thomas' Forest,* by the Rt. Rev. Bishop Kemp, on Thurs., 28th Oct, to Miss Fanny T. D. Owings, of Baltimore Co. (*BPAT* 2 Nov 1819).
Taylor, John S., was m. at Elkton on Thurs., 18th inst., by Rev. Gideon Ferrall, to Miss Ann, second dau. of Zebulon Beeston (*BPAT* 23 Nov 1819).
Taylor, Joseph, was m. last Thurs. by Rev. Mr. Duncan to Miss Margaret Wightman, all of Baltimore (*FGBA* 20 July 1818; *BPAT* 17 July 1818).
Taylor, Lemuel G., of Baltimore, was m. [date not given] in Annapolis to Miss Ann Rawlings of the latter place (*BA* 11 Nov 1817; *BPAT* 10 Nov 1817).
Taylor, Mr. Levi, was m. last Thurs. eve. by Rev. Dr. Roberts to Miss Catherine Ash, all of this city (*BPAT* 23 Dec 1817).
Taylor, Mrs. Margaret, wife of Lemuel Taylor, d. last Thurs., with scarce an hour's warning [Long obit and memorial verse] (*FBGA* 22 April 1817; *BPAT* 25 April 1817). Her death was recorded in the class lists of the Baltimore City Station of the Methodist Church (PedenM).
Taylor, Samuel G., merchant of Accomack Co., Va. and Maria, dau. of Zachariah Keene of Baltimore Co., were m. last Tues. eve. by Rev. Rev. Bartow (*BPAT* 12 Aug 1819).
Taylor, Mr. William, was m. by Rev. Glendy last Mon. eve. to Miss Margaret Byrnes, all of Baltimore (*BPAT* 30 Oct 1817; *BA* 30 Oct 1817).
Taylor, Capt. William S., was m. last Sat. by Rev. Glendy to Catherine Rawlings, all of Baltimore (*FGBA* 28 July 1818; *BPAT* 28 July 1818).
Tebo, Miss Mary Ann, dau. of Peter, d. 17th inst., after a short illness, in her 4th year (*BA* 21 Jan 1817; *BPAT* 21 Jan 1817). Peter Tebo, a native of France, and resident of Baltimore Co. and Baltimore, filed his Declaration of Intention 13 Aug 1816 (Baltimore Co. Court of Oyer and Terminer and Goal Delivery: Docket Minutes 1816).
Teneyck, Daniel W., of Baltimore, and insolvent debtor, has applied for benefit of the insolvent laws of Maryland (*BPAT* 25 March 1817)..
Terry, Mr. William, was m. last eve. [Thurs.] by Rev. Mr. Healey to Miss Elizabeth Brown, all of Baltimore (*BPAT* 31 Oct 1817).
Tesson, M. Pierre, formerly of Baltimore, d. at St. Louis Mo., on 17th March (*FGBA* 2 April 1818; *BPAT* 3 April 1818).
Thayer, Mr. Laban, of New York, was m. on Sat., by Rev. Mr. Davis to Miss Mary Ann Louis [or Tows], of Baltimore (*BPAT* 1 July 1817; *BA* 1 July 1817).

Biographical Data from Baltimore Newspapers, 1817-1819

Theker, Mrs. Jane, consort of Walter Theker of this city, d. Mon., 13th inst., in her 49th year, after a lingering illness, leaving a husband and four children (*BPAT* 14 Dec 1819).

Thieneman, Charles, was m. Thurs., 30th ult., by the Rev. Mr. Duncan, to Miss Ann Cunningham of this city (*BPAT* 10 Feb 1817; *BA* 10 Feb 1817).

Thomas, Miss Ann, dau. of Rev. James Thomas, d. at Centreville, [date not given] (*BPAT* 18 Sep 1818).

Thomas, Mr. Argalus G. D., was m. last eve. [Thurs.] by Rev. Stephen Rozzell to Miss Rebecca Shade, all of Baltimore (*BPAT* 7 Nov 1817).

Thomas, Mr. Isaac, was m. last Thurs. eve. at Lanvale, by Rev. Mr. Reed. to Miss Elizabeth Bowler, both of Baltimore Co. (*BPAT* 5 April 1817; *BA* 5 April 1817).

Thomas, Col. James, of Bangor. District of Maine, was m. at Washington, [date not given] to Miss Ann Davis, dau. of Mr. John Davis of that city (*BPAT* 11 Nov 1818).

Thomas, Jim, a mulatto boy, aged about 20 or 21 years, ran away from John Bausman living 14 miles from Baltimore. He has a mother living at Snow Hill, Princess Ann Co. [*sic*] (*BPAT* 10 June 1817).

Thomas, John, of West River, was m. on Wed., 21st Dec. by Rev. Dr. Wilson to Miss Elizabeth Murray, dau. of Commodore Alexander Murray (*BPAT* 7 Jan 1818).

Thomas, John, of Baltimore Co., is an insolent debtor (*BPAT* 28 Dec 1819).

Thomas, Thomas S., and Ann, eldest dau. of the late William E. Sewell, Esq., were m. Tues. eve., 21st inst., at North East, Cecil Co. (*BPAT* 27 Dec 1819).

Thomas, William, servant of J. Eichelberger, left the house of his wife last Sat, eve., about 9 o'clock for the purpose of attending a religious meeting about two or three mikes from the house. His master fears he may have been kidnapped or have run away, and offers a reward. Thomas was 27 or 28, but appears no more than 23 or 24; black, straight, and well-proportioned (*BPAT* 28 May 1818).

Thomas, William, b. in Penna., aged 19, has served part of his time to the blacksmith's business in Old Town, deserted from my Rendezvous, Light St., on 13 Dec. /w/ James H. Hook, Capt., 4th Infantry (*BPAT* 9 Jan 1818).

Thompson, George, aged 21 years, b. in N. Y., a laborer, deserted from Fort Covington, on the 16th inst. /s/ James H. Hook, Capt., 4th Inf. (*BPAT* 24 Jan 1818).

Thompson, George, was m. by Rev. Dr. Glendy last Thurs., to Mrs. Sarah Jordan, all of Baltimore (*BPAT* 2 Nov 1819).

Thompson, Israel P., of Alexandria, D. C., was m. last Thurs. by Dr. Inglis to Miss Angelica Robinson, dau. of Alexander Robinson of Baltimore (*BA* 31 March 1817).

Thompson, James, d. last Thurs., aged 24 (*BPAT* 11 May 1818).

Thompson, Lieut. John W., of the U. S. Ordnance Corps. was m. last Tues. by Rev. Bishop Kemp to Miss Ann Beam, dau. of Maj. George Beam of Baltimore Co. (*FGBA* 23 Jan 1818; *BPAT* 22 Jan 1818).

Thompson, Joseph, of Queen Anne's Co. has died. Charles A. C. Thompson, admin. advertised he would settle the estate (*BPAT* 29 Nov 1817).

Thompson, Martin, was m. last Tues. eve. by Rev. Healy to Miss Sarah Davis, all of Baltimore (*FGBA* 26 Feb 1818).

Thompson, Samuel, was m. last Mon. eve. by Rev. Mr. Hargrove, to Mrs. Sarah Brown, all of this city (*BPAT* 15 Jan 1817; *FGBA* 15 Jan 1817).

Thompson, Samuel, was m. last Thurs. eve. by Rev. Force to Miss Ann Lock all of Baltimore (*FGBA* 10 July 1819; *BPAT* 9 July 1819).

Thompson, Thomas, and Miss Mary Ann Allender were m. last eve. [Thurs.] by Rev. Dr. Roberts (*BPAT* 1 Oct 1819).

Thompson, Thomas F., was m. last Thurs, by Rev. Dr. Roberts to Mary W. Bowen, all of Baltimore (*BA* 17 April 1819; *FBBA* 16 April 1819; *BPAT* 17 April 1819).

Thomsen, Laurence, of the House of Labes and Thomsen, and His Danish Majesty's Consul for MD, d. Sat. in his 30th year, after a short illness (*BA* 20 April 1819; *BPAT* 19 April 1819). (For the will of Lawrence Thomson, filed in 1819, see BAWB 10:613)

Biographical Data from Baltimore Newspapers, 1817-1819

Thomson, Mr. William A., was m. last eve. [Thurs.] by the Rev. Mr. Valiant, to Miss Ann Hendrickson, all of Baltimore (*BPAT* 16 May 1817).

Thornton, Francis A., Esq., of the U. S. Navy, was m. [date not given] at Philadelphia, to Miss Sally Ann D. Heap, of Wilmington, De. (*BPAT* 23 Nov 1819).

Thum, George, of Philadelphia, was m. Thurs. eve. by Rev. Henshaw to Maria Warner, dau. of George Warner of Baltimore (*BA* 14 Nov 1818).

Tickey, Mr. Frederick, was m. at Fells Point last Tues. eve. by Rev. Mr. Eli, to Mss Mary Little both of Baltimore (*BPAT* 18 Nov 1819).

Tiernan, Sarah, dau. of Luke Tiernan, d. Sun. night n her 16th year (*BA* 12 May 1819; *BPAT* 12 May 1819). Sarah Tiernan, dau. of Luke, aged 16 years, d. 9 May 1819 of consumption and was buried 11 May 1819 in the Cathedral Cemetery (Grogaard).

Tilden, Miss Mary Ann, d. 28th ult. in Chestertown on the Eastern Shore of Md. (*BA* 8 Aug 1817; *BPAT* 7 Aug 1817 contains a long obit).

Tilghman, Mrs. Ann Maria, wife of Col. Frisby Tilghman, d. Fri. eve. last in Washington Co. (*BPAT* 28 Feb 1817).

Tilghman, Edward, Esq., of Kent Co. was m. at the "White House," Queen Anne's Co., the seat of Mrs. Eleanor Tilghman, of Tues., 21st inst., by Rev. Mr. Moynihan, to Anna Maria Tilghman, only dau. of the late William Tilghman, Esq. (*BPAT* 24 April 1818; *BA* 24 April 1818).

Tilghman, Col. Frisby, of Rockland, Washington Co., was m. at Cumberland [date not given] to Miss Louisa Lamar, dau. of Col. William Lamar (*BPAT* 1 Oct 1819)

Tilghman, James, of Worcester Co., has died. Levin Cottingham, exec., will settle the estate (*BPAT* 4 June 1817).

Tilton, Mrs. Mary Elizabeth, consort of Dr. James Tilton, Jr., d. at Peach blossom, Talbot Co., on Mon., 20th inst., leaving a husband (Long obit) (*BPAT* 28 Oct 1817).

Tilyard, Philip, was m. last Tues. by Rev. Neal to Miss Martha Moale, both of Baltimore (*BA* 20 Feb 1817).

Timanus, Jesse, owes taxes for the years 1813, 1814, 1815, on 11 or 12 a. *The Tanyard,* in the 1st Dist. (*BPAT* 7 Jan 1819).

Tingey, Commodore Thomas, of the City of Washington, was m. on the eve. [Wed.] of the 19th inst., by the Rev. J. Kirkpatrick, to Miss Ann Craven, dau. of Dr. Craven of Amwell, N. J. (*BPAT* 3 April 1817).

Tisdale, Mr. Reuben, was m. last Thurs. eve. by Rev. Dr. Roberts, to Miss Sarah Scudder, all of Baltimore Co. (*BPAT* 13 Oct 1817).

Todd, Miss Eliza, d. Sun., 5th Dec., in her 25th year (*BPAT* 13 Sep 1819). She d. on the 4th inst., in her 26th year, dau. of the late Thomas Todd of Elk Ridge Landing (*BPAT* 15 Sep1819).

Toole, Mr. Martin, was m. last Thurs. by Rev. Mr. Fenwick to Miss Mary Cloherty (or Clougherty) (*BPAT* 28 June 1817; *BA* 2 July 1817).

Topken, Gerhard, d. 1st inst., of dropsy; a native of Bremen, but for many years a resident of Baltimore. He leaves a widow (*BA* 6 Nov 1818; *BPAT* 6 Nov 1818). For the will of Gerard Topkin, filed in 1818, see BAWB 10:533.

Toso [Tooso?, Tuso?], Mr. Lewis, was m. last Thurs. eve. by Rev. D. E. Reese to Mrs. Harrietta Floote all of Baltimore (*BPAT* 10 Nov 1817; *BA* 11 Nov 1817).

Towne, Mr. John, was m. last eve. [Wed,] by Rev. John Hargrove, to Miss Sarah Robinson, all of Baltimore (*BPAT* 1 May 1817; *FGBA* 1 May 1817).

Townsend, Benjamin, was m. last Thurs. eve. by Rev. B. Waugh to Miss Ann Maria Townsend, both of Baltimore (*BPAT* 14 June 1819).

Townsend, Nicholas Waln, eldest son of Mr. Joseph Townsend of this city, d. last Tues. eve., 6th inst., in Chester Co., PA, in his 28th year, after an illness of four days (*BPAT* 9 Jan 1818; *BA* 9 Jan 1818).

Townsend, Perry R., was m. last Monday by Rev. Henshaw to Miss Anna M. Duncan, dau. of Rev. William Duncan, rector of All Hallows Parish, Anne Arundel Co. (*FGBA* 20 Jan 1819; *BPAT* 19 Jan 1819).

Towson, Mr. James, was m. last Thurs. eve. by Rev. Mr. Glendy to Miss Sarah Root, all of Baltimore (*BPAT* 1 Nov 1817; *FB BA* 1 Nov 1817).

Towson, Mr. Thomas, was m. last eve. [Thurs.] by the Rev. Mr. Kurtz, to Miss Henrietta Grubb, all of Baltimore *(BPAT* 17 Oct 1817; *FGBA* 17 Oct 1817).

Toy, Mr. John D., and Miss Margaret Smith, all of Baltimore, were m. Thurs. eve. by Rev. Joseph Toy *(BPAT* 13 Nov 1819).

Trace, or Tracey, Charles, recruit of the 4th Inf., b. in Bucks co., Pa., aged 27 years old, by profession a cooper, has been in the Marine Corps for the past five years, deserted from the detachment under my command at Fort Covington on 3rd of March. /s/ James H. Hook, Capt., 4th Inf. *(BPAT* 13 April 1818).

Tracey, James, was m. last Mon. eve. by Rev. E. J. Reis to Laura Cole, both of Baltimore *(FGBA* 3 Dec 1818; *BPAT* 3 Dec 1818 gives the bride's name as Lavinia Cole).

Travers, George, attorney at law, d. yesterday by his own hand at his father's house in Georgetown, leaving a father and mother *(FGBA* 12 March 1819; *BPAT*12 March 1819).

Treadwell, Mr. Alexander Philip Socrates Emilius Caesar Hannibal Marcellus George Washington, m. [date not given] at New Orleans, to Miss Caroline Sophia Maria Juliana Wortley Montague Joan of Arc, all of that city *(BPAT* 26 Feb 1817).

Trego, Mr. Samuel, was m. last Thurs. eve. by the Rev. Dr. Roberts, to Miss Eliza Nichols, all of Baltimore *(BPAT* 27 June 1817; *BPAT* 28 June 1817).

Tricket, John, (*alias* John Cricket), about 20 years of age, apprentice to Benjamin Hardester, ran away from his master's bed and board *(BPAT* 21 Jan 1817).

Trimble, William, d. suddenly of an apoplectic fit, in his 75th year; he was a member of the Society of Friends *(FGBA* 31 May 1819; *BPAT* 31 May 1819). For the will of William Trimble, filed in 1819, see BAWB 10:611,

Trott, Capt. William H., was m. Thurs. eve. by Rev. Dr. Glendy to Miss Elizabeth McDermott, of Baltimore *(FGBA* 28 Aug 1819).

Trowbridge, Mr. Reubin, was m. last Tues. eve. by Rev. Glendy to Miss Eliza Smith, both of Baltimore *(FGBA* 1 Jan 1817, *BA* 2 Jan 1817).

Trum, Dr. George, of Philadelphia, and Maria, dau. of George Warner, Esq., of Baltimore, were m. last eve. [Thurs.] by Rev. Henshaw *(BPAT* 13 Nov 1818)

Trumblingson, William, was m. last Thurs. by Rev. Davis to Miss Elizabeth Reade, all of Baltimore *(BPAT* 16 May 1818).

Trumbo, Adam, owes taxes for the year 1816 on 1½ a. of land from Thomas Carroll, in the 1st Dist. *(BPAT* 3 Aug 1819).

Tschudy, Mr. Samuel, was m. last (Thurs) eve. at Mt. Prospect, by Rev. Mr. Rossell, to Miss Eliza Clemm, all of Baltimore Co. *(BPAT* 21 March 1817; *BA* 22 March 1817).

Tuchson [Tuchstin, Tutchson], Nathan, was m. Thurs. eve. by Rev. Mr. Parks to Elizabeth Allen, all of Baltimore *(BA* 8 Dec 1818; *BPAT* 8 Dec 1818).

Tucker, Mr. Joseph, was m. last Tues. eve. by Rev. Mr. Force, to Miss Ann Young *(BPAT* 3 Dec 1819).

Tull, William, was m. last Sun. by Rev. Dr. Roberts, to Miss Elizabeth Todd, both of Baltimore *(BA* 1 Dec 1818).

Tunis, Samuel, of Baltimore Co., was late an imprisoned debtor of Baltimore Co., is discharged from Prison *(BPAT* 5 June 1818).

Turner, Daniel, late of the State of Del., d. intestate, leaving the following children and heirs at law, who reside beyond the State of Md.: Ebenezer, Sarah Ann, Benjamin, William, Elizabeth, and Lydia, and a widow Elizabeth *(BPAT* 15 Oct 1815).

Turner, Miss Mary C., dau. of Samuel Turner of Georgetown, D. C., d. 30th ult., aged 17 years, from mistakenly taking Tartar Emetic instead of magnesia *(BPAT* 4 Sep 1819).

Turner, Mrs. Ruth, d. last Tues., aged 50, after a long and painful illness *(BA* 21 May 1819; *BPAT* 21 May 1819). Her death was recorded in the class lists of the Baltimore City Station of the Methodist Church (PedenM).

Turner, Capt. Samuel W., was m. 5th inst. [Sun.] by Rev. John Glendy, to Miss Margaret Evans, all of Baltimore *(FGBA* 9 Jan 1818; *BPAT* 8 Jan 1818).

Biographical Data from Baltimore Newspapers, 1817-1819

Turner, Mr. Thomas, d. last Fri., aged 64, formerly of Portland, D. M. [District of Maine?] (*BPAT* 3 March 1817).
Turner, William, d. 6th inst., at Chaptico, Md., in his 35th year, a merchant of the firm of Josiah Turner and Co. (*FGBA* 1 Jan 1819; *BPAT* 15 Jan 1819).
Turreau [Turgeau?], Gen., late French minister to the U.S., d. at Normandy, France (*BPAT* 8 March 1817).
Tuttle, Daniel, was m. last Thurs. eve. by Rev. E. J. Reis to Miss Teresa Davis, all of Baltimore (*FGBA* 16 June 1818; *BPAT* 15 June 1818).
Tyson, Charles J., d. 11th inst., after a distressing indisposition, in his 10th year, son of the late Nathan Tyson, leaving a bereaved mother (*BPAT* 16 Sep 1819).
Tyson, Elisha, Jr., was m. 19th inst. [Tues.], at Friends North Meeting House in Philadelphia, to Sarah S. eldest dau. of Thomas Morris, Esq., of that city (*BPAT* 21 Oct 1819).
Tyson, George, merchant, of Baltimore, d. yesterday of an inflammation of the lungs (*BPAT* 18 Oct 1819).
Tyson, James Wood, son of Isaac Tyson, Jr., of Baltimore, d. 10th inst., at Woodfield, Gloucester Co., N. J., aged 7 mos. (*BPAT* 27 Sep[1819).
Tyson, Mr. Jonathan, was m. last Tues. eve. by Rev. D. E. Reese , to Miss Hedith Barrett, both of Baltimore Co. (*BPAT* 4 Dec 1819).
Tyson, Nathan, merchant of Baltimore, d. yesterday in his 63rd year; he resided at the corner of Hanover and Pratt Sts. (*FGBA* 16 March 1819; *BPAT* 16 March 1819).

"U"

Uhler, George, d. yesterday, aged 34. The funeral will be from his residence, 55 N. Hanover St. (*FGBA* 24 Jan 1818; *BPAT* 24 Jan 1818). For the will of George Uhler, filed in 1818, see BAWB 10:411.
Umbaugh, Mr. Michael, and Miss Jane R. Herbert, were m. [date not given] at Hagerstown (*BPAT* 17 July 1819).
Underwood, John, Jr., and Miss Louisa Walker, all of Baltimore, were m. last eve. [Thurs.] by Rev. Dr. Jennings (*FGBA* 19 Dec 1817; *BPAT* 20 Dec 1817).
Updegraff, Samuel, and Miss Susan Boyd, were m. [date not given] at Hagerstown (*BMC* 17 May 1819).
Urquhart, Mr. John, was m. Mon. eve. by Rev. Dr. Inglis, to Miss Ann Murray (*BPAT* 27 March 1817; *BA* 27 March 1817).

"V"

Valdenegro, Capt. Don Eusebeus, a native of Monte Video, d. at Philadelphia, of a pulmonary complaint, aged 35 years. He was among those noble spirits who first attempted to raise the standard of Liberty in the South. He leaves a wife and two children, the eldest of whom is not yet seven years of age (*BPAT* 24 Feb 1818).
Valentine, Rezin, a Negro land about 18 years of age, ran away from Joshua Young, living on Elk Ridge, Patapsco Mills (*BPAT* 19 Sep 1818).
Vallett, Charles, d. Mon. last, after a painful illness, in his 44th year (*BA* 18 Nov 1818; *BPAT* 18 Nov 1818). Charles Vallett d. 16 Nov 1818 of a bilious fever and was buried 17 Nov 1818 in the Cathedral Cemetery (Grogaard). S. and J. Cole, the auctioneers, advertised a sale of Vallette's household goods, furniture, and merchandize, at Vallette's late residence on Market St. (*BPAT* 27 Nov 1818).
Vanbibber, Ab. (and his heirs) owe taxes for the years 1814, 1815, on 87¼ a *Pimlico* in the 1st Dist. (*BPAT* 7 Jan 1819). Vanbibber and Smith owe taxes for the years 1814, 1815, on 624¼ a. of the Company's Lands (*BPAT* 7 Jan 1819). In 1816 his heirs owed taxes on 66⅓ a. *Pimlico,* 16 a. *Peace and Good Neighborhood,* and 5 a. *Tom's Choice,* all in the 1st Dist. (*BPAT* 3 Aug 1819). For the will of Abraham Van Bibber, filed in 1805, see BAWB 7:436.

Biographical Data from Baltimore Newspapers, 1817-1819

Vanbibber, Washington, owes taxes for the years 1814, 1815, on 879 a. of Company Lands transferred in the 1st Dist. (*BPAT* 7 Jan 1819). In 1816 he owed taxes on land in Randall's Town in the 7th Dist. (*BPAT* 3 Aug 1819).
Vance, Mrs. Ann, relict of the late William Vance of Baltimore, d. in Philadelphia (*BPAT* 3 March 1819).
Vance, Thomas, was m. last Tues. eve. by the Rev. John Glendy, Miss Elizabeth Smith, all of this city (*BPAT* 7 Feb 1817; *BA* 7 Feb 1817).
Vance, William, dec.; Christopher Deshong advertised the sale of a black man and a lot of ground on Aisquith St., belonging to the deceased's estate (*BPAT* 16 March 1818). Later Deshong advertised the lease of 140 feet of ground on King George St. and 50 feet on Prince and Granby Sts., as well as a lot, 50 feet on Aisquith St., belonging to the said Vance (*BPAT* 21 April 1818). On 17 Aug 1818, Deshong and Henry Thompson, execs. of William Vance, sold a lot at the intersection of Aisquith St. and Hall's Lane to John S. Young, and commissioners would meet on 1 Sep next to establish the lines of the lot (*BPAT* 24 Aug 1818). For the will of William Vance, filed in 1816, see BAWB 10:182
Vanderford, Henry, of Baltimore, and Miss Eliza Whittington of Queen Anne's Co. were m. Thurs., 23rd July, by Rev. Mr. Reed (*BA* 3 Aug 1818).
Van Horn, Archibald, d. last week at his res. in Prince George's Co., a member of the Maryland Senate, and formerly a Member of Congress from Maryland (*FGBA* 4 March 1817; *BPAT* 3 March 1817).
Van Horn, Capt. Jonathan, was m. on 6th ult. [Wed.] by Rev, Dr. Glendy to Miss Ann Rhoday (*BPAT* 7 Oct 1819).
Van Riper, John, of Patterson, N. J., and Miss Letitia McKee of Baltimore, were m. Thurs. eve. by Rev. Bartow (*BA* 21 Nov 1818; *BPAT* 21 Nov 1818).
Van Weazle, Mr. Moses Davis, and Miss Rebecca Conley (Condley), all of Baltimore, were m. last Sun. by Rev. Mayberry Parks (*BA* 11 Aug 1818).
Van Wyck, Mrs. Elizabeth L., d. yesterday morning, in the 60th year of her age, widow of the late Wm. Van Wyck. Her funeral will be this afternoon (*BPAT* 24 Dec 1819). Elizabeth Van Wyck, aged 60 years, was buried 24 Dec 1819 from St. Paul's Parish (ReamySP). For the will of Elizabeth Van Wyck, filed in 1820, see BAWB 11:94.
Van Wyck, Stedman, died last 15 July. He was formerly a captain of the Washington Guards and recently a merchant of St. Thomas. He was born on 8 Sep 1794 (*FGBA* 11 Aug 1819; *BPAT* 10 Aug 1819).
Van Wyck, William, d. this morning, of the typhus fever, aged 69 (*FGBA* 3 May 1817; *BPAT* 3 May 1817). A res. of Baltimore Co.; John C. Van Wyck and Louis Barney, admins., advertise they will settle the estate (*BPAT* 20 May 1817).
Varner, Robert, a stout well made fellow, apprentice to the Morocco Business, ran away from Lewis Kalbfus, on the Reisterstown pad, about one mile from Baltimore; a reward of six cents is offered (*BPAT* 20 June 1817).
Vaughen, John, of Baltimore Co., is an insolvent debtor (*BPAT* 19 Nov 1819).
Vermilion, John, aged about 18 years, an apprentice to the boot and shoe making, ran away on 9 Aug, from John Davis on Bridge St., Baltimore, who offers a reward of 100 cents. He may have gone towards Frederick Town, where he has some acquaintance (*BPAT* 3 Sep 1818).
Viers, Samuel C., of Rockville, Montgomery Co., and Miss Juliana Diffenderfer of Baltimore, were m. last Tues. by Rev. Healey (*FGBA* 11 April 1818; *BPAT* 11 April 1818).
Vidal, Mrs. Antoinette, d. last Sun. eve., after a short illness, in her 84th year (*BPAT* 17 April 1817; *FGBA* 17 April 1817).
Villard, Martha, of Baltimore Co., dec.; Rachel Charlotte Jones, admx., advertises that she will settle the estate (*BPAT* 12 Oct 1818). For the will of Martha Villard, filed in 1818, see BAWB 10:512. (See Mrs. Mary Villard, below).
Villard, Mrs. Mary, d. yesterday, aged 43 years, after a long and painful illness, long a resident of this city (*BPAT* 25 Aug 1818). (See Martha Villard, above).

Biographical Data from Baltimore Newspapers, 1817-1819

Virtue, David, and Miss Ellen Lynch, were m. last Sat. by Rev. Glendy (*FGBA* 14 Sep 1818).
Vosburg, Abraham, and Miss Priscilla Roberts, all of Baltimore, were m. last Sun. by Rev. McCollister (*BMC* 18 May 1819; *BPAT* 24 April 1819).

"W"

Wagner, Mr. John Christian, a native of Frankfort, Germany, and late of Baltimore, d. at New Orleans in his 58th year (*BPAT* 25 Nov 1819).
Wagner, Peter A., editor of the Orleans *Gazette,* was m. [date not given], at New Orleans, to Miss Sidonia, dau. of J. Lewis, Esq., Judge of the District Court of La. (*BPAT* 18 Aug 1819).
Wakeman, Dr. Banks, of Kent Co., was m. Tues., 10th last, by the Rev. Josephus Bulkeley, to Miss Araminta Hynson, of Queen Anne's Co. (*BPAT* 18 June 1817).
Waldron, Benjamin, aged 60, was m. at Ovid to Miss Sally Hawkins, aged 22 (*BPAT* 17 Feb 1817).
Walker, Emanuel, of Cecil Co., dec.; John Conrad, his administrator, will settle the estate (*BPAT* 2 Sep 1819).
Walker, John James Augusts, a native of Dublin, is a swindler who has made his appearances in Lancaster, Carlisle, Chambersburg, etc. Innkeepers, Merchants, and Washerwomen are particularly warned to be on their guard (*BPAT* 16 July 1819).
Walker, Margaret Mary, d. 5th inst., dau. of Charles Walker of Baltimore Co. (*BACDA* 7 July 1819; *BPAT* 6 July 1819).
Walker, Samuel, was m. last Thurs. by Rev. D. E. Reese to Mrs. Mary Morrow, both of Baltimore Co. (*FGBA* 25 July 1818; *BPAT* 25 July 1818 states she was Miss Mary Morrow).
Walker, Thomas, of Baltimore, was m. last 30 Oct [Thurs.] at St. Francisville, La., to Miss Mary Coralie Beauvais (*BA* 19 Dec 1817; *BPAT* 19 Dec 1817). He d. at St. Francisville, on 17th Sep last in his 24th year, leaving a widow and an infant son; he was for many years a resident of Baltimore (*BPAT* 18 Oct 1819).
Walker, Dr. Thomas C. was m. Tues., 17th inst. by Rev. Armstrong, to Miss Catherine Cradock, all of Baltimore Co. (*BA* 18 Feb 1818; *BPAT* 18 Feb 1818). For the will of Thomas Walker, filed in1818, see BAWB 10:520.
Walker, William, father of William Walker, sail-maker, with whom he had lived for the last fifteen years of his life, d. Tues. eve. in his 89th year (*BPAT* 2 May 1817).
Wallace, Joseph A., of Baltimore, was m. Tues. by Rev. Wheaton to Rebecca Maria, elder dau. of the late Mr. Henry McCoy of Elk Ridge (*BPAT* 1 April 1818).
Wallace, Mrs. Maria, consort of Joseph A. Wallace, d. 10th inst., leaving a husband and child (*FGBA* 12 Jan 1819; *BPAT* 13 Jan 1819). "Mrs. Rebecca Maria Wallace, consort of Joseph A. Wallace, who was born 15 August 1794 and departed this transitory life 11 Jan 1819, aged 24," is on the tablet where she is buried in Westminster Presbyterian Churchyard, Baltimore (HaywardW).
Wallace, Mr. Solomon, merchant of Baltimore, and Miss Ruth E., dau. of Mr. John E. Stansbury of Baltimore Co., were m. Tues. eve. last by Rev. Mr. Burch (*BPAT* 17 Sep 1819).
Wallace, Thomas, late collector to this establishment, d. last Thurs., in his 22nd year (*BA* 20 June 1818; *BPAT* 20 June 1818).
Wallace, Capt. Thomas, d. Sat., 6th inst., at his residence in Culpeper Co., Va., in his 57th year, one of the surviving officers of the Revolutionary War (*FGBA* 12 June 1818).
Waller, Bazil, was m. last eve. [Thurs.] by Rev. D. E. Reese, to Miss Susan Stewart of Anne Arundel Co. (*BA* 5 Sep 1817; *BPAT* 5 Sep 1817).
Waller, William, late Sheriff and Collector of Somerset Co., was to have an act passed to allow him further time to complete his collections (*BPAT* 10 Feb 1817).

Biographical Data from Baltimore Newspapers, 1817-1819

Wallis, Mrs. Louisa Chew, consort of Mr. John Wallis, Jr., of this city, d. 2nd inst., in her 21st year, of a lingering illness. She left a husband and infant son (*BPAT* 5 Dec 1817).

Wallow, Abraham, was m. last eve. [Thurs.] by Rev. Hargrove, to Miss Amey Chapman, all of Baltimore (*BA* 27 June 1817; *BPAT* 27 June 1817).

Walls, Mr. William, son of the Rev. John Walls of Baltimore Co., was m. last Tues. eve. by the Rev. James Smith to Miss Eliza Munn, dau. of the Rev. Benj. Munn, late of N.J. (*BPAT* 19 March 1818; *BA* 19 March 1818).

Walmsley, Mr. John Gooding, of Baltimore Co., was m. last Tues. eve. by Rev. James Megraw, to Miss Harriet Simes of Cecil Co. (*FGBA* 15 May 1817; *BPAT* 16 May 1817 gives the bride's name as Simco).

Walsh, John Francis, second son of Robert Walsh of Baltimore, d. last eve. in his 27th year (*FGBA* 12 March 1818; *BPAT* 13 March 1818). John F. Walsh d. 2 [*sic*] March 1818 aged 27, of consumption; he was buried 3 [*sic*] March 1818 in the Cathedral Cemetery (Grogaard).

Walter, William, of Baltimore Co., is an insolvent debtor; a trustee will be nominated on next 1 Oct (*BPAT* 6 Dec 1819).

Walters, Benedict F., was m. last Tues. in Harford Co. to Miss Milcah Matthews; all of Harford Co. (*BPAT* 28 Nov 1818).

Walters, Mr. Corbin, and Miss Catherine Roof, both of the state of Va., were m. [date not given] at Hagerstown (*BPAT* 8 Oct 1819).

Walters, William, was m. last Thurs. eve. by Rev. Benjamin Richardson, to Miss Ann Ford, all of Harford Co. (*BA* 4 Oct 1817; *BPAT* 4 Oct 1817).

Waltham Charlton M., of Abingdon, Harford Co., was m. Mon. eve. by Rev. D. E. Reese to Miss Hester Taylor, of the same place (*BA* 18 March 1818; *BPAT* 18 March 1818).

Wanhill, Capt. Thomas, of the British ship *Garland*, now in this port, d. yesterday morning, after an illness of two days (*BPAT* 27 Aug 1819). Capt. Thomas Wanhill [*sic*], was buried 26 Aug 1819 from St. Paul's Parish (ReamySP).

Wampler, J. Lewis, at 6 N. Liberty St., advertises for the return of four deeds and a patent relative to land lying on the east side of Hanover Lane, now called Hanover St. (*BPAT* 14 April 1818).

Ward, John W., was m. last Thurs. eve. by Rev. Mr. Wyatt to Elizabeth Roberts, all of Baltimore (*BA* 10 Dec 1818; *BPAT* 9 Dec 1818).

Ward, Nathan, of Philadelphia, was m. last Tues. by Rev. Glendy to Miss Elizabeth Peck of Baltimore *BA* 1 May 1818; *BPAT* 1 May 1818).

Ward, Patrick, of Philadelphia, was m. Thurs., 10th inst., by Rev. Parks, to Miss Lilly Boyle of Baltimore (*BA* 12 April 1817; *BPAT* 12 April 1817).

Ward, Rebecca, late of Philadelphia, d. last eve. in her 18th year (*BPAT* 2 Jan 1818).

Ward, Robert, Esq., was m. last eve. [Fri.] by the Rev. Mr. Matthews, to Miss Mary Baker, both of Baltimore Co. (*BPAT* 22 March 1817; *BA* 22 March 1817).

Ward, William H., and Joseph M. Sanderson, of Baltimore Co., are insolvent debtors (*BPAT* 6 Oct 1819).

Ware, Thomas, a tailor by trade, and a native of White Haven, Eng., came to this country in 1818 and was in Augusta, Ga., last 19 dec., and has not been heard from since; his wife and two children are now in Baltimore, and need his presence (*BPAT* 20 May 1819).

Warfield, Daniel, of Anne Arundel Co., was m. last Tues. by Dr. Inglis to Miss Ann Mactier, of Baltimore (*FGBA* 16 Feb 1819; *BPAT* 12 Feb 1819).

Warfield, Elisha, a native of Md., d. 16th ult. in Fayette Co., Va., in his 78th year (*BA* 10 Aug 1818; *BPAT* 10 Aug 1818).(For the will of Elijah Warfield, filed in 1818, see BAWB 9:531.

Warfield, John Marriott, was m. last Thurs. eve. by Rev. Mr. Stigers, to Miss Ann Hammond, all of Anne Arundel Co. (*BPAT* 17 March 1817; *BA* 17 March 1817).

Warfield, Lewis, eldest son of G. F. Warfield, d. 19th Sep in Baltimore in his 20th year, leaving his parents, and five brothers and sisters. (A long obit gives details of the fatal accident). (*BA* 22 Sep 1818; *BPAT* 23 Sep 1818). Lewis Warfield, aged 20 years, was buried 20 Sep 1818 from St. Paul's Parish (ReamySP).

Warfield, Philemon, and Miss Ann Wright of Annapolis, were m. at that city on last Sun. eve. by Rev. Mr. Watkins (*BPAT* 29 Oct 1819).

Waring, Mr. George W., Esq. and Miss Sarah, dau, of Caleb Dorsey, Esq., of Anne Arundel Co., were m. Tues. eve. by Rev. Mr. Wheaton (*BPAT* 3 Dec 1819).

Warner, William, son of Michael, d. yesterday in his 19th year. The funeral will be from his father's residence, Washington St., in the Western Precincts (*BA* 14 Aug 1817).

Warrington, Capt. Lewis, of the U. S. Navy, was m. at Norfolk, 13th inst. [Thurs.], at Norfolk by Rev. Low, to Miss Carry King, dau. of the late Miles King, Esq., of Norfolk (*BPAT* 20 March 1817; *BA* 20 March 1817).

Washington, Laurence, Esq., was m. Tues., 26th Oct.. at Harwood, Westnoreland Co., Va., by the Rev. Dr. Wilmer, to Sarah T., dau. of the late Col. Wm. A. Washington (*BPAT* 3 Nov 1819).

Waterhouse, Elias B., of Portland, Me., was m. [date not given] in Alexandria, to Miss Alice Cartwright (*BPAT* 10 Feb 1818).

Waters, Col., of Baltimore, was m. Sun., 20th inst., at the seat of H. Hollyday, Easton, to Miss Eliza J. Boyle of Dorchester Co. (*BA* 29 Dec 1818; *BPAT* 29 Dec 1818).

Waters, Edward, member of the Society of Friends, d. 31st ult., in his 73rd year. He leaves a widow (*FGBA* 7 Oct 1818; *BPAT* 7 Oct 1818).

Waters, Mrs. Elizabeth, consort of Hezekiah Waters, Esq., d. last Thurs. eve. in her 31st year, of lingering consumption. She left a husband and five children (*BPAT* 6 July 1818).

Waters, Mr. John, was m. Thurs. eve. by Rev. Dr. Roberts, to Miss Ann Carson (*BA* 23 Nov 1818; *BPAT* 20 Nov 1818).

Waters, Joseph, d. 4th ult., at New Orleans, of the prevailing fever, in his 25th year; formerly a resident of Baltimore (*BPAT* 12 Oct 1819).

Waters, Patrick, of Worcester Co., dec.; Samuel H. Smith and John S. Martin, admins. with will annexed, will settle the estate (*BPAT* 11 May 1818).

Waters, Richard, was m. last Thurs. by Rev. Glendy, to Miss Mary Brown (*FGBA* 14 Sep 1818; *BPAT* 14 Sep 1818).

Waters, William, d. at Abingdon, Harford Co. on Sun., 27th inst., after a distressing illness, in his 41st year (*BA* 31 Dec 1818).

Waters, William D., was m. last eve. [Wed.] by Rev. Hargrove, to Miss Sarah Gettis, all of Baltimore (*BA* 2 Oct 1817; *BPAT* 2 Oct 1817).

Watkin, Asa T., was m. 19th ult. [Fri.], by Rev. John Glendy, to Miss Maria Duvivier (*BA* 9 Oct 1817; *BPAT* 8 Oct 1817).

Watkins, Gassaway, is an insolvent debtor of Baltimore Co. (*BPAT* 13 Nov 1819).

Watson, John, was m. last Wed. eve. by Rev. Glendy to Miss Jane Campbell, all of Baltimore (*BA* 8 Nov 1817; *BPAT* 8 Nov 1817).

Watson, Mr. Joseph, was m. [date not given] at Annapolis to Miss Elizabeth Mace, both of Annapolis (*BPAT* 21 Nov 1817).

Watts, David, Esq., for many years, an eminent Attorney at Law, d. at Carlisle, Pa. (*BPAT* 20 Sep 1819).

Watts, Ezekiel, d. last evening. Funeral from his late dwelling, corner of Sharp and Camden Sts. (*FGBA* 16 Jan 1818; *BPAT* 17 Jan 1818). For the will of Ezekiel Watts, filed in 1818, see BAWB 10:408.

Watts, Frederick J., was m. last Sun. eve., by Rev. Mr. Wells, to Miss Julia Ann Parks, all of Baltimore (*FGBA* 2 June 1817; *BPAT* 3 June 1817).

Way, Mr. George, of Washington, d. last Thurs. in Philadelphia (*BPAT* 31 May 1819).

Way, John D., was m. Thurs. eve. by Rev. Bartow to Miss Ann Green, all of Baltimore (*BA* 22 May 1819; *BPAT* 22 May 1819).

Wayman, Miss Milcah, d. Tues., 12th ult., at the residence of her brother, Henry Wayman, near Poplar Springs, Anne Arundel Co., in her 37th year, after an illness of twenty-one days (*BPAT* 11 Nov 1819).

Biographical Data from Baltimore Newspapers, 1817-1819

Wayne, Francis, merchant of Washington, D. C., d. there of a pulmonary disease (*BPAT* 20 Dec 1819).

Weatherby, William, was m. 6th inst. [Tues.], by Rev. John Glendy, to Miss Sarah Ann Turner (*BA* 20 May 1817; *BPAT* 20 May 1817).

Weaver, Mr. Jacob, was m. last Thurs. eve. by Rev. Mr. Duncan, to Miss Elizabeth Reed, both of Baltimore (*BPAT* 28 Feb 1818; *BA* 28 Feb 1818).

Weaver, James, was m. last eve. [Tues.] by Rev. Hargrove to Miss Mary Ann Jackson, all of Baltimore (*BPAT* 8 April 1818).

Weaver, John, of Baltimore. was m. Sun., 12th inst., by Rev. Mr. Zeilly, to Miss Elizabeth Sparr of Carlisle, at the latter place (*BPAT* 24 June 1819).

Weaver, William, a resident of Georgetown, D. C., and a Lieutenant in the U.S. Navy, is to be arrested and brought to trial for stabbing the 19 year old son of James Power with a sword so that the young man is dangerously wounded. The notice gives details of how Weaver befriended the youth and invited the son to take a walk, and when he got to a convenient place suddenly attacked the young man. /s/ James Power (*BPAT* 27 June 1817).

Webb, Charles, was m. last eve. [Fri.], by Rev. Waugh, to Miss Clarissa Legg, of Baltimore (*FGBA* 22 May 1819; *BPAT* 22 May 1819).

Webb, Mr. Gideon, was m. last eve. [Wed.] by Rev. Hargrove, to Mrs. Sarah Drummond, all of Baltimore (*BA* 13 Nov 1817; *BPAT* 13 Nov 1817).

Webb, Mr. Henry, merchant, of Baltimore, was m. last Tues. eve. by Rev. Mr. Wyatt, to Miss Elizabeth Robinson of Philadelphia (*BA* 11 Oct 1817; *BPAT* 11 Oct 1817).

Webb, William, aged about 58 years, left the house of Catherine Webb, North St., on Friday evening in a fit of derangement; any information will confer a favor on his disconsolate wife. /s/ Catherine Webb (*BPAT* 27 Oct 1819).

Webber, Mrs. and Miss, just arrived from England, intend opening a school for the education of Young ladies in needlework of all kinds, and in English, Arithmetic, Geography, History and Chronology; the School is in Queen St., at the corner of Albemarle, Old Town (*BPAT* 3 Nov 1818).

Webster, Charles, a stone mason from Litchfield, Eng., d. yesterday of an apoplectic fit. He was in the employ of Mr. Diffendall, and was about 35 years of age. he leaves a wife and two children in England (*BPAT* 8 Aug 1818).

Webster, Toppan, of Washington, was m. last Tues. by Rev. Stephens, to Miss Mary Chauncey, of Harford Co. (*BA* 22 April 1817; *BPAT* 19 April 1817).

Weed, Mr. Ezra, and Miss Juliann Gafford, all of this city, were m. last eve. [Thurs.], by Rev. Mr. Burch (*BPAT* 8 Oct 1819).

Weedon, Mr. Jonathan, was m. [date not given] at Annapolis, to Miss Margaret Hutton (*BPAT* 6 Aug 1819).

Weems, John, owes taxes for the years 1813, 1814, 1815, on 541½ a. of *Edwards and Wills Valleys and Hills* in the 1st Dist. (*BPAT* 7 Jan 1819).

Weir, Benjamin, d. 10th inst., in Philadelphia., in his 42nd year (*BPAT* 20 Feb 1818).

Weise, Augustus, a native of Saxony, d. Thurs., 6th inst., in his 42nd year. His funeral will be from his late dwelling house, 78½ Market St. (*BA* 8 Nov 1817; *BPAT* 7 Nov 1817). Susannah Louisa Weise, extx., advertised she would sell a house and lot of ground at 140 Market St. (*BPAT* 10 March 1818). For the will of Augustus Weise, filed in 1817, see BWAB 10:381.

Weise, Godfrey, of Frederick Town, was m. last eve. [Tues.] by Rev. Hargrove to Miss Susanna Louisa Weise of Baltimore (*FGBA* 28 July 1819).

Welling, Samuel L. P., of New York, was m. Thurs. eve. by Rev. Dr. Roberts, to Miss Hannah Hussey, of Baltimore (*FGBA* 20 Sep 1817).

Wellmore, Mrs. Ann, consort of Robert, d. last Tues. eve., aged about 75 years (*BA* 19 Dec 1817; *BPAT* 19 Dec 1817).

Wellmore, Robert, d. Friday eve last, in his 76th year, an inhabitant of Baltimore for the last 34 years (*FGBA* 8 Jan 1817; *BPAT* 9 Jan 1817).

Wells, Charles, dec,; his estate owes taxes for the years 1813, 1814, 1815, on 35 a., Part of *Wells Manor* in 1st Dist. (*BPAT* 7 Jan 1819).

Biographical Data from Baltimore Newspapers, 1817-1819

Wells, Daniel, late Captain of the Artillery Co. of Annapolis, where he had been a citizen for 50 years, d. there on 21st inst., leaving a wife and six children (*BPAT* 27 Jan 1818; *FGBA* 28 Jan 1818). Daniel Wells, aged 55 years, was buried 16 Jan 1818 from St. Paul's Parish (ReamySP).

Wells, William, Jr., of Baltimore, was m. on Tues. eve. by Rev. Dr. Davis to Miss Eliza Pickard of New Haven, Conn. (*BA* 14 May 1818; *BPAT* 13 May 1818).

Welsh, Charles, owes taxes for the years 1813, 1814, 1815, on 70 a. *Warfield's Forest* in the 6th Dist. (*BPAT* 7 Jan 1819).

Welsh, Mrs. Elizabeth Hallock, d. yesterday morning, of pulmonary consumption, she was the consort of Rev. John Welsh, aged 22 years and 1 day (*BPAT* 10 Feb 1817).

Welsh, Jacob, Esq; dec.; his valuable estate on the Conewago Creek, near Berlin, Adams Co., Pa., will be sold. It consists of 183 a., a saw mill, and a dwelling house; for terms apply to Anna Maria Welsh or Charles Welsh on the premises or to Henry Welsh at Hanover (*BPAT* 23 Feb 1818).

Wenn, Elisha, was m. last Sun. eve., 19th inst., by Rev. Mr. Richards, to Miss Polly Shaw, all of this city (*BPAT* 24 Jan 1817).

Werdebaugh, John, merchant, was m. last Thurs. by Rev. Kurtz, to Miss Amelia Ratien, all of Baltimore (*BA* 15 Nov 1817; *BPAT* 15 Nov 1817).

West, Stacy, of Harford Co., and Miss Susannah Hopkins, were m. last Thurs. by Rev. Valiant (*BA* 11 Jan 1819; *BPAT* 11 Jan 1819).

West, William, who resided on Bridge St., d. yesterday, aged about 35 years (*BA* 5 Jan 1819; *BPAT* 5 Jan 1819).

Westby, Hugh, died; by order of the Baltimore Co. Orphans court, Mary Kindall, admx., and John Ash, admin., will sell his property at the corner of Paca and Pratt Sts., including a two story brick house and a frame house (*BPAT* 6 April 1818). [See Hugh Westley. below].

Westley, Hugh, of Baltimore Co., dec.; Jacob Myers, administrator *de bonis non,* advertises the sale of three lots of ground at Pratt and Paca Sts. (*BPAT* 5 April 1819). [See Hugh Westby above]. His name is given as Hugh Wesby in *BPAT* 29 April 1819).

Weston, Miss Mary, late of Baltimore, d. yesterday (from the Alexandria *Herald*) (*BA* 12 May 1817).

Wetherly, Bristo, and Miss Clarissa Peters, all of Baltimore, were m. last Thurs. by Rev. Wyatt (*BMC* 12 April 1819; *BPAT* 10 April 1819).

Weymouth, Mr. Dean, of the War Dept., Washington City, was m. Sat. eve. last by the Rev. Mr. Allen, to Miss Maria Hamilton, eld. dau. of Mr. James Hamilton, Principal of the Hamiltonian School in this city (*BPAT* 6 Sep 1819)_.

Wharfe, Joseph, was m. at Emmittsburg, [date not given] to Miss Teresa C. Nevitt, of Frederick Co. (*BMC* 17 May 1819).

Wheeler, Mr. Benjamin, was m. last eve. [Mon.], by Rev. Mr. Fry, to Miss Mary Ann Johnson, both of Baltimore (*BPAT* 1 Sep 1818; *FGBA* 1 Sep 1818).

Wheeler, Benjamin, late of Baltimore, was m. on 28 Feb [Sun.] by Rev. D. E. Reese to Sarah Ogden, of Baltimore Co. (*BA* 6 March 1819; *BPAT* 6 March 1819).

Wheeler, Mr. Odel, of Montgomery Co., was m. Tues., 24th Nov., by Rev. Mr. Hood, to Miss Caroline, 2nd, dau. of Col. Richard Dorsey, of Elk Ridge, MD (*BPAT* 9 Dec 1818; *BA* 10 Dec 1818).

Wheland, Peter, an apprentice to the coopering trade, ran away from James Daly, on Spear's Wharf. A reward of six cents and a basket of chips is offered as a reward (*BPAT* 8 May 1817).

White, Charles, late of Philadelphia Co., has died. Claimants to shares of his property include Joseph Montgomery on behalf of his wife Margaret, late Margaret Blanchard, and Catherine Roberdeau and all others claiming to be heirs, representatives and next of kin of said Charles White (*BPAT* 16 June 1817).

White, Edward, aged 16, indented apprentice to the cordwaining business, ran away from William Elliott, Duke St., Old Town near the Circus (*BPAT* 2 Sep 1818).

Biographical Data from Baltimore Newspapers, 1817-1819

White, Francis, son of Gideon White of Baltimore, d. Wed., in his 21st year (*FGBA* 8 May 1819; *BPAT* 8 May 1819).

White, Mrs. Hannah, consort of Gideon White of Baltimore, d. in her 46th year (*FGBA* 23 Aug 1819; *BPAT* 24 Aug 1819).

White, Mr. James, was m. on Thurs. by Rev. Healy. to Miss Catherine Fulmer, all of Baltimore (*FGBA* 20 March 1819; *BPAT* 19 March 1819).

White, Joshua, son of Daniel White of Townsend, Mass., left his father's house about two years ago, and has not been heard of since. He is about 19 years old and is supposed to be in some of the southern states (*BPAT* 2 May 1818).

White, Samuel, d. 1 March at Liverpool, Eng., aged 18 years and 11 mos., nephew of Mr. Isaac Redgrave of Baltimore (*BA* 20 May 1819; *BPAT* 21 June 1819).

White, Samuel K., of Baltimore Co., is an insolvent debtor (*BPAT* 1 Jan 1819.

White, Thomas, aged about 18 years, apprentice boy, ran away from Wm. P. Barnes, No. 45 Fell's St., Fell's Point; a reward of ten dollars is offered (*BPAT* 4 June 1818).

White, Thomas, and Miss Mary Atkinson, both of Annapolis, were m. there on Thurs., 14th inst. (*BPAT* 15 Oct 1819).

White, Thomas, states that his wife Mary has left his bed and board without any just cause, and he will not pay her debts (*BPAT* 3 Dec 1819).

White, William, aged 17 years and 10 mos., apprentice to the cordwaining business, ran away from John Williams, living on Gallows Hill (*BPAT* 11 Jan 1819).

Whitney, Mr. Ephraim, of Baltimore, d. last Thurs. morning, after a lingering illness, aged 40 years (*BPAT* 13 Jan 1818; *FBA* 12 Jan 1818). Ephraim Whitney, aged 40 years was buried 8 Jan 1818 from St. Paul's Parish (ReamySP).

Whittle, Clarissa, wife of Nicholas Whittle, of Elkridge, Anne Arundel Co., was killed by a stroke of lightning, leaving five children "from the *Fed. Gaz.*" (*BPAT* 31 July 1819).

Wichelhause, Mr. Jacob, was m. last eve., [Thurs.] by Dr. Glendy, to Miss Henrietta Dukehart, dau. of the late Henry Dukehart of Baltimore (*BPAT* 15 May 1818; *FGBA* 15 May 1818). He may be the Jacob Wickethausen of the Austrian Empire, who was born in the City of Bremen, and filed his Declaration of Intention in U. S. Circuit Court on 6 May 1818and was naturalized ion 7 Dec 1824; witnesses were Conrad Henry Daumenen and John N. Dacey (Baltimore Co. Court Naturalization docket 1:91).

Wightman, Capt. John, was m. Sun. eve. by Rev. Force, to Miss Ann Marie Askew, both of Baltimore (*FGBA* 7 April 1819).

Wilcox, Anthony, resided in Westmoreland Co., Va., and left his wife, Phoebe, about fourteen months since, during a severe spell of illness, with two small children to support; he was seen in Norfolk about six weeks since, and it is believed he went to Richmond in some vessel; he took with him, his eldest child, a boy about seven years of age. /s/ Phebe Wilcox (*BPAT* 22 Oct1819).

Wilhelm, Jane, owes taxes for the years 1813, 1814, 1815, on 47 a. *Poor Dependance* in the 3rd Dist. (*BPAT* 7 Jan 1819).

Wilkins, William, of Pittsburgh, was m. [date not given] at Philadelphia, to Miss Matilda Dallas, dau. of the late A. J. Dallas (*BPAT* 7 Oct 1818).

Wilkinson, Charles, d. Sat., 13th inst., a native of Ireland (*BPAT* 17 Nov 1819). For the will of Charles Wilkinson, filed in 1819, see BAWB 11:72.

Willat, William, left Manchester, Eng., at the age of 24; if now living he must be 83 years, He will hear something to his advantage if he applies to the office of this advertisement. His friends would like any knowledge of him, living or dead (*BPAT* 26 Oct 1817).

Willey, Mrs. Mary, d. last Thurs. eve. after a short but painful illness, in her 70th year (*BPAT* 1 Jan 1818).

Williams, Amos A., of Baltimore Co., is an insolvent debtor (*BPAT* 14 Oct 1819).

Williams, Mr. Baruch, of Baltimore, d. at Havana on 27 Jan 1818, leaving a wife and two children [long obit] (*BPAT* 13 Feb 1818; *FGBA* 13 Feb 1818). His business, at

9 South St., will be continued by Abel Marple and Barrett Williams (*BPAT* 6 June 1818). For the will of Baruch Williams, filed in 1818, see BAWB 10:424.

Williams, C. D., of Baltimore Co., is an insolvent debtor (*BPAT* 19 Oct 1819).

Williams, Ebenezer, of Baltimore, d. at Washington on Sat., leaving a mother and sister (*BPAT* 15 April 1819; *BMC* 16 April 1819).

Williams, Mr. George, was m. last Thurs. eve. by Rev. Mr. Bartow to Miss Eliza Bevans, all of this city (*BPAT* 8 July 1818; *FGBA* 8 July 1818).

Williams, George, of Baltimore Co., is an insolvent debtor (*BPAT* 19 Oct 1819).

Williams, Henry, a bright mulatto boy (who may also call himself Henry Bordley), aged about 20 years old, a good waiter, but given to drink, has been enticed away from L. & J. Barney; he had some old clothes, marked with his owner's name (*BPAT* 26 Jan 1818).

Williams, James, aged 77, d. 18th inst., at Annapolis (*BPAT* 24 April 1818). For the will of James Williams, filed in 1818, see AAWB JG#3:218.

Williams, Mr. James W., of Baltimore, was m. last Thurs. eve. by the Rev. Mr. Stephenson, at Stafford, Harford Co., to Miss Hannah C. Stump, of the latter place (*BPAT* 20 Oct 1817; *BA* 20 Oct 1817).

Williams, Mr. Jesse, was m. last Thurs. eve. by Rev. Mr. Valiant, to Miss Elizabeth Green, all of Baltimore (*BPAT* 18 May 1818).

Williams, Mr. John, was m. last Sun. eve. by Rev. Mr. Hagerty, to Miss Mary Evans, all of this city (*BPAT* 11 Sep 1817).

Williams, John, aged 25, light complexion, 5 feet, 6 inches in height, born in France, a blacksmith, deserted from my recruiting rendezvous on 19th inst. Williams may be a fictitious name. /s/ J. H. Hook, Capt., 4th Infantry, Baltimore, 27 Sep. (*BPAT* 3 Oct 1817).

Williams, John, of Cecil Co. was to have an act passed to confirm his title to certain lands in said co. (*BPAT* 10 Feb 1817).

Williams, Capt. John, and Mary Williams, all of Baltimore, were m. Thurs. eve., 23rd inst. by Rev. Mr. Beal (*BPAT* 25 Sep 1819).

Williams, John J., was m. last Sun. by Rev. Hagerty, to Miss Mary Vans, all of Baltimore (*BA* 11 Sep 1817).

Williams, Mr. John Mason, was m. last Thurs. eve. by the Rev. Mr. Hargrove, to Miss Sarah [Furber?], all of this city (*BPAT* 17 June 1817; *BA* 17 June 1817).

Williams, Otho H., youngest son of the late Gen. Otho Holland Williams, d. at Charleston, S. C., on 16th inst., in his 23rd year (*BA* 26 March 1818; *BPAT* 26 March 1818).

Williams, Mr. Richard, was m. last Thurs. eve. by Rev. Mr. Jennings, to Miss Mary Wells, both formerly of Annapolis (*FGBA* 21 Feb 1818; *BPAT* 23 Feb 1818).

Williams, Samuel, and Miss Ann Ford, all of Baltimore, were m. last Tues. by Rev. Healy (*BMC* 16 April 1819; *BPAT* 15 April 1819).

Williams, Capt. Thomas, d. at the Borough of Norfolk on Wed., 16th ult., aged 70, for many years a respectable sea captain of that port and formerly of the Navy, commander of the U. S. Brig *Norfolk* (*BPAT* 7 March 1817).

Williams, William, Jr., Esq. of Somerset, was m. last eve. [Tues.] by Rev. Mr. Glendy to Miss Adeline Pechin, second dau. of Maj. William Pechin of Baltimore (*BPAT* 29 Oct 1817; *FGBA* 29 Oct 1817).

Williams, Mr. William, was m. Thurs. eve, last by Rev. Dr. Davis, to Miss Maria Hooker, both of Baltimore (*BPAT* 19 Jan 1818; *FGBA* 17 Jan 1818).

Williams, Mr. William B., of Georgetown, D. C., was m. [date not given] to Miss Ann Dorsey, dau. of Henry W. Dorsey, of Montgomery Co. (*BPAT* 26 June 1817).

Williams, William C., Esq., of Woodstock, Shenandoah Co., [Va.], d. 4th inst.; for a long time a gentleman of extensive practice at the bar of the Virginia Superior Courts (*BPAT* 25 Oct 1817).

Williamson, Mrs. Sarah, d. 28 April, leaving a husband and four children (*BPAT* 6 May 1819).

Biographical Data from Baltimore Newspapers, 1817-1819

Willis, Francis Asbury, d. Thurs., 22nd. inst., near Frederick Town, of pulmonary consumption, in his 16th year (*FGBA* 24 July1819; *BPAT* 26 July 1819).

Willson, Mrs. Ann, relict of Capt. James Willson, d. yesterday morning, leaving children (*BPAT* 24 July 1818; *BA* 24 July 1818).

Willy, Mrs. Mary, d. last Thurs. eve. in her 70th year (*FGBA* 31 Jan 1818).

Wilson, Mr. Alexander, and Miss Margaret Ann Boyce, all of Baltimore, were m. last Tues. by Rev. Mr. McJilton (*BPAT* 20 Sep 1819).

Wilson, Aquila, was m. [date not given] by Rev. M'Cormick, to Miss Eleanor Talbert, both of the District of Columbia (*BPAT* 2 Feb 1818).

Wilson, Mr. Edward M., was m. last Sun. by the Rev. Mr. Richards, to Miss Sarah Linton, all of this city (*BPAT* 11 June 1817; *BA* 11 June 1817).

Wilson, Henry G., was m. last Tues. by Rev. Ryland, to Miss Mary Kennedy, both of Georgetown (*FGBA* 12 Jan 1818; *BPAT* 10 Jan 1818).

Wilson, Mr. James, was m. last Tues. eve. by Rev. Mr. E. J. Reis to Miss Mary Ann Baillet, all of Baltimore (*BPAT* 6 May 1818).

Wilson, Mr. James R., of New York, formerly a Purser in the Navy, d. in Georgetown, D.C., on the 17th inst., after a long and painful illness (*BPAT* 20 Aug 1819).

Wilson, Mr. John, was m. last evening [Fri.], by Rev. Dr. Jennings, to Miss Hannah M'Intire, all of Baltimore (*BPAT* 2 May 1818; *BA* 4 May 1818).

Wilson, John, a respectable merchant of Baltimore, died the eve. of 31st ult. (*BPAT* 3 June 1819). For the will of John Wilson, filed in 1819, see BAWB 11:20.

Wilson, Mr. Robert, of Baltimore, was m. on Thurs., 15th inst., by Rev. Mr. Johnson, to Miss Tacy Thomas, dau. of Dr. David Thomas, of Upper Oxford, Pa. (*BPAT* 27 Oct 1818; *BA* 27 Oct 1818).

Wilson, Robert, and Miss Margaret Pendegrass, were m last eve. [Tues.] by Rev. Dr. Roberts (*FGBA* 14 July 1819; *BPAT* 15 July 1819).

Wilson, Robert R., aged 23, d. last Fri. of the prevailing fever, which he contracted at Fell's Point (*BPAT* 13 Sep 1819).

Wilson, Samuel, and Miss Mary H. Gatchell, were m. Sun. eve. by Rev. Bartow (*FGBA* 17 Feb 1819; *BPAT* 15 Feb 1819).

Wilson, Mrs. Sarah, native of Ireland, d. last Tues. eve. in her 68th year, at the house of her son (*BPAT* 26 Sep 1817; *BA* 26 Sep 1817).

Wilson, Thomas, was m. last Thurs. eve. by Rev. Glendy, to Miss Mary, eld. dau. of Major James Haslett, both of Baltimore (*BPAT* 27 Feb 1818; *FGBA* 9 Feb 1818).

Wilson, Thomas, Mayor of Richmond, d. at that city last Sun. (*BPAT* 7 May 1818).

Wilson, William, d. last Thurs. at his residence in Harford Co., leaving a wife and children (*FGBA* 4 May 1819; *BPAT* 4 May 1819).

Winchester, David, Jr., was m. last Thurs eve. at Reisterstown, by Rev. Mr. Wyatt to Miss Sarah Forney (*BPAT* 12 Nov 1817; *FGBA* 11 Nov 1817).

Winchester, Richard, late of Md., d. Friday, 18th June, near Louisville, Ky. (*FGBA* 17 July 1819; *BPAT* 13 July 1819).

Winchester, Mr. Samuel, was m. last Thurs. eve. by the Rev. Dr. Inglis, to Miss Frances, eld. dau. of Alexander Mactier, Esq., of this city (*BPAT* 10 Oct 1818; *BA* 10 Oct 1818).

Winckler, George, of Baltimore Co., is an insolvent debtor (*BPAT* 25 Nov 1819).

Winder, Maj. Gen. Levin, of Somerset Co., d. in Baltimore, on 1st inst. He was born on 4 Sep 1757 and fought in the Revolutionary War. He was Governor of the State during the late War with England [long obit] (*FGBA* 5 July 1819; *BPAT* 2 July 1819, 3 July 1819). For the will of Levin Winder, filed in 1819, see BAWB 11:31.

Wininger, Mr. Lewis, was m. last Thurs. eve. by Rev. Mr. Healy, to Miss Eliza Loudenslager, both of this city (*BPAT* 3 Dec 1817; *BA* 4 Dec 1817).

Winn, Elisha, was m. last Sun., 18th inst., by Rev. Richards, to Miss Polly Shaw, all of Baltimore (*BA* 24 Jan 1817).

Winsor, Arnold T., was m. [date not given] to Mrs. Mary Riley, both of Montgomery Co. (*BPAT* 29 Aug 1818).

Biographical Data from Baltimore Newspapers, 1817-1819

Winston, Edmond, late judge of the Circuit Court for this district, died 18th last at an advanced age, at the residence of Dr. George Gable. "Lynchburg Press" (*BPAT* 29 Aug 1818).

Winthrop, George W., aged about 33, d. 22nd inst., at the house of a friend in Va. (*BPAT* 2 Aug 1819).

Winton, Joseph S., and Miss Ann Maria Pierce of Baltimore, were m. [date not given] in New Orleans (*BPAT* 31 Jan 1818).

Wirgman, Peter, Esq., a native of Eng., aged 36, d. yesterday (*FGBA* 16 Aug 1819). Peter Wingman [*sic*], aged 36 years, was buried 15 Aug 1819 from St. Paul's Parish (ReamySP). His elegant brick dwelling on Washington Square, and several articles of household furniture, will be sold at public auction next Saturday (*BPAT* 8 Dec 1819). For the will of Peter Wirgman, filed in 1819, see BAWB 11:43.

Wistar, Dr. Caleb, d. at Philadelphia, late Professor of Anatomy at the University of Pennsylvania, and President of the American Philosophical Society [long obit] (*BPAT* 27 Jan 1818).

Witmer, Daniel, innkeeper, d. at Hagerstown last Sun., in his 60th year (*BPAT* 19 June 1819).

Witmer, Mrs. Mary, consort of Henry Witmer of Philadelphia, d. there last Tues., leaving her husband (*BA* 18 Nov 1817).

Witwell, Capt. Thomas, a native of Boston, a swindler, tried to cheat Elijah R. Sinners out of a sum of money, and borrowed $6.00 from Mrs. Sinners (*BPAT* 15 April 1818).

Woelper, George, is an insolvent debtor of Baltimore Co. (*BPAT* 4 June 1818).

Wood, James, and Miss Mary King, dau. of the late William King, all of Baltimore, were m. last Tues. by Rev. Hemphill (*BA* 21 Feb 1817; *BPAT* 21 Feb 1817).

Wood, James P., and Miss Mary Whittiker, both of Baltimore, were m. Thurs., 28th inst., by Rev. Dashiell (*FGBA* 30 Jan 1819; *BPAT* 30 Jan 1819).

Wood, Thomas, d. Monday, 2nd, inst., leaving a widow and several children; another Revolutionary patriot gone! (*FGBA* 5 Aug 1819; *BPAT* 5 Aug 1819). He is buried in Mt. Olivet Cemetery, Baltimore (MOLL).

Woodburn, Mr. John, was m. last eve. [Thurs. or Sat.] by Rev. Mr. Wyatt to Miss Sarah Thompson, both of Baltimore (*BPAT* 7 Aug 1818; *FGBA* 8 Aug 1818).

Woodhouse, Capt. Samuel, of the U. S. Navy, was m. [date not given] at Philadelphia, to Matilda, dau. of the late Michael Roberts of that city (*BPAT* 27 June 1818).

Woodland, Mr. Ezekiel, and Miss Sarah Ann Cox, all of Baltimore, were m. last Wed. eve,. by Rev. Mr. Rev. Bartow (*BPAT* 27 Nov 1819).

Woods, Gen. John, of Pittsburgh, Pa., Member of Congress from that state, d. at the residence of William Wilkinson of Brunswick Co., Va. (*BPAT* 6 Jan 1817).

Woodward, Mr. Amin [Amon?], was m. [date not given] at Washington to Miss Sarah Martin, both of that city (*BPAT* 29 Dec 1817).

Woodward, Dr. Edward, native of Delaware Co., Pa., and late Surgeon of the U. S. Frigate *Constellation,* d. last Mon. at Norfolk (*BPAT* 30 Jan 1818).

Woody, William, of Baltimore, and formerly of Va., was m. on Thurs., 12th inst., to Miss Ruth B. Atkinson, dau. of Joseph Atkinson of Elk Ridge (*BA* 19 June 1817).

Woodyear, Mr. Thomas, was m. Tues. eve. last, by the Rev. Mr. Henshaw, to Miss Elizabeth Yellott (*BPAT* 8 Sep 1817).

Woolford, Levin, eldest son of Dr. John Woolford, d. 2nd inst., in his 21st year, of a pulmonary complaint, at the residence of his father in Somerset Co. (*BPAT* 17 Nov 1819).

Woolfolk, John G., Esq., d. at his seat in Caroline Co., Va., on Fri., 16th inst., in his 70th year (*BPAT* 20 April 1819).

Worley, Henry, about 18 years old, apprentice to the combmakng trade, ran away from William Disney, 80 Conway St.; he may have made for Washington, Georgetown, or Alexandria (*BPAT* 13 June 1818).

Worman, Andrew, has died. By decree of the Hon. The High Court of Chancery, H. S. Pigman, trustee, is authorized to sell at public auction, a half lot of ground on the southwest corner of Lombard and Hanover Sts. (*BPAT* 22 April 1817). Pigman advertised the sale of and which had formerly been conveyed by William Goodwin and Thomas Russell to Andrew and Jacob Worman (*BPM* 28 Nov 1818).

Worten, Thomas, aged 17 years, apprentice to the ship joiner's business, ran away from William Denny, Wolf St., Fell's Point; a reward of $20.00 was offered (*BPAT* 25 Aug 1818).

Worthington, Mr. Charles, of Montgomery Co., was m. [date not given] to Miss Mary Ann Thomas of Cumberland, MD (*BPAT* 29 Aug 1818).

Worthington, Thomas I., of Anne Arundel Co., and Miss Henrietta Warfield, 2nd dau. of Alexander Warfield, of Sams Creek, Frederick Co., were m. Tues., 9th inst. by Rev. Steven Roszel (*FGBA* 15 Feb 1819; *BPAT* 16 Feb 1819).

Wray, John, who resided at 28 N. Baltimore St., d. yesterday, in his 68th year (*FGBA* 13 March 1819; *BPAT* 13 March 1819).

Wray, John, Jr., d. 5th inst. in his 31st year (*FGBA* 9 April 1819; *BPAT* 10 April 1819).

Wright, Mr. A. T., (a minor) of Kent Co., will have his property sold at auction, including (1) Water Lots 22, 23, 24, 25, and 26 on the Plot of Chestertown; a two story brick house at the corner of Front and Cannon Sts., formerly the residence of Richard Tilghman, Esq.; (2) one-half of Lot # 5, on Front and Cannon; (3) Residue of lot # 5; (4) Part of Lot # 1; (5) Adjoining No. 2, 3, 4; (6) Adjoining Lot # 4. . . . (9) Twenty-five acres of wood and timber land in Quaker Neck, part of *Chigwell* (*BPAT* 17 July 1818).

Wright, Felix, plasterer, d. suddenly on the evening of the 14th inst., leaving a widow and one child in Philadelphia, from which place he came to this city (*BPAT* 16 July 1818).

Wright, George, and Miss Rebecca Leaf, both of Baltimore Co., were m. last Thurs. by Rev. George Grice (*FGBA* 30 Nov 1818).

Wright, Dr. Thomas H., and Miss Mary F. Norwood, dau. of the late Col. Edward Norwood, were m. 19 June [Thurs.] (*FGBA* 20 June 1817; *BA* 21 June 1817).

Wyant, Mr. Peter, who resided on Hanover St., d. 22nd inst., one of the oldest and most respectable inhabitants of Baltimore (*BPAT* 24 Oct 1817; *BA* 23 Oct 1817). For the will of Peter Wyant, filed in 1817, see BAWB 10:373.

Wyatt, Mary, of Caroline Co., was to have an act passed for her benefit (*BPAT* 10 Feb 1817).

Wymbel, Mr. James, and Miss Rachel Maxwell, both of Baltimore, were m. Mon. night by Rev. Dr. Burgess (*BPAT* 29 Sep 1819).

Wyrick, Caspar, a German redemptioner, aged about 26 years, speaks French and German and somewhat broken English, employed in the baking business, ran away on 27 Nov from Peter Snyder, who offers a reward of $20.00 (*BPAT* 4 Dec 1817).

Wyvil, Darcy, late of Dorchester Co., dec.: Levin Keene, exec., was ordered to advertise that he would settle the estate in the Baltimore and Easton newspapers for three successive weeks (*BPAT* 4 Sep 1817).

"Y"

Yates, Mrs. Mary, d. Tues., in her 50th year (*FGBA* 10 April 1818; *BPAT* 10 April 1818). For the will of Mary Yates, filed in 1818, see BAWB 10:458.

Yeates, George, of Baltimore, d. 2nd Feb last at Aux Cayes. He was b. in Kent Co., Md., a son of Col. Donaldson Yeates of the Revolutionary War. In 1804 he came to Baltimore at the request of his friend, James Corrie, who was in declining heath. A long obit is given (*FGBA* 12 March 1819, 17 March 1819; *BPAT* 11 March 1819).

Yeates, Jasper, late a Judge of the Pennsylvania Supreme Court, d. at Lancaster, Pa., on Fri., 13th inst., in his 73rd year ("Philadelphia, March 20" (*FGBA* 21 March 1817; *BPAT* 19 March 1817).

Yeiser, Jesse, aged about 17, apprentice to the cordwaining business, ran away from Samuel Clayton, at 111 Camden St. (*BPAT* 14 June 1819).

Biographical Data from Baltimore Newspapers, 1817-1819

Yellott, George, d. this morning, aged 41 years. His funeral will be from his late residence, at 45 Pratt St. (*FGBA* 7 April 1818; *BPAT* 7 April 1818).

Yeohannes, Mr. Charles H. d. yesterday morning, aged 32 (*BPAT* 25 June 1818).

Yeomans, Charles H., d. this morning, aged 32 (*FGBA* 24 June 1818).

Yerkins, David, d. last Sat. eve., of an apoplectic fit., in his 65th year. He was a native of Pa., and a member of the New Jerusalem Church. He leaves a wife and family (*FGBA* 27 Jan 1818; *BPAT* 27 Jan 1818).

Yokel or Yokeley), Thomas, was m. last Sun. eve. by Rev. D. E. Reese, to Miss Julian Rutter, all of Baltimore (*BPAT* 24 Sep 1817; *BA* 24 Sep 1817).

Young, Benjamin, born in Pa., aged 21 years, by profession a cooper, deserted from the detachment under my command at Fort Covington on 3rd March. He is supposed to have gone to Philadelphia, where he has relations living. /s/ James H. Cook, Capt. (*BPAT* 13 April 1818).

Young, Duncan, and Miss Henrietta Brensinger, both of Baltimore, were m. last Thurs. by Rev. Dr. Jennings (*FGBA* 1 May 1819; *BPAT* 3 May 1819).

Young, Gen. Henry, d. about the 15th ult., at his seat in King and Queen Co., Va., an old Revolutionary officer, in the 76th year of his age (*BPAT* 6 Dec 1817).

Young, Mrs. Mary, relict of John Young, formerly of Philadelphia, d. last Wed., 4th inst., aged 72 years and 8 mos. (*FGBA* 7 June 1817; *BPAT* 5 June 1817).

Young, Mrs. Rebecca, a native of Philadelphia, d. last Sat., in her 80th year (*BPAT* 9 Feb 1819).

"Z"

Zachary, Peter, d. yesterday, in his 59th year, leaving a wife and six small children (*FGBA* 21 April 1818; *BPAT* 22 April 1818). For the will of Peter Zacharie [*sic*], filed in 1819, see BAWB 10:465.

Zimmerman, George, Sr., of Baltimore, d. Fri. eve. aged 86 years and 11 mos., leaving a wife with whom he had lived for 50 years, 7 children, 45 grandchildren, and 12 great-grandchildren, nearly all of whom attended the funeral (*BA* 24 June 1817; *FGBA* 23 June 1817; *BPAT* 24 June 1817).

Zimmerman, Mr. Henry W., and Miss Lydia Culin, were m. last eve. [Thurs.] by Rev. Mr. Shane (*BPAT* 12 June 1818).

Zimmerman, Mr. Jacob, and Miss Amelia, eld. dau. of Major Steiger, all of Baltimore, were m Thurs. eve. last, by Rev. Mr. Richards (*BPAT* 31 Oct 1818; *BA* 31 Oct 1818).

Zollickoffer, Dr. William, was m. last Thurs. eve. by the Rev. Stephen G. Rozzell, to Miss Sarah Edwards, all of Baltimore (*BPAT* 20 Oct 1817; *FBA* 11 Oct 1817).

Biographical Data from Baltimore Newspapers, 1817-1819

People with One Name

It should be noted that not all of the individuals in this list are slaves. There is at least one indentured white servant. Slaves who had two names are listed in the main portion of the text.

Aminta, a house servant, a tall thin woman about 30 years of age, absconded on the 8th inst., carried off her son, who is about nine years old and has an impediment in his speech. John Graham of Washington D. C. offers a reward (*BPAT* 14 June 1817).

Ann, a dark mulatto girl about 14 years old, absconded from Daniel Pendleton on Granby St., near the Green Tree bump [?]; a reward of $5.00 is offered (*BPAT* 16 Jan 1818).

Annette, a French slave, about 40 or 50 years old, does not speak English, ran away from Mr. Lavignac, Bond St., Fells Point (*BPAT* 16 Oct 1817).

Anthony, Negro man about 18 or 20 years of age, "tolerably black," bought from Mr. John Etherington, of Kent Co., Eastern Shore of Maryland, ran away from James Hooper, No 16 Light St., Baltimore (*BPAT* 13 Jan 1817).

Anthony, a Negro man, a good rough carpenter, ran away from Alexius Edelen, near Newport, Charles Co..; he was raised in Charles Co., near Newport, by Mr. Leon Wood who sold him to Edelen about five years ago.; he may have obtained free papers under the name of John Thomas, and may be on his way to Philadelphia, by way of Baltimore (*BPAT* 24 June 1817).

Anthony, a young Negro man, aged about 21. Ran away from Andrew Skinner, living in Talbot Co. He may have gone to Baltimore (*BPAT* 12 Nov 1818).

Auguste, aged 11 years old, apprentice to the segar making business, speaks French and English languages, ran away from P. Seguin (*BPAT* 13 Jan 1817).

Ben, a Black slave, about 21 years of age, ran away from Robert Casey, 10 Hanover St., Baltimore; he may have gone to the Camp Meeting (*BPAT* 31 Aug 1818).

Benjamin, a mulatto man, about 40 years of age on 8th Oct last; he was at Rock Point on Sunday last. He may be lodged in jail, or delivered to John Keys, Dugan's Wharf, and a reward will be paid by Levin Jones, Castle Haven, Dorchester Co. (*BPAT* 20 Nov 1819).

Betty, a Negro woman, aged about 18 years of age, ran away from James T. King, near Lower Marlborough, Calvert Co.; she may have gone to Baltimore or Washington City; she has a father, by name of Richard Harris, living in Old Town, Baltimore (*BPAT* 19 May 1818).

Bill, aged 27 to 30 tears old, had been raised to the water business, not to follow the seas, but the in the Sounds and Country ran away from William and John Howard at Occdock Bar [N. C.], on the night of 8 June 1817 (*BPAT* 23 June 1817).

Bill, a Negro boy, about 14 years of age, ran away from James Jenkins, Southeast; has run away frequently, and has been caught several times on the York Road, about 15 to 20 miles from the city (*BPAT* 25 July 1817).

Bill, a small Negro boy, about ... years old, has gone missing. A liberal reward id offered by Jacob Baer, 26 Pratt St. (*BPAT* 13 May 1818).

Bill, a bright mulatto man, about 26 years old, was committed to the Harford County jail on 6th inst... He says that he formerly belonged to John Hinton, dec. , who sold him to Mr. Cutler, who sold him to Thomas Morgan who sold him to John Amey of Northampton Co., N.C., which is where he now belongs Joshua Guyton asks his owner to come and release him, or he will be sold to pay his jail fees (*BPAT* 17 June 1819).

Biographical Data from Baltimore Newspapers, 1817-1819

Brezine, a mulatto woman, aged 30 or35 years old, pregnant, speaks little English, took with her three children, a mulatto girl, 5 or 6 years old, a black girl, 3 years old, and a black boy, about 18 mos. old, ran away from Mr. Lavignac, Bond St., Fells Point (*BPAT* 16 Oct 1817).

Caesar, about 30 years of age, ran away from John G. Baptist of Mecklenburg Co., on the 25th of last month; has been employed as a wagoner, and is well acquainted with Richmond, Petersburg, and some of the northern towns (*BPAT* 24 July 1818).

Celestine, a French slave, about 28 or 30 years old, speaks pretty good English, took with her a little girl about 6½ years old, ran away from Mr. Lavignac, Bond St., Fells Point (*BPAT* 16 Oct 1817).

Charles, Negro, aged about 16, ran away from Elizabeth Thompson, living at Chestertown (*BPAT* 13 Sep 1817).

Charles, Negro, aged about 35 years, ran away from Samuel Maccubbin on Sun., 13th inst., formerly the property of Mr. Gassaway Rawlings; some years ago was taken up at Frederick Town; he has one wife at William Stewart's Quarter, and another at Levey [Levi] Stansbury's; he may have obtained a pass and may make for Baltimore or Washington; calls himself Charles Emberson (*BPAT* 12 Oct 1818).

Charles, Negro, aged 25 or 26, ran away from Jeremiah or H. Doxy, Cotaco Co., Alabama on 29th Aug last; He may attempt to return to Richmond, as he was purchased last winter from Mr. Wooldridge, near the Coal Mines in the vicinity of Richmond (*BPAT* 16 Nov 1819, 14 Dec 1819).

Charlotte, a stout Negro girl, between 19 and 20 years of age, a slave for life, ran away from her master's house in Franklin St. She was born on Sharp's Island and was purchased about five years ago from estate of Mr. Thomas (*BPAT* 17 April 1818).

Clemm, Negro, aged about 22, ran away from Walter Wilburn, Calvert Co., near Plumb Point; may have a forged pass and may make for the Delaware (*BPAT* 9 Sep 1817).

Commodore, a Negro man about 36 years of age, five-foot-six or seven inches in height, who has a wife and children belonging to Mr. James Sterling near Baltimore, and has been in the habit of visiting them with a pass every holiday for several years, ran away from Jacob Franklin near West River (*BPAT* 21 March 1817).

Daniel, a Negro man, aged 21 years, ran away from John W. Dorsey, living near Ellicott's Mills, Anne Arundel Co. (*BPAT* 14 March 1818).

David, a Negro man, aged bout 24 years, has a free mother living; he ran away from Edward Stevenson, living near the Old Liberty Road, bear Mr. Denning's Tavern (*BPAT* 16 March 1818).

Dolly, a Negro woman, about 31 years old, may have left here in the Queenstown packet as she has a mother and child living with R. C. Tilghman on the Chester River, and a husband living with Mr. Neale, stone cutter; Apply to the editors of *The Patriot* (*BPAT* 6 Jan 1817).

Eliza, a Negro woman, 19 years of age, about five-feet-five or six inches high, ran away from John Bausman of Baltimore Co., near Reisterstown; she was formerly owned by Joseph B. Brooks of Kent Co., Md., and sold by Eli Clagett to Mr. James Jackson, from whom Bausman bought her (*BPAT* 31 Dec 1818).

Esther, a Negro woman, aged 22 or 23, ran away from Parran Taylor, living at Church Hill, Queen Anne's Co.; it is presumed she will make for Baltimore (*BPAT* 27 June 1817).

George, aged about 23 years of age, sailed under the employ of Capt. Gilmore from Susquehanna, attempted to pass himself as a free man, was discharged, and has since been employed in the Fishery on the Susquehanna. Tho. W. Turner, at the head of Pratt St., near Lilly's Tavern, offers a reward (*BPAT* 28 May 1818).

Getty, negro woman, aged about 25 years old; had not been long from the country, ran away from Capt. Wright's in Albemarle St. She has lived with Mr. Jarrett Bull in Light St., Mr. Jacob Pattison, Sharp St., and Capt. Wright, Old Town. /s/ Josiah Hubbell, Light St. Wharf (*BPAT* 23 March 1819).

Biographical Data from Baltimore Newspapers, 1817-1819

Harriot, aged nine years old, ran away from Jas. L. Hawkins; she was purchased from Mrs. Latimer who owns her mother; the child may be somewhere in Baltimore or Annapolis (*BPAT* 1 Jan 1819).

Hercules, a Negro man about 25 years of age, five-foot-seven or eight inches tall, ran away from the schooner *Collector*, lying in the port of Alexandria, last 29 Nov. /s/ Joseph Robinson of Gloster [*sic*] Court House Va. (*BPAT* 7 Jan 1817).

Hercules, a Negro man, 27 years of age, ran away from Luke Robinson and Z. Keene, at No. 98 Dugan's wharf; he was seen on Fell's Point last week (*BPAT* 31 July 1817).

Hester, a dark mulatto woman, aged about 27 years, ran away from Henry Gable, living at the Lower Ferry, Anne Arundel Co. She took with her three children, all boys, the eldest about seven years old, named Benjamin, the next named Bazil, about six years old, and the youngest named Charles, about 14 mos. old (*BPAT* 20 Dec 1819).

Hetty, a dark mulatto girl, about 20 or 22 years of age, ran away from the subscriber last Sat. night, formerly owned by Rev. John Hargrove, and then George Warner, from whom W. M'Jimsey, 115 Howard St., her current owner, purchased her (*BPAT* 29 April 1817).

Isaac, a black man about 23 or 24 years old, purchased from Hugh Fenix, blacksmith, of Kent Island; he was formerly owned by a Mr. Horton; he ran away from William Norris, Jr., whose farm is four miles from Baltimore (*BPAT* 9 May 1817).

Isaac, a Negro boy, 20 years old, ran away from the subscriber, on 30 May last; he may be in Baltimore, "Salisbury, July 9" (*BPAT* 16 July 1817).

Jacob, a Negro man, aged about 21, ran away from E. S. Thomas two miles from town in the York Turnpike. He was lately the property of Mr. Walker, corner of Chesapeake and Calvert Sts., but formerly belonged to Lloyd Nicholls, Esq., of Easton. He has a mother and brother living at Centreville, and other relations living at different places on the Eastern Shore (*BPAT* 23 July 1817).

Jacob, a boy, about five feet high, was enticed or ran away last 29 July. Owen Allen purchased him about six years ago from Mr. Wilmer of the House of Wilmer & Paler, for a house servant (*BPAT* 19 Sep 1818).

James, aged about 22 years old, ran away from Augustus Cabarrus, Jr., at Occdock Bar [N.C.]. (*BPAT* 23 June 1817).

Jeniseh, Master of Languages, has lately arrived from Germany, and will give information [instruction?] in the English, French, Italian and German languages. His aim is to "accomplish all the duties of a faithful and diligent preceptor." He is lodging at Mr. Gotolet's, 22 Fell's St. (*BPAT* 10 Feb 1818).

Jenny, Negro, aged about 19 years old, and apparently pregnant, and her child Paul, ran away from Jeremiah or H. Doxy, Cotaco Co., Alabama on 29th Aug last. She may attempt to return to Richmond, as she and her child, Paul, were purchased last winter from Mr. Macon's estate, Orange Co. (*BPAT* 16 Nov 1819, 14 Dec 1819).

Jerry, a Negro who absconded from the sloop *Saucy Whig*, is about 15 or 16 years old. John and Aaron Levering offer a reward (*BPAT* 21 Aug 1817).

Jesse, a Negro man, formerly the property of Dr. Sullivan of New Market, Dorchester Co., about 38 years old, ran away from Thomas Seales on their way to Sparta in Georgia (*BPAT* 23 Jan 1818).

Jim, Negro, aged 24 or 25 years old, ran away from Jeremiah or H. Doxy, Cotaco Co., Alabama on 29th Aug last. He may attempt to return to Richmond, as he was purchased last winter from William Littles of Richmond Co. (*BPAT* 16 Nov 1819, 14 Dec 1819).

Jim, a Negro who ran away on the 6th of this month from the farm of William Norris, Jr. He is about 10 years old, and was purchased of Mr. Grafton of Baltimore, who purchased him from Mrs. Johns of Harford Co. He has relations living near Belle Air, and also near the Conowingo Bridge (*BPAT* 14 April 1818).

Joe, Negro, about 23 years old, ran away from John Shortt at the Mineral Water Manufactory on South St. His wife is also gone and is supposed to be with him, lurking somewhere about the City (*BPAT* 22 March 1817).

Biographical Data from Baltimore Newspapers, 1817-1819

Joe, a Negro boy, about 16 years old, ran away from Conrad Schultz on Wed., 16th inst. (*BPAT* 28 July 1817).

John, a Negro, aged about 20, ran away from Walter Wilburn, Calvert Co., near Plumb Point; may have a forged pass and may make for the Delaware (*BPAT* 9 Sep 1817).

John, a genteel back fellow, aged about 30 tears old, ran away from Pes [?] Spain at Lynchburg about last 1 Nov. He was raised by Dr. Hardaway of Dinwiddie, and belonged to Benjamin W. W. Leigh, Esq. of Richmond, and has a wife at P. Nicholson's (*BPAT* 26 Aug 1819).

Levi, aged bout 19, ran away from A.&S. Woolfolk, Alexandria, D. C., may be harbored in or near Baltimore; was purchased from a Mr. Pendle, an agent of Kinsey Harrison, Queen Anne's Co., Md., formerly belonged to the estate of Widow Write [Wright?], who was married to the said Kinsey Harrison (*BPAT* 16 Oct 1819).

Levi, Negro, aged about 20 years old, ran away from Jeremiah or H. Doxy, Cotaco Co., Alabama on 29th Aug last. He may attempt to return to Richmond, as he was purchased last winter from Abner Mitchell of New Kent Co., whose mother lives in Richmond (*BPAT* 16 Nov 1819, 14 Dec 1819).

Levia, Negro, aged about 17 years, ran away from Rezin Pool on 24th ult.; took with him a number of clothing (*BPAT* 25 Sep 1817).

Lewis, aged about 23, had been raised to the water business, not to follow the seas, but in the Sounds and Country ran away from William and John Howard at Occdock Bar, [N. C.] on the night of 8 June 1817 (*BPAT* 23 June 1817).

Limus, a Negro man, aged about 25 years of age, sometimes calls himself James, ran away from James Burton on 16th inst., having stolen $179.00; has been seen in Baltimore, dressed very fine, with a watch in his pocket (*BPAT* 27 Aug 1818).

Margery, a Negro girl aged from 14 to 15 years old, has run away from the service of Mr. Richard Cutts. She is well known in Alexandria, having resided for several years in Mr. John Roberts' family. /s/ Richard Bland Lee (*BPAT* 24 June 1817).

Mary, a dark mulatto girl, aged about 12, four-feet-eight or nine inches tall, ran away from Wm. Burk (*BPAT* 13 March 1817).

Nancy, a Negro girl about 21 years old, was raised in Frederick Co. near New Town, ran away from Jas. L. Hawkins (*BPAT* 26 Aug 1818).

Nancy, aged 21, Negro woman, ran away from Jas. L. Hawkins on last 24 Aug, and may have gone to Philadelphia or somewhere in New Jersey (*BPAT* 1 Jan 1819).

Ned, Negro, aged about 20 years old, ran away from Thomas Johnson living about eight miles from Baltimore on the Falls Turnpike Road (*BPAT* 27 May 1819).

Nicholas, a small sized yellow man, fond of his enemy, strong drink, ran away from William Norris, Jr., 66 Baltimore St, (*BPAT* 11 March 1817).

Peter, a black man, aged about 22 years ran away from H. G. S. Key, of Leonardtown, St. Mary's Co., and has been seen in this and Calvert Counties almost ever since. (*BPAT* 28 May 1818).

Phaeton, a Negro about 30 years of age, ran away from Sarah B. Blake of Kent Co.; may be making for the State of Delaware (*BPAT* 9 Sep 1817).

Rachel, a Negro about 16 years old, ran away from H. N. Sands, 60 N. Liberty St., may have gone to Annapolis, where her father, Samuel Bulling [Billing?], is (*BPAT* 13 Nov 1817).

Richard, a Negro, aged about 26 years old, ran away from Thomas Johnson, living eight miles from Baltimore o the Falls Turnpike Road. He had run away in 1814 and was taken up in Pennsylvania at the house of a Mr. Gross, where he learned the distilling business (*BPAT* 27 May 1819).

Rose, a dark mulatto girl, ran away from Capt. Dunkin living on Fell's Point (*BPAT* 7 July 1817).

Ruthy, a bright colored Negro woman, ran away from W. Pechin's farm, about two miles from Baltimore (*BPAT* 15 Sep 1818).

Sam, aged about 28, a cooper, ran away from Charles P. Goodall at Hanover, Va. (*BPAT* 7 July 1817).

Sam, aged about 20, brought up to plantation work, son of Andrew, living on Carroll's Manor, ran away from Thomas Hall Dorsey living near Annapolis, on 29 Aug last (*BPAT* 4 Sep 1817).

Sam, a likely Mulatto boy, aged 17 or 18, lately owned by Dr. Foucher of Richmond, Va., ran away from J. Echols of Richmond, Va. (*BPAT* 10 Sep 1819).

Sanon, a mulatto man, about 35 years old, a caulker by trade, who may assume the name of Samuel Adams, ran away from G. Leoni (*BPAT* 4 Nov 1817).

Shep, aged about 18, ran away from William and John Howard at Occdock Bar [N. C.], on the night of 8 June 1817 (*BPAT* 23 June 1817).

Solomon or **Saul,** a Negro man, about 22 years old, who goes by the name of John Jackson, the property of James Layton of Dorchester Co., Md., ran away shortly after coming into this port from a Patriot brig on a cruise, and is known to harbor in and about Petticoat Alley, Fell's Point. A reward is offered by Robert Armstrong & Co., Dugan's Wharf (*BPAT* 13 June 1818).

Suck, a house servant, woman of about 25 years of age, absconded on the 8th inst.; John Graham of Washington D.C., offers a reward (*BPAT* 14 June 1817).

Suzette, a Swiss by birth, aged 19 years of age, an indented white servant girl, ran away from P. A. Guestier (*BPAT* 16 Aug 1819).

Terry, a Negro woman, aged 22 or 23, belonging to the estate of Wm. Buschonell, dec., ran away from Jonathan Harris, near Chestertown, Kent Co., last 10 March; she may have gone to the state if Delaware to see an acquaintance named Sam Goulden, a free Negro who is a blacksmith (*BPAT* 16 June 1817).

Washington, a Negro man, aged 28 years, ran away from John Hammond, living near the Head of Severn River, Anne Arundel Co.; he has a number of relations and friends in Baltimore (*BPAT* 31 Dec 1819).

Wat, a Negro man about 30 years of age, 5 feet, 9 or 10 inches high, ran away from Francis W. Hawkins, living near Port Tobacco, Md. (*BPAT* 16 April 1818).

William, a black man, 5 feet, 6 or 10 inches high, about 35 or 40 years of age, but looks younger, ran away from Benjamin Brookes, living in Lower Marlborough, Calvert Co.; may be headed for Philadelphia (*BPAT* 31 March 1818).

William, a bright mulatto slave, aged about 24, ran away from David Porter in the District of Columbia; he formerly belonged to Gen. John Mason, where he was brought up as a waiter, and where he has a wife; his mother lives with Mr. McKenney at the back of Georgetown (*BPAT* 28 April 1818).

Biographical Data from Baltimore Newspapers, 1817-1819

Notes on the Maryland Ministers Mentioned in the Text

Sources and Abbreviations:

Barnes, Robert W. *Marriages and Deaths from the Maryland Gazette, 1727-1839.* Baltimore: Genealogical Publishing Co. © 1973.

Erdman, Lorrie A. E. *Abstracts of Marriages and Deaths in the (Baltimore) American and Commercial Daily Advertiser, 1831-1836.* Westminster: Willow Bend Books, 2003. Cited as BACDA in the text.

FTM CD#521: Maryland Settlers and Soldiers. Baltimore: Genealogical Publishing Co.

Kanely, Edna Agatha. *Directory of Ministers and the Maryland Churches They Served.* Westminster: Family Line Publications, 1991, hereafter cited as Kanely.

Who Was Who in America, 1607-1896. Chicago: A. N. Marquis Co., 1963

Abbreviations Used:
BA: Baltimore American.
BACDA: Baltimore American and Commercial Daily Advertiser.
BAWB : Baltimore Co. Will Book
BPAT: Baltimore Patriot and Mercantile Advertiser.
Md. Gaz. Annapolis Maryland Gazette

Allen, Rev. John, A.M., Prot. Epis., served St. George's Parish, Harford Co., 1795-1815, St. John's Kingsville, Baltimore Co., 1800-1805. [1] John Allen, Professor of Mathematics at the University of Maryland, died 16 March 1830 in the 71st year of his age.[2]

There was also a John Allen, Meth. Epis., who served the Baltimore Circuit in 1790, but Kanely lists nothing for him after that until 1843.

Allison, Rev. Dr. [-?-], 1819, D. C. (No other data found).

Amery, Rev. [-?-], (No other data found).

Armstrong, Rev. [-?-], fl. 1818 in Frederick Co. or Prince George's Co.; in Baltimore Co. in 1818. He may be the Rev. James Armstrong, formerly of Baltimore, who d. at his residence at LaPort, LaPort Co., Ind. on 12 Sep 1834.[3]

Asbury, Francis, b. 20 Aug 1745, d. 31 March 1816, served many charges in Md., was Bishop of the Methodist [Episcopal] Church from 1784 until his death.[4]

Atkinson, Rev. Dr. [-?-], fl. 1819, Georgetown (No other data found).

Baker, Rev Dr. [-?-], fl. 1817, Baltimore (No other data found).

---

[1] Edna Agatha Kanely. *Directory of Ministers and the Maryland Churches They Served.* Westminster: Family Line Publications, 1991, hereafter cited as Kanely, 1:1:8.
[2] *BPAT* 17 March 1830.
[3] *BACDA* 10 Oct 1834.
[4] Kanely, 1:1:17.

Biographical Data from Baltimore Newspapers, 1817-1819

Barbad, Rev. Mr. [-?-], fl. 1818, Baltimore (No other data found).

Bare, Rev. [-?-], 1819 (No other data found).

Barnhard, Rev. [-?-], fl. 1817 (No other data found).

Barry, Rev. E.D., D. D., of Baltimore Co., was m. at St. Paul's Church in Huntington, Conn., on 4th inst., to Miss Cornelia Shelton, dau. of Dr. Shelton of Huntington.[5] Mrs. H. Barry, [the first] wife of Rev. E. D. Barry, recently of New York, d. yesterday, leaving a husband and children.[6]

Bartow, John V., d. 1836; served Trinity Prot. Epis. Church, Baltimore, 1807-1836. John V. Bartow d. 14 July 1836 at Perth Amboy, N.J., in the 48th year of his ministry.[7]

Bausman, John P. (or John T.), served Christ Church Parish, Calvert Co.,, 1815-1825, and 1846-1847; Augustine Parish, Cecil Co., 1838, 1842; and Memorial Episcopal Church, Baltimore, 1862-1864.[8]

Beal, Rev. Mr. [-?-], fl. 1819, Baltimore. (No other data found).

Beare, Rev. John, b. 1794, d. 1878; Methodist Episcopal, was at the Baltimore City Station from 1819; later served other charges.[9]

Becker, Rev. Dr. Christian L., Pastor of the First German Reformed Church in Baltimore, 1806-1818. He d. 12 July 1818 in his 63rd year; he resided on Second St.[10]

Bell, Rev. Mr. [-?-], fl. 1819, Cecil Co. or St. Mary's Co. (No other data found).

Birch, Rev. Thomas; See Rev. Thomas Burch, below.

Bird, Rev. Mr. [-?-], fl. 1818, Baltimore Co. (No other data found).

Blayne, Rev. [-?-], fl. 1818-9, Queen Anne's Co. (No other data found).

Bond, Rev. John Wesley, b. 11 Dec 1784, d. 22 Jan 1819. From 1817 to 1818 he served the Harford Circuit: Bush Forest Chapel and Cokesbury. Rev. John Wesley Bond d. last night at the house of his brother, after a painful illness of 15 days, in his 35th year. He had been an itinerant minister of the Gospel in the Methodist Episcopal Church for ten years. He had been the faithful attendant of the late Bishop Asbury for the two years. The funeral will be tomorrow morning from the residence of Dr. Bond in Charles St., and the funeral discourse will be delivered at Light St. Church.[11]

Bonteyn, Rev. [-?-], Baltimore, 1817 (No other data found).

Brady, Rev. John, Prot. Episcopal, from 1816 to 1822 served William and Mary and St. Andrews Parishes in St. Mary's Co. Mrs. Brady, widow of the Rev. John Brady, late Rector of William and Mary and St. Andrew Parishes in St. Mary's Co., d. Tues. eve.,

---

[5] *FGBA* 12 Jan 1819; *BPAT* 12 Jan 1819.
[6] *FGBA* 24 April 1817.
[7] Kanely, 1:1:34; *BACDA* 19 July 1836.
[8] Kanely, 1:1:37.
[9] Kanely, 1:1:39.
[10] Kanely, 1:41; *FGBA* 3 July 1818; *BPAT* 13 July 1818.
[11] Kanely, 1:59; *BPAT* 23 Jan 1819.

Biographical Data from Baltimore Newspapers, 1817-1819

11th March at the residence of Col,. Joseph Harris, near Leonard-Town. She was the fifth of the same family to die within five months[12]

Brice, Rev. George, fl. 1817, Baltimore Co. [May be George Grice: See below].

Brook, Rev. Thomas, M.A., d. 29 June 1818. He resided on South Eutaw near Lombard St.[13]

Brown, Rev. Clarke, Rector of William and Mary Parish, Charles Co., d. 12 Jan 1817.[14]

Bubad, Rev. [-?-], Baltimore, 1817 (No other data found).

Bulkley, Rev. [William] Josephus, d, 1831, aged 44. Protestant Episcopal. He served St. Paul's Parish, in Queen Anne and Talbot Cos., and Chester and Wye Parishes, from 15 March 1817 to 1820.[15]

Burch (Birch), Rev. Thomas, Methodist Episcopal. He served St. Martin's Circuit in 1806 and the Baltimore City station from 1815, and 1819-1820.[16]

Butler, Rev. William; Meth. Epis.; served various charges in Baltimore Co.[17]

Carback, (Canback), Rev. Dr. Richard; Meth.; served the Great Falls Circuit, Ebenezer, Chase, c1817.[18]

Carbury (Carbery), Rev. Joseph, b. 3 May 1784, d. 15 May 1849; R C., was at St. Inigoe's, St. Nicholas, Mattapany, St. Mary's Co., 1816-1849.[19]

Carney, Rev. [-?-], Baltimore Co. 1818 (No other data found).

Childs, Rev. John, d. 1829, Meth. Ep., Montgomery Circuit: Clarksburg, 1789, 1818; Prince George's Circuit, Ross St., Bladensburg, 1815; Baltimore Circuit: Gans, 1817-1818; Great Falls Circuit, 1819-1820, etc.[20]

Chilton, Rev. Dr. [-?-], Baltimore Co., 1818 (No other data found).

Choate, Rev. Edward, Baltimore Co., 1819, Baptist, was at Taneytown after 1822.[21]

Clay, Rev. John Curtis, d. 20 Oct 1862, Prot. Ep., was at Frederick Parish from 1817 to 1821, and at St. John's Parish, Hagerstown from 1818 to 1821.[22]

Coleman, Bishop [-?-], fl. 1819, Prince George's Co. (No other data found).

Cone, Rev. Spencer H.; Baptist; had been an actor, and then an editor. He later took orders, and for many years was pastor of one of the largest Baptist churches in New York City.[23]

---

[12] Kanely, 1:67; Annapolis *Maryland Gazette* 27 March 1823.
[13] *BA* 30 June 1818; *BPAT* 30 June 1818.
[14] Kanely, 1:79; *FGBA* 27 Jan 1817; *BPAT* 28 Jan 1817.
[15] Kanely. 88.
[16] Kanely, 1:90.
[17] Kanely, 1:95.
[18] Kanely, 1:102.
[19] Kanely, 1:102.
[20] Kanely, 1:116.
[21] Kanely, 1:116.
[22] Kanely, 1:121.

Biographical Data from Baltimore Newspapers, 1817-1819

Craney (or Carney), Rev. [-?-], fl. 1818 (No other data found).

Dade, Rev. Townsend; Prot. Epis.; was at Eden, now St. Peter's Parish, Montgomery Co., 1791-1794. He died 2 Feb 1822 at his seat in Montgomery Co. in the 30th tear of his age.[24]

Dashiell, Rev. George; Prot. Epis,; in 1797 was at South Sassafras Parish, Kent Co.; in 1800 was at Chester Parish, Kent Co.; in 1804 was at St. Peter's Church in Baltimore; in 1816 he left the Protestant Episcopal Church and organized the Evangelical Episcopal Church.[25] Mrs. Esther Dashiell, wife of the Rev. George Dashiell, d. near Louisville, Ky., on 3 July 1834 (). Mrs. Rozetta E. Brown, dau. of Rev. George Dashiell, d. 1 Jan at the residence of her parents in Shelbyville, Ky.[26]

David, Rev. [-?-], fl. 1819 (No other data found).

Davis, John, almost certainly the John Davis who was a Methodist Episcopal Minister who served a number of churches in the Baltimore Circuit; specifically the Wilk St, and Dallas St. Churches, 1817-1819.[27]

Diver, Rev. [-?-], 1817, Anne Arundel Co. (No other data found)

Dodson, Rev. Thomas; Meth. Epis.; Dorchester Circuit: Salem and Federalsburg, 1798; Somerset Circuit, 1799; Queen Anne's Circuit, Dudley's Chapel, 1801.[28]

Duhamel, Rev. Charles, Roman Cath., Hagerstown or Elizabethtown, 1804; later at St. Joseph's, Emmittsburg. He was pastor of the R. C. Church at Emmittsburg. He d. 6 Feb 1818 at St. Mary's Seminary near Emmittsburg, Md.[29]

Duke, Rev. William, d. 1840, aged 83. Meth. Epis., until 1779, then Prot. Epis.; was at St. Anne's Parish, Annapolis, 1803-1806.[30]

Duncan, Rev. John Mason; Presb.; Associated Reformed Presbyterian Church, Fayette St. betw. Charles and Liberty, 1812-1851; Tammany St., east of Forrest Lane, Balto., 1822-24.[31]

Duncan, Rev. William, was born c1764 in Kent Co. and d. 1819. He was ordained a Protestant Episcopal Minister by Bishop Clagett in 1808 and was Rector of Durham Parish; from 1808-1813; All Hallows Parish, Anne Arundel Co., 1813-1819; before 1808 he was a Meth. Preacher. He d. 3 March 1819 at his residence on South River in the 56th year of his age.[32]

Edelen, Rev. [-?-], fl. 1818, Calvert Co. Leonard Edelen, b. 20 Oct 1783, d. 21 Dec. 1823, R. C., served St. Francis Xavier, Newtown, St. Mary's Co., 1810-1823.[33]

---

[23] John Thomas Scharf. *The Chronicles of Baltimore*. (1874). Repr.; Bowie: Heritage Books, 1989, hereafter cited as Scharf, 90.
[24] Kanely, 1:157; *BPAT* 12 Feb 1822.
[25] Kanely 160.
[26] *BPAT* 17 July 1834; *BPAT* 22 Jan 1830.
[27] Kanely, 1:163.
[28] Kanely, 1:178.
[29] Kanely, 1:189; *BA* 2 March 1818.
[30] Kanely, 1:189-190.
[31] Kanely, 1:191.
[32] Kanely, 1:191; *Md. Gaz.* 11 March 1819.
[33] Kanely, 1:198.

Biographical Data from Baltimore Newspapers, 1817-1819

Elbert, poss. Dr. Lodman, d. by Feb 1834. Margaret, dau, of the late Rev. Lodman Elbert, m. Capt. Arthur Forman on 11 Feb 1834.[34]

Eli, Rev. Mr. [-?-], fl. 1819, Baltimore (No other data found).

Elliott, Rev. Dr. [-?-], fl. 1817, Baltimore (No other data found)

Endress, Rev. [-?-], Baltimore Co., 1818, may be in Lancaster Co., Pa. (No other data found).

English, Rev. [-?-], fl. 1818, Baltimore Co. (No other data found).

Fairclough, Rev. [-?-], of Baltimore, 1818 (No other data found).

Fechtig, Rev. Louis R.; Meth. Ep.; Cumberland, Allegany Co., 1805: Baltimore City Station, 1815-1816; Annapolis, 1817. He entered the ministry in 1812 and at the time of his death was Presiding Elder in the Baltimore District of the Methodist Episcopal Church. He d. in Washington, after an illness of ten days.[35]

Fennell, Rev. [-?-], Baltimore Co., 1818 (No other data found).

Fenwick, Rev. Enoch: R. C.; 15 May 1780-25 Nov 1827; St. Peter's Pro-Cathedral, 1809-1820; St. Thomas, 1826-27.[36]

Ferrall, Rev. Gideon, fl. 1819, Cecil Co. (No other data found).

Finney, Rev. William; Presb.; d. 31 July 1873, Harford Co.; Churchville Presbyterian Church, 1813 or 1814 to Oct 1854; Deer Creek, Harmony, Glenville, 1837-1854.[37]

Force, M.; Meth.; Baltimore City Station, 1819.[38]

Franklin, John; R. C.; d. Sep 1819; St. Mary's Co.: St. Joseph's. Morganza, and St. Francis Xavier, Newtown, 1817-1819.[39]

Fry(e), or Frey, Rev. Joseph, b. 1786, d. 1845; Meth. Ep.; Baltimore City station, 1811-1812, 1828-1829; Great Falls Circuit: Bosley and Ebenezer, Chase, 1832; served other churches. Cornelia, wife of Rev. Joseph Frye, d. 23 Oct 1832; her funeral was from the residence of Mr. Jesse Comegys, on N. Calvert St.[40]

Gadsden, Rev. Philip, fl. 1817 (No other data found)

Geiger, Rev. Jacob, d. 19 Oct 1848; Germ. Ref.; served Manchester Charge from c1816 to 1841 or later. Rev. Jacob Geiger of Manchester, was m. to Miss Catherine Seltzer of Baltimore, on Tues., 19th inst., by Rev. Dr. Becker.[41]

Gibson, Rev. William Lewis, d. 1848; Prot. Epis.; He was at St. Anne's in Annapolis in 1806; in Alexandria, Va., in 1807; at St. John's in Harford Co. in 1811; at Havre de

---

[34] *BA* 15 Feb 1834.
[35] Kanely, 1:216; *BPAT* 29 Sep 1823.
[36] Kanely, 1:218.
[37] Kanely, 1:222.
[38] Kanely, 1:229.
[39] Kanely, 1:235.
[40] Kanely, 1:238; *BA* 24 and 25 Oct 1832.
[41] Kanely, 1:248; *FGBA* 21 Feb 1818; *BPAT* 21 Feb 1818.

Biographical Data from Baltimore Newspapers, 1817-1819

Grace, Harford Co. in 1812; at St. Peter's Parish in Montgomery Co. in 1813; in Queen Anne's Parish, Prince George's Co. 1814-1819; All Hallow's Parish 1819-1820.[42]

Glendy, Dr. John, Pastor of the 2nd Presbyterian Church of Baltimore from 1805 to 1826, d. at Philadelphia on 4 Oct 1832. On Sunday, September 11, 1814, as the Citizen Soldiers of Baltimore marched to repel the British invaders, Rev. Glendy stood on the steps of his Baltimore St. residence and blessed the soldiers and prayed for their safety and success.[43]

Green, Rev. Nathaniel, Baltimore Co., 1817 (No other data found).

Greenfield, Rev. Nathan; died by June 1831, when his widow Elizabeth, aged 59 years, died on 15 June and was buried at her residence in Long Green, Baltimore Co.[44]

Grice, George, d. 1826; served Sater's Baptist Church at Chestnut Ridge, Baltimore Co., until 1826.[45]

Guest, Job; Meth. Epis.; served many churches in the Baltimore Circuit, Frederick Circuit and Montgomery Circuit. He d. 1857, aged 72. Elizabeth E., only dau. of the Rev. Job Guest of Annapolis, d. Sun., 2nd Oct. 1831 [Long obit is given].[46]

Hagerty, John, d. Thurs. eve., in his 77th year. He was a minister in the Methodist Episcopal Church for nearly half a century.[47]

Harent, Rev. Joseph; R. C.; d. in Martinico last April, in his 63rd year, one of the members of St. Mary's College, Baltimore. He served St. Francis Xavier, Newtown, St. Mary's Co., 1812-1813.[48]

Hargrove, John, was Swedenborgian Pastor of New Jerusalem Church from 1799.[49]

Hawley, Rev. [-?-]; Kanely lists several but none for this time period.

Healey (or Healy), Rev. John, was Pastor of the 2nd Baptist Church in Baltimore from 1797 to 1848. John Healey d. 19 June 1848. Elizabeth, wife of John Healey, died 11 May 1843.[50]

Helfenstein, Rev. Albert, served First German Reformed Church, Baltimore, from 1818-1825. Catherine, dau. of Rev. Helfenstein of Baltimore, d. last Mon. at Carlisle, Pa., in the 13th year of her age.[51]

Hemphill, Andrew, was a Methodist Minister, ordained in 1803. He served various Methodist charges in Md., from 1819 and was at Baltimore City Station in 1816. He d. 22 Aug 1837.[52]

---

[42] Kanely, 1:252.
[43] *BA* 8 Oct 1832 long obit William Marine. *The British Invasion of Maryland,* 147.
[44] *BA* 25 June 1831.
[45] Kanely, 1:271.
[46] Kanely, 1:276; Annapolis *Maryland Gazette* 6 Oct 1831.
[47] Kanely, 1:281; *BPAT* 6 Sep 1823.
[48] Kanely, 1:293; *BA* 15 June 1818; *BPAT* 15 June 1818
[49] Kanely, 1:294, lists him as John Hargrave,
[50] Kanely, 1:308; Baltimore *Sun* 13 May 1843, 20 June 1848
[51] Kanely, 1:311; *BPAT* 19 March 1830.
[52] Kanely, 1:312.

Biographical Data from Baltimore Newspapers, 1817-1819

Henry, Rev. John, prob. Rev. Joannes Henry, (Cath.), was at St. Francis Xavier, Bohemia Manor, in 1818.[53]

Henshaw, Rev. John Prentice Kewley. d. 1852, Prot. Episcopal, St. Peter's, Sharp St., and German Lane, Baltimore. His dau. Sarah died 23 Jan 1832, aged 7 mos. and 4 days.[54]

Hershberger, Rev. [-?-], Baltimore Co., 1818 (No other data found).

Hitselberger, Rev. [-?-], Baltimore, 1818 (No other data found).

Hoskins, Rev. Nathaniel, MO, 1819 (No other data found).

Hunter, Rev. Dr. [-?-], fl. 1819 (No other data found).

Inglis, Dr. James, D.D., was Pastor of the First Presbyterian Church, Baltimore, from 1802 to 1819. Rev. James Inglis died 15 Aug 1819. Mary S. Inglis, second dau. of the late Rev. Dr. Inglis, d. Mon., 20th inst., in her 21st year. George S., son of the late Dr. James Inglis, m. Kezia Martin, dau. of Rev. Dr. Martin of York Co., Pa., on 16 Oct 1834.[55]

Jackson, Rev. Joseph, d. 1820, Prot. Epis. In 1818 and 1819 he was at St. Thomas, Garrison Forest in Baltimore County.[56]

Jenkins, Rev. [-?-], Baltimore Co., 1818 (No other data found).

Jennings, Dr. Samuel K. (No other data found).

Johnson, Rev. Matthew, d. 1825, Prot. Epis., was at St. John's, Kingsville and St. James, My Lady's Manor, from 1615 to 1818 or 1819.[57]

Keith, Rev. Mr. [-?-], 1818, Baltimore American (No other data found).

Keller, Rev. Isaac; was m. to Miss Margaret Schnebley, at Hagerstown.[58]

Kemp, Bishop James, d. 28 Oct 1827, aged 62. He was a Protestant Episcopal Rector of St. Paul's Parish, Baltimore, from 1812; in 1814 he was Suffragan Bishop of Md., and in 1816 was Bishop.[59]

Kieffer, Rev. Daniel H., was m. to Miss Elizabeth Storm, all of Baltimore, last Thurs. eve. by Rev. Dr. C. L. Becker.[60]

Kohlman, Rev. [-?-], Prince George's Co. (No other data found).

Kurtz, Rev. Johann Daniel; Luth.; was Pastor of Zion Lutheran Church, Baltimore, from 1785 to 1833.[61]

---

[53] Kanely, 1:314.
[54] Kanely, 1:315; *BA* 27 Jan 1832.
[55] *FGBA* 16 Aug 1819; *BPAT* 25 Jan 1834; *BA* 25 Jan 1834, 18 Oct 1834.
[56] Kanely, 1:1:349.
[57] Kanely, 1:1:360.
[58] Baltimore *Maryland Chronicle* 17 May 1819
[59] Kanely, 1:378
[60] *FGBA* 13 April 1818; *BPAT* 11 April 1818
[61] Kanely, 1:400.

Biographical Data from Baltimore Newspapers, 1817-1819

Lauston, Rev. in Frederick Co. c1818 (No other data found).

Lemmon, Rev. George; Prot. Epis.; 1813-1816, Christ Ch., Queen Caroline Parish Howard Co., and Zion, Prince George's Co., and Montgomery Co.; by 1822 was in St. John's Parish, Hagerstown.[62]

Linthicum, Rev. [poss. William B. F.; Meth.; who was at the Severn Circuit in 1834: fl. 1819 at Anne Arundel Co.[63]

Lucas, Rev. Thomas, Meth. Epis.; served many churches. He d. 11 Jan. 1819, in Baltimore Co., in his 87th year; for many years he was an itinerant preacher of the M. E. Church.[64]

Luck, Rev. Mr. [-?-], fl. 1817, Baltimore; may be Rev. Thomas Lucas, see above.

Lyon, Rev. Mr. [-?-], was last Sun. by the Rev. Mr. Parks, to Mrs. Ann Linch, both of this city.[65]

Magraw, Rev. James, (Presbyterian), served West Nottingham Cecil Co., 1804-1821, Charlestown and Port Deposit, from 1822; he d. as a result of a fall from his dearborn [a type of carriage] on 1 Oct 1835.[66]

Mann, Rev. Charles; Prot. Epis.; was at William and Mary Parish, Charles Co., from1817 to 1831.[67]

Marechal, Archbishop Ambrose, from Bohemia, R. C. Archbishop of Baltimore, 1817-1828.[68]

Markland, Rev. [-?-], fl. 1818 at Baltimore. (No other data found).

Martin, Rev. [-?-], fl. Frederick Co., 1818. (No other data found).

Martindale, Rev. Mr. Stephen; Meth. Epis.; from 1818 to 1819 was at Queen Anne';s Circuit: Dudley's Chapel, Sudlersville.[69]

Matthews, Rev. Edward: Meth. Epis.; served various charges in Baltimore and elsewhere. Rev. Edward Matthews of the Methodist Episcopal Church, d. 26 Nov 1833, aged 71 years.[70]

McCollister, Rev., fl 1819, Baltimore (No other data found).

McJilton, Rev. [-?-], fl. 1819, Baltimore Co. (No other data found).

Megraw, Rev. James, fl. 1817, poss. Cecil Co. (No other data found).

---

[62] Kanely, 2:16.
[63] Kanely, 2:23.
[64] Kanely, 2:32; *FGBA* 12 Jan 1819; *BPAT* 13 Jan 1819.
[65] *BPAT* 17 June 1817.
[66] *Baltimore American* 20, 27 Oct 1835; Kanely, 2:41.
[67] Kanely, 2:44.
[68] Kanely, 2:46
[69] Kanely, 2:51.
[70] Kanely, 2:54; *BA* 28 Nov 1833 long obit.

Biographical Data from Baltimore Newspapers, 1817-1819

Merts/Mertz, Rev. John Nicholas; R. C.; was born 26 April 1764 and died 10 Aug 1844, served in Baltimore for 15 years and at Conewago for 3 years.[71]

Montgomery, Rev. J.; Meth.; served in the Baltimore City Station in 1817. However there was also a Rev. Robert Montgomery of the First Congregation Reformed Presbyterian Church, who d. 20 March 1836.[72]

Moore, Rev. Mark, fl. Baltimore, 1817. Mary B. Moore, dau. of the Rev. Mr. Moore, all of this city, was m. last eve. by Rev. Dr. Roberts, to Thomas Lynch.[73]

Moranvillie, Rev. John Francis; R.C.; served St. Peter's Church, 1794 or 1795-; St. Patrick, at Bank and Market Sts. 1804-1824. He d. at Amiens, France, last 17 May [1824], late Rector of St. Patrick's Church, Fells Point, in the 53rd year of his age.[74]

More, Rev. [-?-], fl. Baltimore, 1817 (No other data found).

Morse, Rev. |-?-|, fl. 1818, Baltimore Co. (No other data found).

Neal, Rev. Abner; Meth.; Baltimore, Dec 1817-1818; d. 1824.[75]

Neale, Most Rev, Leonard, Archbishop of Baltimore, died Wed., 18th inst., in the 71st year of his age, after a short and painful illness of only 36 hours. He succeeded Dr. John Carroll in the Archepiscopal See.[76]

Nind, Rev. William; Prot. Epis.; Rector of St. Stephen's Parish, d. last Fri. morning at his residence in Cecil Co., leaving a wife and six children.[77]

Norris, Rev. Oliver; Prot. Epis.; served Queen Carolina Parish. Christ Church in Anne Arundel [now Howard] Co., and Zion Parish in Prince George's and Montgomery Cos.1809-1812; d. 1825, aged 39.[78]

Orrell, Rev. |-?-|, fl. Anne Arundel Co. 1819. (No other data found)

Orem, Rev. |-?-|, fl. 1819, Talbot Co. (No other data found)

Parks, Rev. Maybury; Meth. Epis.; Rev. Maybury Parks d. 28 Oct 1834, aged 58 years, minister of the M. P. Church. His funeral was to be from his late residence, Exeter St.[79]

Paxton, William; Presb.; b. 1 April 1760, d. 16 April 1845. He served Lower Marsh Creek from 1792 to about 1831.[80]

Peyton, Rev. Yelverton; Meth.; b. 1797, d. 183' served the Frederick Circuit in 1818. He d. last Sat. evening, in his 34th year. His funeral will be from his late dwelling in Exeter St. and a funeral will be preached at the Old Town Church on Tues. morning.[81]

---

[71] Kanely, 2:83.
[72] Kanely, 2:97; *BA* 19 March 1836.
[73] *BPAT* 28 March 1817.
[74] Kanely, 2:102; *BPAT* 15 July 1824.
[75] Kanely, 2:118.
[76] *BPAT* 20 June 1817; see also *FGBA* 20 June 1817.
[77] *BPAT* 19 Sep 1822.
[78] Kanely, 2:128.
[79] *BA* 29 Oct 1834, obit in *BA* 1 Dec 1834.
[80] Kanely 2:149.
[81] Kanely, 2:155-156; *BPAT* 17 Jan 1831.

Pfeiffer, Daniel; United Brethren; served Hagerstown Circuit, Bethel, Chewsville, and St. Paul's, 1819; served Mt. Hebron, and Salem, Keedysville, 1819-1820.[82]

Pfeiffer, Rev. Henry H.; Prot, Epis.; served Grace Ch., Baltimore, 1819-1826. Mr. Henry H. Pfeiffer and Miss Dorothy S. Bausman were m. last eve. [Thurs.] by the Rev. John P. Bausman. His wife Dorothy died 27 Jan 1828 after a short illness. Her friends are requested to attend her funeral this afternoon at 3:00, from the corner of Lee and Sharp Sts.[83]

Phinney, Rev. Mr. [-?-], fl. Dec 1819: See **Finney, Rev. William.**

Poteet, Rev. Thomas, fl. 1819, Baltimore Co. (No other data found)

Reed, Rev. James; Meth. Epis.; he served the Great Falls Circuit: Bosley, Ebenezer/Chase, Algire and Brown's Mtg. House, 1818-1819.[84]

Reed, Rev. Nelson, b. 27 Nov 1751, d 20 Oct 1840; Meth. Epis.; he served various Methodist stations.[85]

Reese, Rev. D. E.; Meth. Prot.; Kanely does not describe where he was from 1817 to 1819. Caroline Barnes Reese, dau. of the Rev. D. E. Reese, m. Robert Nicholas Loyd of Talbot Co. on 23 July 1836. Rebecca Rhodes Reese, dau. of the Rev. D. E. Reese, m. William E. Clemm on 24 Feb 1835.[86]

Reily, Rev. J. H., 1819. Washington Co. (No other data found).

Reis, E. J. [Edmond J. or Edward J.]; Bapt.; served First Baptist Church, Baltimore, Front and Wapping Sts., 1815-1821.[87]

Reynolds, Rev. Caleb, b. 1785, d. 7 Oct 1827; Meth. Epis.; served the Frederick Circuit, 1817, 1825-1826.[88]

Richards, Rev. Lewis; Bapt.; fl Baltimore, 1817-1819. The venerable Lewis Richards, for many years pastor of the First Baptist Church in this city, died 1 Feb 1832, aged 80.[89]

Richardson, Rev. Benjamin; Meth. Prot.; was at Union Chapel in Joppa, 1821.[90]

Ridgely, Rev. Greenbury, fl Baltimore, 1819 (No other data found).

Robbins, Rev. [-?-], Kanely lists several.

Roberts, George M.; Meth Epis.; served the Baltimore City Station from 1807 to 1828.[91]

Roberts, George C. M., Meth. Epis., served the First Methodist Ch., Baltimore, from 1847 to 1846.[92]

---

[82] Kanely 2:156.
[83] Kanely, 2:156; *BPAT* 5 Nov 1816, 28 Jan 1823.
[84] Kanely, 2:183.
[85] Kanely, 2:183.
[86] *BA* 26 Feb 1835, 35 July 1836.
[87] Kanely, 2:189.
[88] Kanely, 2:191.
[89] *BA* 3 Feb 1832.
[90] Kanely, 2:195.
[91] Kanely 2:203
[92] Kanely 2:203.

Biographical Data from Baltimore Newspapers, 1817-1819

Rooker, Rev. James, late of Baltimore, and Miss Smart of Germantown, were m. there last Thurs. by Rev. Charles Dupuy. Rev. James Rooker, late Pastor of the Presbyterian Church in Germantown, Pa., d. there suddenly, in the 74th year of his age. Mr. James C. Rooker, son of Rev. James Rooker, late of Baltimore, d. at New Orleans on 4 Sep, after an illness of four days.[93]

Roszel (Rossell, Rozzel), Rev. Stephen George, b. 8 April 1770, d, 14 May 1841, Meth, Epis., served the Baltimore City Station from 1816 to 1817, and the Frederick Circuit in 1818. Sarah A. A. Roszel, dau. of the Rev. Stephen G. Roszel, m. Solomon Corner of Wheeling W.Va., on 31 March 1836.[94]

Schaeffer, Rev. Baltimore, 1817; Kanely lists several.

Sewell, Rev. Baltimore, 1817 (No other data found).

Shane, Rev. Joseph, Meth. Epis., served First Methodist, in Baltimore from 1806 to 1854 and the Baltimore City Station from 1806 to 1829. Samuel Shane M.D., son of Rev. Joseph Shane, d. in Vicksburg, Miss., on 5 Nov 1836, aged 32 years (*BA* 29 Nov 1836). He married on 10 Nov 1831, Rachel H. Roberts, dau. of the late Rev. George Roberts (*BA* 11 Nov 1831). Rachel H. Shane, wife of the late Samuel Shane, d. in Vicksburg, Miss., on 6 Nov 1836.[95]

Sharpley, Rev. John, Meth. Epis., served various Eastern Shore churches between 1808 and 1815; served the Cecil Circuit; Zion and Elkton, 1816 to 1817.[96]

Shaw, Rev. Neill (or Neale) Hammond, Prot. Epis., d. 1832, He served King and Queen Parish, St. Mary's Co., from 1813 to 1821.[97]

Sickles, Rev. Jacob, fl. 1817 poss. DE (No other data found).

Sigler, Rev. [-?-], fl. 1817 (No other data found).

Sinclair, Rev. Dr. [-?-], fl. Baltimore Co., 1818. Rev. Dr. Sinclair, a native of Ireland has died. He left his native country during her noble but ill-fated struggles for independence.[98]

Slemons, Rev. John Brown, d. 1832, Presb; served Manokin and Princess Anne in, Somerset Co. from 1799 to 1821; also Salisbury in Wicomico Co. from 1797 to 1821.[99]

Smith, Rev. James, an eminent itinerant Minister of the Gospel of the Methodist Episcopal Church, d. 9 April 1826. A funeral discourse will be delivered by Bishop Soule at the Light St. Church. Ministers of the Gospel are invited to meet at the house of Mr. Thomas Whittington in Hill St. He was in his 42nd year and had been stationed a minister in this city [Annapolis] in the past year. Rev. James Smith of Annapolis and Mrs. Mary Childs of Anne Arundel Co. were m. last Monday evening by Rev Battee.[100]

---

[93] *FGBA* 25 Jan 1819; BPAT 25 Jan 1819, 5 Oct 1819, 12 Dec 1828.
[94] Kanely, 2:212; *BA* 12 April 1836.
[95] Kanely, 2:241; *BA* 11 Nov 1836, 29 Nov 1836.
[96] Kanely, 2:242.
[97] Kanely, 2:243
[98] *BPAT* 13 Nov 1830.
[99] Kanely, 2:255.
[100] BPAT 10 April 1826, Md. *Gaz.*16 March 1826, 13 April 1826.

Biographical Data from Baltimore Newspapers, 1817-1819

Snethen, Rev. Nicholas, Meth. Epis., served various churches in Baltimore and Frederick Counties.[101]

Snyder, Rev. John M. (Schneider, Johann), b. 1767, d. 2 June 1845, United Brethren; served Otterbein Church, Baltimore, from 1817 to 1825.[102]

Sparks, Rev. Montgomery Co. 1819; Kanely lists several.

Stansbury, Rev. Daniel, a minister of the Methodist Episcopal Church, d. last Sun. morning in the 52nd year of his age, and on the same day, his dau. Mariah, aged 10 years. He leaves a wife and four children.[103]

Stephenson/Stevenson, Rev. Sater, d. last Tues., at his farm in Baltimore Co., last Tues., 2nd inst., aged 77 years and one month. He was a preacher in the Methodist Society and started preaching before the Revolutionary War.[104]

Stevens (or Stephens), Rev. Daniel, d. 1851, Prot. Epis., served Havre de Grace Parish, Harford Co. from 1815 to 1819 or 1820.[105]

Stigers, Rev. [-?-], fl. Anne Arundel Co., 1817 (No other data found).

Styres, Rev. [-?-], fl. Anne Arundel Co., 1817. (No other data found).

Thomas, Rev. James; Meth. Epis.; served various parishes on the Eastern Shore of Md. from 1791 through 1828. His dau. Ann d. at Centreville, [date not given].[106]

Tidings (Tydings), Rev. Richard; Meth. Epis.; was on the Baltimore Circuit from 1818 to 1819.[107]

Toy, Rev. Joseph, b. 1747, d. 28 Jan 1826; Meth. Epis.; was on the Baltimore Circuit from 1813, the Harford Circuit in 1816 and 1817, and in 1819 served the Prince George's Circuit.[108]

Valiant, Rev. [-?-]; Kanely lists several.

Viers, Rev. Healy, prob. Montgomery Co. (No other data found).

Walch, Rev. [-?-], fl. 1819 at Anne Arundel Co. or Prince George's Co. (No other data found).

Walls, Rev. John, fl. Baltimore Co., c1818. (No other data found).
  Mr. William Walls, son of the Rev. John Walls of Baltimore Co., was m. last Tues. eve. by the Rev. James Smith to Miss Eliza Munn, dau. of the Rev. Benj. Munn, late of N.J. (*BPAT* 19 March 1818; *BA* 19 March 1818).

Watkins, Rev. [-?-], Anne Arundel Co., fl. 1819. (No other data found).

---

[101] Kanely, 2:266.
[102] Kanely, 2:232.
[103] *BPAT* 3 Nov 1828.
[104] *BPAT* 5 Dec 1817; *FGBA* 5 Dec 1817; *BA* 5 Dec 1817.
[105] Kanely, 2:280.
[106] Kanely, 2:306; *BPAT* 18 Sep 1818.
[107] Kanely, 2:323
[108] Kanely, 2:317.

Biographical Data from Baltimore Newspapers, 1817-1819

Waugh, Rev. Beverly; Meth. Epis.; served various Meth. Epis. Churches in Baltimore.[109]

Weems, Rev. John, late Rector of Port Tobacco Parish, Md., where he had been the officiating minister of the Protestant Episcopal Church for more than thirty years, d. 2 Nov 1821 in his 57th year.[110]

Welsh, Rev. Robert, a respectable and useful local preacher of the Methodist Episcopal Church, died Sunday, 2nd inst. at his residence in Anne Arundel Co., aged 50 years. Mrs. Sarah Welch, relict of the late Rev. Robert Welch, d. last Fri. on Magothy River, in her 54th year.[111]

Wells, Rev. George, a Minister of the Associated Methodist Church, and long a resident of Annapolis, died last Sun. morning (*BPAT* 15 Dec 1830). He was a native of England and had been a resident of Annapolis for many years; he d. Sat eve., 11th inst., in his 55th year.[112]

Wells, Rev. Joshua, b, 1764, d. 25 Jan 1862: Meth Epis.; served various churches in Baltimore and Harford Cos[113]

Welsh, Rev. John, fl. 1817 . Mrs. Elizabeth Hallock Welsh d. yesterday morning, of pulmonary consumption, she was the consort of Rev. John Welsh, aged 22 years and 1 day.[114]

Westerman, Rev. William, d, 1859; Prot. Epis.; before 1818 he was a Methodist preacher; from 1819 to 1821 he served the Episcopal parish of St. Mark's. Petersville, Frederick Co.[115]

Wheaton, Rev. Nathaniel S.; Prot. Epis.; he served at Christ Church, Queen Caroline Parish, Anne Arundel Co. (now Howard Co.), from 1817 to 1819; also Zion Parish, in Prince George's Co. and Montgomery Co. from1817 to 1818, and St. Bartholomew's Parish, Montgomery Co., 1818-1819.[116]

Whitefield, Rev. James, Archbishop of Baltimore, d. yesterday. His funeral service will be solemnized tomorrow morning at the Cathedral.[117]

Williams, Rev. Samuel, fl. 1817. Rebecca, wife of the Rev. Samuel Williams, d. last eve., in the 57th year of her age. Rev Samuel Williams m. Mrs. Maria Wehner on 9 Aug 1832.[118]

Williamson, Rev. [-?-], fl. Baltimore, Sep 1819 (No other data found).

Wilson, Rev. James, fl. 1818, Anne Arundel Co.? (No other data found).

Wyant, Rev. [-?-], Baltimore, 1819 (Could he be Rev. Wyatt; see below).

---

[109] Kanely, 2:347.
[110] *BPAT* 15 Nov 1821.
[111] *BPAT* 10 July 1826; *Md. Gaz.* 6 July 1826, 23 April 1829.
[112] *Md. Gaz.* 16 Dec 1830.
[113] Kanely, 2:353.
[114] *BPAT* 10 Feb 1817.
[115] Kanely, 2:355.
[116] Kanely, 2:357.
[117] *BPAT* 20 Oct 1834.
[118] *BPAT* 23 Aug 1831, *BA* 10 Aug 1832.

Biographical Data from Baltimore Newspapers, 1817-1819

Wyatt, Rev. [-?-], Baltimore Co., 1817. Charles Handfield Wyatt, son of the Rev. Dr. Wyatt, aged 5 years, d. 13 Jan 1834 of scarlet fever. Mr. Mary Wyatt, aged 84 years and 6 mos., d. at the residence of her son, Rev. Dr. Wyatt on 6 July 1833.[119]

---

[119] *BA* 8 July 1833, 14 Jan 1834.

Biographical Data from Baltimore Newspapers, 1817-1819

CEMETERIES

This list of cemeteries is based on a "Report of Interments from the 1st Day of January 1818 to the 1st Day of January, 1819, taken from the records of the Board of Healh," published in the *Baltimore Patriot* of 8 January 1819. The locations of cemeteries of Baltimore City in 1806 are shown on an adaptation of Warner and Hanna's Plan of the City [and] environs of Baltimore, 1801.[120]

Alms House (See Potter's Field, below).

Baptist: In October 1818 The Standing Committee of the Church advertised that persons who have friends or relatives interred in the burying ground of the Baptist Church, corner of Front and Pitt Sts., Old Town, are respectfully informed that arrangements have been made to sell the said property, and it is necessary to remove the remains of the persons interred therein. The Standing Committee is authorized to remove persons who are interred here to the new burying ground near Ridgely's Cove after the 15th of November next.[121]

First: The Baptist Meeting House owned a one-half acre lot, suitable for a house of worship and a burying ground, was located on Fayette and Front Sts., and remained until 1828 when the present Shot Tower was built.[122]

Second: The cemetery was located on Broadway; now site of Johns Hopkins Hospital.[123]

Dunkards

In 1787 John Eager Howard sold land to Abraham Sitler, trustee for the Society of German Baptists, commonly called Dunkards. In 1801 this cemetery was bounded by Cyder Alley, Paca St., Lombard St., and half a square east of Paca. It is now the site of the University of Maryland.[124]

Episcopalians

Christ Church: The cemetery was established in 1795 and was located east of Broadway, about where Johns Hopkins Hospital now stands. The last interment was in 1851.[125]

St. Paul's: The original cemetery was located adjacent to the church, but by 1806 had moved to a new location south of Baltimore St.

---

[120] *Memoirs of the Dead and the Tomb's Remembrancer.* (Baltimore: 1806). Transcribed by Martha Reamy and Marlene Bates. © 1989 by the Transcribers. Westminster: Family Line Publications, 1989.

[121] *Baltimore Patriot* 23 October 1818.

[122] *Memoirs*, 264.

[123] Joseph B. Legg. "The Burying Grounds of Baltimore." Unpublished typescript, n.d.; Maryland Historical Society.

[124] *Memoirs*, 266.

[125] *Memoir*, 261-262; See also Edna A. Kanely. "Old Christ Burial Ground," *Notebook* [of the Baltimore Co. Genealogical Society] 3 (3) 3. Mary P. Brunell. "Old Christ Church Burial Ground, Baltimore, Maryland," *Maryland Genealogical Society Bulletin* 29 (1) 12-15.

St. Peter's: The Warner and Hanna Map shows the cemetery located south of Baltimore St., between Hanover and Sharpe Sts., and their records date from 1803.[126]

Trinity: The cemetery was at Belair Road and Chase St.[127]

Friends: In October 1793 the Society of people called Quakers gave notice they intended to present a petition to the General Assembly of Maryland to confirm their title to several small lots of ground, whereon is their present meeting house, and burying ground.[128]

East of Jones' Falls: In 1781 the Patapsco Meeting was moved to Aisquith and Front Sts.[129]

West of Jones' Falls: No other data found.

German

Lutheran: The graveyard of the German Lutheran Church was at Gay and Holliday Sts.[130]

Reformed: There were German Reformed Cemeteries at Scott and St. Peter's Sts., and at Aisquith and Jefferson Sts.[131]

Evangelical Reformed: The German Evangelical Cemetery was at Scott and Wicomico Sts.[132]

Jews:
There was a Jewish Cemetery at Fayette, Fairmount, and Orleans Sts.[133] (L.).

Methodist: In March 1818 the male members of the Methodist Episcopal Church of thru\e City and Precincts of Baltimore , in order to prevent a nuisance, have determined to fill up their old Burying Ground on Lombard and Paca Sts.. The filling up will commence on the 15th of April next. The Trustees and Stewards state that ground free of expense will be furnished for the remains of the dead who may be removed in either of the other grave yards belonging to the Church.[134]

African: The Sharp Street United Methodist Church Cemetery (col.), was located at Chase, Md.

Bethel: No other data found.

Eutaw: No other data found.

Fell's Point: This cemetery was located at Wilks St. (Eastern Ave).[135]

Light Street: Interment records of the Light Street Meth. Epis. Church, 1823-1833, are at the Maryland Historical Society.

Old Town: No other data found.

New Jerusalem Temple
The cemetery was at Broadway and Old Joppa Road.[136]

---

[126] *Memoirs,* 262.
[127] William N. Wilkins. "Early Baltimore City Burial Grounds and Their Interment Records, 1834-1840.: Typescript, MHS. See Ella Rowe and F. Garner Ranney, "Baptisms and Burials, 1802-1817," *Maryland Genealogical Society Bulletin* 30 (3) 273-294; See also Henry C. Peden, *A Collection of Maryland Church Records.* Westminster: Family Line Publications.

[128] *Baltimore Daily Intelligencer* 13 Nov 1793
[129] *Memoirs,* 265-266.
[130] *Memoirs,* 266.
[131] Wilkins.
[132] Wilkins,
[133] Legg.
[134] *Baltimore Patriot* 20 March 1818.
[135] Wilkins.
[136] Wilkins.

Biographical Data from Baltimore Newspapers, 1817-1819

Potter's Field
  East: In September 1797 the Board of Health ordered that all applications for interment in the Potter's Field on the north side of Hampstead Hill should apply to Edward Agnew, the present grave digger, who is authorized to charge for digging the graves of grown persons, $1.00, and for children, 75¢. If he attends in his carriage to remove the corpse to the grave, he may charge $1.00 more. Grown persons should be buried at a depth of five feet, and children at least four feet. The East Potter's Field was at Chase and Rose Sts., but there was an old Potters Field at Broadway and Orleans Sts.[137]
  West: This may be the cemetery shown on the 1822 Poppleton Map as being Cross, Ridgely, and Stockham (S. Paca) Sts., and is in that area of South Baltimore known as Spring Gardens. Wilkins places the West Potters Field at Cross and Barre Sts.[138]

Presbyterians
  English Presbyterian: is shown on the 1801 Warner and Hannah Map as being located between North St. (now Guilford Ave), East St. (now Fayette), Calvert St,. and north almost to Saratoga.[139]
  First: By the 1780s there was a feeling that graveyards should not be in any town, so two graveyards were acquired: one on the east side for 'strangers,' (*i.e.,* those who did not hold a pew in the church), and one on the west side for pew-holders. This latter was known as the Western Burial Ground. Located at Baltimore, Fayette, and Greene Sts. , it became the site of Westminster Presbyterian Church, which opened in 1852.[140]
  Second: The Second Presbyterian Cemetery, later known as Faith Presbyterian Cemetery, was at Belair Road and Chase St.[141]
  Associate Reformed: The Reformed Presbyterian Cemetery was at Light and Randall Sts.[142]

Roman Catholic: In March 1800 The Mayor and City Council authorized the repair of that part of Charles St. which lies on the east side of the Roman Catholic burial ground, which is rendered impassable by the washing of a gully which extends into the same.[143]
  St. John's: No other data found.
  St. Patrick's: William Fell donated land in 1783 for the purpose of a burial ground. The land was used by the Cathedral Congregation until early in the 19th century when St. Patrick's took it over. The cemetery was located between Star Alley (Chapel St.), South St. (now Lombard), Wolfe St., and Dulany (now Baltimore) St.[144] Wolfe St., was established in 1783 (Memoirs). Legg gives some inscriptions and much history. When the cemetery on Wolfe Street was purchased for a new church, many of the dead were removed to the Holy Cross Cemetery, on Harford Road (Scharf, p. 542); inscriptions in FCA, MHS.
  The records of the cemetery on Philadelphia Road are in Filing Case A at the Maryland Historical Society . The earliest stone was dated 1797, and many bodies were transferred here in 1852. In 1936 when Orleans St. was extended, many graves were removed to Holy Cross Cemetery (*Sunday Sun Magazine*, 28 Nov 1948, p. 2). New Cathedral Cemetery has a section labeled St. Patrick's. See "St. Patrick's Cemetery, Philadelphia Road, Baltimore," *Notebook* (of the Baltimore Co. Genealogical Society) 10 (1) 1-3, 17-20, 31-34, 43-47, 11:5-6; See also Mrs. Frank

---

[137] *Federal Gazette and Baltimore Advertiser* 6 September 1797; Wilkins.
[138] *Memoirs,* 267; Wilkins.
[139] *Memoirs,* 265.
[140] *Memoirs,* 264-265.
[141] Wilkins.
[142] Wilkins.
[143] *Federal Gazette and Baltimore Advertiser* 13 March 1800.
[144] *Memoirs,* 263.

Biographical Data from Baltimore Newspapers, 1817-1819

A. Suter, et al. "[Partial List of Inscriptions of Inscriptions] St. Patrick's Cemetery, Philadelphia Road, Baltimore, Md." typescript. General Mordecai Gist Chapter, D.A.R., Nov 1934; see also "St. Patrick's Cemetery, Philadelphia Road." MGRC 9:123-133.

St. Peter's: No other data found.

Society of Friends

The meeting house at Aisquith and Fayette Sts. Dates from 1781. In 1906 the bodies were moved to the burying ground at 3605 Harford Road.[145] In October 1793 the Society of people called Quakers in Baltimore Town, announced they would present a petition to the next General Assembly to confirm their title to several small lots of ground whereon is their present meeting house and burying ground.[146]

---

[145] *Memoirs*, 265-266
[146] *Baltimore Daily Intelligencer* 13 Nov 1793.

Index

People with one name

Allen 50
Aminta 129
Andrew 133
Ann 129
Annette 129
Anthony 129
Auguste 129
Bazil 131
Ben 129
Benjamin 129, 131
Betty 129
Bill 129
Brezine 130
Caesar 130
Celestine 130
Charles 93, 130, 131
Charlotte 130
Clemm 130
Commodore 130
Daniel 130
David 130
Dolly 130
Eliza 130
Esther 130
George 130
Getty 130
Harriot 131
Hercules 131
Hester 131
Hetty 131
Isaac 131
Jacob 131
James 131, 132
Jeniseh 131
Jenny 131
Jerry 131
Jesse 131
Jim 131
Joe 131, 132
John 132
Levi 132
Levia 132
Lewis 132
Limus 132
Margery 132
Mary 132
Nancy 132
Ned 132
Nicholas 132
Paul 131
Peter 132
Phaeton 132
Rachel 132
Richard 132
Rose 132
Ruthy 132
Sam 132, 132
Sanon 133
Saul 133
Shep 133
Solomon 133
Suck 133
Suzette 133
Terry 133
Washington 133
Wat 133
William, 133

Companies

A. & S. Woolfolk 132
Baynard and Dickenson 7
Brune and Danneman 29
Cedar Coopering Business 8
Chas. Crook and Co. 2
Cole, S. and J. Cole 39
Cook & Taylor 17
Disney & Miller 79
Harrison & Sterett 60, 93
Hazlehurst & Dorsey 26
Higgins, Moore, and Co. 81
James George & Co. 43
Jno Sykes & Son 81
Josiah Turner and Co. 115
L. & J. Barney 123
Labes and Thomsen 112
Lough and McKee 71
Marks, Nones, and Co. 85
Messrs. Ryan, Hampson and Co. 51
Patterson&Brother 35
Pease and Butler 17
Peter Gough & Co. 72
S. & J. C. 42
S. & J. Cole 94, 115
Sanderson and Ward 25
Simkins and Usher 102
Van Wyck & Morgan 48, 60, 77
William Baer & Co. 4
William Wilson & Sons 35
Wilmer & Paler 131
Wm. Cochran and Comegys 24

Individuals

Abbott, Ann 1
  Frances [-?-] 107
  John 1
Abell, Samuel 1
Abercrombie, Elizabeth 50
  Rev. James 1, 4, 50, 78
Ackey, John 1
Ackland, James 28
Acworth, Capt. William 1
Adair, Mary Ann 86
Adam, Elizabeth 1
  Jacob 1
Adams, Phebe 90
  Samuel 133
  Susannah 1
  William 1
Addington, Rt. Hon. John Hilby 1
Addison, Rev. Mr. 66
Adkison, John 1
Aikenbrode, Fredericka 80
Aikens, William 1
Aisquith, Edward 1
  Rev. Grandison 1
  Robert C. 1
Aitken, Robert 1
Alberger, Samuel 1
Albers, Samuel 1
Alexander, James 1
  John 1
  William 1
All, Theresa 44
Allan Mary K. 75
Allbright, Hetty 2
  John 2
Allen, Rev. Mr. [-?-] 121
  Adam T. 2
  Rev. Benj. 8
  Elizabeth 114
  Capt. Ethan A. 2
  James 2
  Capt. James 2
  John 2, 64
  Rev. John 66, 110

Index

Mary Susan 2
Michael 2
Owen 87, 131
Tabitha 2
William W.
Allender [-?-] 48
Allender, William 2
Allendere, Mary Ann 112
Allenson, [-?-] 2
Alley, Micajah 2
Allison, Rev. Dr. 54
William 2
Allmond, Jacob 2
Alvis, Peter M. 2
Amery, Rev. [-?-], 72
Amey, John 129
Amos, Elizabeth 94
James 2
John 70
Amoss, Joshua 2
Anderson, Rev. 52
Catherine 2
Elizabeth 88
Elizabeth Parker 2
Ellen 2
Col. Enoch 88
George 2
James M. 14
John 2
Major John 2
Mary 106
Matthew 2
Michael 2
Robert 2, 3
Sybella 2
William 3
William J. 2
Andeslouis, Adrian 3
Andreas, Rev. 35
Angelucci, N. J. M. 3
Angier, Rev. Mr. 67
Anloes, George 3, 59
Annan, Rev. Robert 3
Anthony, Lieut.
Charles 3
Appleton, William G. 3
Appold, Frederick 3
Arc, Caroline Sophia Maria Juliana Wortley Montague Joan of 114
Arcambal, Felix 3
Archer, Stevenson 60
Ardery, Anne Isabell 31

Argilanders, John 3
Armistead, Elizabeth S. 71
Col. George 3
Robert 3
Armitage, Abigail Lyon 62
Benjamin, 3
Armor, David 3
Armstrong, Rev. [-?-] 54, 117
Amelia 53
Daniel 3
Elizabeth C. 58
Henry 3
Mary Ann 4
Robert 133
Silas 3
Thomas 46
Arnest, Ann [-?-] 3
Dr. John 3
Arnold, Francis 3
Arthur, Damaris [-?-] 3
Asbury, Bishop 11
Ash, Catherine 111
John 121
Ashe, Bernard D. 3
Ashley, David 4
Jane 4
Jane [-?-] 4
Ashmore. Susannah 8
Askew, Alexander 4
Ann Marie 122
Robert 4
Asquith, Eli 4
Atkinson, Rev. Dr. 82
Anselow 4
Isaac C. 4
Joseph 125
Mary 122
Ruth B. 125
Sarah 17
Thomas 4
Attlesperger, John 4
Augustine, Henry 4
Samuel 4
Aull, Ann Jane 21
John W. 4
Ault, Ann Jane 22
Austin, Nancy 70
Thomas 70
Ayres, Capt. James 4
Thomas 4

Babade, Rev. 68
Babe, Elizabeth 4

Babe[?], Luke 4
Bacon, James 4
Dr. James 4
Dr. John 4
Baconais, Mr. Louis 4
Badab, Rev. [-?-] 4
Henry 4
Baden, Lieut. N. 4, 25
Baer, Jacob 129
Baggett, Ignatius 4
Julia 4
Bahler, John 30
Baile, Eliza 15
Bailey, Ann C. 7
Elisha T. 43
Eliza 15
Baillet, Mary Ann 124
Baily, Charity 45
Baker, Rev. Dr. [-?-] 9, 66
Abigail 26
Ann 9
Anna 106
Ellen 99
John R. 99
Mary 105, 119
William 106
Balderston, Jonathan 5
Baldwin, Abraham, 5
Charles 5
Hannah [-?-] 5
Capt. Pierson 5
William 5
Ball, Elisha 5
Elizabeth 9
Evelina 66
Capt. William 66
Ballard, William 5
Balling, William 5
Baltzell, Charles 5
Bandel, William 70
Bangs, Thomas 5
Banks, Rev. C. D. 24, 28
John 5
Bankson, John C. 5
Banning, Henry 5
Bannon, Hugh 5
Bantz, Catherine [-?-] 5
Jacob 5
Baptist, John G. 130
Barbad, Rev. 101
Barber, James 6
Col. Thomas 6
Bare, Rev. 34, 62, 88
Barnard, John 6

Index

Priscilla 6
Sarah 6
William 6
Barnes, Basil 70
Mary 70
Whitley 12
Wm. P. 122
Barney, Major [-?-] 20
Charles 6
Chase 6
Joshua 51
Commodore Joshua 6
Louis 116
Matilda 8
William B. 6
Barnhard, Rev. 28
Barnman, Henry 6
Barrett, George H. 6
Hedith 115
Lieut. John M. 6
Mary 49
Barrickman, Hannah 106
Barroll, James E. 2
William 59
Barron, Ann 6
Rev. Dr. E. D. 6
Elizabeth [-?-] 6
Hepzibah. [-?-] 6
Jane 72
Capt. John Jones 6
Commodore Samuel 6
Col. Standish 72
Thomas J. 6
Wm. H. 6
Bartholomew, Susan 37
Bartleson, William 6
Bartlett, Jonathan 6
Rebecca 86
William 6
Barton, Elizabeth Ann 58
John 6
Bartow, Rev. John 1, 2, 3, 4, 7, 9, 13, 17, 19, 21, 28, 29, 30, 34, 35, 37, 38, 39, 41, 42, 43, 46, 49, 50, 51, 53, 54, 59, 60, 62, 63, 68, 70, 72, 73, 74, 75, 76, 85, 96, 106, 107, 111, 116, 119, 123, 124, 125

Basford, David 7
Batchelder, Smith 7
Bateman, William L. 7
Bates, James 90
Batnett, Hannah 62
Bauer, David 7
Bauhgn, Dorothea [-?-] 7
Bausman, Dorothy S. 89
John 112, 130
Rev. John P. 42, 81, 89
Baxley, Elisha T. 7
John 7
Margaret [-?-] 100
Sally Phillips 7
Bayard, James 7, 80
Mingo 7, 80
Bayley, E. T. 101
Elisha T. 7
Henry E. 7
Sarah Ann 7
Bayly, Elisha 7
Girdin C. 7
Baynard, [-?-] 20
John 7
Bayne, John F. 7
Bays, William 7
Beacham, Eliza 7
William 7
Beacon, Ann [-?-] 44
Beadle, John 90
Beal, Rev. Mr. 123
Beall, Elizabeth Caroline 7
Margaret [-?-] 7
Mary 26
Zadock W. 7
Beam, Ann 112
Conrad 7
Maj. George 7, 8, 112
Sarah [-?-] 8
Susannah H. \8
William 7
Beans, Major Wm. B. 8
Beard, Alex. 57
Harriet Hargrove 56
Mary Ann 100
Beare, Rev. 20
Beatty, Lewis A. 8
Samuel 8
Beausey, Charles 8
Beauvais, Mary Coralie 117

Beauzamy, Rose 34
Beck, Paul 8, 67
Samuel 8
Sarah 8
Susan 67
William C. 8
Becker, Rev. Dr. Christian L. 8, 23, 43, 65, 100
Beckett, John 8
Beckham, Armistead 8
Bedford, Julia 18
Beedle, Thomas 8
Beemis, Nathan S. 8
Beeston, Ann 111
Zebulon 111
Bell, Rev. [-?-] 23, 53, 98
Elisha 8
Hugh 8
John 8
Julia Ann 45
Peter 8
Susan D. 51
Thomas, 8
William D. 8
Belt, Mary 22
Osborn 97
Bemont, Silas 8
Bender, Henry 9
Benjamin, Emily 9
Benner, Elizabeth 4
Bennet, John M. 8
Bennett, Anthony B. 9
Edmund T. 9
Pamela 15
Benning, William 9
Benson, Anna 84
Benson, Eleanor [-?-] 76
Levin 9
Bentley, Israel 9
Benton, Richard 9
Berbage, John 10
Berery, Ophelia 83
Berge, Joseph 9
Berkley, Robert 9
Bernard, Capt. Louis 9
Bernheiser, Sarah 1
Berridge, William 9
Berry, Benjamin, 9
Catherine 10
John 9
Bersch, Henry 9
Bestpitch, Joseph 9
Betts, Catherine [-?-] 9
Enoch 9

155

Index

Betune, Joseph 9
Betz, George W. 9
Bevans, Ann Briscoe 14
   Eliza 123
   Thomas 14
Biays, James 9
Bicknell, Thomas W.
   T. 9
Biddison, Jeremiah 9
Biddle, Susanna 60
Bidgood, Wm. Rodman 10
Biggs, Benjamin 10
Billing, Samuel 132
Billington, William 10
Bilus, Robert 4
Bines, Rachel 87
Binns, John A. 10
Birch, Rev. Mr. [-?-] 65
Birch, Rev.: See also Burch, Rev.
Birckhead, Nehemiah 24, 105
Bird, Rev. Mr. [-?-] 109
   Ann 8
   Charles 10
   Capt. Jacob 10
Bishop, Sophia 100
   Rev. Trueman 71
Black, [-?-] 40
   James 47
   Vachel 10
Blackburn, [-?-] [-?-] 10
Blackburn, Professor [-?-] 10
Blackiston, Doretha M. 10
   Ebenezer 10
   Harriot 10
   Jabez 10
   James 10
   John 10
   Mary 10
   Michael 10
Blades, Ann 49
Blair, William 10
Blake, Hannah Arianna 13
   Dr. James H. 10
   Sarah B. 132
Blaney, Mary 11
Blatchford, Harriot P. 10

Rev. Samuel 10
   Thomas 10
Blayne, Rev. [-?-] 85
Blick, William H. 10
Bliss, Capt. Calvin 10
Blondie, Mary 47
Bloomfield, Antony 10
   Charles 10
   John 10
   Michael 10
Blount, Thomas H. 15
Blow, John 10
   Joshua 10
Blue, Harry 10
Blufford, Mary 56
Blunt, Catherine 81
   John S. 11
Boblitz, Michael 11
Boddily, John 11
Bodenverber, John 11
Boetefuerr, Eliza W. 87
Bogen, Dr. John A. 11
Boggs, Alexander L. 11
Bohn, Charles 11, 27
   Elizabeth [-?-] 11
   Margaret 27
Boisseau, Joseph 11
Bollman, Thomas 11
Bolte, John 39
Bolton, Capt. Henry 11
Bond, Buckler 67
   Jacob H. 11
   James 11
   Rev. John Wesley 11
   Josiah 11
   Lambert 11
   Mary Ann 25
   Oliver 11, 60
   Peter 70
   Rachel 45
   Thomas 11
Bonfanti, Joseph 11
Bonfield, James 11
   Thomas 35
Bonner, Elisha 46
   Hugh, 75
Bonsall, John M. 11
Boone, Mr. Robert 11
Booth, [-?-] 64
   Joseph 12
Bordley, Henry 123
Bose, William 12
Bosley, Ann 12
   William 107

Boss, Hezekiah, 12
Bouldin, Charles D. 12
Bounds, John 12
Bourke, Bridget [-?-] 12
   John 12
   William Y. 12
Bourry, Lewis 12
Boury, Lewis, 12
Bowen, Josias 12
   Mary W. 112
   Sarah M. 97
Bowers, Abraham 89
   Daniel 12
   Mary 98
Bowie, Mary M. 62
   Gov. Robert 12
Bowler, Elizabeth 112
   Rebecca 81
Bowly, Daniel 12
   Wm. L. 108
Bowman, Elizabeth 17
   Capt. Samuel 12
Bowyer, Margaretta 84
Boyce, Eliza 79
   Margaret Ann 124
Boyd, A. 40
Boyd, George 42
   John 12, 26
   Patrick 12
   Susan 115
   Tylinda Delia 26
Boyle, Eliza J.
   Hugh 50
   Lilly 118
   Margaretta 41
   Patrick 12
   Thomas 12
   Capt. Thomas 41
Bradburn, Samuel 12
Braderhouse, William 12
Bradford, John 12
   William 12
Bradley, Jenny 21
   Capt. Peregrine 13
Brady, Rev. [-?-] 62, 90
   Felix 13
   Francis 13
Bragdon, John 13
Brand, David 13
Brandt, David W. 13
   Mahalia [-?-] 13
Brannan, Pritchard 13
Branslan, Patrick 13
Brant, J. 13

Index

Brashears, Richard B. 13
Brass, Joseph 13
Brensinger Henrietta 127
  Mary [-?-] 79
Brent, Eliza [-?-] 13
  George 46
  Robert 13
Brereton, Thomas 13
Breuning, [-?-], 11
Brevitt, Benjamin S. 13
Brewer, [-?-] 332
  Chancy 32
  Lewis 13
  Mary Jane 95
  Nicholas 13, 95
Brewster, Edward 13
Brian, William 13
Brice, Rev. George 57, 110
  John 64
  Mary Clare 64
Bridges, Elias 13
  Harriet 13
  James 13
  Sarah 13
Bridon, Virginie 47
Bridport, George 13
Briggs, Rebecca 89
Briguin, James 13
Briscoe, Ann 14
  Barbara Mackall 105
  Edward Briscoe 105
  George 14
  Margaret 14
  Maria 14
  Moses 14
  Samuel 14
Britten, Edward 14
Britton, Ann M. 88
  Sophia 100
Bromwell, Henry B. 14
Brook, Elizabeth [-?-] 14
  Samuel 14
  Rev. Thomas 14
Brooke, Lieut. Edmund 14
  Richard 14
  Robert 14
Brookes, Benjamin 133
Brooks, Major Alexander B. 14

Joseph B. 130
  R. 14
  William 14
Broom, Lieut. C. R. 14
  Mary [-?-] 23
  T. R. 14
Brotherton, Mary 14
  Sarah 14
  Susannah 53
Broughan, John 14
Broughton, Henry 14
Brow-[?], Elizabeth
  Clayton 22
Brown, Amos 14
  Benjamin 14
  Caroline S. [-?-] 14
  Catherine Hoffman [-?-] 14
  Charles 14
  Rev. Clarke 15
  Elias 15
  Eliza 60, 74
  Elizabeth 15, 66, 103, 111
  Ellen 96
  Elvira 41
  Dr. G. R. 15
  George 15
  J. 74
  Jedediah 15
  John 15
  John D. 15
  John M. 15
  John R. 29
  Louisa W. 29
  Margaret 83
  Margaret [-?-] 15
  Mary 15, 52. 119
  Morgan 15
  Dr. Morgan 14
  Major Moses 15
  Nathan 94
  Nicodemus 15
  Peter 15
  Rachel 94
  Sam'l 109
  Capt. Samuel 15
  Sarah [-?-] 112
  Stewart 15
  Susanna 15
  William 15
Browne, Caroline S. [-?-] 15
  Dr. Morgan 15
Browning, Louisa C. 61
  Mary 16

Peregrine G. 16
Bruff, Maria 96
Brundige, Jane M. [-?-] 16
  William 16
Brunelot, Capt. Francis 16
  Francois Bernardin 16
Brunlot, Francois 16
Brunner, Elias 16
  John C. 37
  Mary Ann 37
Bryan, Santy 16
  Thomas 16
Bryne, Thomas 96, 107
Bryson, Nathan Greg. 16
Bubad, Rev. [-?-] 48
Buchanan, Ann O. 107
  Catherine [-?-] 42
  George 16
  James 16
  Jane 16
  Meliora O., 28
  Thomas 12, 28, 107
  William 16
Buck, Benjamin 55
  Elizabeth G. 54
Bucker, Capt. Samuel 16
Buckingham, Samuel 16
Buckley, Henry 16
Buckmaster, Benjamin 16
Buell, William S. 16
Buffin, John 16
Buffum, Jane [-?-] 16
Bulkeley, Rev. Josephus 117
Bullen, Eliza 25
Bulling, Samuel 132
Bunker, Rachel [-?-] 16
Bunn, Miles 4
Bunson, Tacy [-?-] 102
Burbine, Margaret 98
Burch, Rev. Thomas 25, 37, 54, 101, 120
Burcket, Thomas 16
Burgess, Rev. Dr. [-?-] 126
  Bazil 16
  Elizabeth 54

Index

Elizabeth [-?-] 37
George 16
Burgoyne, Margaret 103
Burk, John 16
Richard 16
Wm. 132
Burke, James 16
John 16
Joshua 17
Patrick 17
Burling, Thomas 17
Burn, Henry 17
Burnes, James 17
Burneston, Mary [-?-] 17
William J. 17
Burnett, Asa 17
Burns, Catherine [-?-] 85
Francis 17
Robert 17
William 17
Burroughs, George 17
Burton, James 132
Mary Ann 46
Buschonell, Wm. 133
Busey, Samuel F. 17
Bush James 17
Bushey, George 22
Busk, John 17
Butler, Rev. [-?-]24
John 17
Capt. John R. 17
William 17
Buttman, David 17
Button, Ann 50
Byer, Henry 17
Byrd, Francis Otway 17
Byrne, Catherine 17
Lawrence 17
Byrnes, Eliza 26
George 26
Margaret 111
Mary Ann 21
Teressa [-?-] 17
Byus, Harriot P. 33
Capt. William 33
Bywater, Elizabeth 19

Cabarrus, Augustus 131
Cabell, Col. Samuel Jordan 17
Cadle, Ambrose 18
Cady, Lavinia 56, 57

Caffert, Thomas 18
Cain, A. 18
John 18
Caldwell, James H. 18
John 18
Jonathan 18
Joseph, 18
Calhoun, James 18
John 18
Lydia 18
William 18
Callender, Thomas 18
Cameron, Hugh 18
Campbell, Archibald 18
Daniel W. 18
Elizabeth [-?-] 18
George 18
Jane 119
Levin H. 18
Margaret 51
Mary 17
William, 18
Camper, Anne Maria 77
Moses 18
Canback, Rev. Dr. 58
Cannon, Mrs. [-?-] 30
Sarah 73
William 19
Canoles, Charles 19
William 19
Cantler, David 19
Capt David 19
Louisa [-?-] 19
Cantwell, Caherine 37
Caphart, Catherine 8
Carbury, Rev. 67
Card, Mary 35
Care, Elizabeth 71
William R. 19
Carlton, Sophia 30
Carman, [-?-] 46
Carmichael, Mary 12
Carnan, Robert N. 102
Carney, Rev. [-?-] 28
Jane 16
Carnighan, Catharine [-?-] 19
James 19
Carns, Capt. John 19
Carpenter, Emanuel 19
Richard 19
Carr, [-?-] 21
Rev. Mr. [-?-] 67
George 19
James 19

John 19
Joseph 19
Carrell, John 19
Mary [-?-] 19
Carrere, John 13, 89
Mary 89
Carrerre, John 24
Carrington, Paul 19
Carroll, Charles 19
Daniel, 19
I. 43
Dr. John 84
Margaret [-?-] 19
Cars, Capt. Thomas 19
Carson, Ann 119
George 19
John 20
Carter, Eliza Hill 109
Nancy 53
Robert 20, 80
Sophia 20
Thomas Burton 20
William Champe 109
Cartwright, Alice 119
Carvalho, Rev. Emanuel Nunes 20
Carver, Elizabeth [-?-] 20
Cary, Joseph 63
Casey, Elizabeth 50
Dr. John A. 20
Robert 50, 129
Cassat, Elizabeth 20
Cassell, Joseph 20
Cassin, Commodore 53
Mary Ann 53
Casson, Henry 20
Cathcart, Rev. Dr. 37, 68
George Latimer 20
James Leander 20
Caton, [-?-] 35
Cavanagh, Bernard 20
Cavanaugh, Peter 20
Cave, Mary Ann 25
Cavenaugh, Bernard 20
Peter 20
Chalmers, John 20
Mary Ann 57
Chamberlin, Philip 20
Chambers, Ann 8
Dyne 21
Ezekiel F. 2, 42
Thomas 21

Index

William 93
Chance, Eugenia M. 35
Chandler, Benjamin 15
Capt. Samuel V. 21
Channing, Rev. William E. 56
Chapman, Amey 118
Chappell, John G. 21
Charlton, Elizabeth 85
Chase, William 21
Chatard, Dr. [-?-] 16
  Maj. Henry 21
Chatterton, Julia Ann 24
Chauncey, Mary 120
Chavis, George 21
Chelly, William 21
Cheney, Mary Ann 41
Chenoweth, John 21
Chesley, Z. C. 21
Cheston, Daniel 21
  Maria 21
Chew, Richard 21
Chibester, Dr. Thomas 21
Chidester, Dr. Thomas 21
Child, William 21
Childs, Rev. [-?-] 21
  Ann Eliza 38
  Benjamin 21
  Samuel 21
Chilton, Rev. Dr. 14
Chinn, John Y. 21
Choate, Mr. 94
Chotard, Maj. Henry 21
Chrisfield, Peregrine 21
Christy, Rt. 43
Churchill, Lucy 95
Clackner, Adam 21
  Catherine 13
Clagett, Ann Louisa [-?-] 21
  Darius 21
  Eli 130
Claggett, William D. 21
Claghorn, John 21
Claiborn, Frances H. 46
Clark, Agnes 21
  Elizabeth 21
  James Cooke 21
  John 21, 22

Joseph 22
Joshua 22
Mary Jane 54
Nelson 22
Patrick Hale 22
Sarah [-?-] 44
Clarke, [-?-] 22
  Daniel 22
  Elizabeth 22
  James Cook 22
  L. 22
  Capt. Matthew 22
  Nicholas 22
Classen, [-?-] [-?-] 22
Claxton, Lt. Comm. Alexander 22
Clay, Rev. 28
Clayton, Joseph 22
  Richard 22
  Samuel 22, 126
Cleghorn, John 22
Clemm, Eliza 114
  William 22
Clendenin, Dr. [-?-] 11
  William H. C. 22
Clendinen, Alexander 22
  Elizabeth [-?-] 22
Clerklee, Ann Russell 25
  James 22, 25
  Margaret Russell 22
Clift, Ann [-?-] 22
Clifton, Arthur 23
Clinch, Col. D. L. 23
Cline, William 23
Cloherty, Mary 113
Clopper, Jane W. 61
Clougherty, Mary 113
Clous, Elizabeth 37
Clouse, Hannah 83
Coal, Skipwith H. 23
Coale, Ann [-?-] 23
  Daniel 23
  John 23
  Dr. Samuel Stringer 23
  William 23
Coates, John 23, 56
  Maria H. 56
Coats, Frederick 23
Cobbett, Wm. 49
Coblentz, Dr. Jacob 23
Cochran, Eliza 41
  Elizabeth Maillard 90
  Grace 43, 90

John G. 23
Capt, Neil 43
Capt. Nichol 90
William 23
Cochrane, James 23
Cocke, Dr. Charles 77
Cockey, John C. 23
  Thomas 23
Cocks, Richard John 23
Capt. John 23
Cockshot, Arthur R. 23
Coe, Maria C. 101
  Wm. M. 79
Coffee, Charles 23
Coffey, Joseph 23
Coffin, Mary [-?-] 35
Cohen, Benjamin I. 23
Coit, Capt. P. L. 23
Coker, Polly 23
Colbert, Levin 24
  Milton Francis 24
Cole, Laura 114
  Lavinia 114
  Patience 26
  Samuel 25, 87
  Capt. Thomas 24
  Vachel 24
Coleman, [-?-] . 24
  Ann Maria 98
  Bishop 24
  Huldah 30
  John 24, 105
  Robert 24
  Sarah 105
  Thomas 24
Coler, Elizabeth [-?-] 87
Colestock, Henry 24
Coliden, Catherine [-?-] 17
Collins, Ann 87
  Benj. 107
  E. Frances 4
  James W. 4
  Sarah M. 110
  Zacheus 87
Colman, Edward 24
Colquohon, Charles W. 24
Colvin, John 24
Colwell, Elijah 24
Comegys, Ann Worrell 24
  Anna W. 96
  Bartus 24

Index

John G. 24
Wm. 65
Comerly, Daniel 24
Compton, Elias 24
  John 24
Conaway, Charles 24
  John 24
  Solomon 24
Condley, Rebecca 116
Cone, Rev. [-?-] 25
  Joseph 25
Conkling, Capt. William H. 25
Conley, John 25
  Rebecca 116
Conn, William D. 25
Connell, [-?-] 25
  Edward 25
  John 25
  Margaret 35
Connelly, William 25
Connor, James 25
  Mary [-?-] 25
Conrad, John 117
Conradt, G. M. 25
Conrey, Capt. Nn 25
Contee, Ann Russell [-?-] 25
  Philip A. L. 25
Conway, Harriet V. 85
Cooch, Zebulon H. 25
Cook, Anthony L. 25
  Eleanor Rebecca 1
  Henry 25
Cook, Capt. James H. 5, 22, 24, 30, 68, 92, 127
  Margaret [-?-] 25
  Mary Ann 35, 37
  Philip 25
  Richard L. 25
  Robert 25
  Samuel 25
  Thomas 25
  William 25, 26, 35
Cooke, Maria 68
  Thomas, 25
  William 26
Coolidge, William 26
Cooper, Catherine Ann 31
  Harriet 45
  Isaiah 26
  Major Samuel 31
  William 26
Corbit, Wm. F. 7
Cord, Mary 35

Corkrell, William 26
Correy, Capt. [-?-] 26
Corrie, J. 26
  James 29, 126
  Mary 29
Corry, Ebenezer 26
Corse, Barney 26
Corum, Ann 42
Corwin, Ann 42
  Elizabeth C. 94
Cosden, George B. 26
Coskery, Bernard 26
  Elizabeth 26
Cotner, Dion 26
Cottingham, Daniel 26
  Levin 113
Couden, Joseph 26
Coudon, Rachel [-?-] 26
Coulter, Dr. [-?-] 92
  Hannah 92
  James 26
Coursey, Ann 85
Courtlan, James 26
Courtney, Rev. [-?-] 99
  Mary 26
  Patrick 26
Covington, Ann 45
Cow, Michael 26
Cowley, Sarah 18
Cox, James 26, 94
  Jane 5
  Jesse R. 26
  John 26
  MacDonald 26
  Rebecca [-?-] 94
  Capt. Samuel 26
  Sarah 110
  Sarah Ann 125
  William 27
Coxe, Edward D. 27
Cradock, Catherine 117
Craft, Thomazine 54
  William 9, 86
Craik, Maria D. 37
Cramer, Cornelius 27
Crandal, Allison 27
Crane, Jesse 27
  Maria 31
Craney, Rev. [-?-] 28
Craper. John 27
Crapster, John 27
Crassey, William 27
Crassmer, William 27
Craven, Dr. [-?-] 113

Ann 113
Crawford, Catherine H. 83
  Edward 83
  James 27
  Dr. John 44
  John F. 27
  Col. Joseph 27
  William H. 27
Creager, John 27
Creagh, John 27
Crevenston, George 27
Crever, Jacob, 27
Crew, Richard 27
Cricket, John 114
Crompton, Thomas 27
Cromwell, [-?-] 27
Cromwell, Capt. Joseph H. 27
Croney, Ann Maria 78
  Maria 89
Cronmiller, Margaret 17
Crook, Eliza 109
  Walter 109
Crosby, James 27
Cross, Lieut. Joseph 27
  Margaret H. 72
  Truman 27
  William 28
Crothers, Margaret 28, 82
Crouch, Elizabeth [-?-] 28
  Samuel 28
Croxall, James 28
  John 28
  Richard 28
Crozier, Jane 75
Cuinand, F. E. 28
Culin, Lydia 127
Cullen, Catharine 49, 51
Cullliden, Catherine [-?-] 7
Cully, Samuel 28
Cummins, Jno. 28
Cunningham, Ann 112
  James 28
  John 28
Curey, Henry 28
Curlet, John 91
Curry, Mary Ann 98
Curtain, James 28
Curtis, Elizabeth 2

Index

Cushing, Dr. Thomas H. 28
Cuthbert, Mary T. [-?-] 28
William 28
Cutler, [-?-] 129
Robert C. 28
Samuel 28
Cutts, Richard 132

Dacey, John N. 122
Daffin, Sarah 28
Dagan, Mary [-?-] 76
Dailey, John 28
Daily, John 28
Dall, John R. 28
Dallas, A. J.122
  Alexander 28
  Catherine R. 7
  Matilda 122
Dalrymple, John 28
  William P. 29
Daly, James 29, 121
  Mary [-?-] 29
Dance, Thomas 29
Dancker, John J. 29
Danneman, C. H. 29
  Conrad Henry 29
Dante, John Baptiste 29
Darcus, Laurena 92
D'Arcy, John M. 29
Darden, John 29
Dare, E. 29
Darllng, John 29
Darnald, Ann 32
Darnel, Capt. Sampson, 29
Darrell, Capt. Sampson 29
Dashiel, Rev. [-?-] 66
Dashields. See Dashiell.
Dashiell, Rev. George 3, 14, 29, 43, 96, 109, 125
  Leah 57
  Rozetta E. 14
Daughaday, Rachel 79
  Sarah 37
Daumenen, Conrad Henry 122
Davey, Henry 29
David, Rev. Mr. [-?-] 30
David, Mary [-?-] 6
Davidge, Francis H. 29

Davidge, Dr. John B. 29, 129
Davidge, Mrs. W. H. 29
Davidson, Ann 40
  Evelina 101
  Job 22
  Thomas 29
Davis, (Rev. Mr. or Dr.)[-?-] 8, 11, 18, 29, 33, 34,41, 42, 45, 56, 58, 63, 65, 67, 70, 73, 76, 79, 81, 84, 89, 96, 98, 102, 103, 104, 106, 107, 108, 111, 114,121, 123
  Ann 112
  Caleb 29
  Charles 29
  Daniel 12
  David 30
  Lieut. E. R. 30
  Elizabeth 30, 110
  George 30
  James 30
  John 102, 112, 116
  Rev. John 94
  John N. 30
  R. 29
  Sarah 112
  Sarah Ann 30
  Teresa 115
  Thomas 18
  William 7, 30
  William M. 30
  Rev. Mr. 106
Davison, Samuel 30
Dawes, Edward 30
  Harrison 30
  Mary 107
Dawson, James 2
  Mary 50
  Mary Ann 27
  Mary Rogers 30
  William 30, 50
Day, Everett 30
  George 30
  Sarah 30
Deakins, Col. [-?-] 52
  Elizabeth 52
Dealing, Abner 30
Dean, Cecilia M. 48
Dean, Kingsmill 33
Deane, James 30
deBuller, Eliza 23
DeButts, John 30

Dechert, Peter S. 30
Decker, Elizabeth 40
  George 32
  Jacob 27
  Margaret 27
  Salome 32
DeGroff, Ann [-?-] 98
Dejarnatt, Daniel 30
Dejean, Peter 30
DeKrafft, Edward 30
Delacour, David 25
  James 30
Delaplaine, John 30
Delavetic, Lucinda 55
Delius, Arnold 30
Dell, Peter 31
Delowshew, Alex. 31
Delpey, Matilda 105
Delrymple, John 28
Demaray, Joseph 31
Dempsey, Eliza [-?-] 51
DenBoer, Abraham, 31
DenBork, Abraham 31
Denker, Johann 30
Denmead, Eliza 110
Denny, William 4, 32, 126
Dennys, Benjamin 31
Dent, Major J. T. 31
  William H. 31
Denys. See Dennys.
Derickson Dr. James 9
  Maria Louisa 9
Derstedt, Capt. John 31
Deschamps, Amelia 72
Deshong, Christopher116
Despeaux, Eli 43
  John 31
  Mary Ann 443
Develin, Patrick 31
DeViar, Joseph Ignacio 31
DeVille, [-?-] 31
Dew, Henrietta Maria [-?-] 31
Dew, James C. 31
deWees, Eleanor 30
  Wm. 30
Dewn, Mary C. 28
Dias, Lopes 31
Dickhut, George 31
Dickinson, Barbary Ann 97

Index

Rebecca Ann [-?-] 31
Susannah 95
William 31
Dickman, T. 32
Dickson, Susannah 95
Didier, Amelia 29
H. 29
Henry 29
Diffendall, [-?-] 120
Diffenderfer, Ann M. 84
Catherine [-?-] 32
Charles 32
Daniel 32
Dorothy 32
John 26, 32
Juliana 116
Michael 32
Dr. Michael 32
Peter 48
Diggs, Esther [-?-] 32
Dillon, Elizabeth [-?-] 71
Mary Ann 70
Dimmitt, Catherine [-?-] 32
Dinges, Caroline 30
Dirickson, Gen. Samuel 32
Disbrow, William 32
Dismukes, John 32
Disney, Wesley 32
William 125
Dison, William 32
Diver, Rev. [-?-] 16
Divers, Elizabeth 59
Mary 8, 5, 59
Dixon, Mary [-?-] 76
Dixson, Thomas 32
Dobbin, Hester [-?-] 17
John 32
Dodson, Rev. Mr. [-?-] 13, 52, 53, 58, 61, 62
Donaldson, Dr. [-?-] 103
Barbara Ann 40
Bathia P. 74
Jane Ann 4, 7
Rebecca [-?-] 32
Richard 32
Sam'l. J. 12
Stephen P. 32
Donavan, Mary Anne 32

Donnell, Elizabeth 110
John 110
Mary 48
Donnellin, Thomas 32
Donohoe, James 32
Donovan, James 32
Margaret 32
William 32
Doonin, Peter 33
Doran, William 16
Dorman, Mary Ann 68
Dorry, Dr. Henry 33
Dorsey, Judge [-?-] 29
Ann 123
Anna Maria 29
Dr. Archibald 33
Caleb 119
Caroline 121
Edward 33
Elisha 33
Elizabeth [-?-] 33
Evelina Mary 24
Everline 92
Hammond 33
Dr. Henry 33
Henry W. 123
Dr. Henry W. 33
Hill 33
John E. 33
John H. 33
Dr. John Syng 33
John W. 130
Margaret [-?-] 33
Mary [-?-] 33
Nicholas 33
Owen 45
Col. Richard 121
Samuel 33
Sarah 119
Thomas Hall 133
William 33
William E. 33
Dougherty, John 33
Mary 103
Rhoda [-?-] 30
Susan 13
Douglas, Isaac 33
Douglass, Fanny [-?-] 71
Dove, William G. 33
Dowell, John 33
Dowerty, Ann 79
Dowlin, Thomas 33
Downes, Dion 26
Downey, William A. 33
Downing, John 34

Downs, Ann 34
James 34
Joshua 34
Robert 34
Dowson, Henry 34
Robert H. 34
Doxy, H. 130, 131, 132
Jeremiah 130, 131, 132
Dreams, Mary E. 87
Driggs, Nath'l 78
Drinkhouse, George 34
Driscoll, Eliza [-?-] 46
Druit, James 34
Drummond, Sarah [-?-] 120
Drury, William 34
Dryden, Capt. [-?-] 35
Dubois, Nicholas 34
Duborg, William 28
Dubourg, Maria Aglae 28
Duchemin, Francis 34
Duesbury, Elizabeth 25
Duffin, James 34
Dugan, Eliza [-?-] 23
Duhamel, Rev. Charles 34, 109
James 34
Duke, Basil 34
Rev. William 79
Dukehart, Henrietta 122
Henry 34, 122
Capt. Thomas 34
Dulany, Col. Daniel 34
DuMaine, Charles Mary Goubert Toubert 34
Dumas. Peter 34
Dunbar, Juliet Ann 71
Duncan, Rev. [-?-] 13, 19, 32, 48, 73, 91, 107
Anna M. 113
Capt. David W. 34
Duncan, Rev. John Mason 37, 41, 42, 65, 74, 75, 77, 78, 86, 89, 103, 111, 112, 120
Rev. William 113
Dungan, Capt. Abel S. 34

Index

Gaynor 16
Mary 16
Dunkin, Capt. 132
Dunlap, Judge 9
Juliet Ann 71
Dunn, Arthur 34
Rebecca 12
Dunning, Samuel 35
Duntze, George 35
Dupont de Nemours,
  Samuel Peter 35
Dupuy, Rev. Charles
  97
  Susan M. 32
Durand, Richard 35
Durang, Richard 35
Durham, M. [-?-] 35
Dusford, Sarah 103
Dusis, Lewis 35
Dutton, John 35
Duval, Cecilia 27
  Charles 27
  E. W. 35
Duvall, Alex'r. J. 35
  E. W. 84
  Edward B. 35
  Nathaniel 98
  Susan T. 84
Duvivier, Maria 119
Dwyer, William 35
Dykes, James 35
Dysart, Moses A. 35

Eagan, Rev. John 35
Eager, Ellen 80
Eagle, James 35
Earlougher, Elizabeth
  16
Eaverson, Joseph 35
Eccleston, Joseph 35
Echols, J. 133
Eckel, Eliza 107
  Philip 107
Eddy, Susan [-?-] 9
Edelen, Rev. Mr. [-?-]
  110
  Alexius 129
  Joseph 78
  Margaret Matilda 78
Edgar, David 35
  Eliza M. 61
Edmondson, James 35
  Peter 35
  William 35
Edward, Jane 35
  Eliza B. 65
  Elizabeth 70

Gouverneur 35
  Sarah 127
  Capt. William 35
Eichelberger, J. 112
  Martin 35
Eicholtz, L. 35
Eickler, C. T. 35
  Sarah 35
Eisler, Mary Magdalen
  97
Elbert, Dr. [-?-] 29
  Rev. Dr. [-?-] 79
  William G. 35
Eldridge, William 35
Eli, Rev. Mr. [-?-] 113
Ellek, Sarah 83
Ellender, Ann 107
Ellicott, Elias 66
  Mary J. 60
  Tacy 66
Elliott, Rev. Dr. [-?-]
  32, 95
  Geo. 71
  Mary Ann 80
  Robert 35
  William 35, 121
Ellis, Rowland 35
  Sarah 58
  William 35
Elridge, William 35
Ely, Christian 35
Emberson, Charles
  35,130
Embry, Eliza 100
Emory, Thomas L. 87
Endress, Rev. [-?-] 6,
  100
English, Rev. [-?-] 95
Ennes, Michael Lucas
  35
  Thomas 35
Ensey, William 35
Ensor, Jemima 24
  John 35
Escaville, Joseph 35
Etchberger, Margaret
  88
Etherington, John 129
Etting, Kitty 23
  Solomon 23
Etzler, Andrew 110
  Rebecca 110
Evans, Andrew P. 35,
  94
  Ann 84, 108
  Daniel 37
  Elizabeth 34

Emily 79
Griffith 27
Hannah 40
Henry 37
James 35
John 35, 37
John K. 37
Margaret 114
Mary 123
Oliver 37
Robert 35
Sarah 35
Thomas 37
Everett, Mary 11
Thomas 37

William B. 37
Everit, Thomas 37
Ewald, Barbara 39
Ewell, Maj. Charles 37
Ewing, Catherine 37

Fache, John 37
Fagan, Andrew 37
Fahnestock, Christine
  55
  Daniel F. 37
  Mary 37
  Dr. S. 37
Fairall, Erasmus 37
Fairbairn, James 37
Fairbank, John 26
  Susannah 26
Fairclough, Rev. [-?-]
  20
Fairing, Augustus 37
Falconer, Abraham H.
  37
  Peregrine 37
Falls, Moor 102
  Sarah 102
Fardon, Aliceanna 49
Farina, [-?-] 37
Farland, Mary Ann
  103
  Joseph 103
Farnandis, Samuel 38
Farquharson, Charles
  52
Farran, Ann [-?-] 38
Farrell, James 38
Farrill, William 38
Farrin, Capt. Thomas
  38
Fausbender, John 38
Fechtig, Rev. 17
Fefel, Joseph 9

Index

Feignahty, John 38
Feinour, Charles 10
Mary Ann 10
Fenix, Hugh 131
Fenn, Lydia Maria 93
Fennell, Rev. [-?-] 7
Caleb 38
Dorcas 71
Fenner, Sally [-?-] 67
Fenton, Thomas 38
William C. 38
Fenwick, Col. Athanasius 38
Rev. Enoch 1, 3, 12, 14, 26, 34, 35, 45, 47, 61, 64, 74, 83, 89, 96, 97, 98, 103, 106, 113
Leo 38
Ferguson, Flora 37
Fernan, John 38
Ferrall, Rev. Gideon 111
Ferran, John 38
Thomas 38
Ferris, Josiah 38
Fessler, Margaret 25
Few, Ann 5
Fields, James 41
Fife, Andrew 38
Figuieres, Louisa 3
Finchmann, Henry 38
Finchnaur, Henry 38
Fincknaur, Henry 38
Finlay, James P. 38
Finley, E. L. 38
Finley, John M. 38
Mary [-?-] 38
Finly, Ebenezer L. 86
Finn, William 38
Finnell, Rev. Reuben 18
Finney, Rev. [-?-] 27
Fishback, Philip 39
Fisher, Ann Mary [-?-] 39
Basil 39
Charles 39
Elizabeth [-?-] 37
George 29
Henry 39
James 39
Robert 39
Sarah 90
Fitch, Thomas 39
Fite, Ann [-?-] 39
Conrad 39

Jacob 39
Fits, Eliza 103
Fitzhugh, George 39
Fitzpatrick, Margaret 58
Flaherty, Catherine [-?-] 39
John R. 39
Fletchall, Col. Thomas 39
Fletcher, William 39
Floote, Harrietta [-?-] 113
Flora, Nancy 1
Floyd, William 39
Focke, Capt. William 39
Folger, Christiana 2
Isabella 95
Folsher, John 39
Foltz, Elizabeth 98
William 39
Fonerden, Adam 39
Fonlevy, Dennis 51
Forbes, Eleanor Brooke Eversfield 9
George 39
Marianne Craik 39
William 40
Force, Rev. M. 2, 5, 32, 43, 51, 58, 66, 77, 95, 98, 103, 112, 114, 122
Force, Peter 40
Ford, Alice Anna C. 106
Ann 118, 123
Foreman, David 40
Forest, Ann Maria 98
Forman, Eliza 44
Ezekiel 40
Rev. John 44
Nelly 40
Forney, Barbara 94
Davis S. 40
Sarah 124
Fornshil, John 40
Forrest, Col. [-?-] 40
John 40
Josiah 30
Rev. Jonathan 3
Sophia 30
Forster, Capt. Francis 40
Fort, Elizabeth 65
Fosdick, John M. 40

Foss, Charles 40
Fossbenner, Andrew 40
John 40
Foster, Charles 40
Eliza 20
Elizabeth 102
Capt. William 40
Foucher, Dr. [-?-] 133
Fought, Thomas 40
Fountain, Sarah 99
Fouse, Henry 40
Fousz, Jacob 40
Fowble, Peter 9, 91
Fowke, Catherine Elizabeth 40
Gerard 40
Mary 40
Mary Bayne 40
Virlinda Stone 40
William Augustus 40
Fowler, Catherine 7
David 40
Rachel M. 52
William 40
Fox, Augusta 106
Frances Ann 102
Capt. Nathaniel 40
S. 41
Foy, Michael 41
Frailey, Philip 41
Frame, Jane 8
France, James 41
John 41
Francisco, Samuel 41
Frank, Ludwick 41
Franklin, Dr. [-?-] 40
Dorcas 105
Jacob 41, 130
John 11
Mary Jane 11
Capt. Samuel 41
Thomas 41
Franzone, Signor Carlo 41
Fraser, John 41
Frazier, Dr. A. 41
Emily 37
Capt. Thomas 41
Freburger, Henry 11
Frederick, Nancy [-?-] 41
Freeburger, John 86
Freeman, Capt. [-?-] 105
Col. [-?-] 51

Index

Carvill 51
Charles 41
Isaac 41, 51
Col. Isaac 41
Isabelle 68
Martha 51
Martha [-?-] 41
William Snow 109
Freer, Peter J. 41
Frey, Rev. [-?-] 65
Frick, John 41
Fricke, Henry C. 41
Friend, John 41
Friendler, Andrew 41
Frisbie, William 41
Fro, Tracy [-?-] 76
Fry, Rev. Mr. [-?-] 47. 94, 121
Frye, Rev. C. 23
Nathaniel 42
Fuller, Ann 55
Nancy 19
Fullington, Lucinda [-?-] 65
Fulmer, Catherine 122
Fulton, Amelia 27
Furber, Sarah 123
Furlong, Capt. William 42
Fyatt, William 42

Gaarde, P. J. 42
Gable, Henry 131
Gadsby, [-?-] 78
Gafford, Emeline 53
Emily 53
Juliann 120
Gailand, John Baptist 42
Gaines, Ann 56
James 56
Galande, Catharine [-?-] 42
J. B. 42
Gale, Martha [-?-] 42
Rasin 42
Gallaway, Jehu 42
Galloway, Ezekiel 42
Hannah 42
Gamble, Darius 8
Greenbury 8
Robert S. 8
Ganteume, Clementine 42
Gantt, Dr. Thomas 42
Thomas T. 42
Garden, William 42

Gardiner, Sarah 15
Gardner, Ann 96
Gardner, Hezekiah B. 42
Col. Robert 42
Sophia 5
Garey, Charlotte 93
Jeremiah 23
Garland, Catherine [-?-] 42
J. B. 42
Garrett, Jesse 42
Robert 42
Thomas 42
Thomas D. 42
Garrettson, Aquilla 42
Gary, Everet 42
Gassaway, Capt. Henry 42
John 50
Gatchell, Mary H. 124
Gatchell, Major Samuel H. 42
Gate, William 42
Gates, Susan 57
Gaunteaume, James 29
Geary, Matthew 43
Geddis, Jane 101
Gee. Cornelius 43
Geiger, Rev. Jacob 43
Geise, Isabella 79
Gelder Van 43
Gendre, Sophia Le [-?-] 68
George, Amelia 42
Harriet 78
Jacob 43
James 43
James B. 43
Gerachty, Capt. Peter 43
Gerahty, Peter 43
Gerard, Mr. 69
German, David 43
Jonathan 43
Gettings, Mahsack 43
Maria 43
Thomas Freeman 43
Gettis, Sarah 119
Getty, Jacob 43
Gettyer, George 43
Geyer, John 101
Ghequiere, Charles 43
Henry Tiernan 43
Tiernan 43
Gibbons, John 43
John N. 43

Gibbs, Elizabeth [-?-] 75
Hannah 43
Gibney, Elizabeth [-?-] 43
Elizabeth Maillard 90
John Francis 90
John Franklin 43
Gibson, Rev. [-?-] 28
Elizabeth 25
James 44
Capt. James 25
John, 44
Joshua 44
Gidney, Dr. Eleazer 44
Giesler, Catherine [-?-] 44
Giffin, John 44
Gilbert, Elizabeth 41
Jesse 44
Gildea, Felix 64
Capt. Reuben 44
Giles, Jacob W. 44
Gill, Ann M'Clain 44
Edward, 44
John 44
Rebecca 24
Stephen G. 44
Gillespie, David 44
Gillespy, E. 93
Gillingham, Elizabeth [-?-] 44
James 44
Gillmeyer, Sarah 109
Gilly, John 44
Gilmor, Jane 57
R. 102
Rev. William 102
William 57
Gilmore, Capt. 130
Gilpin, Mrs. Mary H. 53
Girard, Harriet 67
Stephen 67
Gist, Cornelius H. 39
Pamela 39
William 44
Gittens, J. 44
Gittings, Elizabeth [-?-] 44
Col. James 44
Gladding, Samuel 44
Glandon, Francis 44
Glaspy, George 44
Glass, John 44

165

Index

Glendy, Rev. Dr. John 1, 5, 6, 8, 10, 12, 13, 15, 19, 22, 24, 25. 27, 29, 35, 38, 39, 40, 43, 44, 46, 47, 48, 49, 51, 52, 53, 54, 56, 57, 58, 61, 62, 66, 66, 68, 69, 72, 75, 76, 80, 81, 82, 83, 84, 88, 89, 90. 91. 92, 96, 97, 100, 101, 102, 103, 104, 105, 107, 108, 110, 111, 112, 113, 114, 116, 117, 118, 119, 120, 122, 123, 124
Samuel 44
Glenn, Elias 89
Mary 89
Goddard, Robert 44
William 44
Godefroy, Eliza Anderson 44
Maximilian, 44
Godfrey, Capt. Benjamin 45
Goff, Jacob 45
Goforth, Mary 41
Gohagan, Capt. John 45
Goldsborough, Charles 45
Robert 45
Sarah [-?-] 45
Goldthwaite, Capt. Ezekiel 45
Sarah [-?-] 45
Goodall, Charles P. 132
Mary 70
Gooding, James 45
Richard 45
Sarah 45
Goodrich, Walter 45
Goodwin, Caleb 45
John 45
Oliver 45
William 126
Gordon, Hannah 51
John, 45
Robert 45
Gore, Henry 45
Philip 24
Gormely, Mary Ann 65

Gorsuch, Charles 45
Joseph 45
Rachel 95
Robert 45
Sophia 28
Gorvin, Daniel 45
Gose, John D. 45
Gosse, Adeline 101
Dennis 45
Goswick, Ann 35
Goszler, George 45
John 45
Philip 45
Gotolet, [-?-] 131
Gott, Henrallsia 45
Richard 45
Ruth [-?-] 45
Samuel 45
Gotts, Eleanor 34
Gough, Rachel 29
Gould, Alexander 45
C. C., 45
James 46
James C. 46
James F. 46
John 46
Goulden, Sam 133
Goulding, Mary 12
Gout, Barbara [-?-] 67
Gover, Mary Ann 56
Grace, Ann 94
John 46
Gracie, Henry 46
Graflin, Jacob 53, 54
Grafton, [-?-] 1
Graham, Elizabeth [-?-] 49
Jane 65
Jane Brent 46
John 129, 133
Richard 46
William 46
Capt. William 46
Grammer, John A. 46
Grant, Frances Jane 60
Capt. Henry 46
Mary 33
William 46
Grapewine, Sally 46
Gray, Frederick Christian 46
Capt. French S. 46
Jane 100
John 46
Martha Adeline 43
Susan 42

Graybill, Capt. Philip 46
Green, Ann 119
Benjamin 46
Catherine 72
Charles R. 46
Eliza 62
Elizabeth 57, 123
Isaac 57
Isaiah 46
Isiah 46
John 46
John N. 46
Levin B. 46
Mary Ann 51
Oliver 46
Rebecca [-?-] 107
Susan 11
Susanna Roselba 51
William W. 47
Greenfield, Amos 47
Martha 27
Rev. Nathaniel 10, 48
Greenslaw, James 47
Greenway, Edward M. 47
Greenwood, Elizabeth 33
Grees, Lydia 47
Greetham, William 47
Gregory, [-?-] 25
Lieut. Francis H. 47
Grehum, Frederick 47
Gresham, Margaret [-?-] 47
Gresham, Richard M. 47
Gretham, William, 47
Grice, Rev. George 40, 45, 56, 57, 126
Grice, Susannah 94
Grierson, Andrew 47
Griesley, William 47
Griffen, Mary Ann
Eliza 63
Griffin, William 47
Griffith, Adam 47
Amelia D. 75
Charles 101
David Adam 47
Edmund 37
Edward 47
Hannah E. Stump 47
Henrietta 88
Howard 47
Sarah 50

Index

Griffiths, Richard Eli 47
Griggs, [-?-] [-?-] 47
  James 49, 89
  John 3
Grisas, H. 28
Grisset, William 47
Groome, Elizabeth Black 47
Groome, Harriet Lucinda 47
  Dr. John 47
  Samuel 47
  William 47
Gross, [-?-] 132
  Abraham 47
  Charles 47
Grosvenor, Thomas P. 48
Grouchy, Marshal de 67
Grove, Stephen 48,
Grubb, Henrietta 114
Grundy, George 48
  Mary 48
Gudgeon, Blanche 58
  Jesse 48
Guest, Rev. Job 21, 41, 95
Guestier, P. A. 68, 133
Guhro, Joseph 48
Guinand, Edward F. 48
Guthrot, Joseph 48
Guttry, Eliza [-?-] 48
  Susan 75
Guynn, Dr. John 48
Guyton, Thomas 48
Gwynn, William 18
  Major William 48

Hackney, Elizabeth 50
Haddaway, Lieut. Edward 48
Haff, Priscilla [-?-] 50
Hagerty, Rev. John 1, 3, 40, 41, 59, 60, 70, 97, 123
Hagger, B. K. 51
  Mehitable 51
Hagon, Ann 13
Hagthorp, Thomas 48
Hagthrop, Edw. 18, 38
Haigh, David 48
Haile, Jane 48
Haines, Reuben 57
Hainks, Rachel 14

Hale, Jane [-?-] 48
  Nicholas 48
Hall, Andrew 48
  Benedict W. 49
  Carter A. 48
  Edward 48
  Elias 48
  Capt. Ezekiel 49
  Hannah [-?-] 49
  Henry 49
  Jacob 49
  Jesse 49
  John 49
  Latitia [-?-] 104
  Mary [-?-] 49
  Mary B. 82
  Capt. Nathaniel N. 44, 82, 101, 104
  Nelson 49
  Phebe 62
  Shadrick 49
  Sophia 49
  William I. 49
Hallowell, John 94
  Sarah [-?-] 94
Hamilton, Edward 49
  Eleanor 49
  James 49, 121
  James B. 49
  John 49
  Col. John 49
  Maria 121
  Samuel S. 49
  William 74, 98
Hamlin, Thomas 6
Hamm, Ann 31
  James 31
Hammer, August 49
  Christian 49
  Frederick 49
  Mary [-?-] 66
Hammerton, James 49
Hammon, Joseph 49, 51
Hammond, Ann 118
  Elizabeth 96
  John 50, 133
  Dr. Matthias 50
  Rezin 50
  Vachel 50
Hanby, William 35
Hand, Gen. [-?-] 50
  Edward 50
Handle, John 30, 50
Hands, Louisa 34
  Rose 50
Handy, John 50

  Sarah Custis 50
  William 50
Hanley, Mary 74
Hannah, Eliza 91
Hannaman, Jacob 50
  John, 53, 50
Hanson, Judge [-?-] 48
  A. C. 48
  Alexander C. 50
  Benedict H. 50
  Hantzman, Henry 50
Hardaway, Dr. 132
Hardester, Benjamin 114
  Capt. Benjamin 50
  Isaac 50
Hardesty, Charles R. 50
Harding, Lyman 50
Hardinge, Samuel 50
Hardt, Peter 50
Hardy, Alexander 50
Harent, Rev. Joseph 50
Hargrove, Rev. Mr. John 2, 11, 15, 23, 31, 42, 49, 51, 55, 56, 63, 65, 68, 72, 80, 85, 101, 112, 113, 118, 119, 120, 123, 131
Harkles, Thomas 51
Harkness, Susan A. 51
Harley, Martha 2
Harmon, Zebulon 51
Harner, John 51
Harper, Gen. [-?-] 51
  Caroline M. 17
  Joseph 14
  Mary Diana 51
Harr, Peter 51
Harrington, Peter 51
Harris, Barton 80
  Henry 51
  John 68
  John P. 51
  Jonathan 133
  Nehemiah 51
  Richard 129
  Ruth [-?-] 51
  Samuel 51
  Dr. Thomas 51
  William 2, 59
  William C. 51
Harrison, Elizabeth [-?-] 51
  Harry 51
  John 51

Index

Jonathan N. 51
Kensey 51
Kinsey 132
Robert 51
Robert M. 51
Zebulon 51
Harrod, Lydia 55
Harry, David 30
George I. 51
Mary 30
Susanna 8
Harryman, John, 38
Hart, John 51
Hartshorne, P. S. 51
Sarah [-?-] 51
Harvey, James 52
Harwood, Margaret 49
Richard H. 52
Haskins, Henry 52
Haslet, Andrew 52
Haslett, Major James 124
Haslett, Mary 124
Haslup, Jesse 44
Hasselbach, Catherine 52
  Eliza 46
  John 46, 52
Hatcher, Dr. Hardaway 52
Hathaway, Ebenezer 52
  Capt. John 52
Haubert, Frederick 52
Haugh, William 57
Haveland, Cornelius 52
  James 52
Haven, Elizabeth [-?-] 52
Hawkins, Francis M. 99
  Francis W. 133
  Jas. L. 131
  John 99
  Sally 117
  William 52
Hawley, Rev. 74
Hayden, Clement Whitfield 52
Hayden, Dennis E. 52
Hayes, Belinda [-?-] 52
  John 52
  Sarah 66
  Thomas 60
  William 52

Hays, Archer 61
  Elizabeth 61
  William 52
Hayward, John L. 52
Hazard, Ebenezer 52
Headly, Joseph 52
Heagen, Catherine 23
Healey, Rev. [-?-] 5, 9, 19, 21, 23, 24, 25, 27, 30, 38, 47, 58, 65, 87, 94, 95, 105, 111, 112, 116, 122, 123, 124
Healey, John 13
Heap, Sally Ann D. 113
Heard, Samuel 52
Heath, John P. 52
Hebbelwhite, Benjamin 52
Heck, Ann 53
Hedinger, Catherine 66
Hedrick, Thomas 52, 67
Heide, Ann Maria 25
  George 7
Heister, Barbary Ann [-?-] 52
Helfenstein, Rev. Albert 13, 27, 34, 39, 87
Hellias, John 53
Helm, Leonard 53
Helmling, Anthony 76
Helsby, Mary [-?-] 53
Hemmel, Elizabeth 61
Hemphill, Rev. [-?-] 15, 24, 37, 125
Henderson, Catherine 43
  Frisby 53
  James B. 101
  John 53
  Lieut. John 53
  Dr. Josiah 53
  Peter 101
Hendrick, Manuel 53
Hendrickson, Ann 113
Henisy, Mrs. [-?-] 53
Hennaman, Jacob 5
  John 50, 53
Henning, Benjamin 53
  George 53
Henry, Lieut. [-?-] 53
  Caroline 71
  Rev. John 106

Robert J. 53
Hensel, William 53
Henshaw, Rev. Dr. [-?-] 1, 5, 6, 10, 12, 15, 18, 24, 29, 30, 40, 76, 78, 92, 98, 99. 113, 114, 125
Henwood, Joshua 53
Hepburn, John M. 53
Herback, Mary 9
Herberd, Jane M. 64
  Jane R. 115
  William 53
Herd, James 53
Herford, Henry 53
Heron, Alexander 53
Herrack, George 47
Herring, Alexander 53
  David 53
  Elizabeth 53
  Henry 53
  Ludwig 53
Hershberger, Rev. 10
Hertzog, Rebecca 56
Heslip, Elizabeth [-?-] 54
  John 54
Heuisler, Mary F. 97
Hewes, Daniel 54
  Capt. Daniel 54
  Eunice [-?-] 54
Hewett, Elmer 54
Hewitt, Mary E. 14
Heylands, Elizabeth 17
Heyward, Ann 76
Hickman, Henry 54
  Dr. Joshua 54
Hicks, George 54
Higdon, Richard 18
Higgins, Francis 84
  Harriet [-?-] 54
  Solomon 54
Higinbotham, Ann 86
  Delozier 54
  Ralph 86
Hignat, John 54
Hill, Charles 54
  Elizabeth M. 49
  Capt. John 54
  Margaret [-?-] 54
  Rebecca [-?-] 54
  Richard 54
  Thomas H. 54
Hillard, John 54
Hilleary, Capt. Clement T. 54

Index

Hillen, John 54
Hilliard, Mary [-?-] 54
Hills, Ellen [-?-] 42
Hinchman, Maria V.
  H. 107
Hindes, Wm. 54
Hinds, Jas. 43
Hines, John 54
  Samuel 54
Hinshaw, Rev. [-?-] 5
Hinton, John 129
Hiss, Jacob, 54
  Jesse L. 104
  Joseph 54
Hitchcock, Caleb 54
  Sarah 65, 82
Hitselberger, Rev. [-?-] 42
Hizer, Robert 55
Hobbs, Anne 55
  Charles 55
  Corrilla 20
  Louisa Ann 48
  Nicholas M. 55
Hodgdon, Jane P. 51
  Samuel 51
Hodges, James 55
Hoffman, Ann McKean 55
  David 55
  Elizabeth 93
  George 55
  Henry 55
  Mary 9
  Valentine 14
Hogdstin, James 55
Hohn, John 55
Hoke, Anna Mary 99
  Peter 99
Holbrook, Jacob 55
Holland, George L. 55
  James 55
  Mary [-?-] 55
  William 94
Holliday, John Robert 68
Hollingsworth, Ann Maria 82
  Edward Ireland 55
  Hannah 55
  Henry 55
  Horatio D. 55
  Jesse 55
  Jona. 55
  Rachel Lyde 55
  Capt. William 55
Hollins, Jesse 55

Holloway, Robert 15
Holly, John 55
Hollyday, H. 119
Holmes, Almoran 55
  Henrietta 14
  John 55
  Juliana 55
  L. 49
  Dr. Oliver 55
Holston, Hamilton B. 55
Holtzman, Mary [-?-] 69
Hontsberger, Kitty [-?-] 56
  Peter 56
Hood, Rev. Mr. [-?-] 121
  Catherine D. 88
  Rachel Howard 56
  Col. Thomas 56, 88
Hook, Capt. J. H. 30, 43, 52, 63, 81, 84, 87, 88, 112, 114, 123
  Margaret 23
  Sarah 95
  Thomas 56
Hooker, Maria 123
Hooks, Capt. James H. 49
Hooper, James 129
  John 56
  Mary 23
Hope, William 33
Hopkins, Elizabeth 102
  Greenbury 56
  James 6
  Dr. Joel 56
  John 56
  Margaret 111
  Mary 6
  Nicholas 56
  Richard 56
  Solomon 56
  Susannah 121
Hopkinson, Thomas 23
Hoppe, Frederick 56
  Justus 56
Hopper, Thomas 26
Horn, J. S. 56
  John, 56
  Mary [-?-] 56
Horner, Abel 56
  Bridget [-?-] 99

Elizabeth 56
Job 56
Horsey, Morris 56
  Outerbridge 69
  Smith 56
Horton, [-?-] 131
  A. 56
Horton, James 45. 69
  Lewis 56
  Nicholas F. 56, 57
  William 57
Horze, William 56
Hose, Elias 57
Hoskins, Rev. Nathaniel 35
  Richard 57
Hoskinson, Rev. [-?-] 2
Hough, William 57
Houston, James 57
  Col. John 21, 22
How, John 57
Howard, Agnes 62
  Benjamin C. 57
  Cornelius 57
  Elizabeth 79
  Elizabeth [-?-] 57
  Elizabeth R. 57
  George 50
  Dr. Henry 57
  John 57, 129, 132, 133
  Joshua 57
  Keziah 54
  Lydia 40
  Martha 62
  Rebecca 57
  Robert 57
  Sarah [-?-] 57
  Thomas 57
  Thomas W. 57
  William 129, 132, 133
Howe, Capt. Edward 57
Howell, Catherine 61
  John Brown 57
  Susan 38
  William 61
Hoyland, John 57
Hoyt, Richard C. 57
Hubbell, Josiah 130
  Capt. Josiah 57
Hudson, Henry 57
Hughes Ann Susan 35
  Daniel 96
  Eliza M. 44

Index

Geo. A. 101
Hugh C. T. 57
James 57
Jehu 57
John 57, 58
Maria 106
Richard 58
Richardson 58
Hulett, William 58
Hulse, John 58
Humberstone, Francis 61
Humphreys, Charles 58
Hunt, Capt. Henry 58
  Juliana 71
  William T. 58
Hunter, Rev. Dr. [-?-] 84
  Capt. George 58
  James 58
  Jane [-?-] 58
  Mary 27
Hupfield, Henrietta 39
Hurley, Thomas 58
Hurst, Maria 7
  Susan R. 54
  Thomas 58
Hurtt, John D. 58
Hurxtha, F. 33
Husband, Lydia 90
  William 58
Huschwadel, Christian David 58
Hush, [-?-] 59
Husk, Mary 19
Hussey, George 4
  Hannah 4, 120
Hust, [-?-] 58
Hutchins, Ariel 14
  John 58
Hutchinson, Joseph 58
  Mary [-?-] 58
Hutton, Elizabeth 58
  Margaret 120
  Samuel 58
Huveler, Elizabeth 6
Huxthal, Lewis 58
Hyatt, Henry 58
  Jane 55
  John 58
  Richard 58
  Sarah 33
Hyde, Ann Catherine 76
  Thomas W. 59
Hyland, Horatio 59

Lambert 59
Hynson, Amos 59
  Ann 14
  Araminta 117
  Eliza Rebecca 13
  Robert C. 59
  Temperance 85

Ing, Rebecca Jane 20
Inglis, George 59
  John 59
  Rev. Dr. James 4, 8, 9, 11, 12, 26, 20, 35, 47, 53, 54, 55, 57, 59, 60, 63, 65, 68, 82, 87, 93, 94, 99, 112, 115, 118, 124
Inloes, George 3, 59
Innes, John 59
  Sarah B. 99
Innis, Mary [-?-] 59
Ireland, Edward 59
Ireson, Richard M. 59
Irvin, John 59
Irvine, Alexander 53, 59
  Charlotte Cochran 53
  John 59
  Mary Ann 59
Irving, Thomas Pitt 59
Irwin, Jared 59
  Samuel 59
Isler, Margaretta 12
Isley, Eliza [-?-] 60
  Matthew 60

Jackson, Major [-?-] 60
  Rev. [-?-] 15
  Emily 40
  G. 60
  Gilbert 60
  Henry 60
  Holton 60
  James 60, 130
  Jas. 80
  John 133
  Mary Ann 120
  Nathaniel 60
  Susannah 45
  Tabitha Ann S. 52
Jacob, Samuel 60
Jacobs, Philip 60
  Samuel 60
Jacquett, Ann T. 70

James, George 60
  Henry 60
  Levi 78
  Margaret 68
  Nancy 7
  Rachel [-?-] 60
  Rebecca C. 56
  Samuel 60
  William 60
  Rev. William 23
Jameson, Catherine S. 67
  R. 67
Jamieson, John 60
Jamison, Cecilius C. 60
Jamison, Lieut. William 60
Janeway, Rev. Dr. 67
Janiewar, Jacob 60
Janney, Abijah 60
  Israel 60
Janson, Mr. Raphael 60
Janvier, John 60
  Joseph 61
  Peregrine 61
  Sarah [-?-] 61
  William B. 61
Jarrett, Abraham 61
Jarvis, Ann 29
Jay, Samuel 61
Jefferies, Samuel 61
  Thomas 61
Jeffers, James H. 61
  Rachael 35
Jeffery, Catherine 70
Jeffray, James 61
Jeffrey, Eliza 24
Jeffries, Thomas 61
Jenkins, Rev. [-?-] 14
  Ann 11
  Ann Harrison 61
  Benedict 61
  Custis 61
  Frederick 88
  Henry Neale 61
  James 129
  Thomas 61
Jennings, Dr. [-?-] 19, 65
  Ann 76
  Nathan 61
Jennings, Rev. Dr. Samuel 4, 5, 7, 8, 10, 19, 20, 21, 25, 31, 37, 44, 45, 50,

Index

53, 54, 55, 56, 57, 61, 62, 64, 68, 71, 74, 76, 84, 85, 90, 95, 98, 99. 100, 102, 107, 108, 115, 123, 124, 127
Jeremiah, John 61
Jeys, Thomas 61
John, Amblius 61
Johns, Mrs. [-?-] 131
  Aquila 61
  Hannah [-?-] 61
  Capt. Richard 61
  William 61
Johnson, Gov. [-?-] 69
  Ann 63
  Ann 3
  Ann E. M. 60
  Benjamin 7
  Betsey 62
  Catherine 62
  Charles Henry 62
  David 62
  Edward 62
  Elijah 62
  Fayette 62
  Francis 62
  Henry 62
  Henry Mackubin 62
  Horatio 62
  Isaac 62
  Jacob 62
  James 62
  John 50, 62
  Mary Ann 62,121
  Rev. Matthew 14, 85, 124
  Reverdy 62
  Susanna [-?-] 62
  Thomas 62, 132
  Dr. Thomas 62
  Thomas Rinaldo 62
Johnston, Christopher 53, 62
  Eliza S. 53
  Isaac 62
Jolley, Sarah Ann V. B. 18
  William 62
Jolly, William 62
Jones, Judge [-?-] 99
  Rev. Absolom 63
  Ann B. 99
  Arthur 55
  Aubray 63
  Awbrey 63
  C. L. 63
  Daniel 63
  Capt. Daniel 63
  David 63
  Mr. Edgar S. 63
  Edward S. 63
  Elizabeth 24
  Ellen 35
  Ellis 63
  Hiram 51
  Capt. Jacob 63
  John 63
  Capt. John N. 63
  Levin 129
  Lewis 63
  Lloyd 35
  Mahlon 63
  Mary 16, 54, 63, 68, 91
  Rachel C. 101
  Rachel Charlotte 116
  Rasin 63
  Richard 63
  Richard H. 109
  Col. Roger 63
  Thomas A. 63
  William 51, 63, 91
  Willy Ann [-?-] 40
Jordan, Christiana [-?-] 63
  Fred. 63
  John 63
  Mary Ann 6
  Sarah [-?-] 112
  Capt. William 6
Joy, Edward 64
Joyce, Ann Maria 3
Junge, William H. 64

Kain, Mary 26
Kalbfus, Julian 53
  Lewis 3, 59, 116
Karr, Thomas 64
Karthaus, P. A. 40
  W. 58
Kauffman, John 64
Kean, Robert 64
Kearsley, John 64
Keaver, Samuel 64
Keavin, Samuel 64
Keefer, Jacob 64
Keeho, Catherine 24
Keene, James 64
  Levin 126
  Maria 111
  Col. Richard 64
  Samuel 64
  Z. 131
  Zachariah 76, 111
Keener, Christian 64
  Jacob 64
  Melchor 64
Keeports, Geo. P. 64
Keho, John 64
Keigler, Elizabeth 92
Keilholtz, Elizabeth 99
  John 64
Keith, Rev. Mr. [-?-] 78
  Elizabeth 63
Kell, Juliet 64
  Thomas 64
Keller, Rev. Isaac 55, 64
Kelley, James 64, 65
  Rebecca 24
Kelly, Bartholomew 64
  James 64, 65
  Patrick 1
Kelmeyer, Lawrence 65
Kelsey, Eli 65
Kemp, Rt. Rev. Bishop 3, 4, 9, 12, 15, 18, 23, 24, 26, 29. 38, 40, 51, 69, 74, 75, 79, 82, 83, 86, 88, 92, 101, 102, 106, 109, 110, 111, 112
Kemper, Rev. Dr.98
Kennard, Thomas J. 65
Kennedy, Edmund P. 2, 110
  Mary 124
  William 65
Kennier, Frederick R. 65
Kent, Daniel 106
  Emanuel 65
Kenter, R. 70
Keplinger, Catherine 47
Keppard, Louisa 78
Kerns, John 65
Kerr, Ann 107
  Robert 65
Key, H. G. S. 132
Keys, Bayly 65
  John 129
  Matilda 70
Keyser, Elizabeth [-?-] 65
  Major George 65

Index

William W. 65
Kidd, Pamela A. Hargrove 65
Samuel 65
Kidwell, Robert C. 65
Kieffer, Rev. Daniel H. 65
Kiersted, Emily [-?-] 65
Kilgour, Charles J. 65
Killion, Mark 99
Killmary, Henry 65
Kimmel, Anthony 65
Frederick H. 65
Kindall, Mary 121
King, Rev. Mr. [-?-] 104
Ann 47
Ann Maria 81
Carry 19
Eliza 73
George Wilson 65
Isaiah 65
James T. 129
John 66
John S. 66
Joseph 66
Josias W. 74
Josias Wilson 66
Mary 51, 125
Mary Frances 74
Miles 119
Upthout 66
William 66, 125
Kingsmore, John 66
Kipp, John 44
Margaret Ann 44
Kirk, Aquila W. 66
Samuel 66
Kirke, Mahlon 66
Kirkland, David 66
James 66
Kirkpatrick, Rev. J.113
Kirwan, Capt. Matthias 66
Kitchart, Mary [-?-] 7
Kline, Jacob 66
Klocke, Mrs. Engel Christian 6
Knight, Ignatius 66
Sarah 51
Knox, Ella 19
James 66
Kohlman, Rev. Mr. 75
Kohne, H. W. 66
Kolb, George 66

Michael 66
Rebecca 66
Sarah [-?-] 66
Konig, C. S. 66
Koons, Jacob 66
Kraft, Christian 66
Kraus, Christian 73
Krebs, George 102
Maria 81
Susan 102
Kreider, Martha J. W. 96
Kreps, George 66
Krick, George 66
Kuenstler, A. 67
Kuhn, Magdalena 17
Kuntz, Henry 67
Jacob 67
Kurtz, Rev. Dr. 6, 7, 11, 13, 21, 26, 27, 37, 40, 52, 56, 61, 66, 79, 84, 85, 88, 98, 99, 114, 121

Lacey, John 67
Lacock, Cadet Dryden 67
Lafilly, Martha 13
Lafitte, John 67
Lalellmand, Gen. Charles 67
Gen. Henry 67
Lamar, John 90
Louisa 113
Col. William 113
Lamb, Rebecca 72
Lambert, J. B. 67
Lamborn, Daniel 67
Lammot, Daniel 67
Lammotte, Susan P. Beck 67
Lamotte, Daniel 67
Lamson, Henry 68
Lancaster, Rachel 9
Land, James 2
Landrom, Moses 67
Lane, John 67
Presley Carr 67
Thomas 67
Langley, Hezekiah 67
Capt. Philip 67
Lankford, Jesse 67
Lannay, Louisa 12
Lansdale, Mary 68
Large, James 68
Laroque, Francis 68
J. M. 68

Larrrabe, Daniel 104
Lasquar, John 68
Lastly, John 68
Latimer, [-?-] 131
James B. 68
Jane 87
Susan W. 73
Latour, J. 68
John 68
Lauderman, Susannah 11
Lauston, Rev. [-?-] 9
Lavall, Rodolphe 22
Lavely, Catherine 79
Margaret 79
Lavignac, [-?-] 129, 130
Lavilly, Martha 13).
Law, Eliza 97
Thomas 97
Lawrence, James 68
John M. 68
Lawrenson, Elizabeth [-?-] 68
Capt. James 68
Lawson, Diana [-?-] 68
Elizabeth [-?-] 68
Henry 68
Richard 68
Robert 68
Layman, Jacob 68
Layton, James 133
Leach, Eliza 46
Leaf, Rebecca 126
League, Nathaniel 68
Leahy, Morris 71
Leche, David 68
Lecouet, Thomas 68
Lecoumpt, Philip 68
Ledevidge, Mary 57
Leduc, Theresa 67
Lee, Charles 69
George S. 68
Harriet Ann 106
Maj. Henry 68
James H. 68
Mary Holliday 68
Richard Bland 132
Thomas Sim 69
William 68
Lieut. William Arthur 69
Leek, Cassandra Ann 7
LeFevre, John Brutus 69
Legg, Ann [-?-] 71

Index

Clarissa 120
Legrand, Elenor [-?-] 69
Capt. Samuel D. 69
Legrande, Ellen 56
S. D. 56
Lehmann, Godfrey Daniel 69
Leigh, Benjamin W. W. 132
Leman, Maria 6
Jacob 6
Lemaz, Jacob 6
Maria 6
Lemmon, Geo. 69
Rev. George 69
Moses 69
Richard 69
Dr. Robert 69
Lenox, James 69
Leonard, Elizabeth [-?-] 69
Joseph 69
Leoni, G. 133
Lerew, Abraham 69
Leroy, Alexandra 68
Lervingston, James 69
Lester, Achsah 69
Thomas 69
Lete, Mr. 69
Leuba, Pauline 17
Piere Henry 17
Levely, George 69
William 69
Levering, Aaron 131
Jane Wilson 77
John 131
Levy, Maria 70
Mary 70
Lewis, Maj. [-?-] 38
A. J. 70
Henry 100
J. 117
James 70
James B. 70
Jane 70
Mary Ann 100
Sidonia 117
Simeon H. 70
Liddle, Michael 70
Ligget, Jane 73
Thomas 43
Light, Jacob, 70
Lightner, Catherine M. 33
Deborah 21
Delilah 27

Nathaniel 33
Lily, James H. 70
Linch, Ann Nn 72
Lincoln, Francis 15
Lind, Rev. [-?-] 15
Linderman, John 70
Lindsey, Elizabeth 70
John 70
John G. 70
Lineberger, William 70
Ling, Catherine 10
Joseph 70
Linthicomb, Rev. [-?-] 29
Linthicum, Henrietta H. 85
Linton, Mary 49
Sarah 124
Linvill, James 70
Lipscomb, Overton P. 70
Little, Charles 70
Capt. George 70
Hannah [-?-] 70
James 70
Mary 42, 113
Capt. Thomas 71
William 71
Littlejohn, Dr. 103
Littles, William 131
Littleton, Eliza D. 88
. Thomas 71
Livingston, James 69
Lock, Ann 112
Lockerman, Elizabeth 76
Lodge, Emily M. 67
Logan, David 71
Mary Ann [-?-] 47
Neal 71
Sarah 71
William 71
Lohr, Mrs. 71
Loney, Amos 109
Long, Ann 24
Archibald 71
Eliza C. 33
Margaret 3
R. C. 24
Samuel 71
Longstreth, Esther 52
John 52
Loose, John 71
Lord, Joseph L. 71
Lorman, Wm. 45

Loudenslager, Eliza 124
Lough, John 71
Louis, Mary Ann 111
Love, Dr. John 71
Lovering, Francis 71
Low, H. P. 71
Rebecca [-?-] 71
Rev. 119
Lowe, James 71
John 71
Lowman, William G. 8
Lowry, Robert 71
Lowson, Diana 68
Lucas, Rev. Thomas 71
Luck, Rev. Mr. [-?-] 3, 86
Luneberg, John 71
Lunlay, John 71
Lusby, Ruth 63
William 77
Lyeth, Samuel 71
Lyles, Dennis 72
David C. 71
Lynch, Ellen 117
James 71
Pamela 4
Thomas 72
Lyon, Rev. Mr. [-?-] 72
Catherine H. 68
John 72
Mary [-?-] 72
Major Robert 68
Stephen 72
Lyons, Jeremiah 30
Mary [-?-] 72
Lysles, Dennis 72
Lytle, Thomas 72
Lyvet, Louis Hyppolite 72

M'Arthur, Arthur 72
M'Caffer, John 72
M'Carty. George 72
M'Cawley, Samuel 72
M'Clain, Ann 44
Margaret 15
James 59
M'Conkey, Mary 36
M'Cormick, Rev. [-?-] 124
M'Coy, Capt. John 73
M'Daniel, Walter 73
M'Donald, Isabella 73
M'Dougal. James 73

Index

M'Entire, John 73
M'Fadden, Capt.
  James 73
M'Fadon, Ann [-?-] 73
  Samuel 73
  William 73
M'Farland, Francis
  Frederick 73
  John 74
M'Ferlan, John 74
M'Gowan, Lieut.
  James 74
M'Gregor, [-?-] 20
  Gen. [-?-] 59
M'Guire, Rev. 18
M'Henry, Ann 75
M'Ilvain, Caroline 46
M'Intire, Hannah 124
  Sarah 21
M'Intosh, Samuel 74
M'Jimsey, W. 131
M'Kanna, Ann 20
M'Kay, Benjamin 74
  Mary 38
M'Kean, Sophia Dorothea 74
  Gov. Thomas 74
M'Kee, Cornelius 74
M'Keldin, Frances [-?-] 65
M'Kowan, James B. 101
M'Lanahan, James J. 74
M'Nantz, Charles 75
  Emily 75
M'Pherson, John 75
M'Remick, J. O. 75
Macarty, Charles 72
Maccubbin, Samuel 35, 93, 130
MacDonald, A. 45
Mace, Dr. Charles R. 75
  Elizabeth 119
MacGill, Thomas 75
Mackall, Barbara 105
Mackelfresh, John 75
Mackenheimer, John 75
Mackey, [-?-], 20
  Benjamin 75
  John 75
Macon, [-?-] 131
Mactier, Alexander 124
  Ann 118

Frances 124
Maddigain, Paul 75
Maddigan, Paul 75
Madelaine, Mary [-?-] 75
Magers, William 75
Magill, Basil 75
  Christiana [-?-] 75
  Samuel 75
  Thomas 75
Magness, Ann [-?-] 18
  James M. 75
Magnien, Col. Bernard 75
Magraw (Megraw), Rev. James 33, 118
Magruder, Dr. [-?-] 82
  Dennis 75
  Eliza M. 82
  Frances [-?-] 765
  Henry W. 75
  John M. 75
  Thomas W. 76
Maguire, Ann 10
Mahana, Rebecca 94
Mahanna, Thomas 76
Maher, Margaret 48
  Martin F. 18
Mailard, Elizabeth 90
Maitland, Alexander 76
  Elizabeth 43
Mallory, Carlos L. 76
  Capt. John 76
  Nathaniel F. 76
Mandeville, [-?-] 100
Mangels, John 76
Manigault, Major G. H. 76
Mann, Rev. [-?-] 25
  Catherine Keene 76
  James 76
  Margaret 13
Mannery, [-?-], 76
Manning, Dennis 76
Maranna, Thomas 76
March, Eliza 85
Marcher, George H. 76
Marean, Thomas 76
Marechal, Archbishop 23, 35, 52, 67
Maris, George 5, 76
  Sarah Ann 5
Marking, Elizabeth 46
Markland, Henrietta 15

James 76
Markland, Rev. 22, 33
Marks, William 27
Marple, Abel 123
Marr, William 76
Marrast, Dr. John 76
Marriott, Ann [-?-] 63
  Joshua 76
  Lemuel H. 76
  Thomas 76
Marrow, Isaac 76
Marsh, G. 76
Marshall, Elizabeth 54
  John 76
  Mary 91
  Sarah B. 8
  Dr. William 76
Marston, Major M. 72, 75, 109
Martin, Rev. [-?-] 46
  Jacob 76
  James 77, 83
  John S. 119
  Dr. Samuel B. 24
  Sarah 125
  Simeon 77
  Susan 1
  Thomas 77
Martindale, Rev. [-?-] 84
Mask, Isaac Green 77
Mason, Gen Armistead T. 77
  George 77
  Gen. John 60, 133
  Joseph 77
  Leeanah 6
  Mary 1
  Sarah Ann 62
  Thomson 77
Massey, Elizabeth H. 77
  Joseph 77
Mathews, John 10
Matthes, Priscilla 77
Matthews, Rev. Mr. [-?-] 47, 70, 118
  John 35, 77
  Leonard 77
  Mary 34
  Milcah 118
  Samuel 14
  Samuel P. 77
  Sarah [-?-] 77
  Sophia 14
  William 77

174

Index

Mattison, Daniel Jones 77
  James 77
  S. [-?-] 77
  Sarah [-?-] 77
  William 77
Mauer, John Peter 27
Maul, Susan 34
Maund, Harriet Lucy 77
  John J. 77
  Julia C. 78
Maurer, Caroline 27
  John Peter 38
  Margaretta 38
Maurice, Capt. Theodore W. 78
Maury, Ann R. McCarty 68
  Eliza 78
  Fontaine 68, 78
  Lieut. John M. 78
Maxfield, John 94
Maxwell, Eliza 19
  James 94
  John 14
  Rachel 126
May, Jane 12
Maydwell, James 78
Mayer, Charles F. 78
  Lewis 78
Mayo, Col. [-?-] 100
  Maria D. 100
McAllister, Richard 72
McCall, Nancy 27
McCarty, Ann R. 68
McCausland, Augusta
  Caroline 35
  Alexander 34
  Margaret 34
McCleary, Henry 72
McCleish, Archibald 72
McClelland, Eliza 38
McClennan, Eliza 38
McClish, William 72
McColley, Zedekiah Fletcher 72
McCollister, Rev. 117
  Charity 72
  Clemence 2
  Sarah 1
  Sophia 85
McCombs, John 72
McConkey, James 72
  William 72

McConnell, Priscilla [-?-] 72
McCorkhill, James Douglas 72
McCorkle, William 101
McCormick, Rev. Mr. [-?-] 9, 87, 97, 101
  James 72, 73
  Jane [-?-] 73
  Martha [-?-] 57
  William 73
McCornisky, Mary 73
McCoy, Henry 73, 117
  Isaac 73
  James 73
  Rebecca Maria 117
  Sarah Matilda 8
McCrellen, Effy 61
McCristie, John 73
  Mary [-?-] 73
McCubbin, [-?-] 27
  Moses 73
  William 73
  William H. 73
McCulloh, Dr. James H. 73
McDaniel, Mary Ann 85
McDermett, Grace [-?-] 54
  Elizabeth 114
McDonald, Eliza 73
  Marie 40
McDonaugh, John 73
McDowell, Hamilton 33
McElderry, Elizabeth [-?-] 73
  James 73
  Thomas 73
McFadon, Edward 73
McFerran, John 74
McGay, John 74
McHaffie, James 74
McHenry, Dennis 74
  Francis D. 74
McIlhenny, Louisa 65
McIntosh, Catherine A. 98
  Eliza B. 23
  J. H. 23, 98
McJilton, Rev. [-?-] 58, 124
McKean, Samuel M. 74

McKee, Letitia
McKeldin, Frances [-?-] 65
McKenney, [-?-] 133
McKenzie, Edward K. 74
McKim, John 74
  Mary 13
  Robert 74
McKinley, Isaac 15
  John 74
McKinnen, Mary 15
McKowan, James B. 74
McLanahan, Isabella 15
  John 15
McLaughlin, Ann [-?-] 83
  Mary [-?-] 74
  Peter 74
McLean, Adam 74
  Demarius 74
  John 74
McM'Kirk, Bridget [-?-] 47
McMackan, Alexander 57
McMackin, Silas 75
McMackon, Alexander, 39
McMullen, John 9
  Margaretta 9
McNeal, John 75
McNulty, John 75
McPherson, Henrietta 30
McReding, Edward 75
  Margaret Otheman 75
Meade, Capt. Joseph 78
  Rev. William 63
Mearess, Jacob 78
Mecleve, Elizabeth 62
Medcalf, Abraham 78
  Jemima [-?-] 78
Medcalfe, Catherine 95
Medford, Jane 44
Meech, J. B. 78
Meeks, James C. 78
Meetch, Daniel 78
Megrew. See Magraw.
Meigs, Josiah 9
  Samuel 78

Index

Melish, John 78
Mellen, Henry Orlando 78
Melvin, James 78
Menzies, James 78
Mercer, Elizabeth [-?-] 78
  James 78
  John 78
  Col. John 78
  Sally 78
Merchant, Sarah 89
Meredith, Samuel 79
Merke, Julia Ann 10
Merrick, Mary 79
Merritt, Sarah V. 27
Merryman, Ann 16
  Ann [-?-] 79
  Caleb 16
Merryman, Elizabeth 45
  Job 79
  John 45, 79
  John B. 79
  Dr. Moses 79
Merts, Rev. Mr. [-?-] 41, 107
Messersmith, [-?-] 93
Mettee, Martin 79
Meyer, Capt. James 79
  John James 79
Meyers, Christian 79
  Capt. Daniel 79
  Jacob 79
Michael, Jacob 16
Michel, Mary 104
Mick, Charles 79
Middleton, Dr. [-?-] 9
  Gilbert 79
  Hon. H. 47
  Dr. James 79
  Mary Elizabeth [-?-] 79
Mifflin, Gen. 48
Milborn, York 79
Mileron, Jacob 79
Miles, Margaret 69
  Susan E. 57
Millar, Horatio S. 79
Milledollar, Rev. Dr. 11
Miller, Adeline F. 79
  Alexander 79
  Ann T. 47
  Christopher 38, 40
  Eliza 109
  Francis 80
  George 79
  Henry D. 79
  Howard 59
  Laura 79
  Lewis 70
  Louisa 79
  Mary 58
  Capt. Michael 79
  Peter 79
  Phebe [-?-] 79
  Philey 80
  Reuben C. 80
  Capt. Robert 80
  Ruth [-?-] 80
  Sarah 83
  Susan 80
  Wm. P. 80
Milleron, Jacob 80
Millet, Charles 80
Milliard, Ann 33
Milliron, Jacob 80
Mills, Benjamin 80
  Henry 80
  Capt. James 80
Mines, Rev. Mr. [-?-] 101
Minicks, John 80
Minor, Frances 21
  Maj. Stephen 21
Minskey, Samuel 80
Mitchel, Edward 80
Mitchell, Abner 132
  Alexander 80
  Ann 16, 18
  Maj.-Gen. David 80
  John 80
  Capt. John 18
  Capt. John I. 80
  Margaret [-?-] 80
  Mary 104
  Mary Ann [-?-] 80
  Precilla 80
Moale, Deborah Owings 59
  Martha 113
  Mary 29
  Thomas 59
Moffett, James 80
Moffit, John 80
Mohler, Peter 80
Moke, Keturah 68
Molleston, Del. Henry 80
Mollihorn, Sarah [-?-] 62
Mondel, William 81
Monjef, Samuel 81
Monk, Lieut. James 81
Monks, Francis E. 81
Monro, Dr. George 81
Monroe, Elizabeth 21
  John 21
Montgomery, Rev. Mr. [-?-] 47, 58
  James 81
  Jane 102
  Joseph 121
  Margaret Blanchard 121
  Robert 35
Moodie, Louisa 41
Moody, Mrs. 99
Moore, Rev. Mr. [-?-] 51, 53, 60, 72
  Rev. Bishop [-?-] 35
  Aaron 81
  Ann Giles 48
  Eliza W. 74
  George 81
  Jason 50, 60, 67, 81
  John 81
  Maria 3
  Mary Ann 31
  Mary B. 72
  Philip 48
  Rev. Mark 79
  Robert Scott 81
  Col.. Samuel 81
  William P. 81
Moran, Gabriel 81
  Jane 52
  Thomas 81
  William 81
Moranville, Rev. 3, 21, 28, 31, 46, 48, 57, 62, 66, 70, 80, 91, 98, 106, 107
Moranvilliers, Rev. Mr. [-?-] 40
More, Rev. Mr. [-?-] 46
Morehead, Lewis 81
Moren, Jane 52
Morgan, Augusta 81
  John 81
  Robert 81
  Robert C. 81
  Sarah Ann 81
  Thomas 129
Mork, Lieut. James 81
Morland, Elisha 81

Index

Morris, Alice 17
  Catherine 40
  John B. 82
  Sarah 11
  Sarah S. 115
  Thomas 115
Morrison, Ann [-?-] 82
  David 82
  John 82
  Magaretta 56
  Murdoch 82
Morrow, Mary 117
Morse, Rev. [-?-] 87
Morsel, Tabitha 72
Morton, John A. 82
  Samuel 7
  Susan R. 7
Mory, Capt. Lewis 82
Mosart, John G. 82
Moses, James 82
Mosher, Ann 76
  James 59, 82
  William 82
Mottu, Francis 45
Mountgarret, Thomas 82
Mull, Jacob 82
Mullan, Sarah K. 14
Mullen, [-?-] 41
  Henry 82
Muller, George Henry 82
  Capt. Otto 82
  Theresa Muller 82
Mullikin, Baruch 82
  Basil D. 82
  Belt 82
  Edward 82
  Eliza [-?-] 26
  Henrietta B. 54
  Richard D. 82
Mumma, Sarah 97
Mummey, Joshua 82
  Samuel 82
Muncaster, Sarah 15
Munn, Ann 82
  Rev. Benj. 118
  Eliza 118
  Lindsey 82
Munro, Catherine [-?-] 82
  Robert 82, 83
Munroe, George Marshall 83
  John 83
  Nathaniel 83

Murdoch, George W. 83
  Lavinia 83
  Patrick 83
Murdock, James 83
  Mary Theresa 24
Murduck, James 83
Murphey, Terry 83
Murphy, Adeline 61
  Benjamin 83
  Capt. Isaac 83
  John 83
  Mary [-?-] 83
  Mary Ann 34
  Patrick 83
Murray, Comm. Alexander 112
  Ann 115
  Elizabeth 83, 112
  James 83
  Samuel 83
  Sarah L. 50
  Capt. Thomas Gist. 82
Musgrove, Major [-?-] 35
  Eliza 35
Musket, John 83
Myer, Rev. [-?-] 99
  Thomas 83
Myers, Christopher 83
  Henry 46
  Jacob 21, 121
  Matilda 70
  Capt. Nicholas 70
  Rebecca 21
  William 62

Nabb, John 83
Nagle, David 83
  Henry 83
Nancarrow, John 84
Nantz, John 84
  Capt. John 84
  Sarah [-?-] 84
Nathanham, George 84
Nathstine, Leonard 84
Neal, Rev. Abner 102, 113
Neale, [-?-] 130
  Most Rev. Leonard 11, 14, 84
Needles, Sarah 66
Neely, John 84
Neely, Susanna [-?-] 84

Negley, Barbary 76
Neighbours, Sarah 2
Neill, Rev. Dr. [-?-] 9
  Hugh 84
Neilson, James 84
  Nathaniel 84
Nelson, Jacob 84
  James 84
  Chancellor Robert 84
  Susan 88
  Thomas 84
Neltner, John 84
Neppard, Catherine 13
Nes, Samuel 84
Nesbit, Moses 84
  Wilson 84
Nester, Major Peter 84
Neville, Rebecca 59
  Samuel 84
Nevitt, Teresa C. 121
Nevulle, Hyde de 3
Newell, John 84
Newman, Col. Francis 85
  George 85
  Margaret 103
Newnam, Joseph 85
Newton, Nimrod 86
Nichols, Ann 91
  Eliza 114
  Lieut. W. H. 39
Nicholson, Joseph Hopper 85
  Margaret 16
  P. 132
  Rebecca S. 85
  Sally 81
Nickerson, Elizabeth [-?-] 82
  Capt. Lewis 82
Nickson, Edward 85
Nicodemus, John 85
Nicol, William H. 85
Nicolls, Lloyd 131
Nicols, Charlotte 88
  Hugh 85
  James 88
  Samuel 85
Niles, H. 98
Nimmo, William R. 85
Noble, Alexander 85
Nones, Solomon B. 85
Norris, Bazil 85
  Edward 85
  Eliza [-?-] 85

Index

John 85
Julian 102
Rev. Oliver 105
S. C. 85
William 85, 131, 132
Norton, Mary 53
Norton, Stephen 85
Norwood, Col. Edward 126
John 85
Maria 107
Mary F. 126
Thomas 85
Nowland, John C. 85
Noyes, John P. 86
Nuttall, Christopher 86

O'Bryan, Maryha 34
Ocherman, John 86
O'Connor, Honora [-?-] 86
James 86
Dr. John 86
O'Donald, Elizabeth [-?-] 106
O'Donnell, Eliza W. 38
John 38, 73
Oerstedt, Capt. John 86
Ogden, Amos 86
Col. John Wesley 86
Nancy 86
Sarah 121
Ogilvie, James 86
Ogle, John 86
O'Hare, Hannah 22
Okely, John 86
Oldfield, Granville S. 86
Olems, Thomas 86
Oliver, Isabella 53
Omestiller, Ann Catherine 2
Onderburg, Adrian 86
O'Neale, Capt. Henry 86
Onion, Elizabeth 83
Onis, Chevalier de 86
Onis, Dona Frederica de Merklein y 86
Orem, Rev. [-?-] 87
Thomas 86
William 86
Orrell, Rev. [-?-] 38
Orthoff, Andrew 87

Osburn, Elizabeth [-?-] 72
William 87
Osgood, Rev. Samuel 32
Otheman, Anthony 75, 93
Ourstler, Sarah 70
Overfeld, Martin 87
Owen, Kennedy 87
Owens, Edward 87
Isaac 87
Owings, Caleb 74
Deborah 59
Fanny T. D. 111
Jesse 87
Milcah 74
Richard 87

Page, Jno. 21
Mary Ann 63
William Byrd 63
Pain, Nathaniel 87
Palmer, A. R. 87
Elizabeth 56
Pamelee, Pvt. John 88
Pampilion, William J. 87
Pardy, Elizabeth 33
Pareniere, Joanna 4
Parham, Hannah [-?-] 87
John 87
Parish, John 87
Mark 87
Parisot, John B. 87
Park, Mungo 87
Parker, Rev. [-?-] 27
Ann S. 78
Charles 87
Brig.-Gen. Daniel 87
Ezra 87
John 87
Peter 87
William 87
Parks, Julia Ann 119
Parks, Rev. Maybury (or Mayberry) 2, 26, 35, 37, 45, 55, 63, 72, 84, 89, 99, 114, 116, 118
Sarah 35
Parrish, Margaret 27
Parrott, Eliza [-?-] 88
James 88
Joseph 88

Rebecca 25
Parry, Eliza Ann 101
Parsons, John D. 88
Pascault, Francis 88
Paterson, William 93
Patterson, [-?-] 88
Adolphus 88
Averilla [-?-] 88
James 88
John 88
Joseph W. 88
Keziah 56
Pattinson, Jane 78
William 78
Pattison, [-?-] 88
Jacob 130
Paxton, Rev. William 74
Payson, [-?-] 93
Henry 45
John 88
Peak, Cecelia 106
Pearce, Rachel 41
Sarah S. 107
Thomas 88
William 88
Wm. W. 88
Pearse, Mary 92
Pease, Seth 88
Pechin, Adeline 123
W. 132
Maj. William 123
Peck, Elizabeth 118
I. 88
John 88
John S. 88
Mary 104
Pendegrass, Margaret 124
Mary 39
Pendle, [-?-], 132
Pendleton, Daniel 88, 129
Joseph Jenkins 88
Penhallow, John 52
Sarah Ann 52
Pennington, Capt. Charles 88
William 88
Pennock, Lewis 89
Penquite, Mary [-?-] 89
William 89
Pentland, Brevet Major John 89

178

Index

Peoples, Walter Thomas 89
Peregay. See Peregoy.
Peregoy, Caleb 89
  Charles 89, 92
  Capt. Joseph 89
  Robert 89
  Ruth 89
Peren, John 89
Perine, Ann 21
  David M. 89
  William 21
Perkins, Benjamin 89
  Daniel 89
  Maria 91
  Thomas 89
Perrigo. See Peregoy.
Perry, Elizabeth 54
  Erasmus 54
Peterkin, Sarah Jane 89
Peters, Clarissa 121
Peterson, John 89
  Margaret 89
Pettecord, John 89
Pettigill, John 89
Peyton, John S. 89
Pfeiffer, Henry H. 89
  Margaret 89
Phelan, Elizabeth 89
Phelps, Ann 63
Phillips, Ann 101
  Bathia [-?-] 89
  Isaac 90
  James 89
  John 90
  Sarah 44
  William 90
Phinney, Rev. 99
Phinnezy, Mary H. 35
Pic, Francis 90
Pickard, Eliza 121
Pickersgill, Caroline 92
Pickett, Ann [-?-] 90
  George 90
Pidgeon, Christopher 90
Pierce, Ann Maria 125
  Caroline 90
  Israel 90
Pierpoint, Amos 90
  Julian 35
  Samuel 90
  Thomas 90

Pigman, H. S. 125, 126
Pilch, Eliza Josephine 28, 66
Pilchard, Elizabeth 73
Pilmore, Rev. Dr. 1
Pindell, John 90
Pinnell, F. A. 90
Pitman, Rev. Hipkins 90
Pitt, Rebecca 21
Pizany, Francis 43, 90
Placide, Louisa [-?-] 90
  Louise [-?-] 90
Plains, George 90
Plater, Judge [-?-] 90
  Ann Elizabeth 90
  John Rousby 90
Pleasants, Elizabeth R. 17
  James 90, 91
  John 90
  Joseph P. 90
  Priscilla Lamar 90
  Ruth 47
  Susannah 90
  Thomas 90, 91
  William 90
  Yate 90
Pochon, Charles F. 91
  Harriet [-?-] 90
Poe, Maria 22
Pogue, John G. 91
Points, Harriot 40
Polk, Rebecca [-?-] 29
Pollard, Eliza 68
  Sarah 35
Polley, Henry 91
Pollock, John 91
Pool, Rezin 92, 99, 132
Poole, Edward 91
Poor, Moses 91
Pope, Abner 91
  Joseph 91
Popp, Chas. F. 111
Porter, David 133
  John 91
  Brig.-Gen. Moses 3
Postetru, Catherine 41
Poteet, Keziah 105
  Rev. Thomas 92
Potter, Stephen 91
  Thomas 91
Potts, William 91

Dr. William 91
Pouder, George 91
Mary Fowble 91
Poultney, Elizabeth 68
  Thomas 68
Powell, Albina 66
  Rebecca E. 28
  Thomas 91
Power, Eliza [-?-] 91
  James, 120
  Michael 91
Powers, Richard 91
Powley, George 91
Pratt, James 82
  Capt. James 12, 44, 50, 65, 66, 92, 104, 110
  Susan T. 78
Presbury, George 91
  James G. L. 81
Prestman, George 91
Preston, Benjamin B. 92
  Letitia 92
  William 92
Prevator, Annette 98
Prevost, Col. Andrew M. 92
Price, Andrew 92
  Ann 104
  Rev. Jonathan 92
  Nehemiah 92
  Thomas 92
  William 92
Pringle, Mark 92
Prints, Isabella 90
Pritchard, Charles 18
Pritchett, Caroline 54
  Rebecca 41
Proctor, Elizabeth 69
  Mary 5
Proebsting, Frances [-?-] 92
  Theodore C. 92
Pullen, Robert 92
Pullin, Everet R. 92
Pumphrey, Sarah 102
Purdon, Joseph 92
Purdy, John 92
  Susannah 2
Purviance, John 43
Pusey, Clary 23
Putnam, Rev. Mr. 52

Queen, Catherine Francis 11

Index

Quigley, James 92
Quillon, Ellen M. [-?-] 96
Quinlan, Marcus 92
Quinn, Edward 42, 92
   Thomas 92

Rabb, Leonora 95, 98
Raborg, Catherine [-?-] 93
   Christopher 93
   George W. 93
   George William 93
   John Henry 93
Ramsay, Ann 21
   David 93
   Mary Jane 93
   Thomas 93
Ramsey, Col. Nathaniel 93
Randall, John 93
   Jonathan 93
Randolph, William Elston 93
Rankin, Henry 93
   Mary 25
Ransell, [-?-] 97
Ranton, Eliza [-?-] 96
Rasin, Capt. Samuel 93
   Capt. Thomas 93
Ratcliff, Mary 25
Ratcliffe, Mary 40
Ratien, Amelia 121
   Richard 6
   Sophia 6
Rawlings, Ann 111
   Catherine 111
   Elizabeth [-?-] 84
   Gassaway 35, 93 130
   Stephen 93
Rawson, F. 93
Ray, Miles 93
Read, Rev. [-?-] 9
   William 93
Reade, Elizabeth 114
Reardon, Thomas 93
Reauzamy, Rose 34
Redgrave, John 93
Reding, Edward M. 93
   Margaret Otheman 93
Redman, Catherine Ann 70

Reed, Rev. Mr. [-?-] 112, 116
   Eleanor [-?-] 69
   Elizabeth 120
   Capt. James 94
   Rev. James 55
   John 94
   Rev. Nelson 106
Reeder, Thomas 1
Reese, Rev. D. E. 4, 5, 11, 12, 13, 15, 17, 18, 19, 20, 21, 22, 24, 25, 27, 29, 33, 39, 40, 41, 43, 45, 46, 47, 50, 52, 53, 54, 56, 59, 63, 66, 69, 70, 75, 76, 81, 82, 83, 84, 85, 89, 90, 91, 95, 105, 106, 107, 113, 115, 117, 118, 121, 127
   Eleanor 106
Reeves, John 94
Regester, Samuel 94
Reid, Rev. Nelson 21, 95, 110
Reifsnider, Elizabeth 15
Reily, Catherine 23
   Clagon 94
   Rev. J. R. 1, 23, 51
Reinhart, Elizabeth 66
Reis, Rev. E. J. 7, 13, 16, 28, 35, 41, 44, 57, 65, 77, 88, 114, 115. 124
Reise, Rev. [-?-] 17
Reise, Rev. D. E. See Reese, Rev. D. E
Relf, Samuel 94
Rennalds, Caesar 94
Rennell, John N. 94
Rennells, John N. 94
Rennous, John 94
Renshaw, Thomas 94
Reteu, William 94
Revell, John 94
Reynolds, Rev. [-?-] 57
   Adelia 55
   Elisha 94
   Elisha 94
   Elizabeth 94
   Elizabeth [-?-] 94
   Henry 94

   Immer 94
   Jesse 35, 94
   John 94
   Dr. John 94
   John Brown 94
   John Fough 94
   Leonard 94
   Levi 94
   Lydia [-?-] 94
   Mary 94
   Olivia 94
   Samuel Johnson 94
   Sarah 94
   Sarah [-?-] 94
   Susanna [-?-] 94
   William 94
Rhoday, Ann 116
Rhode, Catherine 89
   Zachariah 95
Ricaud, Annette 13
   Thomas P. 95
Rice, Ann 77
   John 95
   Lewis 95
Richard, Augusta 80
Richards, Rev. [-?-] 21, 22, 25, 35, 52, 56, 76, 84, 96, 99, 121, 124, 127
   John A. 95
   Rebecca 109
   Timothy 70
   William 95
Richardson, Rev. Benjamin 2, 118
   Dr. Charles 95
   Daniel P. 95
   Eliza 47
   J. D. 29
   James 95
   Rebecca 17
   Ricey [-?-] 95
   Major Samuel 95
Richmond, Hannah 5
   James C. 95
Rico, Lewis 95
Riddle, Capt. Edward 95
Rider, Edward 95
   Frederick 95
   Margaret 76
Ridgaway, James 95
   William C. 95
Ridgely, Gov. [-?-] 95
   Charles 95

Index

Col. Charles Sterrett 85
David 95
Elizabeth [-?-] 78
Emily Caroline 55
Rev. Greenbury 95
Judge Henry 55
John 95
John W. 95
N. H. 96
Richard 95
Riggs, Eliza [-?-] 96
George W. 96
Riley, Major Gen. [-?-] 85
Elizabeth 35
Mary [-?-] 124
Michael 96
Rilke, Ellen 107
Rind, William Alexander 96
Rine, Susan 74
Ringgold, Alphonza 23
Ann 83
James W. 96
Jane 12
Maria Virginia 5
Tench 5
Ringler, George 96
Rinker, Susan 75
Riston, Abraham 96
Jesse 96
John 96
Sarah 68
Ritchie, Abner 96
Frances [-?-] 96
Roach, Ann [-?-] 80
John 96
Roache, Mary 28
Robbins, Rev. [-?-] 76
Eliza 96
James B. 96
John L. 96
Roberdeau, Catherine 121
Roberts, Rev. Dr. [-?-] 2, 5, 6, 7, 8, 9, 11, 12, 15, 19, 25, 27, 30, 34, 35, 41, 48, 50, 51, 53. 53, 56, 57, 61, 66, 70, 71, 72, 73, 74, 77, 81, 83, 89, 92, 93, 97, 98, 99, 102, 103, 104, 105, 106,
109, 110, 111, 112, 113, 114, 119, 120, 124
Ann 58
Eliza Ann 38
Elizabeth 84, 118
Rev. George 55, 66, 79, 96
John 132
Capt. John 96
Jonah 96
Joseph 96
Kesiah 47
Keziah, 27
Matilda 125
Michael 125
Priscilla 117
Robertson, George 96
John 96
John Alexander 96
Samuel 8
Robeson, Capt. William [L.?] 96
Robey, Townley 96
Robins, Elizabeth [-?-] 96
Robinson, Alexander 96, 112
Aley 6
Angelica 112
Charlotte 96
Elijah 96
Elizabeth 120
James S. 96
Joseph 131
Joshua D. 96
Luke 131
Sarah 113
Robison, Jesse 96
Roche, John 97
Rockhold, Rev. 54
Rodney, Caesar A. 97
John 97
Roe, Catherine 18
Rogers [-?-] 56
Jacob 96
Lloyd N. 97
Mary 96
Philip 97
Rebecca [-?-] 97
William 97
William C. 97
Wm. 88
Rogge, Charles 97
Roiston, Robert 97
Rollins, Catherine 45
Roney, [-?-] 87
Roof, Catherine 118
Rook, John A. 97
Rooker, James C. 97
Rev. James 97
Root, Sarah 113
Root, William 97
Rose, Ann 25
Catherine 60
Emily 77
Harriet 70
Mary [-?-] 60
Rosensteel, Henry 97
Ross, David 97
Elizabeth [-?-] 97
Capt. John 10
Mary 10
Sandy 97
William 97
Rossell, Rev. Stephen (or Steven) G. 17, 45, 61, 63, 72, 76. 78, 98, 109, 110, 112, 114, 126, 127
Roszel. See Rossel
Rothrock, Jacob 97
Capt. John 63
Rowan, George H. 97
Rowe, Elizabeth [-?-] 97
Elizabeth Ann 97
Capt. John K. 97
Rowles, William 97
Rozel. See Rossell.
Rozenberry, Peter 98
Rozzell. See Rossell.
Rubenthal, John 98
Ruckle, Samuel 98
William 98
Rudenstein, John M. 11
Rudulph, Tobias 79
Rudulph, Zebulon 98
Runnels, Caesar 94
Rush, Catherine [-?-] 98
Russell, Alexander 98
Maj. Benjamin 15
Philip 98
Thomas 126
William 98
William M. 98
Ruth, Catherine Overe 41
Rebecca 84
Rutter, Rev. [-?-] 18

Index

Julian 127
Mary 41
Sarah 30
Thomas 98
Ryan, Amos 101
James 98
Ryder, Frederick 98
Ryland, Rev. [-?-] 124
Margaret 97
Rynd, Bryan 98
Christopher 98

Sadler, Henry 98
Thomas 98
Salenave, James 98
Salges. See Salgues.
Salgues (Salges), John J. 98
John B. 98
Salmon, Valentine 98
Sambourn, Ann 42
Sanders, Benedict I. 99
Maria Louise 3
Sanderson, Joseph M. 99, 118
Sands, H. N. 132
Samuel 99
Sanfer, John 99
Sangston, Eliza 19
Sank, Margaret Ann 32
Sankey, William 99
Sargent, Samuel 99
Saubere, Samuel 99
Saunders, Robert B. 99
Samuel 99
Sauner, John G. 99
Savage, Mrs. [-?-] 99
George 100
John 99
P. 99
Patrick 99
Sayer, Stephen 99
Scaplander, Sarah [-?-] 8
Schaeffer, Rev. Dr. 60, 104
C. A. 99
George B. 99
Jesse 18
Schianeman, Catherine 76
Schleicker, Hannah [-?-] 40
Schley, David 99
Henry 99

Jacob 99
Schliecker, Peter Jasper 99
Schnebley, Margaret 64
Schorr, Sarah 99
Schraer, Louis 99
Schulte, J. E. C. 99
Schultz, Conrad 132
Schultze, J. E. C. 99
Schumacher, Maurice 100
Schunck, John 100
Schwartz, Conrad 100
Schwartzaur, Philip 100
Schwartze, August J. 100
Schwarz, J. E. 100
Schweitzer, Michael 100
Scott, Elizabeth 100
Scott, David 100
Edward 14
Henrietta 95
Henry 100
John 100
Dr. John 100
Louisa [-?-] 100
Margaret [-?-] 100
Lieut. R. I. 100
Sabrett 100
Samuel 100
William 100
Gen. Winfield 100
Scrooby, Amos 101
Scrote, Mathias 101
Scudder, Sarah 113
Seales, Thomas 6, 131
Searl, James 101
Sears, James F. 101
Richard 101
Seaton, Elzie W. 72
Seavers, Christiene 101
Seche, Joseph 101
Sedden, Thomas 101
Sedwic, Caroline Eliza 81
John 91
Seed, Capt. James 101
Seegar, Thomas 101
Seguin, Claude 101
P. 129
Seixas, Rev. L. B. 23
Sellers, Charlotte 28

Sellman, [-?-] 62
John C. 101
Johnzee 101
Jonathan 101
Maria 95
Vachel 101
Seltzer, Adam 22
Catherine 43
Mary 84, 89
Semms, Benjamin 96
Harriet 96
Sergeant, Alling 101
Private William 101
Servant, Lieut.-Col. Richard B. 101
Seth, John 101
Seton, John 101
Sewell, Rev. Mr. [-?-] 95
Ann 112
Benjamin 101
Charles S. 74
George 101
Henry 110
James H. 101
William E. 112
Seymour, Sally [-?-] 101
Shade, Philip 101
Rebecca 112
Shamberg, John 102
Shane, Rev. [-?-] 41, 62, 68, 101, 127
Mary 30
Sarah 35
Sharpless, Priscilla 32
Sharpley, Rev. John 26
Shaw, [-?-] 51
Eliza 38
Elizabeth 47
Commodore John 47
Lieut. John A. 102
Joshua 102
Mary [-?-] 102
Rev. Neale H. 7
Polly 121, 124
William C. 102
Shawen, Ann 88
David 102
Shawler, Eliza [-?-] 100
Sheaffer, Rev. Mr. [-?-] 79
Shed. Capt. James 102
Sheetz, John 102

Index

Sheffield, William
  Robinson 102
Shellman, William 102
Shelton, Dr. 6
  Cornelia 6
Sheppard, Elizabeth 82
  Col. Thomas 82
Sheridan, Abraham 100
  Catherine 100
  Elizabeth 75
Sherlock, John 102
  Louis, 102
  Louisa 102
Shields, James 102
Shilliber, Jonathan 102
Shilling, Henry 102
Shipley, Joseph 102
  Richard 102
Shoemaker, David 102
  Maurice 38
  Samuel E. 102
Shorb, Frances 27
Short, Tom 102
Shortt, John 102, 131
  Mary Ann 79
Shrim, Capt. John 102
Sickles, Rev. Jacob 31
Sides, Catherine 50
Sigler, Rev. [-?-] 68
  Jacob 58
Silverthorn, Henry 102
Simco, Harriet 118
Simes, Harriet 118
Simkins, Eli 102
Simmonds, Elizabeth 75
Simmons, Ann 106
  Catherine 54
  Col. Charles 103
Simms, Joseph 103
  Massey 103
Simons, Ebenezer 103
Sims, Joseph 103
  Robert 103
Sinclair, Rev. Dr. 102
Singleton, Thomas S. 103
Sinners, Elijah R. 125
  Mary [-?-] 103
Sinsner, Jesse, 103
Sitzler, Suzanne H. 45
Skelton, John 103
  Mary [-?-] 94
Skenett, Ruth 103
Skerrett, Mrs. [-?-] 103

Skinner, Andrew 129
  Frederick 103
  Dr. Henry 103
  Zebulon 103
Skipper, David 103
  Thomas 15
Slaytor, John 103
Slemmons, Rev. 2
Sleppy, Jacob 61
  Sarah Lee 61
Sligh, Thomas 35
Sloan, James 103
  William 103
  William J, 103
Sloey, Thomas 103
Small, Elizabeth 84
Smart, [-?-] 97
Smiley, John 103
Smith, [-?-] 115
  Rev. [-?-] 24, 43, 95
  Adam 105
  Ann 103
  Ann P. 67
  Dr. Anthony W. 104
  Rev. Armistead 104
  Caleb 104
  Capt. Charles Henry 104
  Catherine 63
  Daniel 104
  Elie 104
  Eliza 114
  Elizabeth 85, 104, 116
  Elizabeth [-?-] 104
  Ferdinand 104
  George 104
  George C. 63
  Harriet [-?-] 104
  Henry 104
  Jacob 104
  James 104, 111
  Rev. James 16, 33, 45, 118
  James V. 104
  Job 55
  John 101, 104
  Capt. John 104
  Corporal John 104
  Joseph 104
  Capt. Joseph 104, 105
  Juliana 95
  Madison 105
  Margaret 102, 114
  Martha Taylor 111

  Mary 55, 101, 105
  Miranda [-?-] 105
  Polly [-?-] 105
  Robert 67
  Robert S. 105
  Samuel 105
  Gen. Samuel 103
  Samuel H. 119
  Samuel R. 95
  Capt. Shipley Francis 105
  Thomas 105
  W. D. 105
  Walter 105
  William 105
  Col. William 105
  Col. William B. 105
  William M. 105
  Major Wm. R. 105
  Winston D. 105
Smoot, James H. 105
Smother, Daniel 105, 106
Smothers, Mrs. [-?-] 110
  Daniel, 24
Smyth, Dr. James 105
Sneathen, Rev. 47
Snow, Eliza 19
  Lucina E. 91
  William 109
Snowden, Eliza [-?-] 105
  Richard 105
Snyder, Harriet 48
  Rev. John 43, 55
  Peter 126
  Philip Frederick Antes 106
  Simon 106
Solomon, William 106
Soper, James P. 25
Sourhoof, G. 106
Southcomb, Cary 106
Spain, Pes 132
Spalding, Thomas 106
Sparks, Rev. [-?-] 88, 94
  Richard 105, 106
Sparr, Elizabeth 120
Spear, John 106
  Mary 66
  William 1067
Spears, Catherine 62
Speck, William A. 106
Spedden, Edward 106

Index

Lieut. R. 106
Spencer, Elizabeth
   [-?-] 106
   Richard 106
   Robert 106
Sperry, John 106
Spicer, Rebecca 110
Spicknall, Charles M. 106
Spickner, Nicholas 106
Spilman, Thomas F. 106
Sponsler, Joseph 106
Sprigg, Maria 94
   Gov. Samuel 56
Spurrier, James 106
Stables, Amelia C. 4
Stacey, George 72
   Hannah 52
   Melinda 23
Stambaugh, S. C. 106
Stammen, Ulrick B. 106
Standiford, Elizabeth 58
Standley, George 106
Stanes, John 1067
Stanly, Ann E. G. 95
   Capt. Robert 95
Stansbury, Rev. Mr. [-?-] 69
   Catherine 43
   Elijah 107
   Ellen Kent 107
   Capt. James 107
   John 107
   John E. 107, 117
   Levey 130
   Levi 35, 130
   Mary F. 60
   Nicholas 107
   Capt. Robert D. 107
   Ruth E. 117
   Gen. T. E. 31
   Tobias E. 104
   William 107
   William S. 107
   Winifred 107
Stansfield, Louisa Charlotte 104
Stapleton, Jo. K. 100
Starr, William 107
Start, Mary 43
Stattlemeyer, John 17
Staylor, Henry 107
St.Clair, [-?-] [-?-] 98
St.Clair, Major General Arthur 98
Stedel, Harriet 3
Steel, Frances Allenby 109
   Harriet 3, 86
   John 107
   John N. 107
   Ofle 107
Steer, Jacob 107
Steger, Joseph 107
Steiger, Major [-?-] 127
   Amelia 127
   Peter 107
Steinhauer, Rev. Henry 107
Stenon, Capt. 98
Stephens, Rev. [-?-] 120
   Sophronia 57
   William 107
Stephenson, Rachel 84 85
   Rev. Sater 84, 85, 70, 107, 123
Sterett, Benjamin 107
   Margaret [-?-] 107
Sterling, James 130
Sterrett, Augusta Temple 29
   Thomas 29
Stevens Rev. [-?-] 44
   Dolly 107
   Lydia 13
   Mary S.93
Stevenson, Rev. [-?-] 15
   Alexander 108
   Ann 60
   Ann [-?-] 108
   Edward 130
   Maj. George P. 108
   Henry 108
   Sarah Ann 69
   Capt. William 69
Steward, Elizabeth 35
   William 108
Stewart, David 108
   David C. 108
   Ellen [-?-] 108
   Godfrey 108
   James 28
   John 108
   Capt. John 108
   Col. John 108
   John Hathorn 29
   Julia 13
   Mary Ellen 43
   Sarah 27
   Sarah [-?-] 108
   Susan 117
   Thomas 108
   William 35, 108, 130
Stigers, Rev. Mr. 118
Stiles, Ann 91
   Edward 108
   George 108
   William 108
Stinchcomb, Eliza [-?-] 108
Stinson, Thomas 10
Stirling, Elizabeth [-?-] 108
   James 108
Stith, Griffith 108
Stockett, Barbara [-?-] 108
   Capt. Henry 108
   Capt. William 109
   Capt. William S. 109
Stocksdale, Martha Ann 23
Stockton, Frances Arabella Loney 109
   Francis B. 109
Stone, James 109
   John 109
Storm, Elizabeth 65
   James 109
Storrow, Samuel Appleton 109
Storts, Rebecca 18
Stoufer, Elizabeth 42
Stouffer, Henry 66
   Hester 66
   John 109
   Margaret 109
Strachan, Thomas 78
Strause, Henry 109
Strayer, John 106
Street, William 109
Streiby, Adam 109
Stricker Gen [-?-] 12
   Ann Eliza 12
Strike, Nicholas 18
Stringer, Dr. Samuel 109
Strong, William 8
Stroud, Reece P. 109
Stuart, John 109

Index

Stubbs, Joseph 109
Stuffelman, Nancy 43
Stump, [-?-] 93
  Ann Maria 70
  Hannah C. 123
  Hannah Emily 47
  Herman 47
  John 50
Styres, Rev. 45
Sugars, Edward 109
  Joseph 109
Suhr, Jacob 109
Sullivan, Dr. 131
Summer, James 33
Sumner, Frederick A. 39
  Henry Payson 109
Sumwalt, Joseph 100
  Sarah 109
Survilliers, Ct. de 67
Sutton, Samuel 51
Swain, Mary 4
Swan, Emily Augusta 49
  Henry B. 110
  James 110
  William 110
Swaney, Mary 7
Swann, Mary 78
  Thomas 78, 110
Sweadner, Daniel 110
Swearingen, Col. Charles 110
Sweatman, Frances 80
  Willis 110
Sweeny, Edward N. 100
  James 110
Sweeting, Ann B. 90
  John 110
Sweetser, Mary 97
Swell, Henry 110
Swett, Margaret C. 78
Swift, George Washington 110
  Jonathan 110
Switzer, Conrad 40

Tagg, Stephen 110
Tailor, William 110
Talbert, Eleanor 124
Talbot, Elizabeth 41
  Hon. Isham 110
  Jesse 70
  Joshua F. C. 110
  Vincent 110
Tall, William 110
Taney, Michael 75
  Octavius C. 110
Tannehill, George 13
  Tennessee 13
Tanner, Mary Ann 65
Tansfield, Zachariah 110
Tarlton, Richard 110
Tarr, Eli 110
Tatham, Sarah 34
Taylor, Alexander 111
  Charlotte Eliza 77
  Coleman 110
  David 111
  Dilah 111
  Elizabeth [-?-] 111
  Frances 111
  George 111
  Hester 118
  Capt. Humphrey 111
  John 77, 111
  Capt. John 111
  Col. John 111
  John S. 11
  Joseph 65, 111
  Julia 2
  Lemuel 111
  Lemuel G. 111
  Levi 111
  Levin 64
  Margaret 108
  Margaret [-?-] 111
  Maria H. 47
  Mary 111
  Parran 130
  Peregrine, 111
  Priscilla 65
  Robert 111
  Samuel G. 111
  William 111
  Capt. William S. 111
  William W. 47
Teackle, Lavinia 46
  Sarah 78
Teacle, Sarah 78
Tebo, Mary Ann 111
  Peter 111
Tracy [-?-] 76
Teneyck, Daniel W., 111
Tennant, Col. [-?-] 74
  Eliza 74
Tepkin, Caroline [-?-] 11
Terry, Elizabeth 35
  William 111
Tesson, Pierre 111
Tevis, Joshua 102, 103
Thayer, Laban 111
Theker, Jane [-?-] 112
  Walter 112
Thieneman, Charles 112
Thomas, [-?-] 130
  Ann 77, 112
  Argalus G. D. 112
  Dr. David 124
  E. S. 131
  George W. 89
  Isaac 112
  Col. James 112
  Rev. James 112
  Jim 112
  John 112, 129
  Lambert 70
  Lucretia 22
  Maria 79
  Mary 67
  Mary Ann 126
  Sally 87
  Susan 86
  Tach 124
  Thomas S. 112
  William 77, 112
Thomason, Adelaide 110
Thompson, Ann 69
  Charles A. C. 112
  David H. 104
  Deborah [-?-] 40
  Elizabeth 130
  Elizabeth [-?-] 45
  George 112
  Henry 116
  Israel P. 112
  James 112
  Lieut. John W. 112
  Joseph 112
  Martin 112
  Mary 85
  Mary Ann 106
  Samuel 112
  Sarah 125
  Thomas 112
  Thomas F. 112
Thomsen, Laurence 112
  Margaret [-?-] 9
  William A. 113
Thornburg, Isabella 105

Index

Thornton, Francis A. 113
Jane E. B. 21
Sidney E. 85
Thum, George 113
Tickey, Frederick 113
Tidings, Rev. [-?-] 89
Tiernan, Luke 89, 113
  Sarah 113
Tilden, Mary Ann 113
Tilghhman, Anna Maria 113
  Ann Maria [-?-] 113
  Edward 113
  Eleanor [-?-] 113
  Col. Frisby 113
  James 113
  R. C. 130
  William 113
Tilton, Dr. James 113
  Mary Elizabeth [-?-] 113
Tilyard, Philip 113
Timanus, Charles 69
  Jesse 113
Timon, Ann 64
Tingey, Comm. Thomas 113
Tisdale, Reuben 113
Todd, Eliza 113
  Elizabeth 110, 114
  Philip 104
  Thomas 113
Toole, Martin 113
Tooso, Lewis 113
Topken, Gerhard 113
Topkin, Gerard 113
Toso, Lewis 113
Towne, John 113
Townsend, Ann Maria 113
  Benjamin 113
  Joseph 113
  Nicholas Waln 113
  Perry R. 113
Townsley, Louisa 19
Tows, Mary Ann 111
Towson, James 113
  Sarah 2
  Thomas 114
Toy, John D. 114
  Rev. Joseph 114
Trace, Charles 114
Tracey, Charles 114
  James 114
Travers, George 114

Traverse, Jane 34
Travis, Mary 1
Treadwell, Alexander Philip Socrates Emilius Caesar Hannibal Marcellus George Washington 114
Trego, Samuel 114
Tricket, John 114
Trimble, Harriet 21
  William 114
Trissler, Catherine 35
Trott, Capt. William H., 114
Trowbridge, Reubin 114
Trum, Dr. George 114
Trumblingson, William 114
Trumbo, Adam 114
Tschudy, Samuel 114
  Sarah 89
Tuchson, Nathan 114
Tuchstin, Nathan 114
Tuck, Mary P. 89
  Samuel Tuck 89
Tucker, Joseph 114
Tull, William 114
Tunis, Samuel 114
Tupper, Mary [-?-] 52
Turgeau, Gen. [-?-] 115
Turner, Benjamin 114
  Daniel 114
  E. 21
  Ebenezer 114
  Elizabeth 14
  Elizabeth [-?-] 114
  Lydia 114
  Mary Ann 11
  Mary C. 114
  Ruth [-?-] 114
  Capt. Samuel W. 86, 114
  Sarah 14
  Sarah Ann 114, 120
  Tho. W. 130
  Thomas 114, 115
Turreau, Gen. [-?-] 115
Tuso, Lewis 113
Tutchson. Nathan 114
Tuttle, Daniel 115
Tutweiler, Henry 20
Twist, [-?-] 76

Eliza 66
Tydings, Rev. [-?-]12
Tyler, John 13
Tyson, Charles J. 115
  Elisha 115
  George 115
  Isaac 115
  James Wood 115
  John S. 86
  Jonathan 115
  Nathan 115

Uhler, Eliza 52
  George 115
  Philip 52
Umbaugh, Michael 115
Underwood, John 115
Updegraff, Samuel 115
Urquhart, John 115
Usher, Ann Maria 102

Valdenegro, Capt. Don Eusebeus 115
Valentine, Rezin 115
Valiant/Valliant, Rev. John 3, 5, 11, 16, 17,19, 26, 34, 35, 38, 40, 49, 54, 63, 65, 73, 77, 78, 81, 82, 83, 109, 113. 121, 123
Vallett, Charles 115
Vallette, Emilie 3
Van Bibber, Abraham 115
Van Horn, Archibald 116
  Harriet 111
  Capt. Jonathan 116
Van Riper, John 116
Van Weazle, Moses Davis 116
Van Wyck, Elizabeth L. [-?-] 116
  John C. 116
  Stedman 116
  William 116
Vanbibber, Ab. 115
  Washngton 116
Vance, Ann [-?-] 116
  Thomas 116
  William 116
Vandamme, Gen. 67

186

Index

Vanderford, Henry 116
vanLear, Matthew 38
Vans, Mary 123
vanWinckle, Samuel 30
Varden, Sarah 102
Varner, Robert 116
Vaughen, John 116
Vears, Ann 9
Vermilion, John 116
Vidal, Antoinette [-?-] 116
Viers, Rev. Healey 75
  Hezekiah 75
  Samuel C. 116
  Sophia C. 75
  Col. William 75
Villard, Martha 116
  Mary 116
Villaret, L. 3
Vincent, Jane O. 95
  Samuel 95
Virtue, David 117
Voorhis, Johanna 105
Vosburg, Abraham 117

Waggaman, H. P. 52
Wagner, John Christian 117
  Peter A. 117
Wakeman, Dr. Banks 117
Walch, Rev. [-?-] 33
Waldron, Benjamin 117
  Lucy 89
Wales, Emily 59
Walker, [-?-] 131
Walker, Rev. [-?-] 37
  Ann 38
  Charles, 117
  Emanuel 117
  Capt. John 59
  John James Augusts 117
  Louisa 115
  Margaret Mary 117
  Samuel 117
  Sarah 55
  Thomas 2, 117
  Dr. Thomas C. 117
  William 68, 117
Wall, Charlotte 1
  John E. 15

Wallace, Catherine 70
  Joseph A. 73, 117
  Maria [-?-] 117
  Rebecca Maria [-?-] 117
  Solomon 117
  Thomas 117
  Capt. Thomas 117
Waller, Bazil 117
  William 117
Wallington, Capt. Edward 98
  Mary Ann 98
Wallis, John 118
  Louisa Chew 118
Wallow, Abraham 118
Walls, Rev. John 118
  William 118
Walmsley, John Gooding 118
Walsh, John Francis 118
  Robert 118
Walter, Delia 77
  William 118
  Benedict F. 118
  Charlotte 84
  Corbin 118
  William 118
Waltham Charlton M. 118
Walton, Attantick [Atlantgick?] Ocean 80
  Eliza 92
Wampler, J. Lewis 118
Wane, John 71
Wanhill, Capt. Thomas 118
  Mary 39
Ward, Elijah 37
  John W. 118
  Leonora 98
  Martha 88
  Mary 109
  Nathan 118
  Patrick 118
  Peregrine 82
  Rebecca 118
  Robert 118
  William H. 99, 118
Warder, Elizabeth 60
  John 60
Ware, Thomas 118
Warfield, Alexander 57, 126

  Charles Alexander 105
  Daniel 118
  Eleanor Elizabeth 1
  Elijah 118
  Elisha 118
  G. F. 118
  Henrietta 76, 126
  John Marriott 118
  Juliet 57
  Lewis 118, 119
  Philemon 119
  Victoria Louise 105
Waring, George W. 119
Wark, Sarah 19
Warking, Maria C. 82
Warner, George 113, 114, 131
  Maria 113, 114
  Mary 25
  Michael 119
  Sarah [-?-] 68
  Thomas 86
  William 119
Warrington, Capt. Lewis 119
Washington, Laurence 119
  Sarah T. 119
  Col. Wm. A. 119
Waterhouse, Elias B. 119
Waters, Col. [-?-] 119
  Ann 2, 38
  Edward 119
  Eliza 73
  Elizabeth [-?-] 119
  Hezekiah 119
  John 119
  Joseph 119
  Mary 75
  Mary B. 108
  Patrick 119
  Richard 119
  William 119
  William D. 119
Watkin, Asa T. 119
Watkins, Rev. [-?-] 119
  Gassaway 119
Watson, John 119
  Joseph 119
Wattles, Delia 77
Watts, David 119
  Elizabeth 108

Index

Ezekiel 119
Frederick J. 119
Waugh, Rev. Beverly 1, 21, 34, 35, 45, 48, 54, 72, 96, 97, 113, 120
Way, George 119
John D. 119
Wayman, Henry 119
Milcah 119
Wayne, Francis 120
Weakley, Jane 68
Weatherby, William 120
Weaver, Jacob 120
James 120
John 120
William 120
Webb, Catherine 120
Charles 120
Gideon 120
Henry 120
William 120
Webber, [-?-] 120
Webster, Charles 120
Toppan 120
Weed, Ezra 120
Weedon, Jonathan 120
Weems, John 120
Weir, Benjamin 120
Isabella 27
Weise, Augustus 69, 120
Godfrey 120
Susannah Louisa 69, 120
Welden, Ann 3
Welling, Samuel L. P. 120
Wellmore, Ann [-?-] 120
Robert 120
Wells, Rev. [-?-] 119
Ann 13
Charles 120
Daniel 121
Rev. Joshua 2, 21, 33, 35, 37, 39, 40, 42, 44, 46, 70, 82
Mary 123
William 121
Welsh, Anna Maria 121
Charles 121
Elizabeth Hallock [-?-] 121

Henry 121
Jacob 121
Rev. John 85, 121
Wenn, Elisha 121
Wentz, Thos. 9
Werdebaugh, John 121
Wesby, Hugh 121
Wescote, Jane 73
West, Job 9
Stacy 121
William 121
Westby, Hugh 121
Westerman, Rev. Mr. 62
Weston, Mary 121
Wetherly, Bristo 121
Weylands, Elizabeth 17
Weymouth, Dean 121
Weysell, Betsey 95
Whaland, John 14
Whalen, Evalina 45
Wharfe, Joseph 121
Wheaton, Rev. [-?-] 75, 117, 119
Wheedon, Elizabeth [-?-] 29
Wheeler, Benjamin 121
Elizabeth E. B. 104
Odel 121
Sarah 12
Susan 16
Wheelwright, George 17
Margaret F. 76
Whelan, [-?-] 27
Wheland, Peter 121
Whetcroft, Catherine 66
Whiffen, Charlotte 24
Whitaker, Tabitha 43
White, [-?-] 108
White, Right Rev. Bishop [-?-] 47
Ann 9
Charles 121
Daniel 122
Edward 121
Elizabeth 5, 84
Francis 122
Gideon 122
Hannah [-?-] 122
James, 122
Jane 46
Joshua 122

Margaret [-?-] 63
Maria Ann 27
Mary [-?-] 122
Samuel 122
Samuel K. 122
Thomas 122
William 122
Whitefield, Rev. Mr. [-?-] 64, 75, 88
Whitney, Ephraim 122
Whittiker, Mary 125
Whittington, Eliza 116
Mary 2
Whittle, Clarissa [-?-] 122
Nicholas 122
Wichelhause, Jacob 122
Wickes, Simon 8
Wickethausen, Jacob 122
Wielder, Ann 206
Wightman, Capt. John 122
Margaret 111
Wilburn, Walter 130, 132
Wilcox, Anthony 122
Phoebe [-?-] 122
Wilhelm, Jane 122
Wilkins, Elizabeth 47
Margaret 47
Thomas 47
William 122
Wilkinson, Charles 122
Joseph 111
Thomas H. 110
William, 125
Willard, Salem 55
Willat, William 122
Willey, Eliza 81
Mary [-?-] 122
Williams, [-?-] 66
Amos A. 122
Ann 31
Barrett 123
Baruch 122
C. D. 123
Ebenezer 123
Eliza 5, 57
George 123
Henry 123
James 123
James A. 101
James W. 123

Index

Jane [-?-] 44
Jesse 123
John 88, 122, 123
Capt. John 123
John J. 123
John Mason 123
Mary 123
Nath'l 3
Otho H. 123
Richard 58, 123
Rev. S. 60
Samuel 123
Capt. Thomas 123
William 123
William B. 123
William C. 123
Williamson, Rev. 105
Sarah [-?-] 123
Willis, [-?-] 88
Willis, Rev. [-?-] 16
Francis Asbury 124
Willson, Ann [-?-] 124
Capt. James 124
Willy, Mary [-?-] 124
Wilmer, [-?-] 93, 131
Mary Ann 108
Rev. William H.
  100, 105, 119
Wilson, Rev. Dr. 112
Alexander 124
Ann 28
Aquila 124
Catherine 89
Charlotte 91
Edward M. 124
Eliza 19
Elizabeth 76
Henry G. 124
James 124
James R. 124
Jane [-?-] 40
John 124
Juliet 34
Louisa 45
Mary Gover 12
Robert 124
Robert R. 124
Samuel 124
Sarah [-?-] 124
Sarah Jane 21
Susan 91
Thomas 50, 124
William 72. 124
Rev. Mr. Wilson 78
Winchell, J. P. 80
James F. 3

Winchester, David, 124
Gen. James 96
Richard 124
Samuel 124
Selima 96
Winckler, George 124
Winder, Maj. Gen. Levin 124
Winfeld, Eleanor Elizabeth 1
Wininger, Lewis 124
Winn, Elisha 124
Winship, Jona. 102
Winsor, Arnold T. 124
Winston, Edmond 125
Winthrop, George W. 125
Winton, Joseph S. 125
Wirgman, Peter 125
Wistar, Dr. Caleb 125
Witmer, Daniel 125
  Henry 125
  Mary [-?-] 125
Witwell, Capt. Thomas 125
Woelper, George 125
Wolf, Peggy 107
  Susannah 107
Woller, Catherine 70
Wonderley, Sarah 68
Wood, James 125
  James P. 125
  Leon 129
  Thomas 125
Woodburn, John 125
Woodcock, A. & s. 21
Wooden, Julia Ann 46
Woodhouse, Capt. Samuel 125
Woodland, Ezekiel 125
Woods, Gen. John 125
Woodville, Rev. Mr. 109
Woodward, Amin [Amon?] 125
  David 76
  Dr. Edward 125
  Harriet 37
Woody, William 125
Woodyear, Thomas 125
Wooldridge, [-?-] 130
Woolfolk, Austin 18
  John G. 125

Woolford, Dr. John 125
  Levin 125
Working, Henry 46
Workinger, Eliza 66
  Jacob 66
Worley, Henry 125
  Joseph 100
Worman, Andrew 125, 126
  Jacob 126
Wormsley, Maria Carter 18
Warner 18
Worrell, Sarah Maria 99
Worten, Thomas 126
Worthington, Charles 126
  Samuel 81
  Susan 81
  Thomas I. 126
Worts, Catherine [-?-] 29
Wray, John 126
Wright, Capt. [-?-] 130
  Widow [-?-] Harrison 132
  A. T. 126
  Ann 119
  Charity 87
  Maj. Edward 35
  Eliza 40
  Felix 126
  George 126
  Julia Ann 35
  Margaret Elizabeth [-?-] 51
  Martha 81
  Prudence 39
  Dr. Thomas H. 126
Write, Widow [-?-] Harrison 132
Wurts, Mary Campbell 17
Wurts, Maurice Campbell 17
Wyant, Rev. [-?-] 29
  Peter 126
Wyatt, Rev. 8, 22, 23, 27, 55, 57, 59, 73, 75, 80, 85, 108, 109, 118, 120, 121. 124, 125
  Mary 126
Wymbel, James 126

Index

Wyrick, Caspar 126
Wyvil, Darcy 126

Yates, Mary [-?-] 126
Yeates, Col. Donaldson 126
  George 126
  Jasper 126
Yeiser, Jesse 126
Yellott, George 127
Yeohannes, Charles H. 127
Yeomans, Charles H. 127
Yerkins, David 127
Yokel, Thomas 127
Yokeley, Thomas 127
Young, Benjamin 127
  Duncan 127
  Gen. Henry 127
  John 127
  John S. 116
  Mary [-?-] 127
  Rebecca [-?-] 127

Zacharie, Peter 127
Zachary, Peter 127
Zeilly, Rev. Mr. 120
Zimmerman, George, 127
  Henry W. 127
  Jacob 127
Zollickoffer, Dr. William 127

www.ingramcontent.com/pod-product-compliance
Lightning Source LLC
Chambersburg PA
CBHW051644230426
43669CB00013B/2438